THE
NEW TESTAMENT
AND
GNOSIS

THE NEW TESTAMENT AND GNOSIS:

Essays in honour of

ROBERT McL. WILSON

edited by

A. H. B. LOGAN *and* A. J. M. WEDDERBURN

T. & T. CLARK LIMITED

36 GEORGE STREET
EDINBURGH

First published by
T. & T. Clark Limited
36 George Street
Edinburgh EH2 2LQ

ISBN: 0 567 0 9344 1

Typeset by C. R. Barber & Partners (Highlands) Ltd, Fort William,
Inverness-shire

Printed by Billings, London & Worcester

CONTENTS

THE NAG HAMMADI TEXTS AND THE NEW TESTAMENT

FOREWORD

It was indicative of Robert McLachlan Wilson's breadth of interest that when in October 1978 he succeeded Principal Matthew Black to the Chair of Biblical Criticism at St Mary's College in the University of St Andrews he chose as the title for his inaugural lecture 'The Study, the Pulpit and the Pew'. The title reflected his concern to set his scholarship at the service of the Church of Scotland which he had served both as a parish minister and as a teacher at the oldest of her Divinity Faculties. For, after finishing his doctoral research at Cambridge, he served from 1946 to 1954 as minister of Rankin Church, Strathaven, in Lanarkshire. When he was appointed to a lectureship in St Mary's College he was still persistent in his desire to serve the Church of Scotland, as well as latterly the many other denominations whose students were admitted to St Mary's for the study of theology. Constantly he kept the demands of the parish ministry in mind and sought to combine those demands with those of the most exacting scholarship, as well as continuing to serve the Church of Scotland in such demanding work as convening one of its committees.

But it is with Professor Wilson as the scholar that this volume is primarily concerned, a scholar who has received, deservedly, some of the highest honours which can come the way of those engaged in this field: he is, for instance, both a Fellow of the British Academy and was elected President of the *Studiorum Novi Testamenti Societas* for 1981–2. This volume appears at the time of his arrival at two landmarks in his distinguished career: in the autumn of 1983 he steps down from the editorship of *New Testament Studies* and from the Chair of Biblical Criticism in St Mary's College, both of which he inherited from Principal Matthew Black.

It is with some trepidation that the editors of the present volume submit such a collection of articles to this scholar who has himself edited and translated so many volumes in the course of his long career: the English editions of Hennecke and Schneemelcher's *New Testament Apocrypha*, Haenchen's *Acts* and Foerster's *Gnosis*, and, most recently, Rudolph's *Gnosis*, published by the same press as this volume, as well as numerous volumes devoted to Gnosis and Gnosticism and to the Nag Hammadi Codices. But Professor Wilson has made his own distinctive contribution to New Testament and Gnostic scholarship, in his contribution on Mark in the revised Peake's *Commentary* and in a whole series of books and articles on Gnosticism and Gnosis. His influence on scholarship in the latter field is amply attested in the pages of this volume; not only is he without doubt the leading authority on this subject in the British Isles, but worldwide his balanced and judicious assessment of the evidence has been noted and admired both by beginners and experts in this complex and exciting expanding field of studies. But, just as he sought to relate ministry and New Testament scholarship, so his work on Gnosis and Gnosticism has not distracted him from the attempt to assess the relevance of this movement to the interpretation of the New Testament; constantly he has endeavoured to gauge the relationship between Christian Gnosticism and its precursors on the one hand and the world of the New Testament on the other. As a tribute to his contributions to this aspect of the study of Gnosis and Gnosticism we have dared to invert the title of one of his most influential books and to dedicate to him this series of studies on *The New Testament and Gnosis*.

It would be premature to expect a definitive exposition of the topic at this stage. But with the complete Nag Hammadi Library now being accessible and the growing body of scholarly editions of the texts, it seemed appropriate to take soundings of certain key areas as indicative of the present state of opinion. Recent research in the field has perhaps tended to deal with the two areas in isolation, Gnostic scholars concentrating on assessing the significance of the Nag Hammadi finds for our understanding of Gnosis, New Testament scholars limiting discussion to the search for parallels or to the continuation of certain long-running battles. We feel that a volume seeking to relate the two is both timely and a fitting tribute to Professor Wilson. It will be clear from the articles that a consensus has not yet emerged, but we have attempted to ensure that some of the main problems, in particular those with which Professor Wilson has been chiefly concerned, have been dealt with, both at the more general and the more detailed level.

Rather than simply arranging these contributions in alphabetical order, we have sought to group them thematically although our groupings may at times seem rather arbitrary. Following Professor J. M. Robinson's introductory essay which takes stock of the use made of the Nag Hammadi texts by New Testament scholars, a first group of essays deals with various topics concerning the definition and nature of Gnosis and Gnosticism, particularly in relation to the New Testament. The second, 'Gnosis, Gnosticism and Christian Origins', examines the relationship between the early Christian movement, including the New Testament, and Gnosis and Gnosticism. The third, 'The Nag Hammadi Library and the New Testament', is concerned with the relation between certain texts in that collection and early Christianity and the New Testament. We have in some cases translated articles into English in order to make them as widely accessible as possible and we are most grateful to their authors for their assistance in checking our rendering of their texts.

We would also like to thank the many others whose assistance has made this volume possible: Mr R. A. Piper of St Andrews, who has undertaken the considerable task of compiling a bibliography of Professor Wilson's many publications, Dr G. F. Green, who has shown especial qualities of patience, helpfulness and encouragement in guiding this volume through the various stages of its production, and the rest of the staff of T. and T. Clark Ltd, Miss M. C. Blackwood, Mrs K. J. Davies, Miss C. M. Lawson and Mrs E. E. McLauchlan in the St Mary's College office, and Miss M. Faulkner in the Exeter Department of Theology office, who have all cheerfully and efficiently helped with the typing and preparation of material, and also the many contributors to this volume who have often put themselves to considerable trouble to meet fairly tight deadlines; our thanks and sympathy also go to other would-be contributors who for various reasons have been unable to participate in this project, to our disappointment and, even more, to theirs.

Finally, we would like to express our own gratitude to Professor Wilson as both teacher and colleague, and to his wife, Enid; we wish him well in his retirement and trust that it will afford him more time not only for further contributions in pulpit and pew, but also for continued study of the New Testament and Gnosis, and, last but not least, for the challenge of the St Andrews greens.

A. H. B. Logan
A. J. M. Wedderburn

TABULA GRATULANTIUM

James B. Adamson
Hugh Anderson
R. S. Barbour
F. W. Beare
G. R. Beasley-Murray
Pier Franco Beatrice
Hans Dieter Betz
J. Neville Birdsall
Gerald L. Borchert
Peder Borgen
Raymond E. Brown
F. F. Bruce
Donald A. Carson
David R. Catchpole
N. Clark
Raymond F. Collins
Bruno Corsani
John M. Court
C. E. B. Cranfield
Gerhard Dautzenberg
D. G. Davies
M. de Jonge
F. Gerald Downing
John W. Drane
Han J. W. Drijvers
James D. G. Dunn
J. K. Elliott
Eldon Jay Epp
Owen E. Evans
Joseph A. Fitzmyer
Edwin D. Freed
Reginald H. Fuller
Victor Paul Furnish
T. Francis Glasson
J. C. G. Greig
Pierre Grelot
Ferdinand Hahn

S. G. Hall
L. Hartman
Victor Hasler
Charles W. Hedrick
Jan Helderman
A. J. B. Higgins
David Hill
Paul Hoffmann
M. D. Hooker
J. L. Houlden
Hans Hübner
Niels Hyldahl
Marie E. Isaacs
Robert Jewett
Seyoon Kim
A. F. J. Klijn
Otto B. Knoch
Robert A. Kraft
Georg Kretschmar
Jan Lambrecht
Friedrich Lang
Michael Lattke
A. R. C. Leaney
Xavier Léon-Dufour
A. T. Lincoln
Barnabas Lindars
Richard N. Longenecker
Gerard P. Luttikhuizen
U. Luz
J. D. McCaughey
James I. H. McDonald
John McHugh
R. J. McKelvey
Martin McNamara
George W. MacRae
I. Howard Marshall
Dennis M. Maurer

Wayne A. Meeks
Otto Merk
Helmut Merkel
Bruce M. Metzger
W. G. Morrice
Leon Morris
Robert Murray
Peter Nagel
Kenneth V. Neller
Poul Nepper-Christensen
J. C. O'Neill
John Painter
Romana Penna
Ronald A. Piper
Paul-Hubert Poirier
Wiard Popkes
Bo Reicke
Raymond Renowden
John Reumann
Harald Riesenfeld
Michel Roberge
Harry Sawyerr
Wolfgang Schenk
Rudolf Schnackenburg
John H. Schütz
Benedikt Schwank

Stephen S. Smalley
Graham N. Stanton
G. C. Stead
Jane W. Steadman
James S. Stewart
Georg Strecker
Albert C. Sundberg Jr
J. P. M. Sweet
Richard E. Taylor
Theophilus M. Taylor
Einar Thomassen
Margaret E. Thrall
Etienne Trocmé
Karl-Wolfgang Tröger
C. M. Tuckett
Bastiaan Van Elderen
W. S. Vorster
Günter Wagner
Andrew F. Walls
Hans Weder
John William Wenham
D. E. H. Whiteley
Edwin M. Yamauchi
Frances M. Young
J. A. Ziesler

ABBREVIATIONS

For periodicals and serials the abbreviations of the *Theologische Realenzyklopädie*, Berlin/New York 1976, have been used, and for other abbreviations the conventions of the *Theological Dictionary of the New Testament* I, Grand Rapids 1964, supplemented by the revised list of the *Theologisches Wörterbuch zum Neuen Testament* X, Stuttgart 1974, with certain modifications which should be self-evident. For the titles of the Nag Hammadi texts we have generally followed the abbreviations suggested by the Society for Biblical Literature, *Members' Handbook*, Missoula 1980.

Some abbreviations are not covered by the above sources, e.g.:

ALGHJ	*Arbeiten zur Literatur und Geschichte des hellenistischen Judentums*
BCNH Ét	*Bibliothèque Copte de Nag Hammadi; section 'Études'*
BG	Berlin Gnostic Codex (Berolinensis 8502)
BM Or.	British Museum Oriental
Bodleian Hunt.	Bodleian Library Huntington
ET	English Translation
FS	*Festschrift*
log.	logion
NHC	Nag Hammadi Codices
NHS	*Nag Hammadi Studies*
n.s.	new series
ser.	series

TRANSLITERATION

For Hebrew (and Aramaic and Syriac) the conventions used are those of (ed.) H. H. Rowley, *The Old Testament and Modern Study*, Oxford 1951, p. xiii. For Greek the conventions are those of the SBL (see above) except that upsilon is written as *u* and iota subscript as (*i*); a gamma followed by another gamma or a kappa or a xi is written as *n*. For Coptic the conventions are again those of the SBL, but again with the exception of upsilon written as *u*, and with the supralinear written as a supralinear stroke.

Robert McL. Wilson

I

THE NAG HAMMADI LIBRARY AND THE STUDY OF THE NEW TESTAMENT

by

Professor James M. Robinson, Claremont

It is a bit presumptuous to address oneself to this topic after the delivery of Robin Wilson's presidential address on 'Nag Hammadi and the New Testament' before the Society for New Testament Studies in Rome in August 1981.[1] There he presented a magisterial case for the relevance of the Nag Hammadi codices for the study of the New Testament, based on the premise (292):

> Gnosticism is rather older than once was thought, and certainly originated prior to the second century.

Over the past decade or so Wilson and I have been in dialogue concerning the Nag Hammadi texts and the New Testament, both as the two representatives of the English-speaking world on the International Committee for the Nag Hammadi Codices and as colleagues in the Society for New Testament Studies. It has been all the more interesting a dialogue in that we also share a major interest in translating German research into English, even if with the variation suggested by the old maxim: Theology is created in Germany, corrected in Scotland and corrupted in America.[2] For prior to the accessibility of the Nag Hammadi codices the view that Gnosticism was important for the study of the New Testamant was largely confined to German New Testament scholarship and those under its influence.

To be sure, discussions of Gnosticism are not necessarily to be equated with the impact of the Nag Hammadi texts, since Gnosticism had been discussed in relation to the New Testament prior to the accessibility of these texts. Conversely, some of the new texts are not Gnostic, but fall more generally among New Testament apocrypha, and indeed some are not Christian. Yet any discussion of Gnosticism is, explicitly or implicitly,

1

now dependent on the Nag Hammadi texts. Indeed the first effect of the Nag Hammadi discovery may for this very reason have been a wait-and-see attitude, in that one hesitated to continue to make use of the usual construct of 'Gnosticism', based upon inadequate source material, lest the flood of new material, when it was finally released, show up the deficiencies of that traditional approach. Over the last generation this caution has led in many quarters to a decline in the discussion of Gnosticism and the New Testament, a decline that can only to a limited degree be justified as a valid reaction to the excesses of earlier scholarship. Now that the material is fully available, the issue of Gnosticism and the New Testament can be approached with the help of the new primary sources with renewed confidence and real hope of achieving new results.

Rather than again discussing this general issue, superfluous in view of Wilson's address, I propose here to look at the actual way in which New Testament scholarship has begun to make use of the Nag Hammadi codices. The time has not yet come for a general survey of secondary literature on the topic, such as Herbert Braun provided for Qumran and the New Testament.[3] Rather four major Introductions to the New Testament that have appeared over the past two decades are surveyed with regard to their use of the Nag Hammadi texts and their discussion of Gnosticism in relation to the New Testament.[4] To be sure, these works do not discuss all that has been done in this regard, but the survey should suffice to indicate the marked change that the Nag Hammadi codices have already begun to make in our discipline.

It is characteristic of these works that the only position subjected to extensive refutation is the pan-Gnostic theory of Walter Schmithals, which has hung like an albatross around the neck of the Bultmannian tradition. Philipp Vielhauer reserves for it (in his treatment of Galatians) his severest criticism (120–22):

> ... Jewish Christian Gnostics with explicit libertine tendencies. An amazing claim, that finds in Galatians itself only slight support. Schmithals willingly concedes this, and himself emphasizes that Paul thought he had to do with nomists. But Paul was mistaken. ... Here lies the first fundamental mistake of Schmithals's Gnostics hypothesis. ... The bold premise that Paul is poorly informed, Schmithals however quite well informed, and indeed on the basis of Galatians written by the poorly informed apostle, is of course not worthy of discussion. It functions as an alibi for subjective arbitrariness. ... The further methodical mistake is related: the ignoring of the form-critical character of paraenesis. ... Also the individual arguments for the Gnostics hypothesis have little power to convince. ... This argument is based on the untenable thesis of the Gnostic origin of apostleship. ... The Gnostic interpretation of circumcision is an anachronistic insertion of later views and can claim for itself only the consistency of a *petitio principii*. ...

Hans-Martin Schenke is equally decisive (with regard to 1 Corinthians, vol. I, 104–105):

> His presentations are themselves the clear proof that the whole theory of the Gnostic opponents does not work. Schmithals in his treatment takes his point of departure in texts where it is either not at all apparent that Paul is attacking views of opponents or where it is unclear how and against what he is actually polemicizing. He advances the obscure texts at the expense of the clear ones! From these texts he then constructs the mythological doctrine of the opponents of Paul that had thus far been missed. ... To be sure Schmithals bridges the gap between exegetical possibility and necessity with rhetorical decorations. His picture of the whole phenomenon of Gnosticism, which he takes over uncritically from Reitzenstein, Bousset, Bultmann and Jonas, is already as such transcended and out of date. And then he juggles with the ingredients of this picture in an abstract way that must make every person who knows the subject matter lose his or her composure. ... He simply reads a Gnostic meaning into certain Pauline expressions and then takes this to be the terminology and mythology of the heretics. This procedure, of which Schmithals seems not to be conscious, would lead to the outcome of declaring Paul himself to be a Gnostic, i.e. his own opponent. ... Furthermore the work of Schmithals on Corinthians leads to, and stands in the service of, a certain almost 'Lucan' overview of primitive Chrstianity that in our opinion is false. According to that view primitive Christianity would be an internally harmonious, organically developing construction. All conflicts come from outside, namely from Gnosticism. We have here an unstable combination of very critical and very conservative positions.

Similar comments scattered through the works of Werner Georg Kümmel and Helmut Koester indicate that their assessment is basically the same. Schmithals' pan-Gnostic theory does thus serve to mark the degenerate end of the older approach to the study of Gnosticism and the New Testament, so that its crisp repudiation makes way for a new beginning.

Werner Georg Kümmel's references to Nag Hammadi texts were initially limited by the fact that he covered literature only up to 1962, by which time only a few Nag Hammadi texts were accessible. Hence only the Gospel of Thomas and the Gospel of Truth were mentioned, and they somewhat peripherally. For the Gospel of Thomas was dismissed as 'undoubtedly not a later form of the same literary genre as Q, but ... a later, wholly different stage in the development of the tradition of the words of Jesus' (75–76). This assessment is based in part on an appeal to Wilson as of 1960; but in his presidential address of 1981 Wilson introduces precisely those views Kümmel was opposing with the comment (297): 'Today the emphasis has shifted'.

The implications of the Gospel of Truth for understanding the Gospel of John were conceded (228) from an article of C. K. Barrett (to which Wilson also referred):

> C. K. Barrett, in a comparison of John with the Gnostic Gospel of Truth, has shown rather that John consciously employed pre-Christian Gnostic language in an anti-Gnostic sense, because 'Gnosis raised questions that the theologian could not ignore.'

But in the new edition, including literature up to 1971, the role of Nag Hammadi texts for the study of John has been enlarged (227):

> A considerable number of the *ego eimi*-predicates can now be shown in the Gnostic texts from Nag Hammadi. So the fact remains that in this perspective also John appears to have been influenced by Gnostic language.

Kümmel's argument for a Jewish-Gnostic, rather than Qumranian, milieu for the Gospel of John is strengthened by new evidence for non-Christian Gnosticism, in which connection he mentions the Apocalypse of Adam and Eugnostos the Blessed (225–26):

> But the observations already mentioned concerning the existence of Gnostic religiosity in the first century are, besides, supported by establishing Gnostic features for the opponents of Paul in Corinth and Colossae and for the false teachers in Jude and 1 John, and by the not unchallenged probability that some of the Gnostic texts found at Nag Hammadi show no or hardly any Christian influence.

Kümmel's *Introduction* tends to trace the development of Gnosticism from book to book in the New Testament. Whereas he had argued that Paul (*sic!*) in Colossians opposed 'Jewish Christian Gnosis' (1963 German edition, 246), a decade later he considered it 'questionable that the Colossian false teachings are to be characterized as Gnostic' (339, 342):

> Gnosis in the strict sense of the term is scarcely in the picture, since the cult of elements is not comprehensible on that basis. Thus the broad designation of the Colossian error as an early form of Gnosis or as gnosticizing Judaism is not really helpful, ...

But Ephesians 'can only be understood against the background of a christianized mythological Gnosis', in view of 'strong influences of Gnostic mythology' (365). The Pastorals combat 'a Gnosticism more or less influenced by Jewish Christianity', though 'there is then not the slightest occasion, just because the false teachers who are being opposed are Gnostics, to link them up with the great Gnostic systems of the second century' (379). Similarly Hebrews is related to 'the primitive Gnosticism which was originally associated with certain segments of Hellenistic Judaism' (397). Jude combats 'a Gnostic tendency which holds that a real pneumatic existence is not affected in any way by what the flesh does', though 'this characteristic does not fit any particular Gnostic system of the second century' (426). On the other hand in the case of 2 Peter one has to do with a polemic 'against a movement which bears the essential features of second-century Gnosis' (432). Also 1 John combats a mature Gnosticism (442):

> Although the Gnostic false teaching cannot be determined with historical exactitude, it is nonetheless significant that here – unlike the situation in Colossians, the Pastorals, Jude, and 2 Peter – enthusiastic Gnosticism has christological implications, so that here we have to do with a developed form of Gnosticism.

Philipp Vielhauer's volume also appeared before much of the Nag Hammadi library became available. This inhibited a full assessment of the new material (4):

> A special problem is involved regarding which texts from the epoch-making discovery of Nag Hammadi should be considered. It contains Christian–Gnostic and non-Christian–Gnostic writings, and in addition non-Christian writings reworked in a Christian sense, and hence contains compositions that are quite complex literarily and in terms of the history of religions. Many writings are entitled primarily or secondarily as 'Gospel', 'Apocalypse', 'Letter' or 'Acts', without bearing these titles legitimately in terms of genre. The main difficulty consists in the fact that the discovery has not yet been completely edited. Hence a treatment of the edited texts that are certainly Christian–Gnostic in terms of the history of literature would run the risk of writing trash. The Nag Hammadi texts are for the time being the object of monographic analyses. Nonetheless it seemed to me necessary to discuss at length the Gospel of Thomas and the Gospel of Truth, and, warranted by certain reasons, the Apocryphon of James and the Book of Thomas the Contender.

In introducing the Synoptic Gospels the term 'Gospel' and the genre 'Gospel' are discussed. In this connection four Nag Hammadi texts entitled 'Gospel' are discussed, 'The Gospel according to Thomas', 'The Gospel according to Philip', 'The Egyptian Gospel' and 'The Gospel of Truth'. But none are Gospels in terms of genre (257):

> The Gospel of Thomas is a collection of sayings of Jesus, the Gospel of Philip a collection of sayings of quite a different kind, which nonetheless contains a few sayings of Jesus, the Gospel of

the Egyptians is a revelatory writing with liturgical insertions, and the Gospel of Truth is commonly designated a homily.

The title is secondary in the cases of the Gospel of Philip and the Gospel of the Egyptians, but is original in the *incipit* of the Gospel of Truth and, contrary to the commonly-held view, may be original in the case of the Gospel of Thomas. For, again contrary to the commonly-held view that the term was employed to compete with canonical Gospels, Vielhauer attributes the use of the term in Nag Hammadi titles to the survival of the pre-literary meaning of 'good news', to which Saying 1 of the Gospel of Thomas points (258). Thus the Gospel of Thomas is the only one of the four that is classified among 'Apocryphal Gospels' (614), in which connection a whole section is devoted to it (618–35). Regarding the genre of the Gospel of Thomas, Vielhauer argues that it is analogous to Q (621–22):

> The Gospel of Thomas is a collection of sayings and proves conclusively that there were such collections of words of Jesus in primitive Christianity not only as incidental records for private purposes but also as a literary genre with an official purpose, and thereby proves further that the postulated sayings source Q is no 'product of fantasy' [Joachim Jeremias] but a reality. ... It transmits words that Jesus had spoken or was supposed to have spoken during his earthly life and to this extent is a companion piece to Q.

The Gospel of Truth is also treated in a section to itself, among 'Church Orders and Cultic Materials', as a 'homily', 'a model of Gnostic preaching' (W. C. van Unnik) (744–49). The Gospel of the Egyptians, on the other hand, is treated summarily, merely to distinguish it from the previously known childhood Gospel of the same name. The Nag Hammadi tractate belongs to the Gnostic Seth literature not treated in this work (665).

A number of Nag Hammadi texts are 'Dialogues of the Resurrected with his Disciples', a genre whose 'original home' is 'in Gnostic circles' (690). Vielhauer lists (681): the Apocryphon of John, the Sophia of Jesus Christ, the First Apocalypse of James, the Apocryphon of James, the Book of Thomas the Contender and the Apocalypse of Paul. The extent to which the Nag Hammadi texts alter one's understanding of the genre is indicated by Vielhauer (682):

> It is a facile assumption that the Freer Logion is, in terms of the history of traditions, the oldest form of this literature, the Epistula Apostolorum the second, and that, finally, in the Gnostic writings the final phase emerges, namely a genre that has achieved independence over against the Gospels. But the following arguments speak against this view: the oldest of the Gnostic works named above and the Epistula Apostolorum arose very probably in the second half of the second century, but

Codex W, in which the Freer Logion occurs, is significantly younger (5th century). Further, such a dialogue is not necessarily bound to an Easter situation – in the Coptic Apocalypse of Paul [NHC V. 2] the Dialogue occurs at the ascent of Paul (2 Corinthians 12:2ff.). Hence one must at least consider the possibility that in the case of the Dialogues with the Resurrected one has to do with an independent genre.

With regard to specific instances Vielhauer comments (687, 690):

> Among the Nag Hammadi texts there is an interesting formal parallel to the Epistula Apostolorum, the apocryphal Letter of James [NHC I. 2]. It is to my knowledge the only example of a Dialogue of the Resurrected presented in the framework of a letter. ...
> The Book of Thomas the Contender presents not only the simplest, but in my view also the purest (most original) form of the literary type 'Dialogue of the Resurrected with his Disciples', in comparison with which the Freer Logion appears as a reduction, just as the Apocryphon of John, to name only this one, is an amplification, not to speak of the mixed forms of the Epistula Apostolorum and the apocryphal Letter of James.

The four 'Apocalypses' of Codex V are discussed briefly: the Apocalypse of Adam, being non-Christian, does not come up for consideration. The two Apocalypses of James bear such titles 'because they "reveal" soteriological and christological mysteries and gnosis, because they are revelatory discourses; James is not an apocalypticist (seer), but rather a bearer of revelation. ... The Apocalypse of Paul on the other hand can be reckoned literarily with apocalypticism, since it contains traditional elements of this genre' (527). The Apocalypse of Peter is only mentioned to distinguish it from the already-known text of the same name (508), much as the Acts of Peter and the Twelve Apostles is mentioned only to distinguish it from the already-known Acts of Peter (699).

Helmut Koester treats fifteen Nag Hammadi tractates: the Gospel of Truth; the Apocryphon of John; the Gospel of Thomas; the Hypostasis of the Archons; the Book of Thomas the Contender; the Gospel of the Egyptians; Eugnostos the Blessed; the Sophia of Jesus Christ; the Dialogue of the Saviour; the First and Second Apocalypse of James; the Apocalypse of Adam; the Paraphrase of Shem; the Second Treatise of the Great Seth; and the Three Steles of Seth. Thus, to whatever extent the discipline of Introduction to the New Testament does not confine itself to the canonical books but conceives of its more scholarly function as that of a study of the earliest extant Christian literature, some half again the number of canonical books has been added by the Nag Hammadi discovery to the list for which our discipline is responsible!

Koester discusses Gnosticism in one way or the other in connection with Q, John, 1–2 Corinthians, Ephesians, Colossians, Hebrews, the Pastoral

Epistles and 2 Peter. What is more significant perhaps is the way whole sections on Gnosticism are built into Koester's presentation, which is less book-by-book than in terms of geographical areas and historical trajectories. Volume I ends with a major section on the Roman empire, including a section on 'Gnosticism and Hermetism'. The major section on Palestine and Syria in volume II includes sub-sections on Gnosticism under the rubrics 'Jesus as the Teacher of Wisdom', 'The Gnostic Inheritance of John', and 'Syria, the Country of Origin of Christian Gnosticism'. The following major section on Egypt has a section entitled 'Egyptian Gnosticism', which begins with a sub-section on the 'Testimony of the Writings from Nag Hammadi'; the sub-section on 'The Beginnings of Catholicism' also includes a section on the 'Controversy with Gnosticism'. The next major section on Asia Minor, Greece and Rome has sub-sections on 'Apocalypticism and Gnosticism', 'The Struggle against Gnosticism', and 'Apocalyptic Gnosis as Legacy of Paul'. Thus Koester implements the programme set out by Wilson (298):

> We can now explore the whole range from Qumran and the Wisdom literature at the one end, through the New Testament, to an emergent orthodoxy on the one hand and a developed Gnosticism on the other. ... But if the primary significance of the Nag Hammadi library relates more to the context and background of the New Testament, to the climate of that and the succeeding period, there are also points at which the discovery impinged more directly upon New Testament study, and further investigation of these texts may yet have much to teach us.

Koester's own research is more evident with regard to the transmission of the sayings of Jesus as the context in which the Johannine discourses are to be understood. This trajectory is summarized in connection with Syrian Christianity (vol. II, 208):

> In the tradition of the sayings of Jesus, Gnosticism appears in the emphasis upon, and the predominance of, wisdom sayings, and in the spiritualizing of the eschatological sayings of Jesus. The *Gospel of Thomas* offers this interpretation of the sayings under the apostolic authority of Thomas, a tradition that seems to have continued under the name of this particular apostle in communities in Syria. In II CE this is evident in the *Book of Thomas* (NHC II, 7; falsely called the book of *Thomas the Contender*). In early III CE the same tradition reappears in the *Acts of Thomas*, which also draws the aretalogical tradition of the apostles' miraculous deeds into the process of gnostic interpretation: individual miracle stories become descriptions of the encounter of the heavenly world and its messenger with the lower world of demons and transitoriness. Within the circle of the Johannine churches, gnostic interpretation is again tied to

the sayings of Jesus, which were used for the development of dialogue materials in which Jesus speaks about the presence of eschatological salvation, mediated through himself as the revealer from the heavenly world of the Father, the home of all those who are able to hear his voice. The basic concept of the hymn, used by the author of the Gospel of John for his prologue, demonstrates the intimate connection between the myth of Wisdom and the gnostic understanding of Christian revelation. A fully developed gnostic christology, however, does not appear until later among the opponents of 1 John and in the *Acts of John*, where it took shape in explicit controversy with the Gospel's attempts to amalgamate the concept of the gnostic revealer with the kerygma of the death and resurrection of the earthly Jesus.

It is in this broader context that the Gospel of Thomas and the Dialogue of the Saviour are interpreted in a way that is not only relevant to an understanding of the Johannine dialogue but is also important in its own right (vol. II, 154–55):

... A number of newly formed sayings of Jesus are evident [in the *Gospel of Thomas*]. But the majority of the traditional words fit the author's theology very well. Many of these sayings are preserved in a form which is older than the forms of their parallels in the Synoptic Gospels. This is especially the case for the parables, but also for sayings which reject the claim of traditional Jewish piety (6; 14; 27; 104) and which criticize the Pharisees as the guardians of this piety (39; 102). A few sayings in the *Gospel of Thomas* reveal the influence of speculations about the biblical creation story (redemption as the rediscovery of the heavenly prototypes which are superior to the earthly Adam; *Gos. Thom.* 83–85). Such sayings appear to be later interpolations into a document of a Christian church which was interpreting the sayings of Jesus in analogy to a wisdom theology which showed clear gnostic tendencies; nonetheless, this group did not completely reject ecclesiastical authority (12).

... A gnosticizing interpretation of the sayings of Jesus which searches in his words for divine wisdom, recognition of the divine self, and immortality, appears in at least one other document from the library of Nag Hammadi: the *Dialogue of the Savior* (NHC III, 5). In its original form, or in its major source, it must also be dated to I CE; because of several close relationships to the *Gospel of Thomas* and the Gospel of John, a Syrian origin is likely. In its extant form, the *Dialogue of the Savior* clearly bears the signs of a secondary compilation. The introductory gnostic sermon, prayer, and instruction (120, 2–124, 24) contain allusions to the Deutero-Pauline Letters, the Catholic

Epistles, and the Letter to the Hebrews. There are also some other pieces which have been interpolated into the older dialogue, such as fragments of a Genesis interpretation (127, 19–131, 15), a cosmological list (133, 16–134, 24), and a gnostic interpretation of an apocalyptic vision (134, 24–137, 3). But the remaining parts of the writing, about sixty per cent of the extant text (124, 23–127, 18; 131, 19–132, 15; 137, 3–147, 22), are remnants of a more original writing, which is distinguished by the form of a dialogue between Jesus, Judas, Matthew and Mariam, and thus clearly different from the interpolated discourses cited above.

This dialogue has no relationship to the known genres of Hellenistic dialogical literature. It is instead an expanded sayings collection. Sayings are introduced by questions of the disciples; more questions lead to the addition of interpretations, which again use sayings in many instances. The underlying sayings have parallels in the Gospel of Matthew, the Gospel of John, and most frequently in the *Gospel of Thomas*. The intention of the dialogue seems to correspond to the first saying of the *Gospel of Thomas*, namely, to find the interpretation of the words of Jesus and, thus, to overcome death. The themes are arranged according to the themes of the second saying of the *Gospel of Thomas* (in the form in which it is preserved in the Oxyrhynchus Papyri): seeking-finding-marvelling-ruling-resting. The disciples are asked to recognize that they have not yet reached rule and rest, but must carry the burden of earthly labour, which Jesus himself also shares (139, 6–13).

With regard to the history of early Christian literary genres, this dialogue is a significant document because it shows the further development of Jesus' sayings tradition into a new genre, which makes its appearance as the 'revelation dialogue' or 'revelation discourse' in the Gospel of John and in later gnostic revelation writings. In its theological themes the *Dialogue of the Savior* is also an important predecessor of the Johannine theology since it discusses the problems of a realized eschatology for the Christian church. In this tradition of the interpretation of his words, Jesus remains the teacher of wisdom and the living revealer, who challenges his disciples to discover in themselves whether and how the revelation has become a reality in their existence. Only in the recognition of the self does the revelation become effective, because here the believers become equal to Jesus insofar as they know their origin and their destiny. It is exactly at this point that we are confronted with the roots of gnostic theology. With this theology as well as this tradition of interpretation of Jesus' sayings, the Gospel of John, developing in the same context of traditional interpretation, had to come to terms.

Hans-Martin Schenke's *Introduction*, like that of Kümmel, is more strictly confined to the New Testament books than are the *Introductions* by Vielhauer and Koester, which represent somewhat different genres in German New Testament scholarship. Schenke's involvement with the Nag Hammadi texts has been the most intense of the four, in that he directs the 'Berliner Arbeitskreis für koptisch-gnostische Schriften' that has been primarily responsible for German-language Nag Hammadi research both in its own right and in relation to the New Testament. It is all the more interesting that Schenke does not see Paul as facing primarily a Gnostic front, but rather as confronted with a proto-orthodox opposition (47):

> We for our part see the main opposition – with a slight modification of the classical hypothesis in this regard emanating from F. C. Baur – in the clash between the older type of primitive Christianity represented by the congregations in Jerusalem and Antioch, which we name in abbreviated form 'the official church' of that time, and the comparably newer Pauline type.

Thus the Pauline letters are for Schenke hardly involved in the study of the Nag Hammadi texts. But in the deutero-Pauline world, the impact of the new source material is immediately sensed. Colossians, an 'anti-Gnostic polemic' (I, 155), may serve as an illustration, in that a new interpretation of the opponents is defended precisely on the basis of the availability of original Gnostic texts (I, 160–61):

> We ourselves consider a negative understanding of the powers and the worship addressed to them to be correct, a view that has admittedly been considered occasionally in the past ..., but no one has really attempted to carry it through, especially not on the basis of real Gnosticism. It is often said today that the doctrine attacked in Colossians is Gnostic ..., even if this is not meant consistently. For the concept of Gnosticism that is presupposed is often unspecific and fluctuating. But in our opinion it is most appropriate to interpret specifically the worship of angels in a Gnostic way – but not Gnostic in the sense of 'Gnosticism' that had to be invented just for Colossians, but rather on the background of real Gnosticism, if one is to assume that the idea can be carried through. That is in fact the case. And in our view it becomes clear that in this way the problems can be solved better than on the assumption of the positive interpretation! According to the general world view of Gnosticism the Gnostics themselves, though in principle already redeemed, are nonetheless still subject to the domination of the Archons. Between the realm of light and the world of humans lies the domain of the Archons, who are opposed to the light above and to the light that is in humans as soul or spirit. The Redeemer has secretly passed through the realm of the Archons,

has brought humans the redeeming knowledge, and at his triumphal return above has prepared for the Gnostic the way through the realm of the Archons into the realm of light. Nonetheless this way that the Gnostics must travel after death is still very dangerous. ... Probably the 'angels' or 'principalities and powers' to which the 'worship' of our heretics is directed correspond to these Archons of Gnosticism, who as a matter of fact are indeed so designated in original Gnostic texts.

Evidence for such a Gnostic practice is found in Saying 100 of the Gospel of Thomas (I, 161): 'Give Caesar what belongs to Caesar, give God what belongs to God ['in view of the following context this can only refer to the Demiurge'], *but* give Me what is Mine'. Further instances of the use of specific Nag Hammadi texts to interpret the heresy of Colossians are as follows (I, 162–63):

The 'humility' over against the powers is possibly only the outcome of a very specific Gnostic Christology, which seems to be echoed in 'he humbled himself' in Philippians 2:8 ... and is spelled out in the long Redeemer hymn of the Teachings of Silvanus (NHC VII, 110:19–111:13). ... Its crucial point is that the Redeemer (followed by the Gnostics), by his humility before the Archons, puts to shame precisely these Archons, whose essence is pride. Incidentally new light falls from another Nag Hammadi writing on a still further trait of the heresy of Colossians, namely its yearning after 'pleroma' or 'being filled'. In the Apocryphon of James there is talk of a quite similar kind about 'being filled' (NHC I, 2:28–3:11; 3:34–4:22; 12:26–30), and indeed being filled with the kingdom of heaven, where this traditional term serves only as a symbol for the divine Spirit who is potentially always already in mankind, and yet must be brought to maturity through Gnosis. (Cf. also the dialectic of 'in the descent' and 'in the Pleroma' for the soul in Authoritative Teaching, NHC VI, 21:18–19). ... One must also consider that the author of Colossians himself has been very strongly influenced by Gnosticism. Hence we have to do actually with a debate between a moderate form of Christian Gnosticism advocated by the author, and a more radical form. For such moderate forms of Gnosticism in which Gnosticism appears merely as a slightly – even if clearly – gnosticized form of Hellenistic, Jewish Sophia speculation, compare especially the Thunder, Perfect Mind (NHC VI. *2*) and the Teachings of Silvanus (NHC VII. *4*).

Similarly in the case of Ephesians (I, 183):

Again further Gnostic or mythological conceptions are applied to Christ: Ephesians 2:14–18 – the breaking down of the dividing

wall between the world above and the world below by the
Redeemer ...; 4:8–10 – the return of the Redeemer into the
world of light and the triumph over the Archons ...; 5:25*b*–32
the church as the Saviour's female partner to be redeemed. The
Gnostic background of this last passage must of course be seen
much more concretely than it appears, e.g. in Schlier. ... If thus
far one could only reconstruct it from Gnostic texts ..., it has
now become tangibly accessible and clearly visible in the
Exegesis on the Soul.

Schenke traces a bifurcating trajectory of the Pauline school (I, 229):

Within the Pauline school we must assume at least two
directions: a relatively strongly gnosticizing, as it were open
direction, represented by the authors of Colossians and
Ephesians, and an uncompromisingly anti-Gnostic, so to speak
conservative direction, that does its borrowing from the
Hellenistic synagogue, popular philosophy and high religion.

The Pastorals belong to this wing, with a decidedly anti-Gnostic stance (I,
219):

According to all this the heresy fought in the Pastorals is to be
identified as Christian Gnosticism strongly influenced by Jewish
Christianity, i.e. as Gnosticism in a stage where it has long since
penetrated into Christianity and is moving well on the way
towards transforming the whole church in the author's region
(cf. 2 Timothy 2:17). But the Gnostic movement at the time of
the Pastorals has not yet reached its peak. One still finds no
clear play on any typical trait of one of the later great systems.

Nonetheless Paul is championed by Gnostics, a familiar trait since
Tertullian's branding of him as *haereticorum apostolus* (I, 234). But now
new evidence for this Gnostic reception of Paul is found in Nag Hammadi
texts (I, 246, n. 1): the Treatise on the Resurrection (NHC I, 45:23–29), the
Hypostasis of the Archons (NHC II, 86:21–25, 'the great [or greatest]
apostle'), the Exegesis on the Soul (NHC II, 131:2–13); and the Teachings
of Silvanus (NHC VII, 108:30–32, 'Paul who has become like Christ').
It is interesting to see that Schenke finds the Nag Hammadi texts
relevant even for the study of the Synoptic Gospels, where, in distinction
from the Gospel of John, Gnosticism has played hardly any role in the
scholarship of the past (II, 27–28):

Especially Helmut Koester and James M. Robinson have shown
that such collections of sayings [as the Gospel of Thomas], to
which one may also reckon Q, imply, just as in the case of other
genres, a quite specific Christology, according to which Jesus is
understood as the mouthpiece of divine Wisdom. ... According to

this view of things one can take as one's point of departure the assumption that Gnostic tendencies, even if initially only implicitly, inhered in a genre to which Q also belonged, and indeed from the point in time when Jesus was brought into connection with divine Wisdom. Further, this could be a reason why Q became 'lost' and is encountered only in a theological revision in Matthew and Luke. That Q was in fact not the only collection of sayings is shown by writings such as the Gospel of Thomas or the Gospel of Philip. The Gospel of Thomas can serve us as a living illustration of how we have to think of the kind of text Q was.

Schenke also refers to the Teachings of Silvanus to exemplify the attributing of Wisdom sayings to Jesus and the correlative Christology (II, 63, n. 1).

The opening of Mark is also placed in a Nag Hammadi context (II, 76):

Rather we are concerned here with the possible dependence of the Marcan narration of the baptism and sojourn in the wilderness on a myth of the coming of the Redeemer, which has now become very clearly visible in fourteen variations in the Apocalypse of Adam (NHC V, 77:27–82:28). The new text also puts the already known parallels in a clearer light. Recently James M. Robinson has pointed expressly and convincingly to this problem and this relationship. ... Robinson's statements on this theme do not propose to be more than a beginning of the work on this history-of-religions background. Yet it is already clear that the Gospel of Mark does not at all begin simply 'historically', as one usually thinks and says.

In the case of the Gospel of Matthew it is the designation of disciples as 'the little ones' that is put in perspective by a Nag Hammandi text (II, 111):

That we have to do here really with a designation for Christians, that is to say, with a bit of real life, and not something like a redactional artificial product, is surprisingly confirmed by the analogous and fitting re-emergence of precisely this title in the Jewish Christian substratum of the Gnostic Apocalypse of Peter (NHC VII, 78:22; 79:19–20; 80:11). ... Eduard Schweizer seems inclined to find in the expression 'these little ones' in Matthew the whole congregation. But the wording of the passages in question does not quite fit that. Rather the statements would in our view fit better if one would see in 'these little ones' only another designation for the constantly wandering prophets. These homeless prophets are distinguished incidentally from the settled members of the congregation apparently not only by the way they reside, but also, as is really inherent in the

nature of the case, by a yearning after a higher perfection, i.e.
that must have had at least an inclination to asceticism.

Incidentally, the way in which changing the name of Levi the tax-collector
into Matthew (Matthew 9:9) would lead to attributing the Gospel to
Matthew the tax-collector as its author is illustrated (II, 121) by the way in
which the Gospel of Philip receives (belatedly in Schenke's view) its title
because of a passing reference to Philip (NHC II, 73:8). One could also in
this connection think of Saying 13 of the Gospel of Thomas.

Schenke seeks to clarify in a somewhat new way the Gnostic
background of the Gospel of John (II, 188–189, 193):

> The Gnostic element, to the extent it comes to expression in
> the Gospel itself, is in our view not at all describable as
> somehow belonging to the process of the emergence of
> Gnosticism, but rather is the stump of a fully developed
> Gnosticism whose roots and limbs have been cut off in order to
> suspend it in a Christian framework. This is clearest, as is well
> known, in that Jesus in the Fourth Gospel promises again and
> again to reveal what he has seen and heard from the Father,
> without ever fulfilling this promise. In this perspective of the
> toned-down Gnosticism of the Fourth Gospel there may also
> belong a few other of its distinctive traits that, so far as we
> know, are not usually seen in this perspective. The way that the
> Gospel can speak in a levelling, distancing and deprecating tone
> of 'the Jews' is well known. And it is certainly true that the
> 'Jews' are meant as a symbol for the world, to the extent that it
> rejects the revelation, whereas in the vehemence of many
> statements actual conflicts of the Johannine groups with
> contemporary Judaism are attested. ... But one must nonetheless
> ask whether a presupposition of the possibility of thinking these
> terrible things is not also the presence already of the anti-Jewish
> emotions and conceptions of Gnosticism. That would mean that
> in the background of the Fourth Gospel stands a form of
> Gnosticism that has already carried through the turn against
> Judaism. In this connection also the problems of the use of the
> Old Testament in the Fourth Gospel become interesting in a new
> way. ... Perhaps one can explain the really unusual attitude that
> the evangelist himself assumes towards the Old Testament as due
> to a certain influence of the ambivalent Gnostic understanding of
> the Old Testament possibly already present in his intellectual
> environment, according to which it is both a book of revelation
> and also a witness to the religion of the Demiurge. Finally there
> are aspects of the typically Johannine understanding of the death
> of Jesus that may seem to be still obscure. If one asks who really
> 'the ruler of the world' is (12:31; 14:30; 16:11), how it is that he
> is judged by Jesus' death (16:11), and what is really
> 'consummated' on the cross (19:30), then such passages could

appear as remnants of a considerably more mythological, Christian-Gnostic Redeemer myth.

This Gnostic environment of the Gospel of John is for Schenke an alternative to the Qumranian environment that has often been suggested over the past generation (II, 201, 217–18):

> In the question as to the background of the Fourth Gospel, in any case the Gnostic and the Essene thought world must remain alternatives. And against Qumran, which has clear advantages with regard to the age of the attestation, there is the argument that precisely the main point, the special Christology of the Fourth Gospel, is generally recognized to be in no way derivable from Qumran, whereas New Testament scholarship needs precisely a place where the whole of the strange statements of the Fourth Gospel are intelligible. ...
> The author takes up the dualistic conception that every person has a place of origin, be it from God or from the devil, and that one reveals this origin in one's conduct. In the formulation 'to come from', 'to be born from God', the ethical dualism is rooted in Gnosticism, not in Qumran. In Qumran mankind is determined by the power for which one decides: God or Belial. But in Gnosticism on the other hand one is determined by one's place of origin: light or darkness. Or, put otherwise: in Qumran the dualism is an apocalyptic historical occurrence, in Gnosticism a metaphysical definition of one's essence. In spite of all attempts to affirm Qumran as the sphere of influence, one must hold to the view that the Johannine circle is in this matter clearly influenced by Gnosticism. It has taken over this dualism and made it its own, but not in a cosmological interest, but rather in a soteriological and practical, ethical interest.

The Johannine discourses also receive new light from Nag Hammadi texts (II, 181):

> With regard to the dialogues it is least possible to avoid the insight that their compilation did not take place *in* the text, but already behind it. It also appears that the study of certain Nag Hammadi writings – on the one hand such writings that are shown to be related by their substantive statements and formal parallels to the Fourth Gospel (the Second Treatise of the Great Seth; the Thunder, Perfect Mind; the Trimorphic Protennoia), on the other hand writings with a dialogue framework, where the dialogues are often intelligible only on the assumption that the questions are secondary to the relevant 'answers' (e.g. the Apocryphon of James, the Book of Thomas) – can lead to the view that the hypothesis of a Johannine discourse source will rise again in a new form.

The 'beloved disciple' is also illuminated by Nag Hammadi texts (II, 178–79):

> The designation 'the disciple whom Jesus loved' means, as is especially clear in light of the Gospel of Philip (NHC II, 63:34–35), nothing less than 'the disciple whom Jesus loved more than all the disciples'. And in the apocryphal tradition there actually are disciples of whom this is said explicitly or implicitly. The most striking are: Mary Magdalene (especially the Gospel of Philip, NHC II, 59:6–11; 63:32–64:5 and the Gospel of Mary), the Lord's brother James (especially the First and Second Apocalypses of James; the Apocryphon of James; Saying 12 of the Gospel of Thomas) and Judas Thomas (especially the opening and Sayings 1 and 13 of the Gospel of Thomas and the Book of Thomas [cf. especially the framework at the beginning of the text] ...). It is interesting that the motif of their superiority to Peter readily attaches itself to these figures (cf. especially the Apocryphon of James and Saying 13 of the Gospel of Thomas).

This rapid survey of the use made of the Nag Hammadi library in four major 'Introductions to the New Testament' over the past two decades does not exhaust the references to Nag Hammadi texts and to Gnosticism within these four works, much less surveying the specialized studies only in part presupposed and mentioned in these works – or critically sifting such secondary literature as did Herbert Braun for the often overly enthusiastic Qumranian parallelomania. Nor has the process of working through the Nag Hammadi texts in terms of the New Testament been carried through fully, since most of the experts in this field have been thus far engrossed in making the Nag Hammadi library itself available to scholarship. The fact that this quantity of originally Greek literature survived only in Coptic translation has of course inhibited many from working with it. Yet this survey should have scored at least one major point: the study of the New Testament has been decisively changed by the discovery of the Nag Hammadi codices, and cannot in the future be carried on without considerable serious attention being paid to this new source material. We of the English speaking world are primarily indebted to R. McL. Wilson in this regard, and in repeating this main point of his presidential address we do him the honour he so richly deserves.

NOTES

1. R. McL. Wilson, 'Nag Hammadi and the New Testament', *NTS* 28, 1982, 289–302.
2. Most recently J. M. Robinson, 'Sethians and Johannine Thought: The *Trimorphic Protennoia* and the Prologue of the Gospel of John', in *The Rediscovery of Gnosticism: Proceedings of the International Conference*

on Gnosticism at Yale; New Haven, Connecticut, March 28–31, 1978, vol. II, *Sethian Gnosticism, SHR* 41:2, Leiden 1981, 643–62, 'Discussion', 662–70, 'Concluding Discussion', 671–85; Wilson, 'Nag Hammadi and the New Testament', 302, n. 55.

3. H. Braun, *Qumran und das Neue Testament,* Tübingen 1966.
4. W. G. Kümmel, *Einleitung in das Neue Testament* Heidelberg 1963[12]; 1973[17]; ET = *Introduction to the New Testament,* based on the 14th edition of 1965, tr. A. J. Mattill, Jr, Nashville 1966; revised edition based on the 17th edition, tr. H. C. Kee, 1975. Quotation is from the 1975 English edition unless otherwise indicated. Philipp Vielhauer, *Geschichte der urchristlichen Literatur: Einleitung in das Neue Testament, die Apokryphen und die Apostolischen Väter,* Berlin/New York, 1975. H.-M. Schenke and K. M. Fischer, unter Mitarbeit von H.-G. Bethge und G. Schenke, *Einleitung in die Schriften des Neuen Testaments, I: Die Briefe des Paulus und Schriften des Paulinismus; II: Die Evangelien und die anderen neutestamentlichen Schriften,* Berlin 1978–1979. Volume I begins with the earliest New Testament books, the letters of Paul, and continues through the Pauline trajectory; volume II begins with the Gospels and includes the rest of the New Testament (but not, as such, non-canonical books). The work is based on Schenke's lecture course over the years, with his former assistant Karl Martin Fischer (whose premature death shocked us all) composing parts that Schenke had not had time to write (1–2 Peter, 1–3 John, James, Hebrews, Revelation, Jude), while his subsequent assistant H.-G. Bethge prepared for publication his lecture manuscript on the Synoptic problem and Luke–Acts, and his wife (and pupil) Gesine Schenke provided critical (and supportive?) suggestions, read proofs and produced the indices. Helmut Koester, *Einführung in das Neue Testament im Rahmen der Religionsgeschichte und Kulturgeschichte der hellenistischen und römischen Zeit,* Berlin/New York 1980; ET = *Introduction to the New Testament,* Volume I: *History, Culture, and Religion of the Hellenistic Age;* Volume II: *History and Literature of Early Christianity, Hermeneia:* Foundations and Facets, Philadelphia 1982.

GNOSIS, GNOSTICISM AND THE NEW TESTAMENT: DEFINITION AND NATURE

II

'GNOSIS' AND 'GNOSTICISM' – THE PROBLEMS OF THEIR DEFINITION AND THEIR RELATION TO THE WRITINGS OF THE NEW TESTAMENT

by

Professor Kurt Rudolph, Leipzig

The much disputed question of the relation of what experts today call 'Gnosis' or 'Gnosticism' to parts of the New Testament writings in large measure involves not only philological and historical questions, i.e. factual ones, but also questions of terminology and method. All who reflect on the theory of scientific investigation are conscious of this situation and would find it unsatisfactory merely to invoke certain so-called facts. The alternative solutions of this problem are largely determined by the answers given to certain questions of definition and thus have a direct influence on the historical and philological investigation. It is always very valuable to acknowledge this situation and take note of it in advance. Those who would bypass or even exclude the necessity of this clarification of terminology in order to gain direct access to the sources are blind to the task of modern scholarly research; this seeks to apprehend its object by means of various levels of reflective knowledge, including not least that of definitions, that is descriptions of concepts or, according to the original sense of the Latin loanword *definitio* (which found its way into the academic vocabulary of Europe in the fifteenth and sixteenth centuries), demarcations.

In the present case the New Testament has been to a considerable extent drawn into this enquiry since the 'history of religions school' first posed their questions. We can see this happening in Wilhelm Bousset's *Hauptprobleme der Gnosis* (1907, 1973[2]); however we shall not attempt to trace the history of research further here.[1] Bousset uses the term 'Gnosis' in a general sense for what one had called 'Gnosticism' since the eighteenth century. In this he had a predecessor in F. C. Baur (*Die christliche Gnosis*, 1835) as well as in the fact that the two terms were generally parallel and interchangeable in the nineteenth century, at least in the German tongue.

Bousset made it clear to start with that he was not concerned with a system or systems, unlike previous scholars, but rather with common traditions and recurrent fundamental ideas, around which he arranged his account. 'Gnosis is based on a few basic ideas which keep reappearing, sometimes more, sometimes less':[2] the Seven and the Mother (Sophia), the unknown Father, dualism, the Primal Man, elements and hypostases, the Redeemer, the heavenward journey of the soul, mysteries (sacraments). At the very beginning of his article on 'Gnosis' he says, 'Usually now the name G(nosis) is used of that syncretistic religious movement which impinged on Christianity about 100 A.D. (at the latest); their meeting resulted in a variety of compromises and hybrid formations.'[3] Bousset distinguishes this 'Gnosis' in the narrower sense from the 'wider movement of Gnosticism' (yet not always consistently); the former is 'a significant, indeed the most significant factor' in the development of the latter.[4] By the latter he means the great systems of later Gnostic thought which had their primitive beginnings in syncretistic 'Gnosis'. This is for him a 'religious movement which originally had nothing at all to do with Christianity and whose essence is completely explicable without reference to it. Only gradually did first Old Testament and then Christian elements come to penetrate it.'[5] Gnosis is older than Christianity 'and it is as something already formed that it encounters Christianity.'[6] Bousset regards dualism as its fundamental characteristic.[7] The compromise with Christianity visible in the 'great schools of the Gnostics' is an artificial and superficial one, something 'contrived'.[8]

This brief survey of Bousset's views clearly shows how much the problem of (early) Christianity and 'Gnosis' has been affected by them to this day. Coming to us *via* the bridge of the so-called Bultmannian school, Bousset's legacy is still very much alive today – although modified in many details; here the contribution of the circle of Swedish historians of religion gathered round Geo Widengren deserves a mention.[9] 'Gnosis' is seen as an independent, originally non-Christian manifestation of the syncretism of late antiquity; from simple beginnings (in the East) in pre-Christian times it 'developed' – or rather 'proliferated', as Bousset kept emphasizing[10] – into the great, complex systems of the second and third centuries. The name 'Gnosticism' was reserved for these high or late forms; it clearly showed the pejorative nuances of words formed with this suffix, nuances already familiar to the ancient world.[11] Such confidence in the pure origins and in a 'development' to secondary, later stages obscuring the clarity of the beginnings, a dominant conviction of the nineteenth century, fostered these reconstructions every bit as much as did evolutionary theories of history.

Scholarship has grown ever more critical of such a scenario and the often contradictory uses made of it, but has still not been able to dispense with it completely. This is true particularly of German-speaking scholarship. In the Anglo-American world things were from the start rather different: the influence of the German 'Religionsgeschichtliche Schule' ('history of religions school') was not so strong and certain older traditions which regarded 'Gnosticism' as a Christian heresy of a philosophical character were harder to eradicate; an important reason for this was the influence that 'classical' (Greek and Latin) studies had and still have in this area (New Testament studies in Germany seem to me to have broken free from classical philology to a greater degree than in the English-speaking world). To some extent this is true also of French work in this field, even if Bousset's influence here has been stronger (parallel to that of E. de Faye). Robert McL. Wilson, whom this volume honours, was among the first to appreciate the course that scholarship in this area was taking, influenced by these different regional and national traditions, which are reflected in the differences in the terminology used; he has emphasized this aspect in particular in his numerous studies, both large and small. He aimed to restore a certain international unity of approach by means of a clarification of the related key concepts of 'Gnosis' and 'Gnosticism' (in so far as such unity existed until the rise of the 'history of religions school'); his efforts deserve special attention here.

As an attentive and expert observer of the international study of Gnosis, especially that set in motion since the appearance of the Nag Hammadi texts, he sought to integrate certain legitimate concerns which had been expressed in the questions posed by R. Bultmann into the framework outlined by older studies; central for him was the idea of a development from the 'pre-Gnosis' or (as it was later called) 'Gnosis' of the first century into the 'Gnosticism' of the second and third centuries. 'The New Testament itself affords evidence of an incipient movement, which by the second century had grown into a world-religion and constituted a real danger to the Christian faith'; so he wrote as early as 1955.[12] 'It is however suggested that this "pre-Christian" Gnosis, Jewish or pagan, would be more naturally classified not as Gnosticism but as pre-gnosis' (ibid.). This movement is to be dated as more or less contemporary with the rise of Christianity.[13] Possibly there was such a thing as a 'pre-Christian Jewish Gnosticism'.[14] At any rate the Gnostic doctrines of the second century and later are 'clearly the outcome of a long process'.[15] Wilson then gave fuller expression to this view in his well-known book, *The Gnostic Problem* (1958, 1964[2]); there he paid especially close attention to the Jewish contribution to the rise of Gnosticism.[16] In doing so he still stuck to this term as was usual in the English-speaking world and, following A. D. Nock, spoke of the Gnosticism of this time not as a system but as a pervasive atmosphere which enveloped all contemporary religions and philosophies to a certain extent.[17] The Gnosticism of the history of the Christian church is only *one* form of this 'spirit' (as Hans Jonas expressly affirmed!); this 'spirit' remained 'fundamentally alien' despite its connections with Judaism and Christianity (ibid.). 'In short Gnosticism in the broader sense is a general tendency of the period which saw the birth of Christianity, and makes its presence felt in various ways in all the thoughts of the time. In a narrower sense the name is applied to certain types of speculation which appeared in the first two centuries of the Christian era, and whose chief characteristic was the assimilation of Christianity more or less completely to the ideas of the contemporary world. These Christian Gnostics thus apply to the Christian Gospel the ideas of the wider

Gnosticism around them, but in the process the essential message of Christianity is lost.'[18]

R. McL. Wilson has regularly sent me copies of his works during almost twenty years of scholarly contact, and to my knowledge it was in 1964 that he first gave further thought to the varying use of 'Gnosis' in German scholarship in a discussion with G. Quispel:[19] to translate 'Gnosis' in R. Bultmann's writings as 'Gnosticism', as Wilson himself had done, could only lead to confusion amongst English-speakers; for here the traditional view still reigned, according to which Gnosticism was regarded only as the Christian heresy of the second and third centuries.[20] The use of the adjective 'Gnostic' with reference to 'pre-Christian Gnosis' *and* the later 'Gnosticism' could lead to misunderstanding. 'We must distinguish a merely descriptive sense of the term from its use to indicate derivation.'[21] Wilson wished to prevent the danger which he saw in such an unreflecting use of 'Gnosticism' with regard to the New Testament: all that this technical term implied in the second and third centuries might be imported with it into the first century. On the other hand there was an undeniable continuity in the 'Gnostic movement', between the 'Gnosis' of German scholarship and the 'Gnosticism' of English. This is where, in Wilson's eyes, the idea of 'growth' or 'development' already mentioned came in, an idea which he found anticipated by Bultmann.[22] No movement springs up full-grown like Athene from Zeus' head, but develops by stages. We must reckon in 'Gnosticism' with such a 'process of growth and development, of which such documents as we possess may reflect different stages' (ibid.). Hence, he argued, ideas which were later stigmatized as 'Gnostic' may not have struck an earlier period as heretical.[23] It was necessary that 'English-speaking scholars', who were in growing numbers giving their assent to the thesis of a pre-Christian Gnosis, should be able to define this precisely before they could raise the questions of its relation to the New Testament and to later Gnostic schools. This then took place at the 1966 Messina congress on 'The Origins of Gnosticism' (!), where Wilson put forward the view of 'Gnosis, Gnosticism and the New Testament' which he now held:[24] it is legitimate to speak of 'Gnosis' in relation to the New Testament as long as this term does not mean the later Gnosticism; the two are separated by 'a considerable development'.[25] 'It is dangerous in the extreme to assume that what is gnostic (in the sense of gnosis) already implies all that is meant by Gnostic (in the sense of Gnosticism).'[26] In his eyes the danger of 'reading into' the New Testament full-blown Gnostic concepts loomed larger than the attempt to understand with their aid certain characteristics of early Christian thinking.

Proposals were also put forward in Messina for an agreed terminology;[27] these amounted to distinguishing 'Gnosis' as a broader term for 'esoteric knowledge' from 'Gnosticism' as a specific form, i.e. one with a markedly systematic character, a form found in the history of Christianity in the second and third centuries. Elsewhere I have described as dangerous the weakness of this attempt, and especially its separation of the two concepts.[28] Basically, in the specific area in which they have been used till now, they both mean the same thing; but 'Gnosticism' is a modern term, without any basis in the sources (see below). Wilson at any rate would not want to divorce 'Gnosis' from 'Gnosticism' completely; again and again he stresses their genetic connection. 'Gnosticism as such is neither Jewish nor Christian, but a new creation.'[29] But that means that its true roots lie outside these religions, although they contribute to its formation. His revised opinion can be detected even in the title of his *Gnosis and the New Testament* (1968): what was formerly 'pre-Gnosis' or 'Gnosticism in the broader sense' ('atmosphere', 'ways of thought') is now 'Gnosis', a precursor of the Gnosticism of the second and third centuries.[30] 'By Gnosticism we mean the specifically Christian heresy of the second century A.D., by Gnosis in a broader sense, the whole complex of ideas belonging to the Gnostic movement and related trends of thought.'[31] Certain manifestations of the last-named can also be described as 'pre-Gnosis' (e.g. the Dead Sea Scrolls, Philo) but this can be misleading.[32] While 'Gnosticism appears to be roughly contemporary with Christianity, or perhaps a little later, and ... there are signs of an incipient Gnosticism in the New Testament period, ... Gnosis in the broader sense is indisputably older'.[33] He suggests a date for the beginnings of Gnosticism in the last quarter of the first century; possibly they are earlier, 'but the process of transition from Gnosis (or pre-Gnosis) to Gnosticism proper is still obscure.'[34] Wilson argues for a Jewish, pre-Christian Gnosticism (!),[35] inasmuch as its origins are to be found in pre-Christian times; yet he does not want to use the term 'Gnosticism' for this, since there is no evidence of a fully developed form of this at this date.[36] Elsewhere too Wilson seems to chop and change his terminology; he is not always consistent.[37] As a 'working hypothesis' he keeps Bultmann's procedure to some degree and recognizes real 'Gnostic' traits (in the descriptive sense of the term) in various New Testament writings, e.g. certainly in 1 John and the Pastoral Epistles.[38] In others they are of a more general ('gnosticizing') nature, as in John's Gospel ('there are certain affinities'),[39] in Galatians ('some vague traces'), Ephesians and Colossians ('clearer signs ... but still vague and ambiguous')[40] or in the Corinthian church in Paul's time: 'In the broad and comprehensive sense of the term Gnosis, it is perfectly correct to speak of Gnosis at Corinth; but this is not really very helpful unless we can determine the relation between this Gnosis and the latest developed Gnosticism.'[41]

So we can see how terminology controls interpretation. Wilson has subsequently given expression to this insight of his again and again.[42] In reply to my criticism of the 'Messina theses' he affirms that they attempted to recognize a difference and were 'the attempt to trace both the continuity and the discontinuity of the development from Gnosis in its earliest forms into Gnosticism. In terms of monetary exchange, the one currency (Gnosticism) is being pegged at a fixed level, the other (Gnosis) allowed to float until it finds its own appropriate level.'[43] Between the two there is a sort of 'trajectory', a process of crystallization.[44] Thus (in the context of the discussion of a 'Jewish Gnosis') Wilson can say that 'in any case the category of Gnosis should be restricted to material which shows some demonstrable affinity with Gnosticism proper, but in relation to which there is some doubt whether it belongs in the latter category'.[45] Gnosis and Gnosticism are therefore not to be torn apart, and remain related to one another within the context of a fairly long process of development (first and second centuries A.D.). Despite all our efforts they are ultimately 'slippery words', as Wilson has most recently put it;[46] it will take some time to achieve a consensus as to their definition and use.[47] Wilson's labours over many years were thus a beginning, and deserve our continual attention, especially since they encompass the whole international field of studies and enjoin caution. But because he himself gives no clear delimitation or preciser definition of 'Gnosis' and, strictly speaking, sees it too from the perspective of its developed form (as a system or systems of doctrines), the question of what is really common to the two has not yet been answered. Even first century 'Gnosis' is, as a 'way of thinking' (A. D. Nock), inconceivable apart from certain essential convictions (Wilson talks repeatedly of certain 'ideas' held by this early 'Gnosis'). I do not find it very helpful to regard first-century 'Gnosis' as just a general 'way of thinking' lacking any shape (even social!); those who thought thus at any rate existed even if we know very little about them (cf. Simon Magus, Menander, Cerinthus). Without some such assumptions we cannot hope to reconstruct this early stage from later literary sources, including now especially the Nag Hammadi library, and from the echoes of it in certain New Testament texts. The Gnostic 'spirit of late antiquity' (H. Jonas) lacks neither body nor shape, but bears the stamp of a quite specific religious view of the world (see below). German scholarship, inasmuch as it was and still is indebted to the initiatives of the 'history of religions school', has at any rate understood the word 'Gnosis' to refer to what has elsewhere also been described as 'Gnosticism'; it differs from others in that it has sought to trace its beginnings to the period before New Testament Christianity or contemporary with it. We should not forget that the New Testament canon covers a period of nearly a hundred years (50–150 A.D.), yet this has too often been neglected in our discussion. A strictly historical approach does not view the canon as a readymade norm of Christianity or even a dividing line between what is pre-Christian and what is post-Christian; it cannot make a sharp distinction between Gnosis and Gnosticism, for the continuity and the unity between the two looms too large for it.

In view of this disagreement it may help to consider the ancient terminology, even if this is not decisive. This has already been done repeatedly.[48] 'Gnosticism' is a modern, deprecatory expression, a theologizing neologism. In Greek the suffix -ismos is only possible with verbs ending in -izein (Christianismos is the sole exception).[49] Often this ending has an ironic or deprecatory sense, as is still the case today in European languages.[50] Most of these -isms, including 'Gnosticism', have arisen since around 1750 and in increasing numbers: thus man's history has become -istic (F. Dornseiff).[51] Even 'Platonism' can only be traced back to the sixteenth century (first in French).[52] It is hard to shake free from these forms and to return to the old names. For our area of interest only Gnosis and Gnostics (gnōstikoi, gnōstikos) can be shown to have been used at that time. This was not even a general universal self-description.

Gnōsis is an old Greek technical term used since Plato to describe philosophical 'knowledge', the knowledge of what exists as opposed to ignorance of it; knowing and not knowing are distinguished by their reference to what exists and what does not respectively.[53] The term first came to have the sense of an esoteric, revealed knowledge in the Hellenistic period (mysteries, Hermetica, New Testament, magical papyri), a sense adopted also by the Platonic and Neopythagorean traditions (which had long had inclinations to the esoteric). The word is always used positively in the New Testament, even if – in the case of Paul – it is accompanied and controlled by faith (*pistis*) and love (*agapē*); God's knowledge and knowing God as Christian 'knowledge' (*gnōsis*) are as highly prized as 'wisdom' (*sophia*). Only 1 Timothy 6:20 is an obvious exception, with its talk of 'what is falsely called knowledge (*gnōsis*)'. This is the first time that we meet a denunciation of heretical views and those who hold them.[54] This happens at the beginning of the second century (*ca*. 100–110). But already in 1 Corinthians 8 Paul protests at an excessive confidence in 'knowledge' (*gnōsis*).

Irenaeus in the preface to his *Adversus haereses*[55] was the first to lump together the heretics whom he was opposing under the technical term which they used, 'Gnosis' (Latin *agnitio*); thus he laid down the guidelines for later heresiologists until the term 'Gnosticism' was coined in the eighteenth century.[56] In the literature of those thus described knowledge indeed played a dominant role (besides the Greek *gnōsis* there were the Coptic *saune* or *sooun*, the Syriac *īda'ta*, and the Mandean *manda*); yet it did not have its philosophical, gnoseological sense, but meant a saving act which liberated ('redeemed'). 'The beginning of perfection is the knowledge of Man (*anthrōpos*), but the knowledge of God is complete perfection' (Hipp., *Ref.* V, 6:6). 'If anyone has knowledge he is from above' (NHC I. *3*, 22:1ff.). So it was not misleading to give this movement the name of 'Gnosis'; the name expresses a distinctive trait of its ideology.[57] This is confirmed by the term *gnōstikoi* coined by some groups or schools (especially the Ophites). Celsus is the first to attest this (Orig., *Cels*. V, 61), and Irenaeus round about the same time is already using the term quite freely ('the so-called Gnostics': III, 4:3; 11:2).[58] Hippolytus knows it as a designation of the Naassenes and Ophites, but, like Irenaeus, also uses it as a general term (especially *Ref.* V, 23:3; VII, 35:1; 36:2; IX, 4).[59] Tertullian is familiar with it applied to the Ophites or Prodicus (*De anima* 18; *Scorpiace* 1:5; *Val.* 39). Clement of Alexandria tries to distinguish the 'true Gnostics' and the false and so uses the name positively.[60] Finally Porphyry mentions a treatise of Plotinus 'Against the Gnostics'. M. Smith inferred from this that the term was not only Christian but also Platonic, and that Plotinus had a little circle of 'wild Platonists' in mind; the Christian heresiologists, both ancient and modern, had been the first to make of it 'a brand name with a secure market'.[61] However the treatise's contents reveal typical doctrines of the older 'Christian' Gnostic ideology.[62] Even if, as Smith has shown, the expressions *gnōstikos* or *gnōstikē technē* are of Platonic origin and were at home in Platonic and Pythagorean circles, yet it is only amongst the Christian heresiologists that we first meet *gnōstikos* as a widespread self-description of more or less Christianized groups in the history of early Christianity. Otherwise it is conspicuously absent from the rest of contemporary literature and inscriptions.[63] Apart from that we know more today about the real self-designations of these 'Gnostics', thanks to the Nag Hammadi Codices:[64] 'elect', 'sons of light', 'spiritual' (pneumatics), 'holy', 'aliens', 'free', 'seed' (of the Father), 'unchangeable race', 'race of Seth', 'kingless race', etc. But we also find 'Christians', particularly among the Valentinians. Research has to use general terms. Once such terms had been taken over by scholars long ago from ancient traditions, they could hardly be dispensed with again. In our case 'Gnostics' has proved its worth and is very much to the point; this is less true of 'Gnosticism' and we should eliminate it as far as possible, since it is not only pejorative, but also confusing.

It is time to look more closely at the content of this 'Gnosis'. To define its nature it is not enough just to contrast it with 'faith', as was usual already in early Christianity.[65] Bousset, as we saw, listed certain basic ingredients. For a long time the 'redeemed Redeemer' or the 'myth of the Primal Man' was reckoned the principal feature of Gnosis. Their critics have left most of these theories in tatters.[66] Recently C. Colpe has attempted a new approach to this controversial topic; this is noteworthy and deserves a brief discussion here.[67]

Colpe's starting point is that in Gnosis for the first time 'knowledge' becomes an 'organ of knowledge with a substantial character' as the 'self' and is split into two hypostases (540). This hypostatically divided 'self' is the core of all Gnostic systems and an expression of the dualism basic to it. For Colpe 'Gnosticism' is the manifestation of this basic idea in systems. While the Gnostic speculation about the 'self' can be pre-Christian (cf. 559f., 638), when it takes on a systematic form in Gnostic literature it is either subsequent to, or contemporary with, Christianity (542f.). Only parts, aspects of 'Gnosis' are pre-Christian; 'speculation about the self' is a motif which we can trace in the form of various historical processes until it leads us to Gnosticism (543). We must regard as Christian both the Gnosis of the 'Christian heresies' and that of 'Catholic' and early church orthodoxy (544). Colpe wants to define 'Christian' or 'post-Christian' more closely: (1) with reference to chronology (here the content can be non-Christian or contemporary with Christianity) and (2) with reference to content, i.e. (2a) originating from Christian preaching, or (2b) produced by the Gnostic interpretation of a Christian doctrine of that period. Unfortunately Colpe gives no further explanation of what he means by 'Christian', but principally he is thinking of the figure of the Redeemer which first penetrated as a Christian import into the thinking of non-Christian Gnostics with their concentration on the idea of the 'self' (572). Colpe does not deny the existence before Christianity of a 'Gnosis as a world-religion' in the sense of such speculation about the self; its fundamental idea of the two hypostases (the subjective and objective bases of knowledge) can be detected in the first century B.C. (559f.); however it was only when Gnostics took over the Christian concept of the Redeemer that they developed their idea of the *salvator salvandus* (a non-Christian idea! – 572). While the 'Gnostic attitude to life' that underlies the dualistic cosmology of Gnosis is inexplicable, Gnostic soteriology is inconceivable without Christianity (572). Thus Colpe sees a development taking place in Gnosis both before Christianity and contemporary with it and with its assistance. In this development ideas earlier than, or contemporary with, Christianity mingle with Christian ones in various ways. Jewish wisdom speculation is a presupposition of the Redeemer myth (597). The Christian element in it existed in the Pauline and Johannine *corpora* (as soteriological speculations on the 'self', the idea of the macro- and microcosm, and the concept of spirit), but had not taken on a specifically Gnostic sense or become fused with it, so to speak (601ff.). Colpe sees Christian elements operative in many Gnostic systems, but also reckons with the possibility of secondary paganizing to form a 'rival' to Christianity (e.g. Zost. = NHC VIII. *1*; Allogenes, XI. *3* (5)). The historical processes can be gathered 'transcendentally' into three groups (608):

1. Systems earlier than, or contemporary with, Christianity;
2. Pagan or semi-Jewish rivals of the church;
3. (Secondary) paganizations (e.g. in Manicheism).

These distinctions are helpful, but ultimately do not resolve the inherent problem, how far Christian tradition as it formed was enriched by Gnostic ideas, even in its soteriology. If, as Colpe argues, Christ penetrated the Gnostic 'doctrine of the self' (611f.) and transformed it (docetism belongs here), then this affects the figure of Christ and not only the *salvator salvandus*. When the man Jesus is identified with the Gnostic Anthropos (617) and thus becomes a second God (the Son), this is also an activity of Christian theology, and I think that Gnosis had a decisive part in initiating it. I find it surprising that Colpe also ascribes just as important a role to the Jewish components in soteriology (627ff.): the figure of Adam (as Anthropos) enters the 'speculation about the self' (632) and increases its personal character (Colpe calls this 'individuation' – 633). So, without our involving Christian beliefs, various soteriological figures can be explained (Seth, Gnostic prophets): they are 'manifestations of the redeeming call' (634f.). Thus Colpe speaks of the significance of the 'general prophetic impulse' for non-Christian Gnosis (635).

Colpe's article is a step in the right direction, a step away from onesided views and contrasts. His definition of that which is 'Gnostic' by the idea of the divided 'self' is an attempt at a new definition of Gnosis. However it is not wholly satisfactory in so far as the characteristic Gnostic 'division of the self' is the product of its cosmological dualism; the latter, or more precisely their anticosmic dualism with all its implications for speculation and conduct, is therefore the shibboleth of Gnostic doctrine.[68] Even the attempt to understand Gnostic soteriology chiefly as derived from Christian soteriology seems to me still to be influenced by outdated heresiological prejudices. As we saw Colpe himself mentions certain qualifications: the 'speculation about the self' includes a soteriological component and, independently of the Christian idea of the Redeemer, had already spawned the personal and individual forms of various Revealers or Redeemers.[69] We must seek their origins in early Jewish *theologoumena* (especially concerning Wisdom and prophets).[70] In any case, the idea of a descending Redeemer is a strange, Hellenistic one for the original Christian kerygma as well; it is, I think, connected with the beginnings of Gnostic thinking; it is found already in Paul's writings and then above all in the Fourth Gospel.[71] Probably it would still be hard to decide here who gave and who received. At any rate Christology (and soteriology) as attested in the New Testament was born when Gnostic and Hellenistic ideas were already in the air.

Colpe's account clearly combines insights of Anglo-American and German scholarship: he preserves on the one hand the idea of the existence of Gnostic doctrines in the first century – 'speculation about the self', cosmological dualism, the redeeming 'call' and the concept of the *salvator salvandus* – and thus a 'Gnostic atmosphere'; however he gives this a clear, more concrete shape. On the other hand he sees the figure of Christ having considerable influence on the systematization of Gnosis that led to the 'Gnosticism' of the second century. Certainly he reckons with a quite complex process of development on many levels affecting both Gnosis and early Christianity simultaneously; he is concerned to eliminate 'Gnosis' as far as possible from the main New Testament documents (Paul and John) and to find traces of (Gnostic?) reinterpretations of Pauline and Johannine *theologoumena* only in subsidiary traditions (in Corinthians, Colossians, Hebrews, Ephesians – 'a contemporary of John's who continued the work of the predecessors of the Fourth Evangelist', 612). At any rate he still considers the subject of Gnosis highly relevant to the New Testament.

F. Wisse has recently expressed a very different opinion:[72] evidence of opponents in the New Testament is insufficient to characterize them as Gnostics. He cites the optimistic enthusiasm, the denial of the resurrection, libertinism and docetism, and esoteric teaching. None of these can be described as typically Gnostic (repeatedly he cites the Nag Hammadi Codices). What had previously been regarded as Gnosis on this basis 'is a form of pessimistic enthusiasm' (119). The picture which we have had of Gnosis to date is still too dependent on that of the heresiologists (120).[73] As the Nag Hammadi texts in particular show, it is a quite 'polymorphous phenomenon' which we have not yet succeeded in defining. Yet Wisse gives us reason to hope when in tones of a Solomon he says 'that we cannot say with certainty that the opponents, dimly visible in some New Testament writings, were not Gnostics' (120). Such scepticism is all too understandable in view of the proliferation of unanswered questions and contradictory opinions, but it is unproductive. On the one hand Wisse's list of characteristics is incomplete (he omits dualism and soteriology); on the other hand, taken together the list yields a certain coherent picture of the 'opponents' which connects it with what the Nag Hammadi texts (independently of the heresiologists) today reveal to us as 'Gnosis'. This is not just a particular form of pessimism but a special, existential form of religion in late antiquity; this I described in my book on Gnosis (it is visible not least in its protest against the world and society).[74]

We can summarize briefly the stage that discussion has reached by saying that scholars agree that the 'Gnostic problem' is a pressing one today. There is a great variety of solutions to it, depending upon one's subjective bias, theological premises, sceptical reserve or efforts in questions of definition and terminology. We have as yet no detailed investigations of the literary history of, and the traditions behind, the new Nag Hammadi texts, nor a study of the New Testament in the light of these. Historically we cannot treat the New Testament as a fixed and self-contained entity which settles what must be pre- or post-Christian. We have already seen that the New Testament writings span nearly a century: apart from the authentic traditions about Jesus the first of these are the handful of (genuine) Pauline letters (1 Thessalonians, Galatians, 1–2 Corinthians, Philippians, Romans, Philemon); in the middle of the period are the Johannine *corpus* and the Pastoral Epistles (*ca.* 100) and at its end 2 Peter (*ca.* 130–140). This cross-section from that very active period of early (primitive) Christian writing reflects the growth and emergence of Christian thought and conduct in a dialogue with its environment involving agreement and disagreement. Part of this environment was undoubtedly a Gnostic viewpoint, not only in matters of ideology and theology, but also on practical matters, i.e. concerns of ethics and morality and sociology.[75] Impelled by an anticosmic dualism, which also dominated its anthropology, early Gnostic thought, as far as we can tell, concentrated on the liberation of the hidden, divine core of man (the *pneuma*, the 'self'); despite all that happened in the world and history this core remained secretly united with the original above the heavens, of which it was a copy (it is 'speculation about the self'). This involves belief in the original fall of this (secret) core and its eventual rescue ('ascent of the soul'); this belief is made possible by the 'knowledge' of this complex of ideas, 'knowledge' which is a response to the redeeming 'call' of the Gnostic prophet or revealer (revelatory texts with daring exegetical methods are one of the main types of Gnostic writings). The usual response to these concepts is ascetic or encratite behaviour, but the Gnostics could also dispense with the customary moral and (Jewish) legal teachings. The 'kinship of souls' (doctrine of *sungeneia*; cf. Hebrews, John) provided the ideological basis of their communal life; their community centred on the redeemed or 'spiritual' people (pneumatics), while the rest were either unredeemed or still on the way to 'liberation'; thus two sets of moral standards were involved (cf. at Corinth). I think that we must assume these basic features to have existed already in the first century if we are going to understand at all the great systems of the second (which were no longer only anonymous). It is hard to find 'doctrines' of any sort that lack any semblance of system in the sense of an inner logical coherence. We can detect these 'systems' already in writings like the oldest parts or stages of the Apocryphon of John or the tractate On the Origin of the World (early second century). During the same period we also find in the New Testament canon an increase in polemic against 'Gnostics' (Pastorals,

Revelation, Jude, 2 Peter), as well as in some of the so-called 'Apostolic Fathers' (Ignatius, Polycarp).[76] We should not only trace the features discernible here on into the second and third centuries, but also back into the first, to explain some otherwise most puzzling phenomena and the almost inexplicable polemic of the deutero-Pauline (Colossians, Ephesians) and Johannine writings (with their idiosyncratic Christology and world-view); then it will be hard to argue for a 'qualitative' leap from a mere Gnostic atmosphere to a 'Gnosticistic' construction. Rather we will see a smooth transition, more or less completely attested by the New Testament writings: we will see a world-view alien to the (Synoptic) Jesus-traditions entering and engaging Christian thinking in increasing measure; the latter could only resist by adapting itself (formation of a Christology) and rejecting *theologoumena* which attacked or undermined the central Christian message (contained in the Jesus-tradition and its Pauline representation); these included the doctrines of creation and sin, the historicity of the Redeemer, justification, etc. This process cannot be illustrated in detail (the literary remains we have attest only some conclusions to, or crossroads in, its paths), but it largely determined the early history of Christianity. It is already detectable, I think, in Paul's writings, in the Corinthian church and his reaction to it.[77] Whether this involved an 'early form of Gnosis' is uncertain, since we only have the reflection of the church situation in Paul's letters and not the views of the church itself or of groups within it (the situation was similar with our knowledge of the second century before the discovery of the Nag Hammadi texts). The treatment of the emergent (developing) Gnosis as a parallel phenomenon to the also emergent (developing) Christianity which Professor Wilson pioneered is a fruitful working hypothesis offering hope of progress.[78] At any rate it is more help to us in understanding the origins of Christianity than a groundless rejection of the supposition or even running away from it in terror.

NOTES

1. Cf. C. Colpe, *Die religionsgeschichtliche Schule* I, *FRLANT* 60, Göttingen 1961; A. F. Verheule, *Wilhelm Bousset: Leben und Werk*, Amsterdam 1973, 131ff., 159ff.; G. Widengren, 'Die Ursprünge des Gnostizismus und die Religionsgeschichte' in (ed.) K. Rudolph, *Gnosis und Gnostizismus*, *WdF* 262 Darmstadt 1975, 668ff.; K. Rudolph, *Die Gnosis*, Leipzig/Göttingen 1980[2], 35ff. ET by R. McL. Wilson (Edinburgh 1983), 30ff.
2. *Hauptprobleme der Gnosis*, Göttingen 1973 = repr. of 1907[1], 8.
3. *PRE* VII, 2, Stuttgart 1912, col. 1503*a* = repr. W. Bousset, *Religionsgeschichtliche Studien*, ed. A. F. Verheule, *NT.S* 50, Leiden 1979, 44; cf. also ibid. 121f., 132f., 155f. (from the long review of J. Kroll, *Die Lehren des Hermes Trismegistos* in *BGPhMA* 12, 1914, 697ff.), where Bousset sought to distance Gnosis from the general 'mystic thought' as 'reflective religiosity' (132); apart from the

Corp.Herm. the Chaldaean Oracles, Philo, Paul and John were caught up in the influence of this basic way of thinking (133). On the last cf. esp. Bousset's *Kyrios Christos*, Göttingen 1965⁵ = 1921², 191ff., 208ff. *et passim.*

4. *PRE* VII, 2, col. 1544*b* = *Studien*, 93.
5. *PRE* VII, 2, col. 1545*a* = *Studien*, 94.
6. *PRE* VII, 2, col. 1507 = *Studien*, 49.
7. Ibid.
8. Ibid.; cf. also col. 1524 = *Studien*, 70.
9. Cf. n.1.
10. *PRE* VII, 2, col. 1534 = *Studien*, 81.
11. Cf. F. Dornseiff, 'Der -ismus' in (ed.) J. Werner, *Sprache und Sprechender*, F. Dornseiff, *Kleine Schriften* II, Leipzig 1964, 318ff.; H. Dörrie in *ThR* 36, 1971, 285ff.
12. 'Gnostic Origins' in *VigChr* 9, 1955, 193–211, here 211.
13. 'Gnostic Origins Again' in *VigChr* 11, 1957, 93–110, here 109.
14. Ibid., 110 (referring to O. Cullmann); cf. also *The Gnostic Problem*, London 1958, 1964², 261f.
15. 'Gnostic Origins Again', 110.
16. *The Gnostic Problem*, vii and 256ff.
17. Ibid., 261. Cf. A. D. Nock, 'Gnosticism' in *HThR* 57, 1964, 278: 'I should say that in general apart from the Christian movement there was a Gnostic way of thinking, but no Gnostic system of thought with its "place in the sun"; a mythopoeic faculty, but no specific Gnostic myth' (repr. in (ed.) Z. Stewart, *Essays on Religion and the Ancient World* II, Oxford 1972, 958).
18. *The Gnostic Problem*, 263.
19. Response to G. Quispel's 'Gnosticism and the New Testament' in (ed.) J. P. Hyatt, *The Bible in Modern Scholarship: Papers Read at the 100th Meeting of the Soc. of Bib. Lit., Dec. 28–30, 1964*, Nashville 1965, 272–278.
20. Cf. ibid., 274.
21. Ibid., 275.
22. Ibid., 276 (refers to Bultmann's review of J. Dupont, *Gnosis*, 1949, in *JThS* n.s. 3, 1952, 10–26, especially 22).
23. Ibid., 277. The basic statement on this was, of course, made by W. Bauer, *Rechtgläubigkeit und Ketzerei im ältesten Christentum*, Tübingen 1964²; ET by R. A. Kraft and G. Krodel, *Orthodoxy and Heresy in Earliest Christianity*, Philadelphia 1971.
24. (Ed.) U. Bianchi, *Le Origini dello Gnosticismo: Colloquio di Messina, 13–18 Aprile, 1966*, *SHR* 12, Leiden 1967, 1970², 511–527 and Addenda 691–702.
25. Ibid., 515f.
26. Ibid., 516.
27. Ibid., xx-xxxii (in Italian, French, English and German versions, which show certain differences of nuance!).
28. 'Randerscheinungen des Judentums und das Problem der Entstehung des Gnostizismus' in *Kairos* 9, 1967, 105ff. (esp. 106f.) = repr. in *Gnosis*

und Gnostizismus, (see n.1), 768ff.; *ThR* 36, 1971, 18ff.; *Die Gnosis*[2], 64f.; ET 56f.

29. *Le Origini*, 697.
30. *Gnosis and the New Testament*, Oxford 1968, 7ff.
31. Ibid., 9.
32. Ibid., 23.
33. Ibid., 24; cf. 30 and 31.
34. Ibid., 62, 143.
35. Ibid., 59.
36. Ibid., 60.
37. Esp. ibid., 26 and 31ff.
38. Ibid., 35ff., 59. 'In 1 John and the Pastorals we find for the first time real traces of what may be called Gnosticism proper ...'.
39. Ibid., 47f.
40. Ibid., 58.
41. Ibid., 52.
42. 'Gnosticism in the Light of Recent Research' in *Kairos* 13, 1971, 282–288, especially 287; 'Philo of Alexandria and Gnosticism' in *Kairos* 14, 1972, 213–219; '"Jewish Gnosis" and Gnostic Origins: a Survey' in *HUCA* 45, 1974, 177–189; 'From Gnosis to Gnosticism' in *Mélanges d'histoire des religions offerts à Henri-Charles Puech*, Paris 1974, 423–429; 'Twenty Years After' in (ed.) B. Barc, *Colloque international sur les textes de Nag Hammadi, Québec 22–25 août 1978*, *BCNH Ét* 1, Québec/Louvain 1981, 59–67; 'Gnosis at Corinth' in (eds.) M. D. Hooker, S. G. Wilson, *Paul and Paulinism, FS* for C. K. Barrett, London 1982, 102–114; 'Nag Hammadi and the New Testament' in *NTS* 28, 1982, 289–302 (esp. 291f.).
43. *Mélanges Puech*, 426.
44. Ibid., referring to J. M. Robinson and H. Koester, *Trajectories through Early Christianity*, Philadelphia 1971. This work is of considerable importance for a new orientation towards the history of early Christianity, one which incorporates Gnosis.
45. *HUCA* 45, 1974, 189.
46. *ET* 89, 1978, 296–301; here again a good summary of his views, esp. 299f.: 'To cut a long story short, the position advocated here is that the term Gnosticism should be restricted to the "classical"gnostic systems of the second century, and avoided in discussion of first-century documents. The more appropriate term here is Gnosis. It has been objected that this is to tear apart what belongs together, but that is not the case: there is a continuity of development from Gnosis to Gnosticism, although we must allow for some discontinuity as well ... . So far as the New Testament is concerned, what we have is a situation in which Christianity is moving into a wider world, confronted by the competing claims of other religions, including an "incipient Gnosticism" or, more properly, Gnosis in the wider sense. We have to think of a period of mutual interpenetration, in which each in some measure influenced the other, until towards the end of the first century and in the course of the second the lines of distinction begin to

emerge, and orthodoxy comes to stand clearly over against heresy ... . To put it in a nutshell, Gnosticism is a specific Christian heresy ... . This is however only a particular manifestation of a wider movement, roughly contemporary with Christianity and developing alongside it, namely Gnosis. It is now clear that Gnosis is both wider and older than Christian Gnosticism ... .'

47. Wilson is convinced that more and more scholars engaged in this field were coming round to the view 'that it is dangerous to transplant the Gnosticism of the second century back into the first and use second century materials for elucidation of first century documents. Rather are scholars now thinking in terms of developments which culminated in the full-grown Gnosticism of the second century ...' ('Twenty Years After', 67). Yet at the same time he says (ibid., 65): 'There were beyond question trends and tendencies in a gnostic direction in the background of the New Testament period ...'. The relevance of the position of Bultmann and Jonas is undiminished. Cf. also G. W. MacRae, 'Nag Hammadi and the New Testament' in (ed.) B. Aland, *Gnosis, FS* for Hans Jonas, Göttingen 1978, 144–157.

48. Bousset, *Studien* (see n.3), 81ff. (= *PRE* VII, 2, cols 1534f.), 262ff.; R. Bultmann, *s.v. ginōskō* in *ThWNT* I, 1933; R. P. Casey, 'The Study of Gnosticism' in *JThS* 36, 1935, 45–60; Wilson, *The Gnostic Problem*, 107f.; M. Smith, 'The History of the Term *Gnostikos*' in (ed.) B. Layton, *The Rediscovery of Gnosticism: Proceedings of the International Conference on Gnosticism at Yale, New Haven, Conn., March 28–31, 1978*, II, *SHR* 41:2, Leiden 1981, 796–807. The range of meaning in early Christianity can most easily be seen in W. Bauer's *Wörterbuch*[5] *s.v. gnōsis* or in the concordances of the Greek NT of A. Schmoller and K. Aland; cf. also G. W. H. Lampe, *A Patristic Greek Lexicon*, 1978[5], 318ff.

49. Cf. H. Dörrie, *ThR* 36, 1971, 285f.

50. Cf. Dornseiff, op. cit. (n.11 above).

51. Cf. ibid., 327.

52. Dörrie, loc. cit., 287f.

53. *Resp.* V. 477A; VIII. 527B; cf. on this R. Mortley, 'Gnosis I (Erkenntnislehre)' in *RAC* XI, Stuttgart 1980, 447ff.

54. Cf. N. Brox, *Die Pastoralbriefe, RNT* 7, Leipzig 1975[4], 31ff.; 221f.

55. Cf. the Greek text in Epiph., *Haer.* 31, 9:2 (Holl I, 399). In Iren., *Haer.* III, 11:1 the so-called Nicolaitans become a branch of 'what is falsely called Gnosis'.

56. Cf. also M. Smith, loc. cit. (n.48), 804.

57. Cf. Rudolph, *Die Gnosis*[2], 63ff.; ET 55ff.; C. Colpe (in *RAC* XI, col. 540) affirms that in Gnosis knowledge becomes an independent organ of knowledge with a substantial character (see below).

58. Cf. here Casey, loc. cit. (n.48), 48ff.

59. Cf. the Register in Wendland's edition *s.v.* (312*a*).

60. Cf. the Register in O. Stählin's German translation (*Des Klemens von Alexandreia ausgewählte Schriften* V, *Bibl. d.Kirchenväter*, 2. Reihe, Bd. 20, München 1938), 248ff.; M. Smith, loc. cit. (n.48), 802f.

61. Loc. cit., 806.
62. Cf. Rudolph, *Die Gnosis*[2], 69f., 73ff., 241, 287f.; ET 60f., 64ff., 233, 267f.
63. Cf. Smith, loc. cit., 799f. ('total absence from Greek popular usage').
64. *Die Gnosis*[2], 222f.; ET 205f.; B. A. Pearson, 'Jewish Elements in Gnosticism and the Development of Gnostic Self-Definition' in (ed.) E. P. Sanders, *Jewish and Christian Self-Definition* I, London 1980, 151–160, esp. 156ff.
65. Cf. on this contrast R. Mortley, *RAC* XI, 486ff. (see n.53). According to Bousset Hellenistic Judaism had already reflected on the relation of *pistis* and *gnōsis*, 'Eine jüdische Gebetssammlung im 7. Buch der Apost. Konst.', *NGWG. PH* 1915, 466f. = *Studien* (see n.3) 262f.
66. Cf. Colpe, *Schule* (n.1 above); H.-M. Schenke, *Der Gott 'Mensch' in der Gnosis*, Berlin/Göttingen 1962; Rudolph, *Die Gnosis*[2], 140ff.; ET 121ff.
67. 'Gnosis II (Gnostizismus)', *RAC* XI, Stuttgart 1981, 537–659. The complicated and obscure division of the material hinders one's understanding and grasp of the author's arguments. I hope that I have understood them to some extent. Cf. the remarks by the same author also in *JAC* 23, 1980, 108.
68. Cf. my *Gnosis*[2], 68ff.; ET 59ff.
69. Cf. here ibid., 132ff.; ET 113ff.
70. Cf. ibid., 142ff., 300f.; ET 131ff., 280f.; 'Sophia und Gnosis' in (ed.) K.-W. Tröger, *Altes Testament – Frühjudentum – Gnosis*, Berlin 1980, 221–237.
71. Cf. the summary in my *Gnosis*[2], 163f., 174ff., 322ff.; ET 148f., 153ff., 300ff. P. Perkins, 'Gnostic Christologies and the New Testament', *CBQ* 43.4, Oct. 1980, 590–606, very clearly shows the 'un-Christian' element in the Gnostic 'Christologies' of the Nag Hammadi texts and their thoroughly independent structure, without any dependence on the NT: 'Most attempts to accommodate the Christian traditions in gnostic writings seem to represent secondary modifications of an independent system. One might even wish not to speak of "gnostic christology", since the person of Jesus and his relationship to the divine is rarely a matter of speculation' (606). Their origins she sees in Jewish apocalyptic traditions about the Son of Man and Wisdom. I think it certain that it was the Gnostics' interest in Christ that stimulated them to reflect theologically on the relation between God and the Son (Christ, 1st Aeon); cf. *Die Gnosis*[2], 163ff., esp. 174f.; ET 148ff., esp. 153f.
72. 'The "Opponents"in the New Testament in Light of the Nag Hammadi Writings' in (ed.) B. Barc, op. cit. (n.42), 99–120.
73. Cf. on this most recently G. Vallée, *A Study in Anti-Gnostic Polemics: Irenaeus, Hippolytus and Epiphanius*, Studies in Christianity and Judaism 1, Waterloo, Can. 1981.
74. Cf. *Die Gnosis*[2], 76ff., 284ff., 308ff.; ET 67ff., 264ff., 288ff.; R. A. Kraft and J. A. Timbie give a survey of the state of discussion with regard to the Nag Hammadi texts as a whole in *RSR* 8.1, Jan., 1982, 32ff.

75. Cf. *Die Gnosis*[2], 59ff. and 315ff.; ET 53ff. and 294ff.; 'Randerscheinungen' (n.28 above), 108 (773); S. Arai, 'Zur Definition der Gnosis in Rücksicht auf die Frage nach ihrem Ursprung' in (ed.) Rudolph, *Gnosis und Gnostizismus* (n.1 above), 646ff.; H. J. W. Drijvers, ibid., 803ff.; Wilson, *NTS* 28, 1982, 298f.

76. Cf. *Die Gnosis*[2], 324ff.; ET 302ff.; the Corp. Herm. is not considered here, but its Gnostic parts (esp. Tractate I, *Poimandres*) come from the same period (Bousset, *Studien*, 156f., very plausibly suggests a date around 100 A.D.).

77. Cf. *Die Gnosis*[2], 322f.; ET 300f. Even N. Brox writes in his commentary on the Pastorals (n.54 above): 'The characteristics listed are of such a kind as at least to permit, or perhaps even to favour, an early dating of the heretics of the Pastoral Epistles in Paul's lifetime or at the end of the first century' (38). Despite the scepticism with which W. Schmithals' thesis has been greeted, a thesis only modified by L. Schottroff and others, K.-M. Fischer, 'Adam und Christus' in (ed.) K.-W. Tröger, op. cit. (n.70 above), 283–298, continues to invoke 'Gnostic ideas' to explain Pauline *theologoumena* (apropos of Romans 5:12 and 1 Corinthians 15). W. Schneemelcher, *Das Urchristentum*, Stuttgart 1981, 149, says of the Corinthian church: 'This suggests a reversion to the faith of the mysteries, which could also encompass magic and libertinism, or the transformation of the church into a Gnostic club in the form of an elite of *cognoscenti*'. Cf. on this problem most recently R. McL. Wilson, 'Gnosis at Corinth' (see n.42) with a critical survey; he concludes: 'What we have at Corinth, then, is not Gnosticism, but a kind of *gnosis*' (112). In the same way he wrote in *NTS* 28, 1982, 291: 'If it is dangerous to read back second-century Gnosticism into first-century documents, Paul does have quite a lot to say about *gnosis* in his first letter to the Corinthians!' And 297: 'We should then have at Corinth not a full-blown developed Gnosticism but a point on the line of development which led from Wisdom speculation into Gnosticism' (with reference to R. A. Horsley and J. M. Robinson).

78. 'We can only formulate hypotheses', said R. McL. Wilson, 'and must remember that they are tentative, but the fact that adherents of the "narrow" view of Gnosticism explicitly recognize "ill-defined tendencies" or "notions in the air" is significant. We cannot explain subsequent developments without such hypotheses', *ET* 89, 299 (cf. now also *NTS* 28, 1982, 292f.). The fruitfulness of the 'Gnostic' hypothesis seems to me to have been proved, and this is historically decisive.

III

SOME REFLECTIONS ON THE GREEK ORIGINS OF GNOSTIC ONTOLOGY, AND THE CHRISTIAN ORIGIN OF THE GNOSTIC SAVIOUR

by

Professor Ugo Bianchi, Rome

One important contribution of Professor Wilson to the discussion on the origins of Gnosticism is the warning – frequently repeated by him[1] – not to 'read back' Gnostic doctrines and myths into texts belonging to the first century A.D. Another danger of reading back, which scholars have perhaps been equally slow to appreciate, lies in those texts, both Gnostic and non-Gnostic, where 'dualistic' positions, clear in themselves, are not framed by equally clear ontological (cosmological) motivations.

We use here the term 'dualistic' with a meaning which is broad enough to embrace those ideologies and world views in which some basic structures of human existence – e.g. corporeity, sexuality, procreation – are explained, sometimes explained away, as contrary to, or incompatible with, the true essence of man, and are motivated by an 'antecedent fault', that is a fall or a crisis of man or of soul which took place in a kind of 'prologue in heaven'.[2]

Of course, this description of dualism is far from exhausting that variegated family of phenomena which can be so described.[3] (*Inter alia*, it does not fit that unequivocal form of dualism which expresses itself in Zoroastrianism, where the 'doctrine of the two principles' – that is 'dualism' in its broader sense – does not imply anticosmism or a derogatory conception of matter, corporeity and sexuality). But it can apply to religious phenomena – among which Gnosticism, Marcionism, non-Gnostic and non-ditheistic but protologically motivated encratism[4] are the most remarkable – which, different as they are and sometimes mutually incompatible as to their theological implications and practical *ethē*, can and must nonetheless be lumped together – typologically and/or historically – for comparative study. The common element in this series –

we repeat it – is the irreducible opposition between the original essence of man and his actual, physiological corporeity.

As we have said, some of these 'dualistic' trends, both in Gnostic and non-Gnostic literature, are not clearly framed by cosmological motivations, for different reasons. So the Gospel of Truth is not interested in the mythological delineation of an inferior Demiurge, as the Sethian and the Ophite tractates are, but limits itself to the Valentinian concept of Ignorance (and Error) 'fashioning its own matter foolishly' (NHC I, 17:16), whilst in the Epistle of Ptolemy to Flora, be it only for paedagogic reasons, the Demiurge of this world is clearly attested (Epiphanius, *Haer.* 33, 3:6), not precisely in the context of an explicit ontology concerning *pneuma* and *hulē*, but with a view to the opposition (which does not mean mutual exclusion) between the Law (more precisely: its 'imperfections') and the perfection of the Good News. How are we to evaluate the respective cosmologies, since in a Gnostic text which claims to be Christian it is rather difficult to separate cosmology from the Demiurge? Another example, taken from non-Gnostic Christian literature, is the *Liber graduum*, where an equally clearcut opposition between the 'little precepts' (present also in the Christian scriptures) inspiring the 'just ones' and the Paraclete inspiring the 'perfect' – as well as between their respective soteriological expectations – lacks any specific cosmological (and anthropological) motivation, beyond the mere notion of coition being taught by the Devil to Adam, and only secondarily permitted by God.[5]

The opposite case, namely that of fully developed theoretical motivations of an ontological and a cosmological order, is found in most Gnostic tractates and systems (and amongst these Manicheism in particular). Here the ultimate conclusions and implications for anthropology need only be deduced from the respective metaphysics; this did not prevent Manicheism from deriving both the general frame into which that ontology is embedded, and the names of the divine and demonic beings, from religious notions already in existence before the rise of the new religion. We refer to the Zoroastrian concept of the two worlds, of Light and Darkness, and to the polymorphous theonomastics of the Manicheans, utilizing in the different areas of their diffusion names of Judeo-Christian, Zoroastrian or Buddhist origin.

Another kind of opposition is also to be considered here, which only partially coincides with the preceding one, namely that between systems which imply a clearcut concept of an inferior Demiurge, not necessarily demonized but nonetheless strongly contrasted with a Divinity in whom all the supreme attributes of the godhead are found, and – on the other hand – systems which culminate in a 'scientific' and analytical theory concerning the universe in its constituent elements and substances. Our examples here are Marcion, that wild ditheist not so much interested in cosmology and in cosmogony, as contrasted with Mani, a wild anti-cosmicist and an enemy of the body, not very interested in a discussion concerning the God of the Old Testament.

Generally speaking, if we consider the different cases of opposition

discussed so far, we can identify alternative positions at the heart of each
group's views.

So, in the discussion of the God of the Old Testament and the 'economy'
connected with him, we can oscillate between a (relative) condemnation of
him as a 'just' God, with more or less negative connotations, contrasted
with the goodness of the God of Jesus, and a mere opposition (sometimes a
mutual exclusion) between two régimes or economies, that of the Old
Testament and that of the Gospel or – alternatively – that of the 'just' and
that of the 'perfect', but in the context of a theology which is not ditheistic.
As for the systems particularly interested in cosmology and ontology,
systems based on emanation (such as Valentinianism) can be contrasted
with systems based on a radical dualism of primordial substances as in
Manicheism, or more generally in the 'Iranian' branch of Gnosticism, as
well as in the Sethian ('Syrian')[6] Gnosticism and the tripartite Gnostic
systems quoted by Hippolytus.

Things being so, we must try to reassess the question of the essence and
the origins of Gnosticism within the more general framework of a process
which is extended to cover positions not Gnostic in themselves but at the
same time interested in topics crucial for the Gnostics – dualistic in the
broader sense of this term (so e.g. non-Gnostic encratism forbidding or
condemning marriage).

It is difficult to exaggerate here the importance of the Cologne Codex
concerning the life of Mani. The relevance of this text for the study of the
essence and the birth of Manicheism – a Gnostic religion and church with
special characteristics – is clear, as well as its relevance for the study of the
spiritual biography of its founder. In fact, the two issues, the origins of
Manicheism and the spiritual biography of Mani, are one and the same.
They are two aspects of that 'founded' religion, Manicheism, in the context
of which both the 'ethnic' (or better, 'cultural') heritage and the continuity
of a spiritual orientation merge in a message which is new, only
understandable on the basis of the personality of the founder. Broadly
speaking, this is also the case with Jesus and the Buddha (whose discussion
about *samsara*, *karman* and *moksha* is a continuation of the problems
raised in the Upanishads and – at the same time – a revolutionary
interpretation of them, on the basis of the negation of the substantial and
permanent essence of the soul). It is not an accident that the outstanding
relevance of the spiritual biography of a founder is felt precisely in
connection with the personalities of the founders who stand at the
beginning of the three most specific and grandiose examples of
'universalistic religions' (Mohammad and Islam may be added here); and
it is not by chance that precious evidence concerning those lives (spiritual
biographies, i.e. documents carrying the seal of a religious personality of a
specific sort) has reached us (significantly this did not happen with other
cosmopolitan but more properly esoteric messages such as those of the
Ophite and the Sethian schools or of the mystery cults of antiquity).
Moreover, the case of Mani is special in so far as his basic orientation,
which is Gnostic and syncretistic (in the Gnostic sense of this term),

allowed him to present himself both as the 'Apostle of Christ' (whose tragic death, so different from the quiet 'extinction' of the Buddha, is coherent with his message) and as the revealer of a liberating knowledge, founded – as the Cologne Codex puts it – on the 'scientific' analysis of the formative process of his 'body', that is of his earthly existence.

Of course, Mani is primarily a Gnostic doctor, who, because of particular cultural-historical motivations, does not ignore (on the contrary: he fully utilizes and feels inspired by) cosmological and theological conceptions which are understandable in a Mesopotamian milieu, open, at that epoch, to Iranian influences (Iranian in the broad sense of the word, which extends from the radical dualism of substances in the Avestan and Zand scriptures to the metaphysical-cosmogonical theories of a Bardesanes). Now it seems to us that precisely this 'Iranism' (and not only the 'Greek' propensity for ontological argumentation) was responsible for the introduction in a milieu of Aramaic Christian or para-Christian sectarianism of a taste – not so familiar to that milieu – for the analysis of a cosmos and a body which are mixed in their essence and in their formative process.

This analysis is carried out on the basis of the concept of 'substance' (or, better, of substances, Light and Darkness), in the light of their final, mutual separation, in a process not of *purification* of something which had been polluted, but of the inauguration of a differently understood 'purity':

'My lord (Mani) said: "I have had enough debating [with] each one in that Law, rising up and questioning them [concerning the] way of God, [the] commandments of the Savior, the washing, the vegetables they wash, and their every ordinance and order according to which they walk. Now when I destroyed and < put to nought > their words and their mysteries, demonstrating to them that they had not received these things which they pursue from the commandments of the Savior, some of them were amazed at me, but others got cross and angrily said: Does he not want to go to the Greeks? But, when I saw their intent, I said to [them] gently: [This] washing by which you wash your food is of [no avail]. For this body is defiled and molded from a mold of defilement. You can see how, whenever someone cleanses his food and partakes of that (food) which has just been washed, it seems to us that from it still come blood and bile and flatulence and excrements of shame and (the) defilement of the body. But if someone were to keep his mouth away from this (washed) food for a few days, immediately all [these] offals of shame [and] loathsomeness will be known to be lacking and wanting [in the] body ... Now the fact that you wash in water each day is of no avail. For having been washed and purified once and for all, why do you wash again each day? So that also by this it is manifest that you are disgusted with yourselves each day and that you must wash yourselves on account of loathsomeness before you can become purified. And by this too it is clear most evidently that all the foulness is from the body. And, indeed, [you] also have put it (i.e. the body) on. Therefore, [make an inspection of] yourselves as to [what] your purity [really is. For it is] impossible to purify your bodies entirely ... The purity, then, which was spoken about, is that which comes through knowledge, a separation of light from darkness, of death from life, of living waters from turbid ...".[7]

To Mani this is the purity of that substance, or of those elements, whose original brightness has been darkened through an unnatural process of swallowing or infection (mixture) on the part of a contrary substance or a counter-element (dark water or smoky fire as contrasted with the corresponding, pure elements), so that 'through it (i.e. foulness) it (the body) was coagulated and having been founded came into existence'.[8] This attainment of purity, being a separation of substances, and only secondarily a 'purification', is accounted for in the Manichean sources as a process of 'digestion', which is to be understood both in the etymological sense of 'distinction' and in the physiological sense. Given the ontological presuppositions of the system, this is properly a case of *discretio*, not so much of spirits as of substances, in the context of that radical dualism of Kingdoms – of Light and of Darkness – which owes so much to Mazdean systematics, fully 'translated' into Gnostic terms, those of the *pneuma* imprisoned in the *hulē*, which have nothing Zoroastrian in themselves and presuppose *gnōsis*.

Now it is precisely on this Manichean concept of a purity which is not reducible to purification that we would like to insist, in connection with the new evidence afforded by the Cologne Codex concerning the life of Mani who, through his father Patek, had belonged to a sectarian congregation of Elchasaite Baptists, characterized by encratism (sexual and alimentary), as it appears from the 'vocation of Patek' otherwise known. As we have seen, the basic argument of Mani against his old Baptist fellows concerns precisely a theory of the 'purity' of the body which cannot be obtained through those repetitive rituals of purification (both of food and of the body) which were customary to them. This purification is of no use because it does not abolish the very source of impurity: food and body are intrinsically impure; they are defiled in themselves, in their constitution, in their process of 'coagulation' and coming into existence. No ablution will work here; only a drastic separation of substances (and of their responsibilities: see the distinction between *electi* and *auditores*) will bring the faithful Gnostic to a state of purity, in a context in which a special alimentary régime and a proper conduct of life – orientated to that separation of substances – will allow the perfect (directly) and the 'hearer' (indirectly) to attain that goal – a condition of objective and substantial purity – which results in the liberation of the particles of *pneuma* swallowed up in matter.

The objection made by those Baptists to Mani is analogous. So Mani, their former companion, now a heretic, is ranked amongst the 'Greeks', the 'pagans',[9] those who are not observants. The Jewish background of those Baptists is clearly visible in this criticism, fully understandable from their point of view, since this Manichean opposition of substances, and not only of spirits and inspirations, constitutes a novelty which is a real *metabasis eis allo genos*. At the same time the Cologne text enables us to identify the combination, in the person of Mani, of an encratism proper to some fringes of Judaism or of Judeo-Christianity – the abstentions of

Patek and his fellow Baptists – and an encratism based on other presuppositions, those constituting the Greek legacy to Gnosticism, i.e. a theory of substance(s), transcribed into (but not interpreted through) the Zoroastrian radical dualism of Light and Darkness as principles.[10]

Having thus identified, on the basis of an 'histoire d'une âme', that of Mani, the specific nature of this Gnostic *metabasis* of a religious man whose basic experience had been that of a follower of encratism – a non-Gnostic, as it seems, and a non-ditheistic one – we are in a condition to delineate a phenomenological 'triangle': (a) an encratism which is not ditheistic or Gnostic, nor interested in a dualistic cosmology, but not devoid of ontological-anthropological presuppositions (procreation considered as negative, i.e. identified absolutely with *phthora*; femininity substantially connected with concupiscence and defilement; marriage as a devilish invention);[11] (b) Marcionism, ditheistic and encratite, the ontological motivations of which do not go beyond a negative evaluation of corporeity and birth,[12] and whose *pointe* lies in the ethical opposition between the two Gods; this can be seen as the extreme and fully heterodox development of the idea of an opposition between the two régimes, that of the Old Testament and that of the Gospel, or else the 'just' and the 'perfect' as it can be found in the para-encratite *Liber graduum*, not without some partial analogies in some Fathers;[13] (c) non-Marcionite, Gnostic dualism, mostly interested in cosmology and, generally speaking, ontological motivations. These constitute the context into which encratite and ditheistic positions are transcribed and drawn to more or less extreme conclusions. These reach their culmination in the case of Manicheism, with its dualism of substances, whilst other equally systematic formulations (the Sethian and the 'tripartite' doctrines of Gnosticism attested by Hippolytus, as well as the 'devolutionistic' system of Valentinus)[14] admit of a mystical transposition of the themes of marriage and fecundation (respectively, to the realm of the lower world, the *hustera*, fertilized by the *pneuma*, or to the realm of the transcendent couples of eons).

One gets the impression that these different positions – of Marcion, of Valentinus and of Mani (to which a fourth position can be added, that of the Sethian tractates) – though not mutually derivable, are nonetheless characterized by a combination and a selective development of ingredients, the most important of which are the idea of an opposition between the two régimes (not necessarily between the two Testaments) – an opposition drawn to more or less drastic conclusions, in the direction of a ditheism – and a dualism of substances. Ditheism and dualism of substances are variously combined in the different systems with their respective emphases. Marcion and Mani represent here the most pronounced, mutually exclusive formulations, whilst the positions of the Valentinian schools concerning the Demiurge and the pneumatic and psychic substances are more articulate and complex, as well as admitting internal differentiation.

Things being so, it seems to us impossible to explain Gnosticism, that of the sects of the second century A.D., including Marcionism, without having considered those two converging elements: the impact of a 'Christology' which both on the basis of the Christian Gospel but equally on that of a drastic reinterpretation carried on outside the realm of ecclesiastical responsibility both by members of the church and by outsiders, had the effect of a lever strong enough to 'destabilize' the Creator God, depriving him of his continuity with the Saviour God, and at the same time and in the same context, the impact, no less decisive, of a dualistic ontology concerning 'substance', with a programmatic, ontological devaluation of matter. In other words, the Gnosticism of the sects of the second century (Marcionism included) cannot be understood without a reference to the Christian soteriology, the only soteriology which at that time – heterodoxically and syncretistically interpreted – could have been strong enough to 'counterbalance' and drastically reduce (or abolish) the authority of the Creator God (or of the Creator Angel)[15] of the Jewish scriptures and traditions. But at the same time it cannot be understood without reference to a Greek (Orphic rather than Platonic) dualistic ontology (*sōma-sēma*, etc.).

This is why Manicheism, as well as the 'histoire de l'âme' of Mani, can be interpreted in the context of a polarity where the Manichean idea of a 'purity' of the pneumatic substance of Light and of the elements of Light is contrasted with the older encratite ideal of continuously repeated 'purifications', both of body and food, as it is attested in the Cologne Codex for those Elchasaite Baptists. This polarity is not reducible to a mere concept of evolution. It implies a religious revolution, a Gnostic *metabasis eis allo genos*. As for Marcionism, with its emphasis on a dualism of gods and not of substances, it can be seen as another, revolutionary possibility, no less drastic than Manicheism in the direction of radical dualism.

Valentinianism stands here in the middle. It is interested both in an explicit relativizing of the Demiurge and in a theory of substances, as well as in the proper formulation (variously debated between the different Valentinian schools) of the relation between the Demiurge and the substances, both in the cosmos and in man.

We can conclude by saying that the different formulations of the Gnostic revolution, with their different emphases, can explain the self-understanding of Marcion as a polemicist and a 'restorer' of 'Pauline' Christianity, of a Valentinus as a doctor, the 'interpreter' of the Christian Gospel, and of a Mani, as the 'Apostle of Christ', the Paraclete and the 'seal of the prophets', that is the founder of a new religion and a new church.

NOTES

1. So, e.g., *Gnosis and the New Testament*, Oxford 1968, 35.
2. See (ed.) U. Bianchi, *Archē e telos: l'antropologia di Origene e di Gregorio di Nissa. Analisi storico-religiosa*, SPM 12, Milano 1981, 28f. and 312ff.

3. U. Bianchi, *Selected Essays on Gnosticism, Dualism and Mysteriosophy*, *SHR* 38, Leiden 1978, 49–62.

4. i.e. a theoretical and practical attitude condemning or excluding marriage and motivating itself on the basis of the idea of sexual intercourse being objectively connected (or identical) with a primordial fall of man. It must be added that a protological motivation of *enkrateia* (not of encratism as forbidding marriage) is found in some Fathers (the post-lapsarian institution of marriage). See below, n. 11.

5. *Sermo* XV. 336 Kmosko.

6. See our discussion in *Paganisme, Judaïsme, Christianisme, Mélanges M. Simon*, Paris 1978, 75–90, in *Gnosis, FS* for H. Jonas, Göttingen 1978, 33–64, and in (ed.) B. Layton, *The Rediscovery of Gnosticism* I, Leiden 1980, 103–111.

7. *The Cologne Mani Codex 'Concerning the Origin of His Body'*, edited and translated by Ron Cameron and Arthur J. Dewey, *SBLTT* 15, Missoula, Montana 1979, 63ff.

8. Ibid., 69.

9. Ibid., 65 and 71.

10. On Light and Darkness as irreducible substances in the Mazdean theological theory see *Shkand Gumanik Vijar*, as edited and translated by J.-P. de Menasce.

11. On encratism, and the more general concept of the 'tradition of *enkrateia*' see the materials and the discussions published in the Proceedings of the Colloquium on 'La tradizione dell' *enkrateia*. Motivazioni ontologiche e protologiche', held at Milan, Università Cattolica del Sacro Cuore, April, 1982 (in the press).

12. And also of *hulē*. See 'Marcion: théologien biblique ou docteur gnostique?', in *StEv* (= *TU* 103, Berlin 1968), 234 (= Bianchi, *Selected Essays...*, 320–327).

13. See above, n. 11.

14. See above, n. 6 *in fine*.

15. On this notion of the Angel, cf. J. E. Fossum, *The Name of God and the Angel of the Lord: the Origins of the Idea of Intermediation in Gnosticism*, Diss., Utrecht 1982, as well as Segal's *Two Powers in Heaven*.

IV

JUDAISM, JUDAIC CHRISTIANITY AND GNOSIS

by

Professor Gilles Quispel, Utrecht

I

My distinguished colleague, Robert McLachlan Wilson, in 1960 saved the honour of New Testament scholarship. After the Gospel of Thomas was published, quite a few professors considered this writing as nothing but a Gnostic perversion of Holy Writ. But Wilson pointed out that the parable of the Wicked Husbandmen, logion 65, in its Synoptic form has undergone some expansion, and has been converted into an allegory in which the servants represent the prophets. The striking thing about the version in the Gospel of Thomas, as he saw it, only appears when we compare it with Dodd's reconstruction of the original story, in which we should have 'a climactic series of three' – two slaves and then the son. This is, in fact, precisely what we find in the Gospel of Thomas. From this and similar observations Wilson concluded that perhaps we may speak of an element of genuine early tradition, possibly embodying a few authentic sayings, and of an element parallel to but perhaps independent of our Gospels.[1] Recently Antoine Guillaumont, carefully studying the Semitisms in the Gospel of Thomas, has definitively proved that these views were correct.[2]

Wilson also stressed the importance of Judaism for Gnostic studies. He was not the first to derive Gnosticism from Judaism. That was the great Church historian of Berlin, August Neander (David Mendel, 1789–1850) in his book 'Genetic Exposition of the Gnostic Systems' (in German).[3] But the man from St Andrews was probably the first Anglo-Saxon, if not the first of all New Testament scholars, to reconsider this hypothesis after a long eclipse. In 1958 he opined that certain elements of Gnosticism were purely Jewish, and other, pagan elements were also derived from Diaspora Judaism, even although that was not the ultimate source. Thus Diaspora Judaism was established as a contributory source for the development of Gnosticism.[4] Already then he stressed the importance of Philo for Gnostic studies, not because the richest man of Alexandria was himself a Gnostic, but because he was developing, modifying, and generally carrying to a

46

conclusion the work of those who had gone before. Philo did not simply concoct his theories and allegories for himself, but drew upon an existing tradition.[5] This is an excellent vantage-point for considering the special relationship between Gnosis and early Christianity.

Wilson never paid much attention to the rediscovery of Judaic Christianity by Erik Peterson and others, and once frankly told me that he hesitated to follow me in this field. But perhaps he will feel somewhat safer on this treacherous ground now that a mutual friend has set the seal of his approval upon the bold hypotheses of H. J. Schoeps and Jean, Cardinal Daniélou, and their followers.[6]

Marcel Simon starts his survey of the present state of the problem by observing that only a few decades ago nobody spoke about Jewish Christianity, whereas today there is no scholar in the field of early Christian literature who does not think that he has to express his opinion on this question. The result is that the problem has been made extremely complicated. But there can be no doubt whatsoever that there did exist in antiquity sects like Ebionites, Nazoraeans and Elchasaites, which somehow more or less continued the tradition of the primitive congregation of Jerusalem (more especially, I add, the tradition of the 'Hebrews' there, as opposed to the 'Hellenists' like St Stephen and St Paul: Acts 6:1; 7:58).

Schoeps has been criticized for limiting his scope too much when he considered the Jewish Christians (Elchasaites) of the Pseudo-Clementines as the exclusive and direct heirs of these 'Hebrews' or 'Nazoraeans'. Daniélou on the contrary was too broad when he identified every writing before 150 A.D. expressing itself in biblical categories (except the books of the New Testament) as Jewish Christian. More recently the old tradition that the Church in Edessa was founded by a missionary from Jerusalem has been confirmed by new discoveries: the Gospel of Thomas, written ± 140 A.D. in Edessa contains specific typically Jewish Christian material. Mesopotamia and Palestine should be considered as a special, Semitic unit. The shade of Christianity in vogue there should no longer be called Jewish Christian, but rather Judaic Christian. The chronological approach of Daniélou has to be replaced by the new geographical approach to the problem. Syrian Christianity, originally founded by Judaic Christians and always remaining Semitic in spirit, definitely represents the most important form, numerically and historically, of the great and diversified Jewish Christian family.

On the other hand the relationship between Jewish Christianity and Gnosticism is extremely problematic, according to Simon. That would be a deplorable situation for both of us, because one of the writings we edited together, the Apocryphon of James, conveys the impression that it reflects the thoughts of a Valentinian in Egypt, who has grafted his Gnostic experiences onto the root and fatness of a Judaic Christian olive tree. How else could one explain the words: 'become equal to the Son of the Holy Spirit' (6:20), an expression found only in the Armenian Adam books[7] and implicit in the view expressed by several Jewish Christian gospel fragments that the Holy Ghost is the mother of Jesus?

But if we take Judaic Christianity in its limited, geographical sense, then the special relationship between the Egyptian branch of Judaic Christianity and the Egyptian section of Valentinian Gnosis becomes somewhat more plausible. Alexandria is very near to Israel. Tradition tells us that a 'Hebrew' man called Barnabas had come from Palestine to Alexandria to preach the Gospel there for the first time.[8] Who can prove that this is not true? Does not a deviant tradition, at variance with the Catholic myth of Mark coming from Rome to Egypt, deserve our very serious consideration? Other important, quite impressive arguments have impelled C. H. Roberts to assume that at an early date Christianity was introduced to Egypt directly from Palestine. And nobody has refuted or contradicted him.[9] And Birger A. Pearson holds that the writing Melchizedek (IX. *1* of the Nag Hammadi Library) is a Judaic Christian apocalypse, with Gnostic interpolations, written in Egypt at the end of the second or the beginning of the third century.[10] All this seems to confirm that, at least in Egypt, Judaic Christianity did influence Gnosis. Simon was wrong in this respect.

These general considerations may serve as a background for a special case, viz. the concept of deification through vision in Philo of Alexandria and John the Evangelist. Philo never and nowhere cites Ezekiel 1:26: 'and upon the likeness of the throne was the likeness as the appearance of man (Adam, *Anthrōpos*) above upon it'.

And yet he must have been familiar with the exegesis of this verse, already to be found in the Old Testament (Isaiah 40:5), apocalyptic (Eth. En. 46:1) and the New Testament (Revelation 1:13: 'one like unto the son of man'). This transpires from the fact that he calls the Logos: 'Man after his (God's) image' (*Conf.Ling.* 146) or 'Man of God' (*Conf.Ling.* 41). This divine Adam is an idea, incorporeal, neither male nor female, by nature incorruptible (*Op.Mund.* 134).[11] It is possible that the last concept is already to be found in the Septuagint translation of Ezekiel: '*homoiōma hōs eidos anthrōpou*'. In that case, as so often, Philo would have used, developed and modified an already existing tradition. Philo cannot be original, when he speaks about the idea of man: though not present in Plato, it was current in Middle Platonism (cf. the summary of Middle Platonism in the (eclectic) Stoic Seneca, *Ep.* 65:7).

Philo seems also to be polemicizing against an already existing interpretation, when he stresses the fact that God made male and female – 'them, not him' – after his image (*Rer. Div. Her.* 164). There is a variant of Genesis 1:27, attested both by the Pseudo-Clementines and some rabbis: 'male and female created he *him*'.[12] Moreover we find this same concept in the Alexandrian *Poimandres*, according to which the heavenly Man, *Phōs*, is androgynous, both Adam and *Zōē*. Here the ideal Man of Ezekiel 1:26 is held to contain in him the two sexes.

It is certain anyhow that the mystical meditations on the first chapter of Ezekiel were known in Alexandria long before Philo. According to Eusebius of Caesarea, *Praep. Ev.* IX, 29:5, a certain Alexandrian poet, called Ezekiel the Tragedian, who is held to have lived in the second century before our era, in a lost work described events connected with the

Exodus of the Israelite people from Egypt. This is the oldest evidence for the existence of Throne Mysticism, which speculated on the manifestation of the *kābōd* which, according to the prophet Ezekiel, appeared upon the throne of God in the form of a male being.[13] And it is clear that by then the meditations on God's glory were already traditional, because the poet has transposed the scenery to another time and region and man. Among other things he related a dream vision which Moses, not Ezekiel the prophet, experienced, when he was wandering with the flocks of Jethro in the desert. In that dream Moses saw himself on the top of Mount Sinai, and there he beheld a high throne which reached to heaven. On the throne Man (Greek: *phōs*) was sitting, wearing a crown on his head and holding a sceptre in his left hand. Of course this is not God himself, but his anthropomorphic revelation to man, his *kābōd*, the *dᵉmût kᵉmar'ēh 'ādām*, a figure of enormous dimensions as he is also described in later documents of Jewish mysticism like the *Šî'ûr Ḳômâh* (the measure of the body).

With his right hand this Man on the throne is said by the poet to have gestured to Moses to come forward and to approach the throne. Then follows this passage in Greek:

> *skēptron de moi paredōke kai eis thronon megan*
> *eipen kathēsthai· basilikon d' edōke moi*
> *diadēma kai autos ek thronōn chōrizetai.*[14]

This I take to mean: 'And he gave me a sceptre and ordered me to sit upon a great throne. And he gave me a royal crown and rose himself from his throne'.

To understand this passage we must familiarize ourselves to some extent with Jewish mysticism. Its subject is the glory of God, his revelation and manifestation to man in human form, not God himself, who remains hidden. It is the *kābōd* who appears upon the throne in Ezekiel 1 and Isaiah 6. So it is here *ho phōs*, the *dᵉmût kᵉmar'ēh 'ādām*, the god Man who appears upon the throne. In the syncretistic milieu of Alexandria, under the pressure of a rational world civilisation, the Jewish people clung to its living God, but had to admit that ultimately he was an unknown God. Moreover Saul Lieberman has definitively elucidated the meaning of Metatron, the name of the angel of the Lord, also called Jaoel, a prominent figure in Jewish mysticism. Metatron, *metathronos* in Greek, is synonymous with *sunthronos* and indicates a dignitary who is allowed, not to share the same throne as the king, but to sit upon a throne next to the king (as Jesus is said to sit 'at the right hand of God'). Thus Jaoel according to some mystical traditions was sitting in heaven and therefore called Metatron.[15]

The same situation seems to be presupposed in our fragment. The glory of God sitting upon his throne invites Moses to take his place upon a seat next to the royal throne proper. Thereupon, the poet continues, the hosts of the heavenly stars fall down upon their knees before him. They adore Moses as a *deuteros theos*. He has seen the *kābōd* and has become divine. The vision of God achieves deification.

In this passage of Ezekiel Tragicus certain Hellenistic features of later times are absent. Man, divine Man, the manifestation of God, is not yet androgynous, not yet an idea, but the vision of this God makes man divine.

Philo seems to have shared the latter view and to have been familiar with this tradition. He never interprets the glory in a personal way, like the poet Ezekiel before him, but thinks the glory indicates the powers, that is the angels or archetypes of the divine world.[16] And yet he seems to presuppose the same concept as the Alexandrian poet Ezekiel Tragicus. In his *Life of Moses* I, 158 he says:

> Did he not also enjoy an even greater partnership with the
> Father and Maker of the universe, being deemed worthy of the
> same title? For he was named god and king of the whole nation.
> And he was said to have entered into the darkness where God
> was, that is, into the formless and invisible and incorporeal
> archetypal essence of existing things, perceiving things invisible
> in mortal nature. And, like a well-executed painting, openly
> presenting himself and his life, he set up an altogether beautiful
> and God-formed work as an example for those who are willing
> to imitate it' (transl. of W. A. Meeks).

This is a commentary on Exodus 20:21: 'And the people stood far off, and Moses drew near unto the thick darkness, where God was'. A midrashic tradition attested in later times but possibly already known to Philo interpreted Moses' ascent of Mount Sinai as an ascension to heaven. Utilizing this tradition, Philo founds Moses' paradigmatic office on a mystic vision. Owing to that vision (of God) Moses has become a divine king himself.[17]

There are also Jewish documents with a Palestinian background which contain a description of the vision of the *kābōd*. In the first place there is the writing *Šî'ûr Kômâh*, the measure of the body (of God), of unknown date but certainly containing very old traditions.[18] Then there is the vision of Elxai, in the reign of Trajan, of the Messiah, with enormous dimensions, like the speculations of *Šî'ûr Kômâh*.[19] And in the third place there is the Revelation of John the Divine, written in or near Asia Minor, but reflecting Palestinian traditions.

The prophet John sees in the midst of the seven candlesticks one like unto the Son of Man (Revelation 1:13). The underlying idea probably is that Jesus, after his death and ascension, has become identified with the Son of Man, or Man, somewhat like Enoch in a famous passage of the Ethiopic Enoch, 71:14: 'And he came to me (Enoch) and greeted me with his voice, and said unto me: "Thou art the Son of Man" '.

The expression *homoion huion anthrōpou* in Revelation 1:13 refers to the Septuagint translation *homoiōma hōs eidos anthrōpou* of Ezekiel 1:26 or even its Hebrew equivalent. This means that for John the prophet Jesus has become the *kābōd*, the glory of God, which has the figure of Man, and is now the divine, celestial Man as opposed to the earthly, human Adam of Genesis.[20] We find the same curious expression *homoion huion anthrōpou* in

Revelation 14:14. This of course is also a reference to Ezekiel 1:26. But this means that according to this passage also Jesus is the Man, the divine Man, with the golden crown, the royal *kābōḏ*, who reaps the grapes of wrath.

This same figure is described in chapter 14:1: 'and I looked, and, lo, a lamb stood on Mount Zion'. There is no question that this is an allusion to the second coming: Jesus has returned from heaven as the Messiah-king to found his earthly, material, historical kingdom in Jerusalem. But the underlying idea is that this Messiah, at his second coming, is identical with the glory of God. John beholds and anticipates the coming of the glory of the Lord, embodied in Jesus. John the prophet had a vision of the *kābōḏ*, like Moses on Mount Sinai.

There seems to have existed a tradition among the Israelites that the Messiah would manifest himself upon Mount Zion, a hill in the south of Jerusalem in the days of the Apocalypticist. This tradition has been preserved by the author of 4 Ezra (13:35): 'ipse autem stabit super cacumen montis Sion'. For the author of 4 Ezra this Messiah seems to be identical with the divine Man of Ezekiel 1:26:

> Et ecce de mari ventus exsurgebat ut conturbaret omnes fluctus eius. Et vidi et ecce convolabat ille *homo* cum nubibus caeli ... et ecce congregabatur multitudo hominum ... ut debellarent *hominem* qui ascenderat de mari (13:2–5).

And there is no doubt that this Man coming with the clouds of heaven is identical with the *iuvenis* on Mount Zion. Perhaps we may even think of *Šī'ûr Ḳômâh*, when the enormous dimensions of this Messiah are stressed:

> Ego Ezra vidi in Monte Sion turbam magnam, quam numerare non potui, et omnes canticis conlaudabant dominum. Et in medio eorum erat iuvenis statura celsus, eminentior omnibus illis, et singulis eorum capitibus imponebat coronas, et magis exaltabatur (2:42–43).

Curiously enough the counterpart of this view has been preserved by the Samaritans, who of course are nothing but the remnant of the Northern kingdom of Israel and as such a ramification of the religion of Israel:

> Let the Taheb come safely and sacrifice a true offering before Bethel.
> Let the Taheb come safely, that the Lord may have pity and reveal his favour, and that Israel may sacrifice in the evening.
> Let the Taheb come safely and separate the chosen from the rejected, and let this affliction be turned into relief!
> The day which he made the fourteenth is the end of one affair and the beginning of another.[21]

The Messiah is supposed in his prayer to manifest himself in the evening of the 14th (15th) Nisan, when Israel is to kill the Paschal lamb according to the commandment of Exodus 12:6*b*. This will happen on Mount Gerizim (= Bethel), where the Messiah will re-establish true worship and sacrifice. That day, the fourteenth of Nisan, is the end of servitude and the beginning of freedom, because the Messiah is the national liberator of Israel, who has come to scatter the enemies of Israel, who have provoked the ire of God.

II

This passage from *Memar Marqah* shows that among the Samaritans also the view circulated that their Messiah would reveal himself upon their Holy Mountain. A comparison with 4 Ezra suggests that this tradition was intended to rival, and probably was patterned after, the Judaic tradition concerning the revelation of the Messiah on Mount Zion. This implies that this tradition is very old indeed and must go back to a time when the Samaritans, or at least those who gave them their special cult, had not yet been separated from the temple in Jerusalem.

Is this also true of their expectation that their Taheb would come on the eve of Easter? The Jews even today during the Paschal meal leave a chair empty for Elijah, considered to be the forerunner of the Messiah. And this is only consistent, because they celebrate their delivery from Egypt and thus hope that a new, eschatological Moses, a national saviour, will redeem them so as to be 'next year in Jerusalem'. This tradition also was current in antiquity.[22] It was known to St Jerome:

> Traditio Judaeorum est Christum media nocte venturum in similitudinem Aegypti temporis, quando pascha celebratum est (*In Matt.* IV, 25:6; *CChr.SL* 77, 237).

John the prophet, the author of the Apocalypse, probably was a Jew from Jerusalem or at least from Palestine. It is plausible to suppose that he too, like the Jews of his time, expected the coming of the Messiah, his manifestation on Mount Zion in Jerusalem, to happen during the feast of *Pesah*, the only difference being that for him it was the second coming.

But there are also positive indications that he did believe what he is supposed to have believed. According to a letter of Polycrates of Ephesus, the primate of the Asian Church during the second half of the second century of our era (preserved by Eusebius of Caesarea, *Hist. Eccl.* V, 24:3), John used to celebrate Easter on the 14th of Nisan. John was a Quartodeciman, like the Christians of Asia and Mesopotamia in general: and this would explain much of his imagery, expecially that of the Lamb, the Paschal lamb, sacrificed on the 14th of Nisan, just before the meal began and at the time that thousands of lambs were being slaughtered in the temple.

The Quartodecimans fasted during the time that their compatriots celebrated their festival, prayed for the conversion of Israel and celebrated the eucharist/*agapē* in the morning. This is the origin of Lent. Until recently the Western Church still prayed *pro perfidis Judaeis*, for the unbelieving Jews, those of the Jews who did not yet believe in Christ. During their service they read Exodus 12, the story of the delivery out of

Egypt, and explained it in a sermon as a type of the delivery by Christ. The Samaritans and the Eastern Church still do so. They maintained the Johannine chronology of Christ's Passion on the 14th of Nisan, properly speaking the day before *Pesaḥ*.[23] They preserved the eschatological aspects of the Jewish *Pesaḥ*. In the Epistula Apostolorum 17 (28) it is said that the eschatological coming of God (Christ) will take place on the days of the *Pascha*.[24]

The Aramaic Church, centred in Edessa, was also Quartodeciman and preserved these eschatological features. This transpires from the texts of the Manichean *Bema* festival, which was patterned after the Quartodeciman Easter.[25] In one of the Psalms of the *Bema* it is said:

> Thou art glorious, blessed Bema, that shall reign unto the end of world, until Jesus shall come and sit upon it and judge all races.[26]

The *Bema* festival (and the Quartodeciman *Pesaḥ* on which it is patterned) is an anticipation of the second coming of Jesus.

We may be confident that the Quartodeciman *Pascha* has its roots in the congregation of Jerusalem. In fact John the prophet must have been one of those Judaic Christians who brought this special Easter celebration from Jerusalem to Ephesus. And this makes clear what Revelation 14 means to say: the prophet sees in his vision the second coming of Jesus as the embodiment of the *kābōd* and as national liberator of the people of Israel on Mount Zion on the 14th Nisan. We may compare this vision with what Ezekiel Tragicus and Philo say about the vision of the *kābōd* by Moses. What strikes us then is that John definitely does not say that this vision leads to the divinization of the visionary. Like the initiates of Palestinian Merkabah mysticism, John maintains that man remains man even in the ecstasy of the highest vision, when the apocalypticist, or the mystic, beholds the glory of God.

III

The author of the First Letter of John, whom I regard as identical with the last redactor of the Fourth Gospel, also alludes to an eschatological manifestation of the Messiah:

> Dear brethren and sisters, we are already here and now the children of God, although it is not yet evident what will be our ultimate destiny. And yet we know for sure that, when the Messiah shall manifest himself, we shall be equal to him, because we shall behold him in his divine essence (3:2, translation of the author)

The subject of *phanerōthē(i)* must be Christ, not God. This is suggested by 2:28; 3:5, 8 (*ephanerōthē ho huios tou theou*) and Colossians 3:4 (*hotan ho Christos phanerōthē(i)*).[27] Moreover, the above mentioned parallels in Philo and Ezekiel the Tragedian seem to suggest that the true believers will see Christ, not God, whom nobody has ever seen.

The author of 1 John and the redactor of the Fourth Gospel has much in common with the Revelation of John the Divine. I think this is because he heavily edited a Judaic Christian Gospel which John the prophet, also author of Revelation, had written for the congregation of Ephesus. This hypothesis would explain many riddles of the Johannine writings, among others the fact that they proclaim a realized eschatology and at the same time have not eliminated the traces of a realistic eschatology (which cannot possibly be secondary).[28] The prophet John had described a vision of the second coming of the Messiah in Jerusalem. It would seem that this tradition was known to the author of 1 John.

The same man seems to have been familiar with the notion, so dear to John the prophet, that Jesus had identified himself with the *kābōd*. He writes in the Fourth Gospel:

> Isaiah said this because (or: when) he saw his glory and spoke about him (12:41).

This, of course, is an allusion to Isaiah 6, which was interpreted by the Jewish mystics as revealing that the prophet saw the *kābōd* of the Lord, not the Lord himself. C. K. Barrett observes in his commentary: 'the theophany as described in Isaiah 6 could well be termed the "glory of God". But it is to be noted that in the Targum to Isa. 6.5 Isaiah declares that he has seen not "the King, the Lord of hosts" but "the glory of the *shekinah* of the King of the ages" ... It is possible that John was aware of some such version, but not likely that it was the reference to the *shekinah* of God that made him say that Isaiah saw the glory of *Christ* and spoke of him'.[29] We have seen, however, that both Elxai and John the prophet had identified the Messiah with the glory. The redactor of the Fourth Gospel seems to transmit a genuine piece of Judaic Christian tradition.

What is new, however, in 1 John 3:2, as compared with Revelation 14, is the concept that the vision of the divine *kābōd*, the coming of Jesus as divine glory, makes the beholder divine, equal to the divine glory, Christ. This point was not lost on Wilhelm Bousset; in his *Kyrios Christos* he devotes a whole section to the 'Vergottung durch Gottesschau'.[30] He considers 1 John 3:2 as mysticism of God, not of Christ, and relates this passage to the *epopteia* of the Hellenistic mysteries. As examples he quotes among other texts the *Logos Teleios* of the *Asclepius*, as reconstructed by R. Reitzenstein: '*chairomen hoti en sōmasin hēmas ontas apetheōsas tē(i) seautou thea(i)*'.[31] All this is completely wrong. The subject of *phanerōthē(i)* is Christ, not God. Nothing of the kind is to be found in the *Asclepius*. And yet Bousset was basically right.

Thanks to Nag Hammadi Codex VI. *7*, The Prayer of Thanksgiving, we now see clearly that the *Asclepius* does not refer at all to deifying vision and yet is a good parallel to 1 John, because it speaks about God as the source of love, like 'John' (1 John 4:9), and about the seed of God, again like 'John' (1 John 3:9). I give here a personal and paraphrasing translation of the whole passage:

We give thanks to thee
(with) the whole soul and the (whole) heart lifted up to thee,
O unutterable name, honoured with the word 'God' and blessed
    with the word 'Father',
because to every single one and to the universe
(thou showest) benevolence, *eros* and *love* and
whatever may be known that is sweet and simple
by giving us intuition,
    reasoning,
    gnosis:
intuition that we may see thee inwardly,
reason that we may discourse about thee,
gnosis that we may experience thee.
We rejoice because thou hast enlightened us by this thy gnosis,
We rejoice because thou hast revealed thyself to us,
We rejoice because *thou hast made us divine* through
Thy gnosis even though we were still in the body.

This alone is grace in man's relation to thee, that he knows thee.
We know thee, spiritual light,
    life of our life,
    Womb full of sperma,
We know thee, womb pregnant by the phallus of the Father,
We know thee, eternal generation of the begetting Father.

(Thus having) worshipped thy goodness,
we pray thee only this: we want to be preserved in the gnosis of
    thee,
and the one and only guarantee for this is
not to fall away from this way of Life.[32]

It has been hotly debated whether or not *sperma* in 1 John 3:9 really did mean 'male seed'. But this passage of the *Asclepius*, combined with certain parallels in Philo (*Ebr.* 30: '*paradexamenē ta tou theou spermata*'), in Irenaeus (*Haer.* I, 1:1: '*probalesthai ton Buthon ... kathaper sperma tēn probolēn tautēn ... katathesthai hōs en mētra(i) ... Sigēs*') and the Apocryphon of John (Giversen 53:5: 'she became the womb (*mētra*) of the All'), do show that this crude imagery could easily be used by a Hellenistic Jew like the author of 1 John.

IV

In the second place the concept that the vision of a god makes divine is not just Hellenistic, but Hellenic and Greek and mysteriosophic. We have in 1 John 3:2 a classic example of the influence of Eleusis on primitive Christianity.

In the Homeric Hymn to Demeter the initiated who has beheld the mysteries of Mother and Daughter is said to participate in eternal life:

Blessed is he among men on earth, who has beheld this. Never will he who has not been initiated into these ceremonies, who has had no part in them, share in such things. He will be as a dead man in sultry darkness (480–482).

Pindar proclaims:

Blessed is he who, after beholding this, enters upon the way beneath the earth: he knows the end of life and its beginning given by Zeus (Greek in Bowra, fr. 121, *ap.* Cl.Al., *Strom.* III, 17:2).

And Sophocles opines:

Thrice blessed are those among men who, after beholding these rites, go down to Hades. Only for them is there life; all the rest will suffer an evil lot (Greek in Pearson III, 52, fr. 837).

The Hermetic writings too are familiar with this concept:

It is impossible, dear child, that the soul be deified because it has beheld the beauty of the Good, if it still is contained within the human body (Corp. Herm. X, 6; Festugière I, 116).
He who has not ignored these things can know God and even, if I may say so, he can become an eyewitness of God and behold him and he can become blessed, because he has seen him (Corp. Herm. fr. 6:18; Festugière III, 39).

The so-called Mithras Liturgy is a reading mystery, aiming at immortality through inner vision. The process of immortalization is accomplished through a heavenly journey, climaxed by a face-to-face vision of the divinity, in which the divinity of the god appears to confer immortality:

O Lord, I pass away and am born again, I die and grow and grow;
I am passing on, released to death, while being born from a life giving birth, –
as you have established,
as you have decreed,
as you have initiated the mystery (718–723; translation of the author).[33]

The most instructive example for our purposes is a *lekanomanteia*, a revelation of the deity through dish-divination:

I have been united with your holy form,
I received strength from your holy name,

I participated in an emanation of your goodness,
Lord, god of gods, ruler, divinity;
Thereupon come down, having acquired the divine nature
owing to the *lekanomanteia* as an eyewitness and the oracle
of the dead, which is achieved by this mystical union (*P.G.M.*
IV, 216–221; Preisendanz I, 78).

The divinity has manifested itself to the magician in the water of the dish
after he has invoked the god and impelled him to come down. The
magician looks upon the water and sees there the reflection of the Lord:
this vision grants participation in the divine nature (*isotheou phuseōs
kurieusas*).[34] The mirror is a powerful symbol in Greek and Gnostic
religion.[35] Narcissus is said to have jumped into the water and to have
embraced his own shadow and to have drowned, when he looked into the
water and saw his own shadow and fell in love with it. This is not true. For
he was not suffocated in the water, but he contemplated in the transient
and passing nature of his material body, his own shadow, namely the body,
which is the basest *eidōlon* of the real soul. Desiring to embrace this, he
became enamoured with life according to that shadow. Therefore he
drowned and suffocated his real soul and a real and true life. Therefore the
proverb says: 'Fear your own shadow'. This story teaches you to fear the
inclination to prize inferior things as the highest, because that leads man to
the loss of his soul and the annihilation of the true Gnosis of ultimate
reality. Thus the *Anonymus de incredibilibus* IX.[36]

Nonnus of Panopolis tells us that the young Dionysus was looking in a
mirror when the Titans tore him into pieces:

> He did not long occupy the throne of Zeus; Hera in her anger
> moved the Titans, their faces whitened with plaster, to kill him
> with infernal knives while he was looking at his reflection in the
> mirror (VI, 165–173).[37]

The Orphics applied this myth to the dispersion of the world-soul through
the whole creation, according to Proclus, *in Tim.* 33 B. And Olympiodorus,
in his *Commentary on the Phaedo*, B 128, combines this Orphic exegesis
with the myth of Narcissus:

> *Ho gar Dionusos, hote to eidōlon enethēke tō(i) esoptrō(i),
> toutō(i) ephespeto, kai houtōs eis to pan emeristhē.*

Jean Pépin (op. cit., 315) thinks that this combination of the myth of
Zagreus and that of Narcissus goes back to Plotinus, who says that the
human souls, having seen their reflection (*eidōla*) as Dionysus in the
mirror, have hastened to come down from above (*Enn.* IV, 3:12). Pépin has
reason to suppose that this applies to the world-soul too. If that is correct,
Plotinus must have used a tradition older than the *Poimandres* (first
centuries of our era, in Alexandria), because we find the same motif there.

In chapter 14 of the *Poimandres* this theme has been applied to the Anthropos, that is the *kāḇōḏ* of Ezekiel 1:26: he looks through the harmony of the seven spheres and shows his form. Nature becomes enamoured of him, when she sees his reflection in the water and his shadow on the earth. Thereupon Man falls into the irrational body and becomes man. He becomes enamoured of his reflection in the water and wants to dwell there, like Narcissus.

Saturninus of Antioch has preserved a more primitive version of the myth of the divine Anthropos. According to him the *kāḇōḏ* does not fall (a combination of Ezekiel 1 with Genesis 3), but only reveals himself and thus shows the prototype for the body of the first man, earthly Adam: 'The world and everything in it came into being from seven angels, and man also was a creation of angels. When a shining image appeared from the supreme power above, which they were not able to detain, he says, because it immediately sped back upwards, they exhorted one another, saying: "Let us make a man after the image and likeness"'.[38] Moreover, Man, in this case the Idea of Man in the Platonic sense of the word, is not yet identified with Dionysus-Narcissus, the world-soul in exile, an Alexandrian tradition. This proves that the concept is older than Saturninus and to be located, not in Alexandria, but elsewhere in the Diaspora, probably in Antioch. This myth was taken over by other Gnostics in innumerable variations.[39]

This myth is typically Jewish: God reveals himself as the celestial Adam (Ezekiel 1:26), angels create man, a Jewish heresy (Justin, *Dial.* 62:2), the body of man is the image of God, the underlying idea that you can see God only through a glass darkly is expressed with a pun on *rᵉ'î* (mirror) and *rō'eh* (vision).[40]

For our purpose it is important to notice that this myth does not say at all that vision makes the beholder divine. From this we conclude that the author of 1 John is *not* influenced by Gnosticism when he says that in the end the believer, who sees the manifestation of Christ in his divine essence, will be divine like him. 'John' and the Gnostics are familiar with the mysticism of the *kāḇōḏ*. But their concepts of the consequences of this vision for human existence are very different indeed. So even if Gnosticism in Alexandria and elsewhere in the Diaspora might have preceded John, it has not influenced him in his basic tenet, deification through incarnation and vision. This is Hellenic, not Gnostic.

V

With this in mind we turn to the different general studies on the relation of Judaism and Gnosticism.

As long as Protestant scholars from Reuchlin to Knorr von Rosenroth ('Morgenglanz der Ewigkeit') studied Kabbalah and identified Jesus with the Adam of Ezekiel 1, the parallels between Gnosticism and Jewish mysticism could not be left unnoticed.[41] The Enlightenment totally obscured this real insight. Ever since R. Reitzenstein wrote his 'Iranian myth of the Redeemed Redeemer', it was generally held that there once existed a pre-Christian, Aryan myth which could explain Jewish apocalyptic, the New Testament, especially John and Paul, Mandeism, Gnosticism and Manicheism (*excusez du peu*). As Geo Widengren puts it: 'Que cette hypothèse soit fausse tout le monde le pense aujourd'hui'.[42]

As a matter of fact, this alleged and non-existent Iranian myth is the greatest hoax of the twentieth century. And it is of no avail if this scandal is disguised by excluding the experts from the edition of newly discovered texts and launching hypotheses about a pre-Christian Saviour long before the relevant writings have been translated and published. When the Gospel of Truth was discovered (1952), with its elaborate speculations on Jesus as the name of God, it became all of a sudden clear that these views had a Jewish (or Jewish Christian) background. When the Cologne Mani Codex was published, it became certain that Mani had lived from his fourth till his twenty-fifth year in a community of Elchasaites.[43] It was then established that Manicheism, by reaction, had originated in a Jewish milieu. Notwithstanding these undeniable facts some scholars refused to admit that Gnosticism is of Jewish origin.

K. W. Tröger thinks Gnosticism has social origins, being one of the many possible responses to the challenge of the social conditions of late antiquity. According to him it cannot be of Jewish origin, because it is characterized by an anti-Jewish animus; it rejects the world (as no Greek or Jew or Catholic would do), and is aware of a split between the demiurge of this world and the God beyond god.[44]

This is difficult to understand. Catholicism, Mandeism and Manicheism are against the 'Jews', though of Jewish origin. Could not Gnosticism be in the same situation? Alan Segal has definitively shown that certain Jewish '*mînîm*', that is Jewish religious thinkers later considered as unorthodox, used to distinguish between the Unknown God and his vicegerent, the angel of the Lord, his anthropomorphic representative, who, according to some, even created the world: this is certainly the idea underlying the Gnostic split within the Deity.[45] Would it not be wiser to say that apocalyptic, Wisdom schools, Samaritanism, Essenism, Zealotism, Sadduceeism, *mînîm*, the Hellenistic monotheism of Philo and his fellows, magic, syncretism, Merkabah mysticism, Mandeism, Manicheism, Christianity and Gnosticism were all varieties of the religion of the Jews in Palestine ($\pm 500,000$) and the Diaspora ($\pm 10,000,000$), which were suppressed by incipient Judaism ('Frühjudentum' or 'normative Judaism') as it gradually developed from the small group of Pharisees after the fall of Jerusalem in 70 A.D.?

Recently Birger Pearson has given a more sophisticated answer to the same vexed problem.[46] According to him the Gnostic attitude to Judaism is one of alienation and revolt; this, taken together with the massive utilization of Jewish traditions, can only be explained as a movement of Jews. Even their own self-definition turns out to be based to some extent on Jewish tradition. The best possible group of texts to show this consists of those tractates in the Nag Hammadi 'Library' which have been labelled as 'Sethian'-Gnostic (the Apocryphon of John, etc., which have been Christianized slightly, or not at all). They originate in a specific group of Sethians which considered the Old Testament son of Adam, Seth, as a redeemer: there really were, over a period of time, religious communities of 'Sethian' Gnostics, as the Church fathers aver (especially Pseudo-Tertullian, *Adv. omn. haer.* 8; Epiphanius, *Haer.* 39). But, still according to Pearson, this movement of Jews was a movement away from their own traditions as part of a process of religious self-*re*definition. These Gnostics, at least in the earliest stages of the history of the Gnostic movement, were people who can aptly be designated as 'no longer Jews'.

Against this theory it can be observed that the myth of the Apocryphon of John is attributed by Irenaeus (*Haer.* I, 29) to the *Gnōstikoi*, not to the Sethians:

> Super hos autem ... multitudo Gnosticorum [Barbelo] exsurrexit.

The latest editors of Irenaeus' *Adversus haereses* have shown that Barbelo here is an interpolation.[47] And R. A. Lipsius as long ago as 1875 made it perfectly clear that *Gnōstikoi* originally was the name which the adherents of a specific sect gave to themselves.[48] When Irenaeus, in the preface of book II, refers to I, 29–30, he attributes the views contained in them to the *Gnōstikoi tout court*:

> Diximus quoque multitudinem eorum qui sunt ab eo Gnostici.

This is not the place to discuss the numerous passages in Irenaeus where he mentions *reliqui Gnostici* (e.g. II, 13:8). Let it suffice to say that in Greek *Odusseus kai hoi alloi Phaiakes* means: 'Odysseus and the others, namely the Phaiakes'. Liddell and Scott s.v. II:8 mentions for *allos* the meaning: 'as well, besides', in enumerations. We then see that Irenaeus almost always refers to the group of I, 29–30, the group of the Apocryphon of John and its relatives, when he mentions the *Gnostici*. In any case Tertullian did not read Barbelo in his text of (Irenaeus) I, 29; when he alludes to (Irenaeus) I, 29, he only mentions the *Gnostici* as distinct from the Valentinians.[49]

Just as in the past some New Testament scholars have created enormous confusion by calling 'Gnostic' every phenomenon of late antiquity that did not agree with their own kerygmatic theology, now the danger is very real that everything not Valentinian in the field of Gnosticism will be called 'Sethian'. Pearson should have avoided this misnomer.

Moreover a Jew who is alienated from the religious traditions in which he was brought up remains a Jew, because he belongs to a specific nation; a Dutchman who revolts against his Calvinistic background remains Dutch. Let us face it: Mani was a Jew, though he founded a religion which rejected the Old Testament. It is a dangerous fallacy to suppose that all Jews are equal, but that some are more equal than others and excel in Jewishness.

On the other hand Pearson is completely right when he submits the works of Philo to close reading in order to find out what the invisible opposition opposed by this would-be philosopher held about Seth and his offspring, a tradition found very often in the books of the *Gnōstikoi*. In his treatise *On the Posterity and Exile of Cain*, while commenting on Genesis 4:17–25, he remarks that all lovers of virtue are descendants of Seth, in contrast to the wicked race of Cain (42). On the term *heteron sperma* in Genesis 4:25 Philo observes that Seth is 'the seed of human virtue', sown from God (173). One might easily conclude that the Gnostic interpretation of Genesis 4:25 is influenced by, and probably derived from, an exegetical tradition similar to that encountered in Philo.

These views of Birger Pearson agree with the findings of others. Bernard Barc has shown how deeply Gnostic mythology is rooted in Jewish apocalyptic and has its parallels in Philo. In writings like the Gospel of the Egyptians, the Hypostasis of the Archons, On the Origin of the World and the Apocryphon of John (that is in the writings of the specific sect of the *Gnōstikoi*) he finds echoes of the story of Ethiopic Enoch concerning the descent of the angels on Mount Hermon, their union with the daughters of men and the generation of the giants (*nephilîm*). In the opposition of Elohim and Jahwe in the Apocryphon of John he recognizes Philo's distinction between the creative force (*theos*) and the royal force (*kurios*) of God. And he shows that the above-mentioned writings reflect a gradual evolution from Alexandrian Judaism to Gnostic dualism.[50]

In his edition of the Hypostasis of the Archons Barc relates the shadow descending into matter and forming an arrogant being from matter (94:4–19) to the Logos as shadow in Philo which is instrumental in creating the world (*Leg. All.* III, 96).[51] This is very illuminating. The whole of this writing is a meditation on Genesis 1: (a) the Spirit brooding upon the waters and (b) the creation of light. (a) The Spirit upon the waters is the shadow or the *eidōlon* of Sophia which is the Aristotelian form in matter, *to organikon*. (b) The light of the first day, considered as *phōs* (light) and *phōs* (man), is at the same time the Man of Ezekiel 1:26, the light of the *kābōd* in the shape of a man, *to paradeigmatikon*, Plato's ideas.[52] The androgynous monster rising from matter is Phanes, the androgynous demiurge originating from the egg-shell of matter, identified with Yaldabaoth. He receives a form after the shadow. Thus he is the *eidōlon hulikon* of Plotinus (*Enn.* II, 9:12), the *eidōlon eidōlou* of the shadow, who is the *eidōlon en tē(i) hulē(i)* (ibid., 10).

That this is the meaning of this passage, is shown by the parallel in On the Origin of the World:

> Sophia reveals herself on (*hijñ*) the Hyle of Chaos, more
> specifically on the water, by projecting her image on this mirror.
> Thereupon the demiurge, the *tupos* of this *eikōn* (*eine*), arises
> from the water, an androgynous Archon (99:23–100:9).[53]

The author of the common source of the Hypostasis of the Archons and On the Origin of the World, or the tradition he transmits, has transferred the theme of the mirror of Dionysus, already applied to the Man of Ezekiel 1:26 and anthropogony, to the exile of Sophia and her cosmogonic function. The same is found in the views of the Gnostics opposed by Plotinus.

It would seem that the opponents of Plotinus (± 250) were Valentinians who had writings of the *Gnōstikoi*, just as the Valentinians of Lyons had the Apocryphon of John next to secondary Ptolemaeic sources in their library. That was a nucleus of the Gnostic library that was found in the neighbourhood of Nag Hammadi.[54]

Quite often it is said in Gnostic texts that Sophia played a part in anthropogony: she wants to retrieve the power which she has given to the chief Archon and has the *pneuma* transferred into the psychic soul of Adam (Ap. John C II, 19:44); Sophia Zoē sent her breath into Adam (Orig. World 115:14). This seems to be an extrapolation of Ezekiel 37:9ff., where the *Pneuma, Rûaḥ* (fem.) is said to *blow* the life-spirits into the bodies lying motionless upon the earth. In the synagogue of Dura-Europos this Spirit is represented as a winged lady; *Pneuma* and Sophia had been identified long before in the Wisdom literature of Israel.[55]

In a more primitive version of this anthropogonic myth neither Sophia, nor any other female being, plays any part whatsoever. According to Saturninus of Antioch there is one unknown God, who reveals his shining image, the *kābōd* or heavenly Adam, upon the waters of *tōhû wābōhû*. Thereupon the Archons of this world decide to make a material man after the image and likeness of the *kābōd*. When this creature could not stand erect, the Power above (God) sent a spark of life (the *pneuma*) which raised man up (Iren., *Haer.* I, 24:1). When this Anthropos model was combined with the Sophia model (attested by Simon Magus), the conveying of the Spirit in the way described by On the Origin of the World was added by someone who associated the creation of man as described by Genesis 2 with the vision contained in Ezekiel 37. This seems to prove that this Gnostic myth not only originated, but also was transmitted and changed in a Jewish milieu.

It should be noticed, moreover, that the Sophia-Helena of Simon Magus does not fall, but lives in exile, together with the people of Israel (Iren., *Haer.* I, 23:2). Already in apocalyptic *Ḥokmâh* was said to have descended on earth but to have found there no place to dwell and therefore to have returned to heaven (Eth. En. 43). She is a stranger down here on earth. The Simonian Sophia was patterned after this apocalyptic Wisdom.

In the Apocryphon of John, the Hypostasis of the Archons and other writings of the *Gnōstikoi* we find that Sophia has fallen. This notion, an anticipation of Kabbalah, Boehme, Schelling and Hegel, seems to be a secondary development. Plotinus in his work against the Gnostics (*Enn.* II, 9:4) flatly denies that the world-soul has ever fallen. Already in the writings of his youth this philosopher stressed the fact that the world-soul cannot do anything wrong and cannot suffer any predicament (*Enn.* IV, 8:7); this same soul did not come into being nor did it come down (*Enn.* III, 9:3). This is a *petitio principii*: is it not inconsistent to admit that the individual soul has fallen and to maintain that the world-soul did not? Plotinus seems to have reacted from the very beginning to the position of his Gnostic friends. This, much more than the ambivalent argument about the cosmos, is the fundamental difference between Platonic philosophy and Gnosticism. At least one Valentinian, the author of the fifth (fourth) treatise of the Jung Codex, has affirmed that the world, matter, and history have a positive value, because they are instrumental in making the Spirit conscious. And this author belonged to the Italic School of Valentinian Gnosis, which highly appreciated everything 'psychic', the creator, the creation, the true believer, catholics, the Old Testament and Christian morals. Plotinus may have known in Rome Valentinians of this school and this specific writing. It could very well be that he is projecting his own shadow, his dislike of the body, his revolt against history, into his *bêtes noires*, his Gnostic friends.

It would seem that this notion is not Hellenistic. On the other hand Philo seems to polemicize against earlier Gnostics when he paints a favourable image of Hagar, according to him the symbol of *paroikēsis*.[56] In the Prologue of Sirach (34: *tois en tē(i) paroikia(i)*) *paroikia* means Diaspora. The Gnostics of Plotinus (*Enn.* II, 9:6) and the writing Zostrianos also use this term.[57] It is also found in the Unknown Gnostic Treatise of the Codex Brucianus, ch. 20.[58] Could it be that Jewish Gnostics before Philo considered their existence abroad, and perhaps the situation of Sophia, as a life in exile? In that case the historical Diaspora was the basic presupposition for the philosophical tenet that nature is Spirit in exile, being is being in movement and that matter and history are the result of dialectics. The latter in fact is an oriental myth. And it would seem that only the Jewish Diaspora is the historical presupposition for this view. Only in this specific milieu could the awareness arise that the Spirit is in exile in this world.

All this becomes perfectly clear, if only we keep in mind that Philo was not a Gnostic, but a reactionary opportunist, who used and at the same time opposed Gnostic traditions already existing before this time.

Nils Dahl has argued that the target of the Gnostic revolt is the creator of the world rather than the world itself. In fact the world is better than God (I add that in the same way their target was not the Jewish people, but the deficient Law of a tribal god). Dahl shows convincingly that the vain claim of the arrogant demiurge (a Hebrew angel, the Angel of the Lord!) is only understandable as a protest within Judaism.[59] We must remember that the Gnostics were passionately interested in the real and true God, more so than some existentialist philosophers and liberal theologians of our days.

Where do these bright ideas come from? In Alexandria and elsewhere in the Diaspora there lived people even before Philo who taught that the heavenly Adam was androgynous, that Sophia was a passionate female, that the *pneuma* blown into the nostrils of the earthy Adam was divine and that the Angel of the Lord was a *deuteros theos*.[60] We may say then that almost all the elements which made Gnosticism, but not a consistent system, were there already in the Diaspora before Philo and the rise of early Christianity. This, however, has nothing to do with the Christian Saviour, a historical person to whom already existing Hebrew, Israelite notions like Name, Man (Son of Man), *kābōḏ*, Wisdom, Angel were applied, because he was considered to be the Messiah who came in the end of time to save his people. O Lord, save thy people.

NOTES

1. R. McL. Wilson, *Studies in the Gospel of Thomas*, London 1960, 148.
2. A. Guillaumont, 'Les sémitismes dans l'Évangile selon Thomas, essai de classement' in (eds.) R. van den Broek, M. J. Vermaseren, *Studies in Gnosticism and Hellenistic Religions, presented to Gilles Quispel on the Occasion of his 65th Birthday*, EPRO 91, Leiden 1981, 190–204.
3. A. Neander, *Genetische Entwickelung der vornehmsten gnostischen Systeme*, Berlin 1818.
4. R. McL. Wilson, *The Gnostic Problem: a Study of the Relations between Hellenistic Judaism and the Gnostic Heresy*, London 1958, 176.
5. Wilson, *The Gnostic Problem*, 35.
6. M. Simon, 'Réflexions sur le judéo-christianisme' in (ed.) J. Neusner, *Christianity, Judaism and Other Greco-Roman Cults, Studies for Morton Smith at Sixty* II, SJLA 12:2, Leiden 1975, 53–76.
7. In E. Preuschen, 'Die apokryphen gnostischen Adamschriften', *Festgruss B. Stade*, Giessen 1900, 33:3–4.
8. Ps.-Clem. Hom. I, 9:1, *GCS* 42, 27:16–19.
9. C. H. Roberts, *Manuscript, Society and Belief in Early Christian Egypt*, SchL 1977, Oxford 1979.
10. B. A. Pearson, *Nag Hammadi Codices IX and X*, NHS 15, Leiden 1981, 19–40, esp. 38.
11. 'Ezekiel 1:26 in Jewish Mysticism and Gnosis', *VigChr* 34, 1980, 1–13, esp. 4.
12. Ps.-Clem. Hom. III, 54:2, *GCS* 42, 76:28f.: 'For he who created man at first, made *him* male and female'. Cf. the parallels in the Rabbinic literature: b. Megillah 9 a: 'Male and female he created *him*. But they did not write: "created them" '; Gn.r. 8:1: 'R. Jeremiah b. Leazar said: "When the Holy One, blessed be he, created Adam, he created him an *hermaphrodite* (*androgynos*)"'.
13. I. Gruenwald, *Apocalyptic and Merkavah Mysticism*, AGJU 14, Leiden/Cologne 1980, 128.
14. In Eusebius, *Praep. Ev.* IX, 29:5, *GCS* 43:1, 529:11–13.
15. Gruenwald, op. cit., 235.
16. *Spec.Leg.* I, 8, 45; see H. A. Wolfson, *Philo, Foundations of Religious Philosophy in Judaism, Christianity, and Islam* II, Cambridge Mass. 1962[3], 143.
17. W.A. Meeks, 'Moses as God and King' in (ed.) J. Neusner, *Religions in Antiquity, Essays in Memory of Erwin Ramsdell Goodenough*, SHR 14, Leiden 1968, 354–371, esp. 355.
18. Gruenwald, op. cit., 213–217.
19. Hipp., *Ref.* IX, 13, *GCS* 26, 251; cf. G. G. Stroumsa, 'Le couple de l'ange et de l'esprit', *RB* 88, 1981, 42–61.
20. *The Secret Book of Revelation*, New York 1979, 37.
21. J. Macdonald, *Memar Marqah. The Teaching of Marqah*, BZAW 84, Berlin 1963, 33.

22. W. Huber, *Passa und Ostern, Untersuchungen zur Osterfeier der alten Kirche, BZNW* 35, Berlin 1969, 213.

23. See the forthcoming Utrecht dissertation of Gerard Rouwhorst on this subject.

24. B. Lohse, *Das Passafest der Quartadecimaner, BFChTh.M* 54, Gütersloh 1953, 79; Huber, op. cit., 212.

25. G. A. M. Rouwhorst, 'Das manichaeische Bemafest und das Passafest der syrischen Christen', *VigChr* 35, 1981, 397–411.

26. C. R. C. Allberry, *A Manichaean Psalm-Book*, Stuttgart 1938, 25.

27. H. Windisch and H. Preisker, *Die katholischen Briefe, HNT* 15, Tübingen 1951³, 120; R. Schnackenburg, *Die Johannesbriefe, HThK* 13:3, Freiburg 1953, 150 n.4.

28. 'Qumran, John and Jewish Christianity', in (ed.) J. H. Charlesworth, *John and Qumran*, London 1972, 137–155, esp. 140.

29. C. K. Barrett, *The Gospel according to St John*, London 1955, 360.

30. W. Bousset, *Kyrios Christos, Geschichte des Christusglaubens von den Anfängen des Christentums bis Irenaeus, FRLANT* 21, Göttingen 1921², 165ff.

31. R. Reitzenstein, *Die hellenistischen Mysterienreligionen*, Berlin 1920², 137ff.

32 J.-P. Mahé, *Hermès en Haute-Egypte, les textes Hermétiques de Nag Hammadi et leurs parallèles Grecs et Latins*, I, *BCNH* 3, Québec 1978, 161–165.

33. A. F. Segal, 'Hellenistic Magic: Some Questions of Definition' in Broek and Vermaseren, op. cit. (n.2), 349–375, esp. 354.

34. For hydromantic see Varro *apud* Aug., *Civ. D.* VII, 35.

35. A. Delatte, *La catoptromancie grecque et ses dérivés*, Liège/Paris 1932.

36. A. Westermann, *Mythographoi*, Brunswick 1843, 323.

37. C. Kerenyi, *Dionysos, Archetypal Image of Indestructible Life, BollS* 65:2, Princeton 1976, 267; J. Pépin, 'Plotin et le miroir de Dionysos, *Enn.* IV, 3 [27], 12, 1–2)', *RIPh* 24, 1970, 304–320.

38. Translation of R. McL. Wilson, in W. Foerster, *Gnosis* I, Oxford 1972, 41.

39. Iren., *Haer.* I, 29:2 (Ap. John); I, 30:3 (*Gnostici*); *Act. Archelai* 67:8 (*Gnostici* according to Basilides); R. *Ginza* V, 1 (Lidzbarski, 174); Plotinus, *Enn.* II, 9:10 (*Gnostici*); Pist. Soph. 27 (Schmidt-Till, 23); Gos. Eg. 57 (Robinson, 201); Hyp. Arch. 87 (Robinson, 153); Orig. World 98 (Robinson, 162); Great Pow. 38 (Robinson 285); Paraph. Shem 12 (Robinson, 314, 315, 319); Zost. 10 (Robinson, 372); 27 (Robinson, 376); Trim. Prot. 36 (Robinson, 462).

40. M. Meslin, 'Significations rituelles et symboliques du miroir' in *Perennitas, studi in onore di Angelo Brelich*, Rome n.d., 327–341.

41. G. Scholem, *Die Erforschung der Kabbala von Reuchlin bis zur Gegenwart*, Pforzheim 1969.

42. G. Widengren, 'Les origines du gnosticisme et l'histoire des religions', in (ed.) U. Bianchi, *Le Origini dello Gnosticismo: Colloquio di Messina 13–18 Aprile 1966, SHR* 12, Leiden 1967, 28–60, esp. 35.

43. A. Henrichs and L. Koenen, 'Ein griechischer Mani-Codex', *ZPE* 5,

1970, 97–216; ibid. 19, 1975, 1–85; ibid. 32, 1978, 87–200; ibid. 44, 1981, 201–318; cf. A. Henrichs, 'The Cologne Mani Codex Reconsidered', *HSCP* 83, 1979, 339–367.

44. K. W. Tröger, 'The Attitude of the Gnostic Religion towards Judaism as Viewed in a Variety of Perspectives', in (ed.) B. Barc, *Colloque international sur les textes de Nag Hammadi (Québec, 22–25 août 1978), BCNH Ét.* 1, Québec/Louvain 1981, 86–98.

45. A. F. Segal, *Two Powers in Heaven: Early Rabbinic Reports about Christianity and Gnosticism, SJLA* 25, Leiden 1977.

46. B. A. Pearson, 'Jewish Elements in Gnosticism and the Development of Gnostic Self-Definition', in (ed.) E. P. Sanders, *The Shaping of Christianity in the Second and Third Centuries*, London/Philadelphia 1980, 151–160; 241–245.

47. A. Rousseau and L. Doutreleau, *Irénée de Lyon, Contre les hérésies* II, *SC* 264, Paris 1979, 358.

48. R. A. Lipsius, *Die Quellen der aeltesten Ketzergeschichte neu untersucht*, Leipzig 1875, 190.

49. G. Quispel, 'African Christianity before Minucius Felix and Tertullian' in (eds.) J. den Boeft and A. H. M. Kessels, *ACTUS – Studies in honour of H. L. W. Nelson*, Utrecht 1982.

50. B. Barc, 'Samaël-Saklas-Yaldabaôth. Recherche sur la genèse d'un mythe gnostique' in Barc, op.cit. (n. 44), 123–150, esp. 128–130.

51. B. Barc, *L'hypostase des archontes: Traité gnostique sur l'origine de l'homme, du monde et des archontes, BCNH* 5, Québec/Louvain 1980, 31.

52. W. Theiler, *Die Vorbereitung des Neuplatonismus*, Berlin/Zürich 1964, 21.

53. On the *Eikōn* of Sophia in Zost. 10:16 and the *eidōlon eidōlou* in the same writing see H.-Ch. Puech, *En quête de la Gnose* I, Paris 1978, 114 and V. Cilento, *Paideia Antignostica, Ricostruzione d'un unico scritto da Enneadi III 8, V 8, V 5, II 9*, Florence 1971, 256–257.

54. 'Valentinian Gnosis and the Apocryphon of John', in (ed.) B. Layton, *The Rediscovery of Gnosticism, Proceedings of the Conference at Yale March 1978* I, *SHR* 41:1, Leiden 1980, 118–132; C. Elsas, *Neuplatonische und gnostische Weltablehnung in der Schule Plotins, RVV* 34, Berlin 1975, 5–10. Plotinus seems to have known Valentinians of the Italic School in Rome:

a.   He reports that Sophia created to be honoured (*Enn.* II, 9:11: *hina timō(i)to*); the best parallel for this is Hipp., *Ref.* VI, 30:7 (Italic School, cf. Elsas, op. cit., 201).

b.   According to his opponents Sophia brings forth a *logos* after her fall (*Enn.* II, 9:5); this corresponds to the doctrine of Valentinus that the spiritual body of Christ was brought forth after the fall (Iren., *Haer.* I, 11:1). This, however, is also found in Tri. Trac. (Heracleon (?), Italic School) 81:21; 82:2–3; 115:23–28 (with my notes).

c.   These same opponents hold that the Pronoia of God takes care only of the elect (*Enn.* II, 9:16). This agrees with the view of Tri. Trac. 66:19ff. (God the *pronoia* for those for whom he is *pronoia*). The same in the Valentinian *Excerpta ex Theodoto* 74 (the Lord himself, men's guide, who came down to earth to transfer from fate to his Pronoia those who believed in Christ). See J. Zandee, *The Terminology of Plotinus and of some Gnostic writings, mainly the Fourth Treatise of the Jung Codex*, Istanbul 1961, 30. Plotinus seems also to have read writings of the *Gnōstikoi*:

d. The demiurge defects from his mother (*Enn.* II, 9:10) as in the Apocryphon of John in Codex III, 15. This is unique: elsewhere the demiurge arises from matter.

e. The reflection in the water of Chaos (*Enn.* II, 9:10) as in the Hypostasis of the Archons.

f. Exile, resipiscence and antitypes, as in Zostrianos.

Plotinus has confused the views of the Valentinians and the *Gnōstikoi* in order to create the impression that his opponents had a muddled mind. If only he had used the *Tractatus Tripartitus* as a source, a writing more rational, consistent and optimistic than anything Plotinus wrote!

55. C. Kraeling, *The Synagogue* (= *The Excavations at Dura-Europos, Final Report VIII*, New Haven 1956), plate LXX. In the Mandean religion, as with Saturninus, it is God himself, not *Rûhâ* (= the Holy Spirit = Sophia), who gives the divine spirit to Adam (Maria Vitoria Cerutti, *Dualismo e Ambiguita*, Rome 1981, 19: 'Interviene allora il padre degli *'utria*, spiriti della vita e della luce, il quale immette in Adamo l'anima (*nišimta* o *mana*)'). This seems to show that the role of Sophia in the process of anthropogony is secondary, rather late and perhaps to be located in Alexandria, the place of origin of the Apocryphon of John and related writings.

56. R. A. Bitter, *Vreemdelingschap bij Philo van Alexandrië. Een onderzoek naar de betekenis van paroikos* ('Alienship' in Philo of Alexandria. An investigation into the meaning of *paroikos*), Diss. Utrecht 1982, 182–183.

57. Cf. Zost. 5:24ff. (Robinson, 370): 'I ascended to the *Transmigration* (*paroikēsis*), which [really] exists. I was baptized and [...] world. I ascended to the Repentance (*metanoia*) which [really] exists [and was] baptized there four times'; 8:15f. (Robinson, 371): 'Concerning the *Transmigration* and the Repentance and the Creation of [aeons]'; 12:8ff. (Robinson, 372): 'They come into being and are removed, one by one, first from the copy of the *transmigration* up to the *Transmigration* which really exists, then from the copy of repentance up to the Repentance which really exists'; 27:13ff. (Robinson, 376): 'for there are three forms of [immortal] souls: those who have taken root upon the *transmigration*, because they cannot beget'; 43:13f. (Robinson, 379): 'Now concerning the man in the *Transmigration*'.

58. C. Schmidt and W. Till, *Koptisch-Gnostische Schriften* I: *Die Pistis Sophia, die beiden Bücher des Jeû, unbekanntes altgnostisches Werk*, GCS 45, Berlin 1954², 362: 'danach die Wohnung in der Fremde, die Reue, innerhalb davon die selbstgezeugten Gegenbilder'.

59. N. Dahl, 'The Arrogant Archon and the Lewd Sophia: Jewish

Traditions in Gnostic Revolt' in Layton, op. cit. (n. 54) II, *SHR* 41:2, Leiden 1981, 689–712.
60. 'Gnosis', in (ed.) M. J. Vermaseren, *Die orientalischen Religionen im Römerreich*, *EPRO* 93, Leiden 1981, 413–435, esp. 422.

V

AN ARAMAIC ETYMOLOGY FOR JALDABAOTH?

by

Professor Matthew Black, St Andrews

The etymology of the name of the Gnostic Demiurge Jaldabaoth has been the subject of much speculation since Franciscus Feuardentius first suggested reading it as Jaldaboth, *a patribus genitus*, in his 1575 edition of the works of Irenaeus.[1] Much later, in the early nineteenth century, a popular view was to connect the second element in the name, *ba[h]ōṯ*, with *bōhû* in the well-known *tōhû-wā-bōhû* phrase of Genesis 1:2 (*ba[h]ōṯ* was explained as a plural form), a view for which at least one modern scholar can still express a certain sympathy.[2] Some of the most notable among earlier scholars in the field, such as Mosheim and Bousset, preferred to maintain a prudent silence on the subject, and, in this respect, they have been followed by one modern Gnostic expert, Søren Giversen, who remarked 'It is safest to say, as Sagnard said of Barbelo ... "En réalité on ignore l'origine de ce nom".'[3] Nevertheless, one explanation of the enigmatic name has come to enjoy a wide consensus of scholarly opinion, ever since it was endorsed and largely promulgated by its authoritative adoption by Hilgenfeld[4] and Leisegang,[5] the two foremost experts at the end of the nineteenth and the beginning of the twentieth century in the field of Christian, and, in particular, Gnostic heresies. It is 'the long suspected etymology ... (which) has sought to derive the name from *jalda bahoth*, "son of Chaos".'[6] It is fair to say that it is this explanation alone which, out of its many predecessors, has survived the critical attention of post-Nag Hammadi scholars.

The first of the Nag Hammadi generation of scholars to comment on the name was Hans-Martin Schenke in his translation of *The Untitled Document* (Orig. World): the best scientific explanation of the name, according to Schenke, was that approved by Hilgenfeld and Leisegang; it corresponded perfectly (*entspricht ausgezeichnet*) to the description in the new text of the Demiurge or Archigenetor as emerging out of Chaos.[7] The explanation was accepted by Böhlig and Labib in their edition of *The*

Untitled Document,[8] and in his influential paper on the Jewish and Jewish Christian background in Gnostic texts from Nag Hammadi Professor Böhlig sought to support 'the long suspected etymology' by fresh Aramaic evidence, the alleged occurrence of the abstract noun *bāhûṭâ* in the Targum of Proverbs 26:21, meaning 'chaos'.[9]

Shortly after the appearance of the Böhlig-Labib edition of *The Untitled Document* Gershom Scholem wrote: 'The current etymology of *Yaldabaoth* as "child of chaos" ... is nonsense. In imitation of Sabaoth the magicians introduced theophoric *nomina* ending with -*ōth*. This syllable becomes the "magic suffix" par excellence ... It has no connection with the purely hypothetical word for chaos that has been invented *ad hoc*. The Aramaic noun *behath* means "shame" not "chaos".'[10] After the publication of the Böhlig paper, endorsing this etymology, Scholem returned to the question in a closely argued and detailed exposition 'Jaldabaoth Reconsidered' in the Puech *Festschrift* (referred to on p.72, n.1). As he was able to point out there, Böhlig's philological support for his theory consisted of a non-existent Aramaic noun *bāhûṭâ'* which had been invented by the lexicographer Jastrow in his Dictionary[11] as an emendation of the noun *kāhûṭâ* 'strife' in the Targum of Proverbs 26:21, the word and meaning which both the Hebrew and the Targum require.

Before proceeding to develop his own ideas about the etymological problem, Scholem examined in detail the arguments from the texts, in particular the contexts, where this *nomen dei* Jaldabaoth appears, and came to the conclusion that 'the new texts bear out the hypothesis ... that Jaldabaoth is not the son of Chaos, but more likely its source. At least two texts call Jaldabaoth or Saklas "King of Chaos" ... These are documents belonging to the first stages of the Gnostic systems ... it is irrelevant to review later developments ...' (ibid., 415f.). Moreover, so far as one other putative Aramaic derivation is concerned, the result is unimpressive: 'To consider the imperative "cross over"(*diaperan*, Orig. World 100:13) as a rendering of a Semitic (Hebrew) *be'oṭ*, the only meaning of which is to trample or to kick, is unwarranted and sounds rather fantastic' (ibid., 413).

In his own explanation of the origin of the name Scholem proceeds from the assumption of a composite *jald-abaoth*, rather than from the usual division into Aramaic *jalda' baoth*, and he explains the element *jald*, not as 'son', but as 'begetter', corresponding to the designation of the deity as archigenetor, 'the first begetter'; thus the Sophia of Jesus Christ speaks of 'the archigenetor whom they call Jaldabaoth.' (ibid., 419)* Both Hebrew and Aramaic, it is argued, use the verb *yālaḏ/yᵉlaḏ* of the function in procreation of both parents. The second element *Abaoth* appears, especially in magical texts, apparently as an abridged form or substitute for *Sabaoth*, one of the six archons generated by the Archigenetor, and a name clearly deriving from the Biblical 'Lord of saba'oth'. *Jaldabaoth* is

---

*[Ed.: the name 'Jaldabaoth' used by Scholem, Adam and the author derives from a transliteration of *yôḏ* by a *j*; in keeping with conventions elsewhere in this volume *yôḏ* is otherwise represented by a *y*.]

the 'Begetter of (S)abaoth', the archon who is assigned the chief role among the six produced by the Archigenetor.

A similar type of etymology has been suggested in a study by A. Adam who explained the *jalda* component similarly but took it as meaning 'generation' (*Erzeugung*); the second component is claimed to be Aramaic, *'abāhûṭâ'*, 'fatherhood' (*Vaterschaft*) understood as the power of generation (*Erzeugungskraft*). The name then means something like 'the production of the power of generation (*die Hervorbringung der Vaterkraft*)'.[12]

The objection has been made to the claim that *yalaḏ/yᵉlaḏ* can have such a force,[13] but, in fact, the use of this semitic verb 'to beget' as well as 'to bear children' is firmly attested (e.g. Targum Zechariah 13:3, Proverbs 23:22), although it is the Hiphil (Aramaic Aphel) which is more commonly used of the male. There are two objections, however, to the Scholem theory, the second of which may oblige us to set aside yet another brilliant guess. If the original etymology was *jalda abaoth*, as Scholem assumes, to get *jald abaoth* we are required to assume that the final syllable of the first noun has coalesced with the first syllable of the second. A more serious, if not fatal, objection seems to me to be that, on this theory, we have an explanation which assumes that the Archigenetor was named as the begetter of one only of the six archons he produced; and the objection is not removed by pointing out that (S)abaoth is the most powerful of the six.

In the course of his convincing case against the 'long suspected etymology' Scholem has noted that the 'only Aramaic and Syriac word which comes near *bāhûthā* (in which the *th* is no part of the root) is *behûthā* or *bāhāthā* (where the *th* is part of the root). In Jewish Aramaic the only and exclusive meaning of this word is "shame" or "disgrace" ...' (ibid., 408). The observation is not further pursued, but it is one which is well worth a second look, since these Aramaic nouns, in particular *bêhûṭâ'*, are the equivalents of Hebrew *bōšeṯ*, a word meaning 'shame', but also with special associations with idolatry, originally with the Israelite Baal cults which were particularly abhorrent to the worship of Jahweh, and not least in the sexual aspects of these Canaanite nature religions. The substitution in proper names of *bōšeṯ* for *ba'al* (e.g. 2 Samuel 2:8; cf. 1 Chronicles 8:33; 2 Samuel 11:21; cf. Judges 6:33) is evidence enough of ancient Israelite reaction to these local *ba'alîm* cults. The best known passage is Hosea 9:10 where Baal-Peor is actually described as Bosheth 'shame'. In Hosea's eyes Israel's submersion in Canaanite nature cults is 'harlotry', deserting Jahweh to 'play the harlot', where 'the term expresses the idea of ... Jahweh's abhorrence of the fertility rites and sacred prostitution of the cult of Baal.'[14]

There is no need to stress the point that the same kind of ethos is shared by the sects of the Gnostics. The suggestion of this essay is that Jaldabaoth was originally named 'the son of Shame, Bêhûṯ/Bošeṯ/Baal'. The name would commend itself since the Aramaic word for shame *bêhûṯ(â')* would be readily conformed to the magical terminology ending in *ōth*.

The other names for the Demiurge have a similar Aramaic origin. In *The Untitled Document* the second designation given to Jaldabaoth, Samael, is a formation from Aramaic *samâ'*, *samyâ'*, 'blind' with the regular theophoric ending *el*; he is 'the blind one'. Again the designation Saklas is best explained as a graecized formation of the Aramaic noun *saklâ'* 'fool', although here the word *sakal* is also Hebrew. Jaldabaoth's partner Sambathas is also a graecized form and is almost certainly to be traced to an Aramaic *šabbaṯâ'* 'sabbath' or *šᵉbî 'aṯâ'*, *hebdomas*, with an inserted mim as in Sambatyon for Sabbatyon, the mythical 'Sabbath river' in rabbinical traditions.

NOTES

1. For a detailed survey of these putative etymologies from the earliest period, see Gershom Scholem, 'Jaldabaoth Reconsidered', in *Mélanges d'histoire des religions offerts à Henri-Charles Puech*, Paris 1974, 406f.
2. G. Quispel in 'The Demiurge in the Apocryphon of John' in (ed.) R. McL. Wilson, *Nag Hammadi and Gnosis, Papers read at the First International Congress of Coptology (Cairo, December 1976)*, NHS 14, Leiden 1978, 22.
3. *Apocryphon Johannis ... with Translation, Introduction and Commentary*, Copenhagen 1963, 200.
4. A. Hilgenfeld, *Die Ketzergeschichte des Urchristentums*, Leipzig 1884, 238, 243.
5. H. Leisegang, *Die Gnosis*, Leipzig 1924, 176.
6. R. Bullard, cited by Scholem, op. cit., 410.
7. *ThLZ* 84:4, 1959, 251, n.39.
8. (eds.) A. Böhlig and P. Labib, *Die koptisch-gnostische Schrift ohne Titel aus Codex II von Nag Hammadi*, *VIOF* 58, Berlin 1962, 42.
9. 'Der jüdische und judenchristliche Hintergrund in gnostischen Texten von Nag Hammadi' in (ed.) U. Bianchi, *The Origins of Gnosticism: Colloquium of Messina, 13–18 April, 1966*, *SHR* 12, Leiden 1967, 115, esp. n.9.
10. Scholem, *Jewish Gnosticism, Merkabah Mysticism, and Talmudic Tradition*, New York 1965², 71–72, n. 23.
11. *Dictionary of the Targumim, the Talmud ... and Midrashic Literature*, Vol. I, 142.
12. 'Ist die Gnosis in aramäischen Weisheitsschulen entstanden?' in *The Origins of Gnosticism*, 291–301.
13. Adam, loc. cit. (n. 12), 300.
14. G. von Rad, *Old Testament Theology*, ET, Edinburgh 1965, II, 142.

VI

PHILO, GNOSIS AND THE NEW TESTAMENT

by

Professor Birger A. Pearson, Santa Barbara

The title of this article, assigned to me by the editors of this volume, might imply a wide-ranging treatment of a multitude of topics within three different and very large areas of study, or it might imply an attempt to find a connecting thread running through Philo, Gnosis, and the New Testament. One might also look upon one of them as the connecting link between the other two, e.g., 'Gnosis' as that which holds Philo and the New Testament together in some way. However one proceeds, though, it will be inevitable that the massive contribution of him to whom this volume is dedicated will necessarily be in evidence. I count it an honour and a privilege to dedicate this little study to Professor Wilson, who has written and spoken much about Philo, about Gnosis, about the New Testament, and about a host of other important things as well. Indeed, it will be evident that his insights have contributed much to what I have to say here.

In this article I shall attempt to find a way of integrating the three items in its title, i.e. to take the second option indicated at the beginning. In so doing I shall begin in Corinth and move to Alexandria. There will also be a movement in time, from the first century to the end of the second. Two of the Nag Hammadi tractates will be taken briefly into account: the Testimony of Truth (IX. *3*) and the Teachings of Silvanus (VII. *4*).

1—'GNOSIS' IN CORINTH?

In an article published some ten years ago Professor Wilson poses the question, 'How Gnostic were the Corinthians?'[1] Focussing on 1 Corinthians he mentions in the course of his article the various motifs which have frequently been taken to reflect Gnostic influence amongst the Corinthians: a tendency to division, the terms 'wisdom' and '*gnōsis*', alleged libertine tendencies, denial or misunderstanding of the resurrection, spiritual enthusiasm, realized eschatology, misuse or misunderstanding of the sacraments, contrasts between *psuchikoi* and *pneumatikoi*, and the typology of Christ and Adam. Wilson grants that these items may add up to 'what A. D. Nock[3] called "a gnostic way of thinking", such as we find later in the developed gnostic schools of thought' (70–71). He adds that the use of the term 'Gnosis' is legitimate as a general description of the Corinthian situation (71). He even concedes that Paul himself 'appears to be moving in a gnostic direction' in his view of the resurrection body (66–67). But he vigorously argues that it is illegitimate to read the developed Gnosticism of the second century back into first-century Corinth. 'Gnosis in the broader sense is not yet Gnosticism' (71). What one finds in first-century Corinth, he concludes, is 'only the first tentative beginnings of what was later to develop into full-scale Gnosticism' (74).

The careful distinction Professor Wilson wants to make between the religion of the Corinthians, which he calls 'Gnosis', and 'Gnosticism' is surely cogent enough. I share his conviction that the religion of Paul's Corinthian congregation cannot reasonably be defined as 'Gnostic' in the conventional sense of the term,[4] though I hasten to add that I make this judgment on exegetical grounds, leaving open the question whether 'developed Gnosticism' actually existed in the first century.[5] But is 'Gnosis' a better designation for the Corinthian situation than 'Gnosticism'? Is this 'Gnosis' simply a step in the direction of the 'developed Gnosticism' of the second century? Professor Wilson does make an important observation, with specific reference to 'Wisdom Christology', to the effect that 'something has happened to break the continuity of development and divert gnostic thinking into a different channel' (73), an important caveat against concluding that the religion of the Corinthians represents a point along a set 'trajectory' leading inevitably to the 'Gnosticism' of the second century. But then two items need further clarification: 1. In what specific first-century religious context should the Corinthian situation be placed? 2. What is that 'something' which 'divert(s) gnostic thinking into a different channel'?

Setting aside the second question for now, I want to take up the first, and reiterate here some points I made some years ago on the subject, viz. the historical contexts of the Corinthians' supposedly 'Gnostic' traits.[6] In so doing I shall also call attention to some recent contributions which shed additional light on this question.

The logical place to begin in an appraisal of 'Gnosis in Corinth' is the single passage in 1 Corinthians where *gnōsis* is discussed and even defined, viz. 1 Corinthians 8. The burning issue in that chapter is whether or not it is permissible to eat meat which has been sacrificed to pagan gods ('idols', v. 4). The *gnōsis* on the basis of which certain Christians in Corinth felt free to eat such meat is specified as the knowledge that 'there is no God but One', knowledge which Paul and his Corinthian opponents have in common (v. 1). The *gnōsis* in question is that insight which enables Christians to make practical decisions in the community, based on the knowledge of God.[7] This kind of *gnōsis* is that which pervades biblical and post-biblical Jewish thought, and has nothing whatever to do with Gnosticism.[8]

R. A. Horsley, in a recent article on 'Gnosis in Corinth', [9] has come to similar conclusions. But he makes some very interesting elaborations by putting the whole argument in 1 Corinthians 8:1–6 squarely in the context of Hellenistic Jewish thought, especially as it is represented by Philo of Alexandria and the Wisdom of Solomon. It is in this context, too, that he places the *logos/sophia* Christology reflected in v. 6. I cannot take up his arguments in detail here; suffice it to say that his understanding of the background of Paul's argument in 1 Corinthians 8 is basically persuasive.

If one can speak of a 'Gnosis' in Corinth in the sense that Wilson does, i.e. as a 'knowledge reserved for an elite',[10] it must be added that such 'gnosis' among the Corinthians was focussed on the term *sophia* ('wisdom') rather than *gnōsis*. This is made abundantly clear especially in 1 Corinthians 1–4.[11] This passage (i.e. 1:10–4:20) constitutes a personal *apologia*, wherein Paul not only seeks to correct some fatal flaws in his Corinthian congregation's theology and conduct but also defends his apostolic authority against opponents who are challenging this authority. As part of their challenge they are claiming a special 'wisdom' (*sophia*) and a special status as 'spiritual' (*pneumatikoi*) and 'perfect' (or 'mature', *teleioi*) men, in contrast to others in the congregation who are still 'babes' (or 'immature, *nēpioi*). Paul cleverly takes his opponents' terminology, in which they express their elitist claims, and turns it back against them. Paul's opponents are using categories derived from Hellenistic Jewish wisdom, such as is represented especially by Philo of Alexandria and the Wisdom of Solomon. Paul himself argues out of a religious background which is more akin to Palestinian Apocalypticism than to the speculative wisdom of his Corinthian opponents. I have discussed all of this in previous studies, and therefore do not wish to repeat the arguments here.[12] However, I do want to call attention, once again, to the recent work of R. A. Horsley, in which he comes to the same basic conclusions while providing additional arguments and evidence.[13]

To be sure, Horsley has taken issue with some of my contentions regarding the contrasting terms *pneumatikos* and *psuchikos* as used in 1 Corinthians (2:13–15; 15:45–57); so I should like to take this up briefly here, particularly because this is the most important item brought up by those who want to point to an alleged 'Gnostic' influence in 1 Corinthians.[14] My argument, in summary, is that the *pneumatikos-psuchikos* terminology derives from Hellenistic Jewish exegesis of Genesis 2:7, wherein a differentiation is made between 'spirit' (*pneuma*) and 'soul' (*psuchē*). The starting point for this observation is 1 Corinthians 15:44–47, where Genesis 2:7 is the focal point of the argument. Paul's eschatological targum on that passage is meant to counter his opponents' use of Genesis 2:7 to prove that man has an immortal element (*pneuma*) in him which is capable of surviving physical death. This is part of their argument against the resurrection of the body. Paul's point, based on his appropriation and reinterpretation of Palestinian resurrection traditions in which Genesis 2:7 is interpreted eschatologically, is that Christ is the 'last Adam' and the 'lifegiving spirit' whose resurrection is the basis of future resurrection and eternal life for all believers. The best analogies to the Corinthians' interpretation of Genesis 2:7 are found in Philo and Wisdom.[15] Paul's opponents use the same Hellenistic Jewish exegetical traditions to bolster their classification of people in the community as 'spiritual' (*pneumatikoi*), those who live on the plane of the spirit (*pneuma*) by their devotion to wisdom, in contrast to those who live on the plane of their lower soul (the *psuchikoi*) by not seeking after the higher wisdom.[16]

Horsley's critique of my argument consists of three points: 1. The specific *pneumatikos-psuchikos* contrast does not occur in Philo or in other Hellenistic Jewish writings. 2. There is no fundamental contrast between 'soul' and 'spirit' in Philo or Wisdom. 3. There is no evidence in Philo or Wisdom for a preference of the term 'spirit' instead of 'mind' (*nous*) as a designation for the higher part of the soul.[17] The first point is obviously correct, nor did I ever claim to find that specific contrast in Philo or other Hellenistic Jewish writings. I did, and do, claim that the adjectival terms are based on a contrast between *pneuma* and *psuchē*, analogous to the differentiation made in popular Greek philosophy of that era between the *psuchē* of man and his rational *nous* ('mind').[18] Point three of Horsley's critique is conceded. I should not have said that a 'preference' for the term *pneuma* instead of *nous* is observable in Hellenistic Judaism.[19] But I still do contend that the *locus classicus* in the LXX for a contrast between the soul and the spirit in man is Genesis 2:7, precisely the text whose interpretation is the bone of contention between Paul and his opponents in 1 Corinthians 15:44–47. There is no question but that Philo uses the term *nous* for the higher faculty of the soul more frequently than he does *pneuma*, but even Horsley concedes that Philo uses *pneuma* for the higher soul sometimes; he counts 'a dozen times' and cites as one of the texts *Spec. Leg.* I, 171, which refers to 'the rational spirit in us' (*tou en hēmīn logikou pneumatos*, cf. *Spec. Leg.* I, 277).[20] As for point two, it is obvious that there is no consistent or 'fundamental' contrast between 'soul' and 'spirit' in Philo or Wisdom – the terms are frequently seen as interchangeable, as Horsley rightly points out[21] – but it can hardly be denied that the contrast occurs in Philo. Genesis 2:7 (LXX) is certainly suggestive of such a contrast: God's inbreathing of the 'breath of life' (*pnoē zōēs*) into man makes him a 'living soul' (*psuchē zōsa*). It is noteworthy that Philo sometimes substitutes the term *pneuma* for *pnoē* in his rendition of the passage (e.g. *Op. Mund.* 135; *Leg. All.* III, 161). And while it is true, as Horsley argues, that Philo often understands *pneuma* as the substance (*ousia*) of the soul,[22] consonant with a basic body-soul dualism, he can also differentiate between a lower (animal) soul and a higher soul (*Det. Pot. Ins.* 79–95; *Spec. Leg.* IV, 123). In sum, while it is true that the contrast between a higher *spirit* and a lower *soul* is not a fundamental and exclusive one in Philo or Wisdom, such a contrast *is* fundamental to the contrast between the terms *pneumatikos* and *psuchikos* as used by the Corinthian opponents of Paul.

Horsley does go on to show in an entirely convincing way that the contrast between the *pneumatikoi* and the *psuchikoi* made by Paul's Corinthian opponents is ultimately based on Hellenistic Jewish categories, including exegesis of Genesis 2:7.[23] Horsley rightly sees Philo and Wisdom, in general, as providing the best analogies to the kind of religion espoused by the Corinthians, as reflected in Paul's argumentation.[24] This, then, brings up a basic historical question: how do we account for the similarities between the Corinthians' 'gnosis' (which I prefer to refer to as Christianized Hellenistic Jewish wisdom) and the religion of Philo? Paul's *apologia* in 1 Corinthians 1–4 provides a good basis for answering this question. It seems clear in his argumentation that he is especially concerned about the role of Apollos in the Corinthian congregation (esp. 3:5–4:5). He wants to express his collegiality with Apollos, but at the same time he expresses his apostolic superiority to him in no uncertain terms. This suggests that the highly-developed wisdom speculation in Corinth can be attributed to the teaching activity of Apollos. If we recall that Apollos was an Alexandrian Jew and a learned and eloquent teacher of scripture (Acts 18:24–26), we have a very plausible link between the religiosity of the Corinthians and that of Alexandrian Judaism as represented by Philo.[25] I am in any case convinced that virtually *everything* in 1 Corinthians thought to represent a 'gnostic way of thinking'[26] can be explained on the basis of Hellenistic Jewish speculative wisdom such as that encountered in Philo.[27]

With this observation we move from Corinth to Alexandria.

2—HOW 'GNOSTIC' IS PHILO?

If the 'Gnosis' of the Corinthians has basic affinities with the religiosity of Philo – which has been argued above – the extent to which Philo himself can be called a 'Gnostic' becomes an issue. Here, again, we can profitably turn to what Professor Wilson has written on the subject. I refer especially to his 1972 article on 'Philo of Alexandria and Gnosticism'.[28] In that article he reduces the various scholarly opinions on Philo's relation to Gnosticism to two: 1. Philo is part of the Gnostic movement.[29] 2. Philo is a 'precursor' of the later Gnostic movement. Wilson prefers the second option, and in that connection makes the usual distinction between 'Gnosis' and 'Gnosticism'. 'Philo is not a gnostic in the strict sense of the term, although he does have affinities with Gnosticism' (215). Philo marks 'one of the preliminary stages' on the way to Gnosticism, but 'he belongs mostly to Gnosis, not to Gnosticism. Indeed the case of Philo is one of the best examples of the value of this distinction' (ibid.).

Wilson specifies three 'affinities with Gnosticism' found in Philo: 1. Emphasis in both on the complete transcendence of the supreme God. 2. Interposition of a series of intermediaries between the supreme God and our world. 3. A general disparagement of the sense-perceptible world (216). The first point is further elaborated by pointing to Philo's unqualified denial of the possibility of knowing the divine essence and his tendency toward a *theologia negativa*, features which he has in common with the Gnostics. Wilson adds that Philo does not use the term *agnōstos* ('unknowable') of God, 'a point on which the gnostics were to carry the Platonic tradition further than either Plato or Philo ever did' (ibid.). But even the use of the term *agnōstos* of God is no necessary proof of Gnosticism. Josephus uses it of God (*Ap.* II, 167), and he can hardly be called a 'Gnostic'. Wilson's main point, however, is right: Philo's doctrine of the transcendence of God is based on a combination of Platonic philosophy with Old Testament theology (ibid.). The same, of course, could be said of the Gnostics' doctrine. So it is their radical dualism which separates the Gnostics from Philo, as Wilson rightly perceives (ibid. and 219).

Wilson's second and third points bear upon the same basic issue, the radical dualism of the Gnostics *versus* the modified Platonism of Philo: Philo's intermediaries are not the wicked and rebellious archons of Gnostic myth (217–219), and Philo's disparagement of the sense-perceptible world – a basic feature of Middle Platonism[30] – is far removed from the Gnostic myth of a pre-mundane Fall which places the world and its creator in the realm of evil (218).

All of this Wilson has stated with great perspicacity and eloquence. But then in what sense can one put Philo into the category of 'Gnosis' at all, as Wilson does? If Philo has 'not yet' taken the step toward Gnosticism (218),[31] under what circumstances *would* he have taken that step? Is it that Gnosticism had 'not yet' developed in the first century?[32] Or rather is it something in Philo's own religious make-up which prevented him from *ever* taking that step?[33] I think the latter is the case, and Wilson himself seems to share this view, when he says of Philo: 'he was a Jew, and it is difficult to imagine him having any sympathy for the gnostic repudiation of the God of the Old Testament' (219). Even if simply being a Jew did not necessarily preclude the possibility of his espousing Gnosticism – though such a step would surely involve apostasy from Judaism – we know what *kind* of Jew Philo was, one ultimately faithful to the religion of his people and totally committed to the one eternal God, Creator of and Provider for the world.[34]

There is, to be sure, a sense in which Philo's religiosity can be called a '*gnōsis*', in the sense of 'knowledge reserved for an elite'. For Philo does, throughout his writings, distinguish between an elite group in his community of persons who are capable of achieving 'wisdom' (*sophia*), the 'wise' or 'perfect' (*teleioi*), *versus* the 'immature' (*nēpioi*) who must be kept on a strict diet of milk (*Migr. Abr.* 28–29; *Leg. All.* I, 90–96; *Agric.* 8–9; etc.).[35] This is a feature which Philo shares in common with the Corinthian opponents of Paul, discussed above. Another definition of the kind of 'Gnosis' represented by Philo has been put forward by A. Wlosok, i.e. a 'philosophical Gnosis' involving a type of religious speculation based on Platonic themes and characteristic of first-century (and later) Alexandrian philosophy.[36] But all of this is considerably removed from the religious thought-world of the Gnostics. Though Philo's 'Gnosis' shares many themes with that of the Gnostics, there is a 'new element' (as Wilson puts it) in Gnosticism: 'the radical dualism which rejected this world and its creator, the divine tragedy, the tragic split in the Deity' (219). Wilson concludes his article with the observation that 'this is something that still awaits explanation' (ibid.).

In order to get a clear grasp on what it is that separates 'Gnosticism' from 'Gnosis' (as defined above) it is necessary to take a look at actual Gnostic texts. In the following section we shall stay in Alexandria, but move in time to the end of the second century, while taking a backward look at Philo and the New Testament.

3—PHILO, GNOSIS, AND THE NEW TESTAMENT IN SECOND-CENTURY ALEXANDRIA: TWO DOCUMENTS

The two documents to be taken up briefly here are meant to illustrate the distinction drawn by Wilson and others between 'Gnosis' and 'Gnosticism', as it may be applied to a situation late in the second century when everyone agrees that 'Gnosticism' is flourishing. To be sure, many examples could be cited to illustrate this, but I have chosen for this purpose two texts from the Nag Hammadi corpus: NHC VII. *4*: The Teachings of Silvanus, and NHC IX. *3*: The Testimony of Truth. Both of these tractates presumably come from the same general milieu, viz. Alexandria in Egypt; and they are roughly contemporaneous, i.e. datable to the end of the second century (the Teachings of Silvanus may be a little earlier). Both of them represent a milieu in which traditions from Hellenistic Jewish speculative wisdom and Middle Platonic philosophy are used to propagate a message in which Jesus Christ plays a central role; hence they are undeniably 'Christian' texts. In both of them one can find numerous parallels to, if not actual use of, the writings of Philo. And both of them make use of the New Testament. But one (the Testimony of Truth) is clearly a Gnostic text; the other (the Teachings of Silvanus) can hardly be called 'Gnostic' in any technical sense.

We consider first the Testimony of Truth,[37] a document which has aptly been called 'one of the best examples of Christian Gnosticism'.[38] It is a homiletic treatise in which its author contends vigorously on behalf of 'the Truth' (as he understands it) against 'the Law' and those who follow it. 'The Law', for our author, is epitomized in the commandment given by the Creator 'to take a husband (or) to take a wife, and to beget, to multiply like the sand of the sea' (30:2–5; cf. Genesis 1:28; 2:24; 22:17). The tractate advocates an extreme encratism based on a radical dualism between 'Imperishability', 'Light', and the 'world' (30:12–21; cf. 40:27–28; 44:24–30; etc.), and between the 'God of Truth' and the 'God' who created the world and gave the Law (41:5; 45:3, 24, etc.). Much of the tractate is devoted to the person and work of Christ, but it is nevertheless fair to say that it grounds salvation squarely on *gnōsis*: Christ will bring to eternal life in heaven those who have achieved *gnōsis* (36:2–7; 38:22–27). What sort of *gnōsis* this might be is not left in doubt:

> This, therefore, is the true testimony: When a man knows
> himself and God who is over the truth, he will be saved, and he
> will be crowned with the crown unfading. (44:30–45:6)

In typically Gnostic fashion our tractate equates knowledge of God with knowledge of the self.[39]

All of this I have treated elsewhere;[40] what is of interest here is the tractate's reminiscence of, if not use of, Philo. The following examples are illustrative of this point: in the opening passage our author addresses 'those who know to hear not with the ears of the body but with the ears of the mind' (29:6–9). The distinction between 'the hearing of the mind' and the 'hearing of the (bodily) ears' is made in Philo, too (*Decal.* 35). In similar fashion the Testimony of Truth refers to the 'eyes of (the) mind' (46:7) in its midrashic quotation of Genesis 3:5; Philo interprets the opening of the eyes referred to in Genesis 3:7 as 'the vision of the soul' (*Quaest. in Gen.* I, 39). According to our tractate the 'mind' (*nous*) of man is male (44:2–3); Philo routinely refers to the *nous* as male and sense perception (*aisthēsis*) as female (e.g. *Leg. All.* II, 38; III, 49–50; *Op. Mund.* 165).[41] Our tractate's denigration of the corruptible world of the flesh (40:27; 42:6) is almost matched in Philo (e.g. *Plant.* 53), as is its denigration of the body and its pleasures (e.g. 30:32–31:1; cf. *Gig.* 13–15; *Leg. All.* III, 77). To be 'stripped' of the body is the goal of the Gnostic (37:2), and this is a goal not far removed from Philo, who in fact uses precisely these terms in describing the glorious end of Moses (*Virt.* 76). Our tractate speaks of the 'dividing' power of the 'word (*logos*) of the Son of Man' (40:23–41:4) in a manner reminiscent of Philo's discussion of the 'cutting' and 'dividing' power of the Logos (*Rer. Div. Her.* 130–140).[42] Numerous other parallels could be cited between the Testimony of Truth and Philo, but let it suffice finally to point out one final feature which they have in common, i.e. the use of the allegorical method of interpreting scripture.[43]

All of this does not show that Philo is a Gnostic. It shows, rather, that this Gnostic text has utilized traditions, conceptions, and terminology at home in a milieu in which Hellenistic Jewish wisdom has been fused with Middle Platonic categories. The metaphysical dualism reflected in the Philonic texts cited above is typical of the Platonic philosophy of the day. The Testimony of Truth has utilized the same conceptions in the service of a radical Gnostic dualism profoundly different in spirit and intentionality from Philo's religiosity and Platonist philosophy.[44] The two parallels cited first are cases in point: in the first (*Decal.* 35) Philo is describing the scene of the giving of the Law on Mount Sinai (Exodus 20), and he says that the miraculous voice of God created in the souls of the Israelites a hearing superior to the hearing of the ears, i.e. a hearing of the mind, wherewith properly to understand and obey the divine commandments. The Testimony of Truth, in contrast, has nothing but contempt for the Law. In the second (*Quaest. in Gen.* I, 39) Philo allegorically interprets the opening of the eyes of Adam and Eve (Genesis 3:7) as 'the vision of the soul' which can perceive good and bad. The Testimony of Truth, on the other hand, describes the entire paradise story in such a way that the Creator becomes the villain and the serpent the hero.[45] Here we have, in a nutshell, a prime example of the 'revolutionary' character of Gnosticism,[46] that 'new element' which according to Wilson[47] marks 'Gnosticism' off from mere 'Gnosis'.

Similar observations can be made regarding the extensive use of the New Testament in the Testimony of Truth. All four Gospels are used, as well as Acts, the Pauline literature, Hebrews, James, 1 Peter and Revelation. The Fourth Gospel and Paul have provided the greatest theological influence: the Son of Man Christology of John is very prominent in the document, and Paul's doctrine of the Law seems to have played a role in its depreciation of the Law and those 'under the Law' (29:22–25; cf. Romans 6:14; Galatians 4:4–5, 21).[48] But the basic religious stance of the Testimony of Truth is ultimately as alien to the New Testament it appropriates as it is to Philo.

We now turn to the other document, the Teachings of Silvanus.[49] This document, the only non-Gnostic tractate in NH Codex VII, is an example of early Christian 'wisdom', modelled upon the wisdom literature of Hellenistic Judaism and showing particular affinities with the Wisdom of Solomon. Loosely structured, it consists of admonitory sayings and proverbs, frequently introduced in typical wisdom style with the address, 'my son', exhortations modelled on the Stoic-Cynic diatribe, and hymnic passages in praise of God and Christ. It has aptly been described as representing 'a Christianized form of Jewish wisdom which prepared the way for the thought of the great Alexandrian theologians of the third century'.[50] Clement of Alexandria, indeed, shows manifest affinities with the Teachings of Silvanus,[51] but it is also of interest that a passage from the tractate (97:3–98:22) has been shown to have been used later in a sermon attributed to St Anthony.[52] The author, of course, is unknown. The document is pseudonymously attributed to the companion of Paul and amanuensis of Peter mentioned in the New Testament (1 Thessalonians 1:1; 2 Thessalonians 1:1; 2 Corinthians 1:19; 1 Peter 5:12; referred to in Acts 15–18 as 'Silas').

Numerous points of contact have been noticed between the Teachings of Silvanus and Philo, and some of these have been explored in an article by J. Zandee on the Teachings of Silvanus and Philo published in the Puech *Festschrift*.[53] Zandee is careful not to claim that Philo's writings were definitely known to the author of the Teachings of Silvanus (338), but he shows that they are remarkably similar both in method and specific content. Comparing specific passages in the Teachings of Silvanus with texts in Philo, Zandee demonstrates that they have much in common in their conception of the transcendence of God, based on Platonic categories (338–339),[54] their doctrine of the personified 'Wisdom' (340–341), their anthropology, also based on Platonism but showing Stoic features as well (341–342), their stress on morality and the struggle against the passions, coupled with a decidedly negative attitude toward the body (343–344), and their use of the allegorical method of interpreting scripture (344–345). It can easily be concluded, on the basis of Zandee's study, that the Teachings of Silvanus exudes the same intellectual and religious atmosphere as Philo. The only basic difference between them in this regard is that the Teachings of Silvanus is a Christian document whereas Philo is Jewish. Thus, for the Teachings of Silvanus it is Christ who is the ultimate teacher of wisdom (90:33–91:1; 96:32) instead of Moses:

> Know who Christ is, and acquire him as a friend, for this is the
> friend who is faithful. He is also God and Teacher. This one,
> being God, became man for your sake.   (110:14–19)[55]

Indeed the Logos and Sophia of Philo have become identified with
Christ in the Teachings of Silvanus: 'He is Wisdom; he is also the Word'
(106:23–24). In this connection the author can paraphrase Paul's[56] words
on the wisdom of God (1 Corinthians 1:20–25): 'For since he (Christ) is
Wisdom, he makes the foolish man wise' (107:3–4; cf. 111:22–29). He can
also paraphrase the praise of Sophia in Wisdom (7:25–26) in a hymn of
praise to Christ:

> For he is a light from the power of God,
> and he is an emanation of the pure glory of the Almighty.
> He is the spotless mirror of the working of God,
> and he is the image of his goodness.
> For he is also the light of the Eternal Light.   (112:37–113:7)[57]

As has already been noted, the Teachings of Silvanus is not a Gnostic
document; indeed, it shows some definitely anti-Gnostic features. It warns
the reader not to be 'defiled by strange kinds of knowledge (*gnōsis*)'
(94:31–33). And Gnostics who refer to the Creator of the world as
'ignorant'[58] are undoubtedly in view in the following warning: 'Let no one
ever say that God is ignorant. For it is not right to place the Creator of
every creature in ignorance' (116:5–9). Nevertheless some 'Gnosticizing'
features have been found in it by W. Schoedel and others, 'notably in the
tripartite anthropology which has to do with the "three races" from which
man originated (92:10ff.)'.[59] A brief consideration of the passage in
question (92:10–94:29) will therefore be in order before we bring this study
to a close.

The key section of this passage reads as follows:

> But before everything (else), know your birth (*souōn pekjpo*).
> Know yourself (*souong*), that is, from what substance (*ousia*) you
> are, or from what race (*genos*), or from what species (*phulē*).
> Understand that you have come into being from three races
> (*šomet ñgenos*): from the earth, from the formed (*ebol hm̄
> peplasma*), and from the created (*ebol hm̄ pteno*). The body has
> come into being from the earth with an earthly substance, but
> the formed, for the sake of the soul, has come into being from
> the thought of the Divine (*hm̄ pmeeue m̄ptheion*). The created,
> however, is the mind (*nous*), which has come into being in
> conformity with the image of God (*kata thikōn m̄pnoute*). The
> divine mind has substance (*ousia*) from the Divine, but the soul
> is that which he (God) has formed (*pentaf̄plasse*) for their own
> hearts.   (92:10–29)

This section is an exhortation to self-knowledge, considered as a prerequisite to living a 'rational' (*noeron*, 94:14–17) life of 'virtue' (*aretē*, 93:2).[60] It consists of an interpretation of the Delphic maxim, *gnōthi sauton*,[61] amplified by a piece of Genesis exegesis focussed on Genesis 2:7 and 1:27. It is a typical piece of Hellenistic Jewish wisdom, and reproduces concepts which are well-known to Philo, if not in fact derived from him.[62] The exhortation to self-knowledge here is similar to Philo's injunction, 'know thyself (*gnōthi sauton*) and the parts of which thou dost consist, what each is, and for what it was made, and how it is meant to work ...' (*Fug.* 46). For Philo, as for the Teachings of Silvanus, the highest 'part' in man is 'the Mind that is in thee' (*ho en soi nous*, ibid.).[63] The three 'substances' or 'genera' (*genos*, translated 'race') are read out of Genesis 2:7 (LXX): 'earth' (*choun apo tēs gēs*), the 'formed' 'soul' (*eplasen ... psuchēn*), and the 'created' 'mind' (*nous*) which has 'substance from the divine' (cf. *enephusēsen ... pnoēn zōēs*). Genesis 1:27 is also brought in, not only with the observation that it is the mind 'which has come into being in conformity with the image of God', but also that it is the mind which is 'created' (cf. Genesis 1:27: *kat' eikona theou epoiēsen auton*). Much of this exegesis is found in Philo, and in fact may reflect influence from Philo. Some of the relevant Philonic texts have been mentioned already.[64] Philo says, for example, that the mind has for its 'substance' (*ousia*) the spirit breathed into man by God (*Rer. Div. Her.* 55–56). Philo also speaks of the mind (*nous*) as that which is created in the image of God (*Leg. All.* I, 90; *Plant.* 18–20; cf. *Rer. Div. Her.* 56–57). And Philo makes the distinction, observable here in our text, between that which is 'formed' by God (*eplasen*, Genesis 2:7) and that which is 'created' (*epoiēsen*, Genesis 1:27; see e.g. *Leg. All.* I, 53).[65]

The main point of this passage is that man has the innate capacity in him either to 'live according to the mind' (93:3–4) or to live on a lower level of existence. If one cuts off the 'male part' (i.e. the mind),[66] one becomes 'psychic' (*psuchikos*, 93:13–14), or worse yet 'fleshly' (*sarkikos*), taking on 'animal nature' (*phusis ñtbnē*, 93:20–21). 'God is the spiritual one (*pneumatikos*). Man has taken shape (*morphē*) from the substance of God' (93:25–27). In sum, 'you will take on the likeness of the part toward which you will turn yourself' (94:3–5). Therefore 'turn toward the rational nature and cast off from yourself the earth-begotten (*ñjpo ñkah* = *gēgenēs*, cf. Philo, *Op. Mund.* 136; *Leg. All.* I, 31) nature' (94:16–19).

This brings us, as it were, full circle, back to the range of ideas at the heart of the controversy in Paul's Corinthian congregation. We see in this passage in the Teachings of Silvanus (and in others as well)[67] the same kind of speculative wisdom as was apparently taught in Corinth by Apollos of Alexandria, still vibrant for the second-century author of the Teachings of Silvanus. Whether this can be called 'Gnosis' or 'Gnosticizing' is a matter of semantics. If there was a 'Gnosis' in Corinth, or in Philo, there is the same kind of 'gnosis' in the Teachings of Silvanus.

CONCLUSIONS

In this survey, touching upon aspects of first- and second-century Christianity, the speculative wisdom of Hellenistic Judaism, and second-century Gnosticism, we have had occasion to test the distinctions made by Wilson and others between 'Gnosis' and 'Gnosticism'. These distinctions are valid to a point, in that 'full-blown Gnosticism' was not found in the New Testament (i.e. in 1 Corinthians, our example) nor in Philo. A kind of 'Gnosis' was arguably present, if one granted the broad definition proposed by Wilson and others, including the Messina Colloquium. But the 'Gnosis' in question, in my view, might better be designated 'speculative wisdom', in that 'wisdom' is a far more central category in the literature in question – 1 Corinthians, Philo and Wisdom, and the Teachings of Silvanus – than 'knowledge' (*gnōsis*). The word 'Gnosis' is too slippery a designation for the religiosity in question and lacks definitional utility, though there are cases where it might be more appropriate, such as the *gnōsis* espoused by Clement of Alexandria.

As for Gnosticism (which German scholars persist in calling 'die Gnosis'),[68] we are dealing with a scholarly construct which has definitional utility so long as the scholarly consensus is there. 'The Gnostic religion' might be a better term, for in effect Gnosticism involves a radically new world-view and symbol-system, and should be defined as a religion in its own right, with clearly recognizable historical parameters.[69]

Finally, we have encountered the tendency to use such terms as 'not yet' to distinguish between 'Gnosis' or 'Gnosticizing' ('pre-Gnostic', 'proto-Gnostic') tendencies, and a 'full blown Gnosticism'. The utility of this usage can also be called into question. In the case of the Teachings of Silvanus, for example, we have a document in which the religiosity of Hellenistic Judaism, as represented also by 1 Corinthians, Philo, and Wisdom, not only did 'not yet' become a full-blown Gnosticism, but also *never* did so. In fine, one cannot project a 'trajectory' from 1 Corinthians or Philo and necessarily expect to find 'Gnostics' at the other end. Nor, for that matter, should we foreclose the possibility that there *was* a 'full-blown Gnosticism' already in Philo's or Paul's time.

To be sure, these and many other related issues remain open for discussion. I conclude this little study with the hope that Professor Wilson will continue to make his important contributions to the discussion for a long time to come.

NOTES

1. 'How Gnostic Were the Corinthians?', *NTS* 19, 1972, 65–74.
2. Wilson rightly observes that 'it is in the first epistle that the gnostic influences are commonly detected' (67).
3. 'Gnosticism', *HThR* 57, 1964, 278.
4. Cf. the well-known formulations found in the 'Proposal for a

terminological and conceptual agreement with regard to the theme of the Colloquium' drawn up at the Messina Colloquium on the Origins of Gnosticism, published in (ed.) U. Bianchi, *Le Origini dello Gnosticismo, Colloquio di Messina 13–18 Aprile 1966, SHR* 12, Leiden 1967, xxvi–xxix, English version. This document distinguishes *gnōsis*, as 'knowledge of the divine mysteries reserved for an elite', from 'the Gnosticism of the Second Century sects'. The latter includes such elements as 'the idea of a divine spark in man', a 'devolution of the divine', and a saving *gnōsis* involving 'the divine identity of the *knower* (the Gnostic), the *known* (the divine substance of one's transcendent self), and the *means by which one knows* (*gnosis*)'. Thus 'not every *gnosis* is Gnosticism'. Professor Wilson refers to these definitions of the Messina Colloquium with approval in several of his writings; see e.g. *Gnosis and the New Testament*, Philadelphia/Oxford 1968, 17. Indeed the distinction between 'Gnosis' and 'Gnosticism' is a basic presupposition of all of Wilson's publications on Gnosticism.

5. Although it is true that we do not have any *primary* textual evidence for Gnosticism earlier than the second century, it need not be concluded that Gnosticism could not have existed as early as the first century. In any case, it can no longer be held that Gnosticism developed as a 'Christian heresy'. On the whole question see now K. Rudolph, *Die Gnosis*, Leipzig/Göttingen 1977, 1980[2] – references in the following are to the 2nd ed. Simon Magus, for example, has been taken by some (not all) scholars to represent a full-blown Gnosticism. See e.g. H. Jonas, *The Gnostic Religion*, Boston 1963, 103–111; E. Haenchen, 'Gab es eine vorchristliche Gnosis?' *ZThK* 49, 1952, 316–349; W. Foerster, 'Die "ersten Gnostiker" Simon und Menander', in *Le Origini dello Gnosticismo* (n. 4), 190–196; and Rudolph, op. cit., 315–319; id., 'Simon – Magus oder Gnosticus? Zum Stand der Debatte', *ThR* 42, 1977, 279–359. It should also be recalled that Wilson himself, in his important book, *The Gnostic Problem*, London 1958, states the following: 'our earliest definite documentary evidence goes back to the middle of the first century, to the New Testament period. It may be that Gnosticism in the full sense is even older, but so far as can be seen at present it is more or less contemporary with Christianity' (68). Cf. also his chapter on 'The Earlier Gnostic Sects', 97–115.

6. B. A. Pearson, *The Pneumatikos-Psychikos Terminology in I Corinthians. A Study in the Theology of the Corinthian Opponents of Paul and Its Relation to Gnosticism*, SBLDS 12, Missoula 1973. See also Pearson, 'Hellenistic-Jewish Wisdom Speculation and Paul', in (ed.) R. L. Wilken, *Aspects of Wisdom in Judaism and Early Christianity*, Notre Dame 1975, 43–66.

7. See my discussion in *The Pneumatikos-Psychikos Terminology* (n. 6), 42–43.

8. Against Bultmann, *TDNT* I, 709, followed by U. Wilckens, *Weisheit und Torheit*, Tübingen 1959, 212, and W. Schmithals, *Die Gnosis in Korinth*, Göttingen 1965[2], 134.

9. R. A. Horsley, 'Gnosis in Corinth: I Corinthians 8:1–6', *NTS* 27, 1981, 32–51.
10. See above, and n. 4.
11. That *gnōsis* in 1 Corinthians (ch. 8) is not the same as *sophia* is evident in 12:8, where the two are distinguished, as well as in 1:5, where Paul praises the Corinthians for their *gnōsis* while proceeding to deny their claim to *sophia* in his main argument in chs 1–4. Cf. *The Pneumatikos-Psychikos Terminology* (n. 6), 42.
12. 'Hellenistic-Jewish Wisdom Speculation' (n. 6); cf. *The Pneumatikos-Psychikos Terminology*, 27–42.
13. In addition to his article cited in n. 9 (esp. 43–51), see 'Wisdom of Word and Words of Wisdom in Corinth', *CBQ* 39, 1977, 224–239; and 'Pneumatikos vs. Psychikos: Distinctions of Spiritual Status among the Corinthians', *HThR* 69, 1976, 269–288, esp. 280–288.
14. H. Jonas takes the *pneuma* (*pneumatikos*)-*psuchē* (*psuchikos*) contrast as a typical expression of Gnostic anthropology; see *Gnosis und spätantiker Geist* I, Göttingen 1964, 210–214. Cf. R. Bultmann, *Theology of the New Testament* I, trans. K. Grobel, New York 1951, 174, 181, 204, with special reference to 1 Corinthians.
15. Cf. The *Pneumatikos-Psychikos Terminology* (n. 6), 15–26.
16. See above, and n. 12.
17. 'Pneumatikos vs. Psychikos', 271.
18. Cf., e.g., *The Pneumatikos-Psychikos Terminology* (n. 6), 9–11.
19. Ibid., 11.
20. 'Pneumatikos vs. Psychikos', 271, n. 8, and 273, n. 10.
21. Ibid., 271–273.
22. Ibid., 272.
23. Ibid., 274–288.
24. Cf. *The Pneumatikos-Psychikos Terminology* (n. 6), *passim*.
25. See 'Hellenistic-Jewish Wisdom Speculation' (n. 6), 46, 59. This point is also made with some force by Horsley, 'Wisdom of Word' (n. 13), 231–232, 237.
26. Cf. discussion above, 74.
27. This is Horsley's basic contention, too, in the three articles treated above.
28. 'Philo of Alexandria and Gnosticism', *Kairos* 14, 1972, 213–219. Wilson treats Philo extensively in his book on *The Gnostic Problem* (n. 5). I have discussed Wilson's treatment of Philo in that book, together with other important studies on Philo's relation to Gnosticism, in my article, 'Philo and Gnosticism', in (ed.) W. Haase, *Aufstieg and Niedergang der römischen Welt* II: 21, Berlin 1982, forthcoming.
29. The most important representative of this view is H. Jonas; see esp. *Gnosis und spätantiker Geist*, II: 1, Göttingen 1954, 38–43, 70–121. See my discussion in *ANRW* II: 21.
30. Philo, in fact, is our earliest evidence for the Middle-Platonic distinction between the *kosmos noētos* and the *kosmos aisthētos* (see e.g. *Op. Mund.* 15–17, 24), but it is probably not original with him. See e.g. J. Dillon, *The Middle Platonists*, London 1977, 158–159, and M.

Baltes, *Timaios Lokros über die Natur des Kosmos und der Seele kommentiert*, Leiden 1972, 105.

31. Cf. Wilson's statement in *The Gnostic Problem* (n. 5), 67–68: 'It must be admitted that there was a good deal of "gnosticizing" thought in the early years of the Christian era, for example in Philo, but this is *not yet* definitely "Gnostic"in the full sense' (emphases mine).

32. Cf. n. 5 above, and n. 33.

33. I have elsewhere explored the possibility whether Philo's own writings betray a knowledge and repudiation of an incipient Gnosticism in first-century Alexandria. See B. A. Pearson, 'Friedlander Revisited: Alexandrian Judaism and Gnostic Origins', *StPhilo* 2, 1973, 23–39, esp. 30–34.

34. See his moving credo at the end of his treatise on the creation of the world, *Op. Mund.* 170–172.

35. These and other texts are discussed in *The Pneumatikos-Psychikos Terminology*, 27–30. Horsley has provided much more evidence in his articles cited above.

36. A. Wlosok, *Laktanz und die philosophische Gnosis*, Heidelberg 1960, 50–114. I have discussed her treatment of Philo in the *ANRW* article cited above (n. 28).

37. See B. A. Pearson, *Nag Hammadi Codices IX and X, NHS* 15, Leiden 1981, 101–203: transcription and translation by S. Giversen and B. A. Pearson, introduction and notes by B. A. Pearson. The English translation is found also in (eds) J. M. Robinson and M. Meyer, *The Nag Hammadi Library in English*, Leiden/San Francisco 1977, 1981[2], 406–416. For other bibliography see D. M. Scholer, *Nag Hammadi Bibliography: 1948–1969*, Leiden 1971, and annual supplements published in *Novum Testamentum*.

38. F. Wisse, 'Die Sextus-Sprüche und das Problem der gnostischen Ethik', in A. Böhlig and F. Wisse, *Zum Hellenismus in den Schriften von Nag Hammadi*, Wiesbaden 1975, 81.

39. Cf. the Messina definition referred to above (n. 4). For other examples of this emphasis on saving self-knowledge in Testim. Truth see 35:22–36:7; 36:23–28; 43:23–26.

40. See my introduction to the tractate in *Nag Hammadi Codices IX and X* (n. 37), 101–120.

41. Cf. R. A. Baer, *Philo's Use of the Categories Male and Female, ALGHJ* 3, Leiden 1970, esp. 38.

42. Cf. D. M. Hay, 'Philo's Treatise on the Logos-Cutter', *StPhilo* 2, 1973, 9–22.

43. The passage just cited on the 'dividing' power of the Logos is an example; the 'saw' used to saw Isaiah the prophet in two 'is the word of the Son of Man which separates us from the error of the angels'. On scripture interpretation in Testim. Truth see B. A. Pearson, 'Gnostic Interpretation of the Old Testament in the *Testimony of Truth* (NHC IX, *3*)', in *HThR* 73, 1980, 311–319.

44. Cf. Plotinus' critique of Gnosticism in his well-known treatise 'Against the Gnostics', *Enn.* II, 9.

45. On the Gnostic midrash embedded in Testim. Truth 45:23–49:7, see B. A. Pearson, 'Jewish Haggadic Traditions in *The Testimony of Truth* from Nag Hammadi (CG IX, *3*)', in (eds) J. Bergman *et al.*, *Ex Orbe Religionum: Studia Geo Widengren* I, *SHR* 21, Leiden 1972, 457–470; and *Nag Hammadi Codices IX and X* (n. 37), 106, 111, 158–169.

46. On the 'revolutionary' character of Gnosticism see e.g. H. Jonas, 'Delimitation of the Gnostic Phenomenon – Typological and Historical', in *Le Origini dello Gnosticismo* (n. 4), 90–104, esp. 101–102; and K. Rudolph, *Die Gnosis* (n. 5), 73.

47. See discussion above, 78 and 80.

48. On the use of the NT in Testim. Truth see *Nag Hammadi Codices IX and X* (n. 37), 110, 112–113, as well as the indices and notes to the text.

49. There is as yet no critical edition of this document, but an English translation, with brief introduction, is readily accessible in *The Nag Hammadi Library in English* (n. 37), 346–361, translation and introduction by M. L. Peel and J. Zandee. I have used their translation in what follows. For the Coptic text see *The Facsimile Edition of the Nag Hammadi Codices: Codex VII*, Leiden 1972. For additional bibliography see Scholer's bibliography (n. 37).

50. W. R. Schoedel, 'Jewish Wisdom and the Formation of the Christian Ascetic', in *Aspects of Wisdom* (n. 6), 169–199, esp. 194.

51. See esp. J. Zandee, *'The Teachings of Silvanus' and Clement of Alexandria: A New Document of Alexandrian Theology*, Leiden 1977.

52. W. P. Funk, 'Ein doppelt überliefertes Stück spätägyptischer Weisheit', *ZÄS* 103, 1976, 8–21.

53. ' "Les Enseignements de Silvanos" et Philon d'Alexandrie', in *Mélanges d'histoire des religions offerts à Henri-Charles Puech*, Paris 1974, 337–345.

54. Cf. also Zandee's article specifically devoted to the Platonism of Teach. Silv.: ' "Les enseignements de Silvain" et le platonisme', in (ed.) J.-É. Ménard, *Les Textes de Nag Hammadi*, *NHS* 7, Leiden 1975, 158–179.

55. Philo (*Vit. Mos.* I, 158) is able to refer to Moses as a 'god and king' on the grounds that he had entered into 'the darkness where God was' (Exodus 20:21), and displayed in his life and career a 'godlike pattern' (*theoides paradeigma*) for others to 'imitate' (*mimeisthai*).

56. Paul is referred to by name at 108:30–31: 'Paul, who has become like Christ'. Cf. 1 Corinthians 11:1.

57. On this hymn see Schoedel, 'Jewish Wisdom' (n. 50), 191–192.

58. This is a familiar topos in Gnosticism. A classic example occurs in Ap. John (NHC II. *1*) 11:15–22; cf. also Testim. Truth (NHC IX. *3*) 47:14–23. Cf. my article, 'Jewish Haggadic Traditions' (n. 45), 466–469.

59. Schoedel, loc. cit. (n. 50), 170. Cf. P. Perkins, *The Gnostic Dialogue: The Early Church and the Crisis of Gnosticism*, New York 1980, 182, n. 19, where influence from Valentinian Gnosticism is posited in this passage. On the three-fold classification of mankind in Valentinian Gnosticism see *The Pneumatikos-Psychikos Terminology* (n. 6), 76–81;

and F.-M. Sagnard, *La gnose valentinienne et le témoignage de saint Irénée*, Paris 1954, esp. 387–415, 567–574.

60. Cf. H. Jonas' remarks on the absence of the concept of virtue (*aretē*) in Gnosticism, *The Gnostic Religion* (n. 5), 266–269.

61. Cf. H. D. Betz, 'The Delphic Maxim *gnōthi sauton* in Hermetic Interpretation', *HThR* 63, 1970, 465–484, esp. 477–482 on Philo. In my view, however, Philo's interpretation is not as close to the Hermetic one as Betz thinks. In the Hermetic (and Gnostic) interpretation self-knowledge *is*, essentially, knowledge of God and salvation; this is far from the Philonic understanding. On the relevant passages in the Poimandres see my article, 'Jewish Elements in *Corpus Hermeticum* I (Poimandres)', in (eds) R. van den Broek and M. Vermaseren, *Studies in Gnosticism and Hellenistic Religions Presented to Gilles Quispel*, *EPRO* 91, Leiden 1981, 346–347.

62. It is curious that these points have been overlooked by Zandee in his article on Teach. Silv. and Philo (loc. cit., n. 53).

63. Colson's translation in the *LCL* ed. Cf. also *Migr. Abr.* 8–13, 137, 185f.; *Somn.* I, 52–60. The two last-cited passages speak of self-knowledge as a prerequisite to knowledge of God. But that self-knowledge is *not the same as* knowledge of God Philo makes abundantly clear in the passage immediately following in *Somn.*: 'This is nature's law: he who has thoroughly comprehended himself, thoroughly despairs of himself (*heauton lian apegnōke*), having as a step to this ascertained the nothingness in all respects of created being. And the man who has despaired of himself is beginning to know Him that IS' (*Somn.* I, 60, *LCL* ed.). On this and similar passages in Philo see my *ANRW* article (n. 28).

64. In our discussion of 1 Corinthians, above, 73–77.

65. This point has been noticed by Zandee; see *'The Teachings of Silvanus' and Clement of Alexandria* (n. 51), 46.

66. Cf. the texts from Philo cited above, 80.

67. For another example, see Pearson, 'Hellenistic-Jewish Wisdom Speculation' (n. 6), 47.

68. Cf., e.g., Rudolph's book, cited above (n. 5).

69. This is the view of Rudolph (ibid.) and many others. See also the very clear statement of the issues by K.-W. Tröger in his article, 'The Attitude of the Gnostic Religion towards Judaism as Viewed in a Variety of Perspectives', in (ed.) B. Barc, *Colloque international sur les textes de Nag Hammadi, BCNH Ét* 1, Québec/Louvain 1981, 86–98.

VII

THE NEW TESTAMENT AND THE CONCEPT OF THE MANICHEAN MYTH

by

Professor Alexander Böhlig, Tübingen

The man we are honouring has particularly devoted himself in his New Testament studies to the question of how far relationships exist between Gnosis and the New Testament.[1] In this he has drawn not only on the patristic sources but also on the recent discoveries at Nag Hammadi. In his work he warns against over hasty conclusions such as the History of Religions School had drawn in their belief that second and third century material could also furnish information about the thought world of the pre-Christian period; what is more, that already in the New Testament controversies with groups like the Gnostic heretics could be discerned. Nevertheless he would not wish to appear biased and recognizes at least limited traces of Gnosis in the Johannine and Pastoral Epistles. However he cautions against reading the New Testament with Gnostic spectacles. That he leaves to the Gnostics themselves. On the question of Christianization or de-Christianization of the tractates, he allows both possibilities, according to the nature of the text under consideration. To determine the *Sitz im Leben* of every Nag Hammadi text or its constituent parts would in my opinion require more thoroughgoing analyses with whose help we could then write a history of the Gnostic tradition.[2] This in turn would form the basis for a history of Gnosticism. But such an enterprise is dogged by one considerable difficulty from the outset; Gnosticism after all in its internal and external form is stamped by syncretism. Pagan religion and philosophy as well as Christian and Jewish elements are to be found in it. It also includes schools which are particularly influenced by Christianity, whose representatives consider themselves the true Christians.[3] Mani too designates himself Apostle of Jesus Christ,[4] and without the knowledge of his teaching one cannot fully judge Gnosticism as a complete system either. His mythological system, with which he believed he could replace Buddhism, Zoroastrianism and

Christianity, was regarded in the first half of our century by several historians of religion and theologians as a source which had preserved ideas emanating from Iran in particular, whose effect could already be traced in the New Testament. All the same, whether Gnosis is pre-Christian or not, Manicheism represents in its system and church formation its culmination. The Iranian influences in it do not contribute to its essential structure; rather it is Gnostic Christianity.

Now in what follows it will be shown that the basic tendency of Mani's teaching derives from the fundamental concepts of Christian soteriology. In his myth Mani reworks various Gnostic and Catholic conceptions of Jesus, with which he became acquainted in his period (third century).[5] In this he is not afraid to split up the person of Jesus.

Mani grew up in a Jewish-Christian Gnostic sect. The Cologne Mani Codex recounts his youth among the Elchasaites and his break with them.[6] From this source we also know of the view according to which Mani calls the earth 'flesh and blood of the Lord'.[7] In this work he attributes this view to Elchasai: 'Elchasai took dust from the earth which had spoken to him, wept, kissed it, placed it in his bosom and began to say: That is the flesh and blood of my Lord.' This idea is to be found, as we shall see later, both in the Roman Empire in the West and in China in the East. The fact that this does not appear so prominently in the earlier strata of the myth, in which it is nevertheless present, is caused by the rather varied form of expression of the myth, in which fundamental problems can be allotted to individual mythologumena and thus furnish a multi-coloured picture.

Already on chronological grounds it would be difficult, indeed strictly speaking impossible, to appeal to Manicheism to illuminate the New Testament.[8] Moreover C. Colpe has demonstrated that the Manichean Primal Man doctrine cannot derive from the Iranian Gayomart concept.[9] Equally the explanation in terms of the dying and rising god Tammuz remains questionable.[10] If we bear in mind that Mani certainly was acquainted with Christianity, and according to the fragments of his letters as well as the introduction to the *Kephalaia*, also knew Paul well and regarded him highly,[11] it would be methodologically more correct to ask first whether the relevant passages in Paul cannot better be explained in terms of his own dialectic and the Jewish background rather than in terms of the ideas of a third century religion, whose elements one would then of course also have to see as already present three centuries previously.

In order to be able to judge the question of a dependence of Manicheism on Christianity correctly, the chief dogmas of both religions will have to be set side by side.

Christianity:

God, the Father and Creator, sends his Son, that is, he himself comes into the world, to free it from sin which entered it through a man. Jesus Christ carries out this commission in human form, he helps men and overcomes the evil spirits, as his healings demonstrate. To save the world he suffers on the cross and by his resurrection wins the victory over sin and death. Those who believe in him, his church, follow in the resurrection to the Father.

Manicheism:

The supreme God of the heavenly realm sends his Son, the First Man, in whom he himself has taken form, into the war with the darkness which threatens him. His struggle with it cripples it, of course, but he and his armour, the soul, are detained in the depths to begin with. Even his liberation and ascent, however, do not prevent essential light elements from still remaining imprisoned. The world is created as a purification machine. However, evil attempts to hamper its operation by the creation of men. But they are enlightened about their situation through Jesus. And Mani leads them back via the church into the realm of light.

In his myth and his theological discourses Mani made Christianity's essential statements of faith the basis of his own teaching too: God as Creator of heaven and earth, the saving activity of God in his Son through struggle, suffering and final victory, the annihilation of death and sin, leading men aloft via the church to God.

Of course, when one compares the Manichean myth with Christian doctrine, the difference appears extraordinarily great. However one should not allow oneself to be deceived by the fact that the mythological manner of presentation appears to make Mani's system a hotch-potch of mythological motifs, but one must observe how strictly Mani's presentation is structured by him. The all-embracing outward form should not make us oblivious to the content. However, one cannot deny that there are also radical differences. Even although Mani calls himself Apostle of Jesus Christ, he is able to give Christian doctrine a new form, which he regards as the authentic Christianity. The Nag Hammadi texts have shown how other Gnostics too have made similar claims. The differences can be found not only in essential but also in formal characteristics.

In contrast to Christianity, Manicheism is stamped by a rigid dualism. From the very beginning there stands opposed to the heavenly realm the realm of evil, darkness, whose goal is the conquest of the realm of light. The purpose of the counter-attack is to immobilize darkness and shut it up in a prison, so that by the final victory final peace will be attained. Whoever knows how this goal can be achieved and what kind of good works he must perform for this purpose, contributes to the conquest of evil Hyle and will be led back into the world of light, while those particular light souls which have achieved too little succumb to eternal imprisonment with darkness.

This dualism is a typically Gnostic mode of presentation.[12] Over against the Christianity of the New Testament, which are concerned with the redemption of man and takes over the problem of sin and redemption from the biblical account, Gnosticism and its culmination, Manicheism, are concerned with the projection of all this onto the universal plane. It is not enough to focus on the life, passion and resurrection of Jesus. Statements such as occur in the Johannine Prologue[13] or at the beginning of Hebrews[14] are not sufficient in this regard, but a description of the world of light must first be given. Although only fragments of the myth are preserved, the doctrinal teachings contained in the *Kephalaia* as well as hymnodic texts offer a plethora of mythological illustrations, so that even the horrors of darkness are depicted in detail.

The confrontation of the two worlds leads to reciprocal activities. From them results the condition from which men must be redeemed. The Gnostic must be well-informed about its presuppositions: without cosmology and anthropology no soteriology is possible for him. As a good physician must first diagnose the cause of an illness to be able to combat its symptoms effectively, so the Gnostic must know about the reason for evil to rescue himself from it. According to Christianity the cause of this evil is the Fall. In Mani it is projected back to an earlier period. If in the primal period of the worlds Rest and Unrest confront each other, it is no wonder that Unrest arms itself to attack and forces Rest to defend itself. God himself takes the initiative and becomes concrete in his Son. In Christianity the corresponding feature to this view is that the Father is revealed in the Son. But in this case the Son is directly the Son of the Father, whereas in Mani's thought the Son is the third person of a triad derived from paganism, which consists of Father, Mother and Son. Here then Mani has used for his presentation a Gnostic model whose competition with the Christian Father – Son – Spirit can be observed in other Gnostic texts too.[15] The notion that God becomes concrete in man is also to be found in Gnostic literature.[16] There it is a matter of a heavenly Man, God himself or also his Son being referred to as 'Man'. The identification of Man and Son of Man corresponds to that of God and his Son. The task of the redeemer, which Jesus Christ has to fulfil, is, in the cosmological view of soteriology, set in a much broader frame than in Christianity, which leads to a division of the action into various operations and to the introduction of numerous mythological figures. The work of Jesus Christ is reduced to certain events and activities; what is more, overlappings of Jesus with other mythological figures can be detected which show that in relation to the Christian kernel the Manichean system is secondary.

The chief self-revelation of God for Mani is not, as for the Catholics and also for certain Gnostic systems, Christ, but the 'First Man'.[17] This circumstance has raised the question as to whether or not the mythological event which can be seen to underlie this figure is a constitutive part of Gnostic thinking in general, which in passages like Romans 5:12, 1 Corinthians 15:20 and 44–49 has either influenced Paul or at any rate in the argument with Gnostics been remodelled by him to suit his theological aim.[18]

The apostle bases his view of the resurrection of the dead[19] on the fact that while only a psychic body is sown here on earth, in the resurrection a pneumatic body will be disclosed. The Old Testament expressed this by means of Genesis 2:7: *egeneto ho anthrōpos eis psuchēn zōsan*, whereas he of course remodels and expands the citation into a theologumenon. Thereby *ho anthrōpos* is altered to *ho prōtos anthrōpos Adam* because *ho eschatos Adam eis pneuma zōopoioun* follows (v. 45). The antithesis 'psychic-spiritual' is represented by the comparison of Adam with Christ. Verse 47 spells this out even more clearly: *ho prōtos anthrōpos ek gēs choikos, ho deuteros anthrōpos ex ouranou.* Two men are contrasted, in chronological sequence, the first and second man, but this latter is simultaneously the last. *Ho eschatos* here could simply be a synonym for *ho deuteros*, but it could also be an appropriate term to express the finality of the eschatological event. The chronological disposition of the saving event is as significant as the qualitative judgment. The earthly man is animated by the soul. Paul, however, sees a limitation in this fact, which he had already clearly expressed in 1 Corinthian 2:14: 'The psychic man does not receive what comes from the Spirit of God'. Therefore there is a fundamental advantage in possessing the animating Spirit. Moreover, origin from the dust is surpassed by that from heaven. This designation of Jesus Christ as *epouranios* and the assimilation of his community to him points to the saving event on earth. The nomenclature of first and second man is thus completely explained in the context of the dialectic with which Paul is going to work out his thesis 'first psychic, then pneumatic'. The argumentation, which sets forth the progression from lower to higher, is already begun in verses 35 to 44.

Paul, granted that he was aware of ideas of a heavenly man which he employed as material to form his model, need not, in his dispute with Gnostics or a heretical group, have taken them over from them. These theologumena could just as well derive from his knowledge of Jewish tradition and exegesis. Finally, after Damascus in fact, Paul had had to realign his theological inheritance as a Pharisee to Christ but had not had to abandon it. The notion of Christ as a heavenly man makes one think of his pre-existence and the associated role of mediator in creation, which indeed is the situation in the New Testament with Paul too. In that case, of course, the heavenly man would have to be the first and not the second man. Just such a conception of two men created by God is in fact found in Philo, who interprets Genesis 1:26 and 2:7 as two different operations. According to Genesis 1:26 a person is created as first man who is made 'in the image of God and in his likeness'. This being in the image is not related by Philo to a man-like form of God or of the man. Here an ideal man originates, whereas Genesis 2:7 speaks about the earthly man[20]: 'In saying this he shows quite clearly that there is a very great difference between the man who has just now been formed, and the man who was made earlier on in the image of God; for the one formed just now was perceptible to the senses, already had a precise constitution, was composed of body and soul, was male or female and mortal by nature; conversely, the one made in the image of God was an idea or generic term or seal, intelligible only, incorporeal, neither male nor female, and incorruptible by nature.' If one were to see the kind of theological conception of two men sketched out above as a background to the Pauline passage, the second man of 1 Corinthians, who, as the heavenly, is really the first, would become the second, because, as eschatological, he becomes chronologically the second, who brings about redemption. That is, he would originally be the Primal Man in whom certain Gnosticizing theologians believe. After all Paul, when formulating his theology anew, was attempting to prove that Christ is the origin and goal of existence.[21] For him he takes the place of Wisdom or the Torah as the mediator of creation. But because the problem facing Paul is the redemption of men through Jesus Christ, who appeared to him, he has to see in him the eschatological redeemer who has overcome sin and death. The correlation first man-second man, earthly man-heavenly man, psychic man-pneumatic man requires for the sake of salvation history the numeration employed by Paul. This is also true of 1 Corinthians 15:21–22: 'For through one man comes death and through one man the resurrection of the dead. For as in Adam all die, even so in Christ shall all be made alive'.

The basis for this optimistic belief is expounded at great length in Romans 5. After the certainty of reconciliation is expressed in verse 11, in verse 12 Adam's fatal transgression and its consequence, death, is set over against the work of the one man, Jesus. Once more this redeeming man has eschatological significance. For him, the one to come, Adam was the (anti)type (*tupos tou mellontos*). The pre-existent Christ appears at the time of fulfilment on earth.[22] In terms of the history of religions there is no need to hark back to Gnosticism for this idea, even if one includes the deutero-Pauline literature. Here too Paul's basic tendency is the transformation of his Jewish belief into a Christocentric one. As mentioned before, the pre-existent Christ appears as the mediator of creation in place of Wisdom or the Torah (which replaced the former in Palestinian Judaism). Adam's sin, which cannot be overcome through the Torah, is overcome through the redeemer Jesus Christ. A man who himself had been a pious Jew and had wholeheartedly accepted the Torah as a creating and sustaining entity must have been faced with the question as to what role it really plays. It is not cancelled or ignored but rather incorporated, inasmuch as it is limited in the answer to the question of salvation to its historical sphere. *Pareisēlthen* can be said of the Nomos which Moses brought. Nevertheless the Law of God as the sum total of his will remains intact. Thus the Law acquires a deepened content. It is *nomos pneumatikos* as *nomos tou Christou*.[23]

In Mani we have, as in Philo, two men, but they are radically differentiated. The heavenly man is Son of God,[24] but the earthly Adam is not a product of God's will. Rather it is in his formation that the resistance to God is manifested. The plural 'let us make man'[25] is reinterpreted in terms of enemies rather than helpers of God. Gods involved in the creation of man are already mentioned by Plato as helpers, who still had to bear the responsibility for deficiencies.[26] The First Man for Mani belongs to the heavenly world while the earthly man is a member of the cosmos, whose saving will be hindered by the propagation of mankind.

The First Man for Mani is equipped with an armament which can also bear the name 'sons of the Primal Man'. Five elements are involved here: air, light, wind, water, fire. They can also bear the collective designation 'living soul', indeed they can even be equated with the First Man. In the portrayal of the elements, not only Gnostic motifs but also philosophical ideas contribute here to the construction of the Manichean myth. Stoic monism is the model for the homogeneity of light. One could speak of materialism but should rather, like modern neo-Gnostics,[27] have to see spiritual elements in the portions of light. When considering the mixture of light and darkness, one might recall the two Stoic *archai*, unformed Hyle and Logos. Just as for the Catholic Church Christ is not only victor but also sufferer, so too Mani allowed the struggle between light and darkness to become a victory and an imprisonment for the light. The victory, however, does not yet mean a final subjugation; it is merely a matter of a crippling or imprisoning of the darkness. The First Man and his sons are imprisoned, but at the same time the darkness is crippled by them. In the case of the First Man his action as warrior is particularly emphasized, whereas in the case of the elements their suffering is thought of. This division allows one to do justice to the historic course of the mythological event, for the period of suffering of the First Man is a great deal shorter than that of the living soul. At the same time, because of the division, greater emphasis is also laid on both, the struggle and the suffering.[28]

In order to free the First Man the Living Spirit arises, who after fetching him home, subjugates the world of darkness and creates this world from the remaining mixture. Since this involves events in the universe, which allow the son of God to appear as First Man, when the world has not yet been created, the duty of mediator of creation only follows the appearance of the First Man. That is, the Living Spirit as the Demiurge sent from God completes a duty which, according to Christian theology, devolves upon Christ. One might compare what is said in the Epistle to Diognetus about Christ:[29] 'But he, the truly almighty and all-creating and invisible Father, he planted among men and established in their hearts the truth and the holy and incomprehensible Logos. He did not, as one might imagine, send men a servant or messenger or ruler, or one of those who carry out earthly duties, or one of those who are entrusted with government in heaven, but the artificer and creator (*technitēs, dēmiourgos*) of the universe himself, by whom he made the heavens, by whom he enclosed the sea in its bounds, whose mysteries all elements faithfully preserve, from whom < the sun > received to keep safe the measure of the courses of the day, at whose command the moon shines at night, whom the stars obey when they follow the course of the moon, by whom everything is ordered and limited and to whom everything is subject, the heavens and what is in the heavens, the earth and what is on earth, the sea and what is in the sea, fire, air, abyss, what is in the heights, what is in the depths, what is in between. This is the one he sent to them.' Of coure, what follows does not apply: 'Did it happen, as a man might suppose, with tyranny, fear and terror? No.' Rather the Living Spirit in the Manichean myth is very cruel in his struggle with the archons: when he makes the heavens from their bodies, and fastens others to the wheel of the stars, he has after all to strip them of the light elements.

For Mani the purifying of the elements from the cosmos has become a very complex process which is split up into several stages. First of all, at the creation of the world, the Living Spirit himself separated off certain amounts of the darkness.[30] Of particular importance, however, is the production of sun and moon from the light. These heavenly bodies, which of course possess a special rank in Greek cosmology because of their quality, are identified with mythological persons. Just as when evaluating the elements we referred to Greek philosophy, so the partition of the cosmos recalls the Aristotelian division into sublunar and translunar worlds, for the elements are escorted via the Milky Way to the moon and thence to the sun. The galaxy[31] bears the peculiar title 'the column of glory, the perfect man'. The *eau* of the Coptic text should perhaps be rendered by 'splendour'. In Parthian texts 'column of splendour' reflects the brilliant character of the Milky Way. Anaxagoras and Democritus see in it a gathering of smaller stars, while according to Parmenides the sun and moon have become separated from it. This tradition may have formed the basis for Mani's view. The souls ascend on the Milky Way (which forms the route of the heavenly ones up to Zeus) to heaven, since the scientific world view had transferred Hades there.[32] The Pythagoreans had already seen it as resting place of the souls. It is also referred to in *Somnium Scipionis* 16: 'ea vita via est in caelum et in hunc coetum eorum, qui iam vixerunt et corpore laxati illum incolunt locum quem vides – erat autem is splendidissimo candore inter flammas circus elucens – quem vos, ut a Grais accepistis, orbem lacteum nuncupatis.' The column of glory is very frequently also designated 'the perfect man'. Mani thereby refers back to a term of deutero-Pauline theology. Ephesians 4:11ff. discusses the building up of the fellowship of Christ and verse 13f. reads: 'until we all attain to the unity of the faith and of the knowledge of the Son of God, to a perfect man, to the measure of the maturity of the fulness of Christ; so that we may no longer be children, tossed to and fro and carried about with every wind of doctrine, by the cunning of men, by their craftiness to the (or according to the) deceitfulness of error'.

The aim is a more secure experience of faith and recognition of the Son of God, not weakened by error. We are concerned here with the totality of believers who are supposed to form a unity. This unity is designated in apposition 'the perfect man', which is followed by a further apposition: 'to the measure of the maturity of the fulness of Christ'. The meaning is in the first place simply that the congregation in its unity should resemble a male adult, as whose measure Christ is specified. Two ideas are connected in these verses. The contrast, adult–childish, is attested by the wish not to be childish. This contrast is used to clarify the wish that the church might reach 'the fulness of Christ'. The *teleios anēr* is in this passage the church summed up in Christ, i.e. a collective entity. No wonder then that Mani regarded the 'perfect man' as such a collective entity of souls, particularly when they were aiming for the moon, in which Christ dwells. This could be compared with Colossians 1:18 where Christ is described as the head of the body of the church. Colossians 1:28 also speaks about the perfection of man (*anthrōpos*, not *anēr*!); this, however, is not concerned with the congregation as a whole, but with the instruction of each person so that he might become a perfect Christian.

The column of glory, the perfect man, forms for Mani the connecting link between the church and the moon.[33] By the fact that it embraces the purified elements, it forms a firm stronghold in the cosmos. It is therefore designated 'rock':[34] 'The first rock is the column of glory, the perfect man, who was summoned by the glorious Messenger and whom he placed in the zone. He extended himself from below to above, he upheld the whole world, became the first of all bearers by his powers, raised himself up through his stability and established all things below and above.' In the Manichean *Psalm-Book* it is characterized as 'the power of God, which upholds the All'.[35] Its characteristic as upholding entity also secures for the column of glory the name 'the great Omophoros' in contrast to Atlas (= Omophoros), the fifth son of the Living Spirit. It has a functional designation, however, not only in Coptic but also in Middle Persian texts. The mythological appellation *Srōšahrāy*, 'the righteous *Srōš*',[36] perhaps alludes to the activity of the column as a judging entity. For *Srōš* is found in the teaching of Zarathustra in Mithra's company as judge; he is simply regarded as an aspect of Mithra.[37] The manner in which the galaxy in its character as way of redemption is connected with Jesus and the First Man is apparent in the Coptic *Psalm-Book*. It is named as the abode where Jesus undertakes the purification:[38] 'O Saviour (*sōtēr*), Son of God, [take] me quickly to yourself, wash me with the dew of the column of glory.' In another psalm Jesus is addressed:[39] 'Perfect Man, haven of my trust, arise! You are the First Man, my true receiver, arise!' In another Jesus psalm he is also directly equated with the column in a section which describes his character:[40]

> Jesus is the first gift which was sent.
> Jesus is the flower of the holy Father.
> Jesus is the first to sit upon the luminaries.
> Jesus is the perfect man in the column.[41]
> Jesus is the resurrection of the dead in the church.

The identification of Jesus with the First Man and his transposition back to the beginning of the universe, to the luminaries, the sun and moon, his identification with the column of glory and as awakener of the dead demonstrates that the whole section from the origin of the First Man to the instruction of the earthly man is a division of Christology into individual spheres of responsibility. The redemptive machinery inaugurated by the creation of sun and moon still needed persons to operate it. The Manichean myth places the Third Messenger in the sun. The First Man was the first messenger, the Living Spirit the second; now there appears a further one who has no particular name but is the Messenger *par excellence* or more precisely the third, whereby the harmony is fulfilled; at any rate the Father of greatness, the Mother of life and the First Man form the first triad, the Beloved of the lights, the great Builder and the Living Spirit the second. While in the Syriac texts Mani is content with the function of the Third Messenger, in Iranian texts he employs not only a functional name of a different sort, namely *Rōšnšahryazd*, 'the God whose kingdom is the light', but also a divine name, *Narisah*, who is the messenger of the gods, but who also seduces the demons by his beauty. In his place there appears in the East the sun god Mithra, since the Third Messenger does indeed sit in the ship of the sun. In North Africa he is replaced by Christ. The Third Messenger, moreover, is also connected with two other figures or groups of figures. If one is being consistent, he is not in fact sufficient on his own because only the sun is occupied by him, whereas the moon must also be occupied. This occurs by the introduction of Jesus. The Iranian doctrinal texts again make use of a functional description as a name: *Chradēšahryazd*, 'the God whose kingdom is intellect'. All other texts employ the designation 'Jesus the splendour'. He dwells with the Virgin of Light and the Nous in the ship of the moon. However the First Man also escorts him instead of Nous.[42] In an account of the stages of redemption he is found between the column of glory (the galaxy) and the Third Messenger (sun), that is, in the moon.[43]

After his journey back to the heavenly homeland the First Man returns yet again into the world to liberate the living soul.[44] He acts like the Jesus of the New Testament here who ascends victorious after his passion and resurrection to the Father, but, conversely, remains with those who believe in him 'till the end of the world'. This parallelism also supports the view that Mani split up the person of Jesus Christ in his myth, something of course he did not achieve with absolute consistency. In addition, the generous assimilation of nomenclature in the mission does not always make it easy to distinguish between fundamental changes and ones adopted solely for evangelistic expediency. Reductions of the mythology sometimes appear to have a purely missionary purpose. However the increased number of sources preserved allow one to establish that such a shortening does not represent any modification in the content, but only a reduction of the more broadly developed mythological system to one which also expresses the theological content adequately. Although the position of Jesus is portrayed entirely adequately in the Coptic-Manichean texts, in the North African Manicheism known to Augustine the mythological figure of Jesus is essentially expanded. In it the suffering light is seen as Jesus *patibilis*, the Christ in sun and moon as *virtus* and *sapientia dei*. That the suffering elements were not first treated as the body of Jesus by the Manichean mission among the Christians is, as noted above,[45] already attested in Mani's case. Particular support for this is found in the Manichean interpretation of Matthew 25:31ff., preserved in Mani's treatise to the Persian high king, the *Šābuhragān*.[46] *Chradēšahryazd*, who is identified with the Son of Man (*märdān pusar*), that is, Jesus, bases the judgement of righteous and unrighteous on their relations to him. In this respect by doing good or evil to Jesus is meant how men have treated the light elements, i.e. whether they have lived sufficiently in accordance with the Manichean ethic. The doctrine of Jesus' unity with the light elements was also carried east, so that it also is to be found in the Chinese hymn book.[47]

If God was Lord of the heavenly world, which is uncreated, he was nevertheless Creator of the cosmos, too. As in Plato a *dēmiourgos* is at work who is a mode of his (God's) being. By this positive evaluation of the Creator God Mani distinguishes himself from certain other Gnostics, Marcion in particular, to whom he is otherwise so indebted,[48] but not from Christianity. Conversely, over the creation of man he takes a negative line. Man, thanks to obscene actions on the part of the archons, is a fleshly being in whom elements of the living soul are imprisoned. He therefore needs *gnōsis*, through which he recognizes his situation. This information he obtains through Jesus. One might at first sight assume that Jesus as teacher is here grafted onto the Manichean mythological system. However his identity with the elements and his cosmological position as victor in sun and moon demonstrate that, to a much profounder degree, he stands behind the whole event. Mythologically this is expressed in terms of his having shone brilliantly in the column of glory, the perfect man – and having descended and having appeared in the world.[49] Already according to the Greek view the gods used the Milky Way as a route down to the world. In the Nag Hammadi Gnostic text, the Second Treatise of the Great Seth (NHC VII. 2), there is a corresponding action. The Redeemer is sent down from the kingdom of light to gather and liberate *ennoiai* (hypostasized ideas) scattered in the world.[50] This section of the Manichean myth recalls Ephesians 5:11f., which calls for separation from the darkness and turning to the light. The link between revelation and light points to the light coming in Christ. If verse 14: 'Wake up, you who are sleeping,[51] and rise from the dead, and Christ will give you light', were indeed an early Christian baptismal formula, this wording would, in a heresy which denied water baptism, also be a point of departure for Gnosis as the spiritualizing of baptism.

That Jesus and the First Man, who are in fact both Son of God, can also be interchanged, is demonstrated by the Persian cosmogonic fragment[52] in which man is instructed about his essential nature by Ohrmizd, as the First Man is called in certain Iranian texts. In this hymn too the result is the resurrection. It was desired to allow the First Man to carry through the role as redeemer, which he plays in this presentation, consistently to the end.

In the eyes of the Manichees instruction has a fundamental effect on man's existence. Manichean anthropology also attaches itself to the Pauline message.[53] In Mani the new man comes into being out of the old through *gnōsis*. In this case too, Mani spiritualizes what Paul has to say about the baptismal experience of the Christian. Romans 6:3ff. is concerned with the resurrection which follows from baptism into the death of Christ: (v. 6): 'since we know that our old man was crucified with him so that the sinful body might be destroyed'. And Colossians 3:9f.: 'Put off the old man and his works, but put on the new (*neos*), who is being renewed in knowledge after the image of his creator.' The image of the creator is Christ; Ephesians 4:20ff.: 'But you have not so learned Christ, seeing that you have heard him and been instructed in him – because truth is in Christ – that you should lay aside the old man, as he (is manifest) in your former mode of life, which is corrupt in deceitful lusts, that you may be renewed in the spirit of your minds and put on the new (*kainos*) man in true righteousness and holiness.' In the Epistle to Diognetus the reader is summoned to purification, through which he becomes a new man as at the beginning of creation.[54] But these statements are not limited to the individual only; the plural forms of address point to the totality of the community. This was already expressed in the passage cited, Ephesians 4:13,[55] where the believers will be united as *anēr teleios*, to which corresponds 2:15, the uniting of the community as *kainos anthrōpos*. In

Mani the antithesis old man–new man is found particularly in the teaching discourses, not only in the Coptic *Kephalaia* but also in the Chinese tractate. But we also come across interesting passages in the hymns. In particular it is the Nous who transforms man. Therefore one can read: 'the new man in whom the Nous finds form'.[56] In a long chapter on the Nous,[57] the imprisonment of the soul by sin is portrayed. The whole process is at the same time compared with the cosmic event, because, of course, man is a microcosm.[58] Sin dwells in the body, but the Light-Nous expels the old body and imprisons the dark elements, in order that the liberated light elements can form the new man. This event is thoroughly speculated on down to the smallest details. In a psalm the new man is compared with a physician who removes painful ulcers with the help of medicine and medical instruments; Mani's books serve that purpose.[59] A *Bema* psalm directed to the Paraclete states, very much in the Pauline style:[60] 'hail, o resurrection of the dead, o new Aeon of the souls, who has stripped us of the old man and dressed us in the new.' How intensively this antithesis was canvassed in the West as well is shown by Faustus of Milevis,[61] who cites the Pauline passages as proof that there are two different bodies, of which only the 'new' is fashioned by God. The similarity to one another of Mani, the Nous and Jesus in Manichean anthropology demonstrates how Jesus Christ has an original character in these conceptions too.

In his youth and by his antecedents Mani had of course got to know various religious currents; Jewish Christianity of a Gnostic stamp was his childhood home; Iranian ideas may have been brought to him by his descent. The world of Buddhism was encountered by him in the east of Iran and in India on his journeys. Perhaps his harsh dualism was influenced by Iranian ideas, as well as certain models, e.g. the great war, the mythology of Persian doctrinal texts and ideas of the ascent of the soul. India may have been responsible for confirming for him the concept of the transmigration of the soul, which he already knew from Greek philosophy, as well as the repudiation of work on the part of the *Electi*. However the basic tendency of the myth, which expresses the central thrust of his belief, is, as I think the above observations make clear, a Gnostic Christianity which represents in broad perspective the way of the Son of God variously incarnated as creator and redeemer, in order, by its *gnōsis* and the resulting consequences, to be led to the Father.

NOTES

1. See his list of publications pp. 245ff. below, esp. *Gnosis and the New Testament*, Oxford 1968.
2. This would also include the setting out of synoptic editions of works surviving in several versions because they allow a better recognition of the elements of the tradition individually and in context, and also allow a better identification of errors in translation and corruptions of the texts.

3. Cf. K. Koschorke, *Die Polemik der Gnostiker gegen das kirchliche Christentum*, NHS 12, Leiden 1978.
4. Cf. A. Böhlig–J. P. Asmussen, *Die Gnosis III: Der Manichäismus*, Zürich 1980, 228; C. Schmidt–H. J. Polotsky, 'Ein Mani-Fund in Ägypten', *SPAW. PH*, Berlin 1933, 24.
5. One might compare the detailed description of Christology in Part 1 (chs 1–3) of A. Grillmeier, *Jesus Christus im Glauben der Kirche* I, Freiburg 1979, 1–280. How extensive the use of the figure of Jesus when named by name already is in our sources is shown by E. Rose, *Die manichäische Christologie*, Wiesbaden 1979. Going beyond Rose, I intend to treat the whole myth from the point of view of Christology.
6. Cf. A. Henrichs–L. Koenen, 'Ein griechischer Mani-Codex', *ZPE* 5, 1970, 97–214, esp. 141–160. The text (hereafter cited CMC) is published in the same journal, 19, 1975, 1–85; 32, 1978, 87–199; 44, 1981, 201–318; 48, 1982, 1–59.
7. CMC 96:21–97:10.
8. As R. Bultmann had attempted to do in his article, 'Die Bedeutung der neuerschlossenen mandäischen und manichäischen Quellen für das Verständnis des Johannesevangeliums', *ZNW* 24, 1925, 100–146. This basic tendency is also retained in Bultmann's *Theologie des Neuen Testaments* (ET *Theology of the New Testament*) in its various editions; indeed it is applied by him to other New Testament writings as well. Attached to the description of the kerygma of the Hellenistic community before and aside from Paul is a comprehensive section, 'Gnostic Motifs', ET vol. I, London 1952, ch. III § 15, 164–183.
9. C. Colpe, *Die religionsgeschichtliche Schule. Darstellung und Kritik ihres Bildes vom gnostischen Erlösermythus*, Göttingen 1961. Cf. also *RAC* XI, 546ff.; H.-M. Schenke, *Der Gott 'Mensch' in der Gnosis*, Berlin 1962.
10. Cf. G. Widengren, *Mani und der Manichäismus*, Stuttgart 1961, 58, but esp. 65 (= ET, London 1965, 54, 61f.). Such a mythology at any rate could have contributed to the depiction of the details of the scene involving the Primal Man.
11. *Keph.* 13, 18ff. See also n. 4 above.
12. It is obvious that Mani inclined towards just such a dualism also out of his awareness of Iranian thought.
13. John 1:1–18.
14. Hebrews 1.
15. Cf. A. Böhlig, 'Triade und Trinität in den Schriften von Nag Hammadi' in (ed.) B. Layton, *The Rediscovery of Gnosticism* II, *SHR* 41:2, Leiden 1981, 617–634.
16. Gos. Eg. NHC III, 49:8–16 = IV, 61:8–18. There the God 'Man' appears as heavenly Adamas to eliminate the deficiency.
17. Cf., e.g., NHC I. *3* (Gos. Truth); VII. *2* (Treat. Seth). Conversely the 'First Man' is Barbelo in Ap. John, NHC II, 25:7 = III, 7:23 = BG 27:19.
18. Cf. W. Schmithals, *Die Gnosis in Korinth*, Göttingen 1969³, 66ff. (= ET, Nashville/New York 1971, 71ff.).

19. On the interpretation of Romans 5:12ff. and 1 Corinthians 15 see also the comprehensive work by E. Brandenburger, *Adam und Christus*, *WMANT* 7, Neukirchen 1962. Through a painstaking enquiry into the religio-historical background the author certainly recognizes the significance of the Jewish background, but he cannot sufficiently detach himself from the Gnosticizing school, which makes use of post-Christian (Mandean) sources for Paul.
20. *Op. Mund.* 134 (following J. Cohn's translation).
21. Cf. 1 Corinthians 8:6.
22. Cf. Galatians 4:4.
23. Cf. Romans 7:14; Galatians 6:2.
24. The Adamas of the Gnostics, who is either God or his Son, is given only a subordinate role in Mani. As one of the sons of the Living Spirit he has to crush the monster who rises from the deep. Cf. Böhlig-Asmussen, *Gnosis* III, 107.
25. Genesis 1:26.
26. Plat., *Tim.* 41a-d; cf. P. Boyancé, 'Dieu cosmique et dualisme' in (ed.) Bianchi, *Le Origini dello Gnosticismo, SHR* 12, Leiden 1967, 340–356.
27. Cf. J. E. Charon, *Tod, wo ist dein Stachel?*, Vienna 1981; R. Ruyer, *Jenseits der Erkenntnis*, Vienna 1977.
28. It goes without saying that, in view of the close connection between the First Man and the elements, this division is not always consistently carried through.
29. Dg. 7:2f.
30. E.g. the three vehicles; cf. *Keph.* chs 42 (106:21–111:17), 43 (111:18–113:25) and 45 (116:1–117:9). Thereby the Living Spirit exercises a judicial function.
31. Cf. W. Gundel, 'Galaxias', *PRE* VII, 560–571.
32. Cf. M. P. Nilsson, *Geschichte der griechischen Religion* II, Munich 1961², 240.
33. *Keph.* 20:21–27. Here the First Man is named as resident in the moon. On the relation of First Man to Jesus see below p. 99f.
34. *Keph.* 155:10–16.
35. *Ps.-Book* 133:24f.
36. Cf. Böhlig-Asmussen, *Gnosis* III, 63.
37. Cf. G. Widengren, *Die Religionen Irans*, Stuttgart 1965, 82.
38. *Ps.-Book* 103:34f.
39. 88:12f.
40. 59:17f.
41. The assumption that Christ was a colossal man-like figure standing between heaven and earth is already found in Elchasai. Mani could have combined this view with the Pauline tradition of the perfect man which he knew via Marcion. Cf. Epiph., *Haer.* 30, 17:6.
42. *Keph.* 37:1f.; 82:33f.
43. 176:4f.
44. Because the First Man thereby in fact redeems a part of himself, he turns out to be genuinely a *salvator salvandus*.
45. See above, p. 91.

46. Cf. *Gnosis* III, 236f.
47. V. 254:
    > (The five lights) and these are Jesus' flesh and blood.
    > Whosoever needs them, can take them as he pleases.
    > However if he is empty and foolish and thankless in heart
    > Then Jesus too is powerless and there is no snow route.
    >
    > (after the German translation by H. Schmidt-Glintzer).
48. I am convinced that the person whom *Keph.* 13:30f. designates as 'really righteous' is Marcion, since that person is directly associated with the proclamation of the kingdom of God. Elchasai is not the subject here. The manner of expression is aimed at outdoing Jewish Christianity dialectically.
49. *Keph.* 37:3ff.
50. NHC VII, 50:1ff.
51. Cf. the passage from the Manichean Psalter cited on p. 98 above, in which Jesus is designated as the resurrection of the dead.
52. S 9; cf. *Gnosis* III, 121–123.
53. This had already been noted by K. Holl in his essay 'Urchristentum und Religionsgeschichte', *Gesammelte Aufsätze II: Der Osten*, Tübingen 1928, 1–32. Cf. also H. H. Schaeder, *Urform und Fortbildungen des manichäischen Systems*, Leipzig 1927, 93 n. 1.
54. Dg. 2:1; 11:4; 12:3.
55. See above, p. 97.
56. *Keph.* 269:19f.
57. *Keph.* ch. 38, 89–102.
58. This kind of observation is particularly favoured by the Chinese tractate as well; cf. 'Un traité manichéen retrouvé en Chine', traduit et annoté par Ed. Chavannes et P. Pelliot, *JA* 1912, 27ff.
59. *Ps. Book* 46:18ff.
60. 25:12ff.
61. Augustine, *Faust.* 24:1 (*CSEL* 25, 717ff. ed. Zycha).

GNOSIS, GNOSTICISM AND CHRISTIAN ORIGINS

VIII

THE *CORPUS PAULINUM* AND GNOSIS

by

Professor Walter Schmithals, Berlin

There are two ways in which the question of the relation between the letters of the *Corpus Paulinum* and Gnosis arises. First there is the problem of the opponents confronted in the letters; how far are they Gnostics (or proto-Gnostics or enthusiasts or the like)? Secondly, there is the problem whether or to what extent Paul or his disciples adopted Gnostic concepts, terms and ideas and made them their own and for what reason or for what purpose. Both problems merge if, as is sometimes suggested, Paul or the deutero-Pauline authors adopted Gnostic concepts, terms and ideas directly from their Gnostic opponents in their argument with them. R. McL. Wilson, to whom this essay is dedicated, has made important contributions, both comprehensive and balanced, to all these clusters of problems.

In view of the limitations of space, this article will in effect be limited to the first problem, and even this cannot, of course, receive an exhaustive treatment. My treatment will be, to some extent, weighted towards the Letters to the Colossians and the Ephesians since I have not previously commented on them. 'Ephesians and Colossians present special problems, in the matter of date and authenticity as well as in regard to possible "Gnostic" influences.'[1]

We have to be very cautious about Paul's direct use of the language, concepts and ideas of those whom he opposes at different times, since, apart from the later stages of the Corinthian correspondence, Paul himself wrote without any personal contact with the false teachers whom he opposed. And the deutero-Pauline Pastoral Epistles react to the false Gnostic teaching by avoiding as far as possible any language of Gnostic provenance, although it had already taken on a Christian colouring.

On the other hand the religio-historical and hermeneutical significance of the Gnostic elements which can be found in a more original form in Paul (and in Colossians and Ephesians) can hardly be overestimated. I have earlier written about this in regard to the authentic Pauline letters;[2] now I want to turn my attention to Colossians and Ephesians as well.

I

Eusebius of Caesarea, in his *Historia Ecclesiastica* (IV, 22:4), tells us, on the basis of the 'recollections' of Hegesippus (*ca.* 180), that the early church was 'called virgin, because she had not been corrupted by futile teachings'. In III, 32:7f. Eusebius explains this statement by saying that the false teachers, 'in so far as they even existed by then', stayed hidden so as to show their unveiled face only after the apostles' deaths and to oppose their 'falsely named knowledge' to the preaching of the truth.

The dogmatic purpose of this view of history is plain: the Gnostic heresy is a defection from the true faith. Where heretical Gnosis appeared unmistakably in the *Corpus Paulinum* (particularly in the Pastorals on account of 1 Timothy 6:20), the corresponding anti-Gnostic polemic was, with the help of, e.g., 1 Timothy 4:1 and Acts 20:29ff., understood as an *anticipatory* rebuttal of false teachers by the apostles. This picture of an apostolic primal age of the church free of false teachings was already dominant in Luke-Acts (Acts 4:32). It was handed down unquestioned in the Middle Ages, and only with the dawn of the modern period was it increasingly seen to be more dogmatic than historical.

Henry Hammond[3] identified Paul's opponents in all his letters (including Galatians and Romans) as Gnostics; these were in fact former pagan Gnostics who had been converted to Judaism in Judaea. Johannes Clericus, who in 1698 published Hammond's work in Latin in Amsterdam, criticized Hammond in his own additions to the work for having found 'his Gnostics' too frequently in Paul's letters; yet he did not dismiss out of hand the assertion that Paul had to contend with Gnostics. The likes of J. L. v. Mosheim,[4] C. W. F. Walch,[5] J. D. Michaelis,[6] and E. Burton[7] came to a similar conclusion and, like Hammond, assumed a pagan and oriental origin for Gnosis. All these scholars arrived at this conclusion while supposing all the letters in the *Corpus Paulinum* to be authentic (except Hebrews); they also interpreted the allusive references to opponents in the earlier letters in the light of the clearly anti-Gnostic later letters, especially the Pastorals.

The perspective was altered by critical scholarship's demonstration of the deutero-Pauline origin of part of the *Corpus Paulinum* and particularly of those letters showing most clearly an anti-Gnostic polemic. J. E. C. Schmidt (1804), F. Schleiermacher (1807) and J. G. Eichhorn (1812) paved the way for an increasing acceptance that the Pastorals were post-Pauline; with Ephesians it was E. Evanson (1792) and W. M. L. de Wette (1826) and with the related Colossians it was Mayerhoff (1838).

This set the authentic Pauline letters at a distance from the post-Pauline ones in the eyes of critical exegetes and thus separated them from the anti-Gnostic thrust of the latter. This distance now allowed a more critical revival of the fathers' vision of a springtime of the church free of Gnostic heretics.

This was the basis for F. C. Baur's 'Tübingen' view of church history. Above all, the anti-Gnostic or Gnosticizing trends in the deutero-Pauline (and Johannine) letters were the reason for his assigning them to a late date in the second century. It was then that Christian Gnosis was spreading, a continuation of the Alexandrian Jewish philosophy of religion emanating from Greek philosophy. The authentic letters of Paul – for Baur Galatians, Romans, 1–2 Corinthians and Philippians – were rather occasioned by his dispute with legalistic Judaizers.

The great influence of this picture of the history of early Christianity, an influence still felt today, rested upon several interrelated factors:

(a) Baur was the first to make the question of the cause or the opposition confronting Paul the key to a historical exegesis of Paul's letters;

(b) he did this within the framework of a comprehensive and philosophically based view of history;

(c) it is historically clear, and this is supported strongly by the texts themselves, that Paul's arguments with his opponents in the principal letters are a unity.

Conservative scholars, on the other hand, concerned to maintain the authenticity of all the Pauline letters, either clung uncritically to the fathers' view of church history and denied any polemic against contemporary Gnostics in the *Corpus Paulinum*, or followed Hammond and his successors in arguing for a single anti-Gnostic front throughout the whole *Corpus*. But neither form of this conservative position had a future in scholarship.

Yet even Baur's unified characterization of the opponents in the main letters as Judaizers did not survive long; it ran counter to too many exegetical data, above all in the Corinthian letters.[8] Few today would still argue that Paul, in the letters which he actually wrote, argued always and only against legalistic Jewish Christians.[9]

W. Lütgert developed a classical counter-position to Baur's analysis of movements in the early church.[10] He detected a single front of Gnostic false teachers who visited Corinth, Galatia, Philippi and Rome and unsettled Paul's churches. Yet Lütgert's insights lacked the penetration of Hammond and his followers and even more that of the insights of the 'History of Religions School' of his own day, to the extent that he did not really reckon with a pre-Christian Gnosis as an independent religious phenomenon with its own missionary movement; rather he regarded the Gnostic traits that he had so acutely observed in Paul's opponents as the result of a disintegration of Paulinism in its Hellenistic environment, a disintegration which occurred spontaneously everywhere in Paul's churches. Lütgert also made a significant concession to the 'Tübingen School': he was forced to recognize that Paul was fighting on two fronts, at least in Galatia and Philippi, against enthusiasts and Judaizers from Jerusalem.

This assumption of two fronts was a dubious one, since Paul nowhere gives any direct evidence of such a situation. Nor have we any evidence of a Judaizing world-mission among the gentiles, apart from the passages of Paul's letters interpreted to that effect. General religio-historical considerations suggest that such a mission was unlikely.

I have therefore tried to show how all the principal Pauline epistles (including 1–2 Thessalonians), which were all written in the period of the third missionary journey, confront a single opposition.[11] In this I am following the suggestions made by Hammond at the start of the modern era as well as presupposing the results of critical analysis of the *Corpus Paulinum*. At the same time I have sought to paint a clear religio-historical picture of early Jewish or Jewish-Christian Gnosis and its mythology. This original proposal has been noted and discussed, but generally not accepted.

Scholars today see things rather differently. They reject the alternatives of defining Paul's opponents as either all Judaizers or all Gnostics (pneumatics, enthusiasts). They unite in dismissing as an unsatisfactory compromise the view of a corresponding twofold opposition. Instead a mass of different, more or less heretical groups appear independently of one another in the various Pauline churches; for 'the opponents of Paul who are mentioned in his letters cannot be assigned to one and the same movement.'[12] The attempt to do so seems rather 'to entail an undue simplification of the probably manifold variety of Paul's readers, and a neglect of their varying background and environment.'[13]

One can compare, for instance, H. Koester's article 'Häretiker im Urchristentum' in *RGG* III (1959[3]), 17–21: here Paul is thought to encounter Judaizers of a syncretistic character in Galatians, non-Jewish Gnostics in 1 Corinthians, Hellenistic-Jewish Christians in 2 Corinthians, Jewish-Christian Gnostics in Philippi. If we included 1–2 Thessalonians and Romans, we could increase the stock of heretical hybrids.

Some argue for a less diverse and relatively unified opposition, identifying the opponents in several letters, e.g. in Philippians and 2 Corinthians or in Philippians and 2 Corinthians 10–13.

The rejection of a unified opposition and in particular that suggested by the Tübingen account of church history is reckoned as an advance amongst scholars: for no longer can one lump together the false teachers whom Paul opposed and dub them 'Judaizers'; moreover was the unity that Baur and others detected in their exegesis not an assumption made on the basis of their philosophy of history?

That is one way of looking at things. Yet we must remember that the similarly unified characterization of the opponents as Gnostics or pneumatics was never linked to a corresponding view of history. Rather, both the 'Tübingen School' and Hammond and also Lütgert based their different theses of a unified opposition in Paul's letters primarily on the *exegetical* observation that the opponents in the different letters were essentially described in one way. Their various studies are in this respect models of comparative exegesis.

In contrast, the dominant view today which sees a great variety of often very loosely described opposing positions in Paul's letters usually rests on the analysis of individual letters *in isolation*. It is often expressly stated to be an improvement in one's methods when a letter or even just a section of a letter is handled without reference even to clear parallels in others.

Such methods are justified as long as one wants to be free of the straitjacket of a system imposed by any philosophy of history. Yet the results obtained by such methods must be critically correlated with one another. This is true because the idea which underlies the dominant view today, that in a limited period of time during the third missionary journey very different false teachers arose independently of each other in the different Pauline churches and then disappeared again, is not particularly probable in itself. Moreover the subsequent history of the church was marked essentially by the clashes between major conflicting systems, and not by a polymorphous profusion of separate movements. So we must take account in our methods of 'the total phenomenon of early Christianity viewed from the particular aspect of the contradictions and conflicts which could, or even had to, have arisen in the course of its development.'[14]

Scholars investigating the opposition to Paul in his churches must do so with this assumption. To what conclusions it will lead in the future is not yet clear.

II

Here the Letter to the Galatians plays a key role. In the 'Tübingen School's' reconstruction it was cornerstone, foundation, pivot and centre to which all gravitated. In their eyes this letter disclosed for the first time in the history of early Christianity that the Jewish Christians in Jerusalem sought to subject Paul's Gentile Christian churches to the Torah contrary to the agreements reached at the so-called Apostolic Council. Whenever today scholars feel led to follow the 'Tübingen School' in postulating solely a critique of the Judaizers throughout the authentic letters of Paul, then Galatians retains this key position, overshadowing the other letters and aligning them with its own position.

For W. Lütgert, too, supported by J. H. Ropes,[15] Galatians was pivotal in his thesis of a struggle with Gnosis that had already begun in the apostolic age. At the same time it was the letter which most clearly showed a division in the church addressed and a corresponding twofold polemic on the part of Paul.

Galatians is also crucial for the dominant view today that Paul faced a variety of opponents; for it extends the spectrum of possible opponents enormously. Without it this spectrum would so contract that it would doubtless be easier to postulate a single opposing position rather than a varied opposition in 1–2 Corinthians, Philippians, Romans 16 and perhaps 1–2 Thessalonians. But Galatians, understood as a polemic against Judaizers, compels one, even if one does not follow the 'Tübingen School', to assume different false teachers.

Yet, for those who follow the 'Tübingen School' in detecting *one* opposition confronted in the authentic letters of Paul, but who describe that opposition as enthusiastic or Gnostic, Galatians still remains the touchstone of their thesis. If it passes the test with reference to Galatians, it can count as having passed everywhere; if it fails here, it fails everywhere.

Professor Wilson gave an apt summary of my attempt to see Galatians as polemic against enthusiasts and assessed and criticized it.[16] He rightly noted that in my essay I had paid insufficient attention to the middle section of Galatians (3:1–5:12): 'One of the main points of the whole letter is in fact the assertion that justification comes not by "works of law", that is by legalistic practice and observance, but on the basis of faith, and in particular faith in Christ.'[17] This observation is a decisive argument for seeing here polemic against Judaizers, even if they were Judaizers 'who may have made room in their theories for some of the speculations which later came to be known as Gnostic.'[18]

If Galatians is thus the point where all conceivable theories about Paul's opponents are most vulnerable then this is because, like Janus, it faces in two directions. To put it otherwise, all depends on the role of chapters 3 and 4 within the letter as a whole.

Were it not for these chapters no one would really imagine that Paul was opposing Judaizers in Galatians; for in Galatians 1–2 and 5:13–6:18 there is no hint of polemic against Judaizers. The beginning and end of the letter suggest rather that those who have infiltrated into the Galatian churches are 'spiritual men'. But the seemingly clear polemic against Judaizers in 3:1–5:12 compels one to align the other parts of the letter with this section.

But is it correct to say that in Galatians 3:1–5:12 Paul defends righteousness by faith against a righteousness based on works of the law propagated or practised in Galatia? Though Paul's argument is usually understood thus, such a view distorts it considerably. In fact Paul poses for the Galatians the *alternatives*, law or faith, and does so with thoroughly traditional material which is not directly related to the situation in Galatia.

Why does he do so? Most scholars answer after little thought that Paul wishes to win back the Galatians for 'faith' because they are in danger of being won over to Judaism. But this answer begs too many questions. That is plain from the fact that nowhere in 3:1–5:12 does Paul assume that Galatians have attacked the idea of righteousness by faith and accordingly he nowhere *defends* this righteousness. Naturally the appeals in 3:1–5 and 4:8–20 are meant to win back the Galatians to Paul's view of justification. However these appeals are inseparable from the following arguments; there Paul states the alternatives of righteousness by the law and righteousness by faith, and states them continuously, repeatedly and emphatically. Such an argument is simply misplaced if directed against Judaizers, for they have always recognized their position in this alternative to righteousness by faith. An appeal based on the proof, first to be forcibly presented by Paul, that 'faith' and 'law' are mutually exclusive ways of salvation, cannot be directed towards Judaizers since they do in fact seek their salvation in the law.

A check confirms this: in Galatians 5:2ff. Paul shows clearly the purpose of his argument in chapters 3 and 4. Christ and circumcision, grace and righteousness based on law are set over against one another as alternatives; the gentile who lets himself be circumcised has taken the law's side (Galatians 5:2–4). The Spirit and faith are God's eschatological ordinances that have exposed the transitory nature of the law; they are lost if the obsolete law is erected as a power for the present. A gentile Christian who lets himself be circumcised is returning to that side of the alternatives that has been supplanted. Circumcision thus means separation from Christ and turning to the law (Galatians 5:5).

But Paul must first summarize Galatians 3–4 and put this fact before the Galatians who are so keen on circumcision: 'Look, I, Paul, tell you ...' (Galatians 5:2). The Galatians' practice of circumcision thus does not imply, as far as Paul knows, this necessary connection between circumcision and the law. Such a way of summarizing Galatians 3–4 in 5:2ff. would be quite unthinkable if Paul's argument were based on the Judaizers' demanding circumcision in Galatia. The middle section of Galatians, to be sure, shows that the new teachers in Galatia propagated circumcision – how vigorously is another matter. Yet Paul's argument, which forces the Galatians to choose between the *alternatives*, law or faith, rules out the possibility that he supposed the false teachers to be Judaizers.

Galatians 6:12f. confirms this: here Paul accuses his opponents of courting the gentile Christian Galatians with the demand that they must let themselves be circumcised in order to benefit the synagogue. That, and no theological reason, was their only reason for wanting their circumcision. Anyone, a Jew or Jewish Christian who was thus subject to the synagogue's jurisdiction, who carried on a law-free mission, was hard-pressed by the synagogue, as Paul must often have found in the Diaspora (cf. 2 Corinthians 11:24). The false teachers in Galatia wanted to avoid this by their practice of circumcision. They themselves are not concerned with the 'Judaizing' observance of the law either (Galatians 6:13). That clearly means that they are no more concerned with their own strict obedience to the law than they were with the Galatians'.

Here too belongs the strange idea which the Galatians have, that Paul was still preaching circumcision (5:11). Irrespective of the reasons which they gave for their idea, they can only have appealed to Paul's example in this way in their wooing of the Galatian churches if, like him, they regarded circumcision, not as the basis of a way of salvation through the law, but as a tactical measure to avert persecution by the synagogue.

Even if the middle section of Galatians does not disclose the whole theological position of the false teachers, it does rule out the possibility that they were Judaizers. Galatians 3:1–5:12 are thus no hindrance to an interpretation of the letter as being at all points a polemic against enthusiastic infiltrators.

III

Frequently scholars who have been prepared to admit that Paul faces Gnostic opponents in his letters have held that these were ultra-Paulinists who developed further the tendencies towards Gnostic ways of thought inherent in Paul's thinking. These opponents thus do not attack the churches from outside but arise within them. Their views, which incline towards Gnosis, can be described as pre-Gnosis, proto-Gnosis or Gnosis *in statu nascendi*.

The Nag Hammadi finds have now disclosed to us a considerable body of original texts of a Jewish Gnosis, and many of their Christian texts are also Jewish Gnostic documents with a thin Christian veneer. These discoveries also let Gnostic texts known earlier appear in a partially new light, a Jewish one, so that the Jewish Gnostic foundations are not eclipsed by those of Christian Gnosticism. This has given fresh impetus to the old thesis that Gnosis is wholly of Jewish origin.

Be that as it may, the fact of a pure Jewish Gnosis found in a broad range of diverse texts rules out a Christian origin for Gnosis. In the recognition of this probably lies the chief significance of the Nag Hammadi discoveries for the topic of 'Gnosis and the New Testament'.

Quite apart from the fact that chronology alone would rule out the derivation of second-century Jewish Gnostic texts from a Christian Gnosis, it is hardly credible, historically and otherwise, that, in a period of increasing separation between Christianity and Judaism, the latter would adapt a Christian Gnosis to any appreciable extent. It is especially hard to imagine a religio-historical process in which the original traces of a Christian Gnosis, both ideas and terms and names, were carefully expunged when these were taken over into Judaism; and then, in a later stage in the history of these religions, the Jewish Gnostic documents which had arisen in this way were appropriated again by their Christian mother with the help of a thin Christian veneer.

This conclusion can only be avoided by postulating a simultaneous and mutually independent rise of Jewish and Christian Gnosis. Such a process might be improbable, but still conceivable, apropos of the Gnostic understanding of existence, but impossible with regard to the characteristic Gnostic myth.

It is thus not possible that the opponents in the relevant letters of Paul represent a Gnosis that arises directly from his thought.

To talk of a 'Gnosis *in statu nascendi*' detectable in Paul's opponents would thus only be meaningful if we were talking of the beginnings of a Christian Gnosis nurtured in the soil of a pagan or Jewish Gnosis. The corresponding terms 'proto-Gnosis' or 'pre-Gnosis' would then mean that Paul's Gnostic opponents did not yet represent a developed Christian Gnosis, but were Christian syncretists more or less influenced by Gnostic ideas.

There is something to be said for this way of looking at things. Anyone who allows that Paul's opponents in his letters were Gnostics or Gnosticizing has to decide how Gnostic they were. Were they only extreme pneumatics? Or were they teaching a developed Gnostic myth? Of course, if one thinks that the opponents entered the churches from outside, the question can be reversed: how great is the Christian element in the views of the Jewish or Jewish-Christian Gnostics who are troubling Paul's churches?

If controversy rages even over the place of these opponents in the history of religion, this is true all the more of an exacter definition of them.

IV

With regard to the Pastoral Epistles we can, with few exceptions, speak of a consensus: today they are usually regarded as deutero-Pauline documents and for many good reasons. The false teachers condemned in them are, as the early church recognized, representatives of a Jewish-Christian Gnosis in the broadest sense.

These teachers are spoken of both as a future development (1 Timothy 1:4) and as a present threat. This points to the post-Pauline origin of the letters, as does the fact that the same heretical movement is confronted in letters ostensibly sent at different points of time to several addressees in different places. Occasionally in the past some have attempted to see different opponents in the various letters but, even when the Pastorals were assumed to be authentic, this thesis was rightly rejected because of the homogeneity of the opponents described.

On the one hand the Pastorals emphasize traditional *teaching in general* (1 Timothy 4:13, 16; 5:17; 6:1; 2 Timothy 2:8, 24; 3:13ff.; 4:2). They do this to combat a Gnostic enthusiasm which replaces traditional teaching with the authority of the free *pneuma*. Thus the Pastorals are strikingly reticent about '*pneuma*'. The word appears in traditional formulae (1 Timothy 3:16; 2 Timothy 4:22; Titus 3:5). Otherwise it is inseparable from traditional teaching (2 Timothy 1:6f., 14; cf. 1 Timothy 1:18; 4:13f.) and exposes false teaching for what it is (1 Timothy 4:1).

On the other hand the Pastorals emphasize *correct teaching*. They have 13 different terms for 'teach': cf. 1 Timothy 1:10; 4:6; 6:3; 2 Timothy 4:3; Titus 1:9; 2:1, 7f. There is hardly any attempt made to expound this teaching, but it is presupposed and occasionally quoted in formulae (1 Timothy 1:5, 15; 2:4ff.; 6:13–16; 2 Timothy 1:9f.; 2:8–13; Titus 2:11–14; 3:4–7). Part of this correct teaching is a right understanding of the Old Testament (2 Timothy 3:13ff.). There is no sign of a direct knowledge of Paul's letters.

The *tradition of teaching* starts with Paul who received true teaching (1 Timothy 1:1, 11f., 16; 2:7; 2 Timothy 1:1, 11; Titus 1:1–3) for all the world (1 Timothy 2:3–7). He passed it on to his pupils Timothy (1 Timothy 1:18; 3:14f.; 4:14; 2 Timothy 1:12ff.; 2:2; 3:10f., 14) and Titus (Titus 1:4; 2:15). They keep it pure (1 Timothy 1:18f.; 6:13f.; 2 Timothy 1:12ff.; 2:8; 3:14–17) until the end (1:12). They are also to pass it on after Paul's death (1 Timothy 1:3; 4:6, 16; 5:22; 6:11; 2 Timothy 2:2, 14f.; 4:2, 5; Titus 1:5–9; 2:1, 15; 3:8).

The *office of teacher* guarantees the authenticity of the tradition of teaching. The church confronts the Gnostic pneumatics with officials ordained with the laying on of hands (1 Timothy 4:14; 5:22; 2 Timothy 1:6), in 'apostolic succession' (2:2; Titus 1:5). Their task is teaching (1 Timothy 3:2, 8; 2 Timothy 2:2; Titus 1:9), and they are paid for it (1 Timothy 5:3, 17f.; 2 Timothy 2:6f.). The Pastorals know of the office of apostle (1 Timothy 1:1, 11f.; 2:7; 2 Timothy 1:1, 11), and of the apostle's pupils (1 Timothy 1:3f., 18; 4:6, 12–5:2; 2 Timothy 1:13f.; 2:15; Titus 2:7f.); there is that of the (one) bishop (1 Timothy 3:1–7; Titus 1:7ff.), the elder (1 Timothy 5:17–21; Titus 1:5f.), the deacon (1 Timothy 3:8–13) and the widow (1 Timothy 5:3–16). These offices do not necessarily presuppose a developed hierarchy; what is really significant is the merging of the tradition and the office of teaching. The Pastorals are accordingly sent to occupants of this office and not to churches as in the authentic letters of Paul.

False teaching is also called by its name (1 Timothy 1:3, 6f., 10, 19f.; 4:1f.; 6:3–5, 20f.; 2 Timothy 1:15; 2:16ff., 25; 3:6f.; 4:3f.; Titus 1:9–16; 3:9–11); yet it is not set out in detail and refuted, as Paul does in the genuine letters. Rather the Pastorals forbid any contact with false teaching (1 Timothy 6:20; 2 Timothy 2:16–23; 3:9). This prohibition of any discussion with the false teachers on the one hand underlines the danger of it (1 Timothy 1:19f.; 4:1f.; 6:3–5, 20f.; 2 Timothy 2:17; 3:6f., 13; Titus 1:10f.; 3:10), but also indicates that the false teachers are not part of the congregation; they are intruders (cf. Ign., *Eph.* 9:1). They are 'imposters' (2 Timothy 3:13) who creep into houses (3:6f.). Accordingly they are accused of seeking their own interests instead of displaying missionary zeal (1 Timothy 6:5ff.; Titus 1:11).

It is not impossible that the false teachers appealed to letters of Paul (cf. 1 Timothy 1:19f.; 2 Timothy 1:15; 4:10, 14f.). In that case one of the purposes of the Pastorals would have been to enlist Paul unequivocally amongst the opponents of heresy.

A precise description of the false teaching is hampered by the lack of discussion of this teaching in the Pastorals.

The false teachers appealed to *Jewish tradition* (1 Timothy 1:7–10; Titus 1:10–16; 3:9). One cannot necessarily infer from this that they were native Jews. They were by no means 'Judaizers'. All the other characteristics of the false teaching are against this last suggestion. Nor is there any evidence for the view found occasionally that the Pastorals deal with both Judaizers and Gnostics (a twofold opposition). The appeal to the Old Testament rules out the attempt to regard the false teachers as Marcionites. The 'antitheses of what is falsely called knowledge' (1 Timothy 6:20) are not a document, let alone Marcion's work of the same name, but the 'empty opinions' of those who wrongly call themselves Gnostics.

The false teachers claim to possess 'Gnosis' or 'knowledge of God' (1 Timothy 6:20; Titus 1:16; cf. 2 Timothy 3:5). 2 Timothy 2:18, the most concrete reference to their false teaching, clearly shows their *basic enthusiastic and spiritualistic posture*. The spiritualizing of the idea of resurrection ('the resurrection has already taken place') is typical of Gnosis (cf. on 1 Corinthians 15:12; also Iren., *Haer.* I, 23:5; II, 31:2; Just., *Dial.* 80; Tert., *Praescr. Haer.* 33:7; Act. P1 7:14; Treat. Res. 49:13ff.; cf. Romans 6:11; John 5:24; 11:23ff.). Their enthusiasm can be inferred indirectly from the emphasis on the idea of a redemption involving the body (2 Timothy 3:2ff.; Titus 2:11–14), from the idea of *universal* judgment (2 Timothy 4:1, 8) and from the criticism of self-conceit (1 Timothy 6:3f.; 2 Timothy 3:4).

Without doubt their enthusiasm lies behind the ascetic tendencies of the false teachers and their depreciation of the gifts of creation (1 Timothy 4:3–5, 8; Titus 1:13ff.; cf. 1 Timothy 2:15; 5:14f., 23). For the same reason they sought emancipation, devaluing the created, the earthly and the bodily in favour of the spiritual. Thus the Pastorals oppose a corresponding 'emancipation' of women. Over against the spiritual assertions of the false teachers Christians are called on to confess in concrete terms their belief in creation, in the value of the body and of the natural distinctions between the sexes (1 Timothy 2:11–15; 5:13; cf. 2 Timothy 3:6; Titus 2:5). The letters oppose the repudiation of the earthly state (1 Timothy 2:1f.; Titus 3:1f.) and of the orders of society (1 Timothy 6:1ff.; Titus 2:9f., 15). They also oppose the ascetic rejection of marriage (1 Timothy 4:3; 5:14f.) and emancipation from the household (as the haven of sound teaching: 1 Timothy 3:4f., 12; 5:3f., 8, 11, 13f.; Titus 2:1–10).

Clearly too they reject the view that the offer of redemption is not extended to all men but only to the pneumatics (1 Timothy 2:1–6; 4:10; 2 Timothy 4:1; Titus 2:11; 3:3).

The author also apparently considered it necessary to emphasize Jesus' humanity (1 Timothy 2:5; 3:16; 2 Timothy 2:8).

What is not clear is the point of the repeated references to 'Jewish myths and genealogies' (1 Timothy 1:4; 4:7; 2 Timothy 4:3f.; Titus 1:13f.; 3:9). Taking these in conjunction with the other evidence, one may suggest that the false teachers used Old Testament passages (e.g. Genesis 4:17ff.; 5:1ff.; 6:1ff.) to present mythical speculations on the aeons like those attested so plentifully in extant Gnostic texts. Jewish Gnostics, who could not postulate an absolute dualism, tried by means of these to explain the emanation of evil from the unity of God.

Thus we will have to regard the Gnosis which the Pastorals oppose as truly mythical. It is not possible to ascribe this Gnosis to one of the second-century Gnostic systems known to us, and for reasons of chronology it would be a mistake to do so.

V

Things are different with the Letter to the Colossians; here there is no consensus in sight as to the opponents. Many problems of method and fact prevent a solution of this problem; above all there is the problem that strikingly heterogeneous traits are mixed up together in the impression which we get of the false teachers at Colossae.

Their activity is described ambiguously. Their fine words and powers of persuasion deceive men (2:4); the vain deceptiveness of their philosophy leads men away from the truth (2:8). Their teaching is unjustly claimed to be wisdom (2:23). They are conceited without cause (2:18). This is all polemical and can only be used with care in describing these heretics.

On the other hand there are important and unambiguous anti-Jewish passages. Particularly characteristic is the heretics' observance of food regulations (2:16, 21), purity regulations (2:21) and the Jewish calendar of feasts (cf. Hosea 2:13; Ezekiel 45:17; 1 Chronicles 23:31; 2 Chronicles 2:3; 31:3; Numbers 28:11ff.). The author criticizes the Jewish pattern of feasts as a 'shadow of what is to come' whereas 'the substance itself' belongs to Christ (2:17; cf. 1 Corinthians 5:7f.; Hebrews 8:5; 10:1). He disparages foodstuffs as transitory things, destined to be used up (2:22a). He describes (critically) Judaizing behaviour as *ethelothrēskia* (2:23: self-chosen or alleged piety), *tapeinophrosunē* (2:18, 23: 'humility' = asceticism, fasting as in Herm., *s.* V, 3:7), *apheidia sōmatos* (2:23: bodily abstinence), and also (ironically?) as *plēsmonē tēs sarkos* (2:23: fleshly pleasure? satisfaction of the flesh?). It is uncertain to what extent he is using his opponents' words here.

The 'human tradition' of 2:8 and the 'human precepts and doctrines' of 2:22 refer to these pious activities. Do these phrases reflect a particular stress on tradition on the part of the false teachers? Or is this just polemic ('only human teaching'; cf. 1 Corinthians 2:5; Galatians 1:11; 1 Thessalonians 2:13; Titus 1:14)?

It is hardly to be inferred from 2:11–13 that they also practised circumcision.

If all this fits the context of a ritualistic Jewish Christianity, the charge of 'worship of angels' (2:18) does not. Is this phrase derived from the false teachers' vocabulary, or from the author's armoury of polemic and irony? In the first instance the angels would be honourable powers venerated by the heretics on a par with Christ. In the second they could be demonic forces whose power the false teachers still had to fear. Others compare the Gnostic idea of emanation and take a mediating position: the 'powers' are arranged in a hierarchy; the more divine they are, the higher they are, but the more evil they are, the closer they are to the world; Christ is their divine head. But which sort are then responsible for their 'regulations'?

The author of Colossians seems to identify the 'angels' of 2:18 with the '*stoicheia* of the cosmos' of 2:8, 20. On the one hand these were created by Christ and are subordinate to him (1:15–20; 2:10), on the other they have been stripped of power by him (1:13; 2:15). This conflicting evidence makes it hard to decide on the sense of the reference to 'worship of angels' on the basis of the author's Christological statements; yet the close proximity of 2:15 and 2:18 suggests that in 2:18 the author was thinking of hostile angelic powers.

When in chapters 1–2 he emphasizes Christ's role as surpassing all powers, almost all exegetes consider that he means to dethrone the 'powers' in contrast to the attitude of the false teachers.

Is the phrase '*stoicheia* of the cosmos' borrowed from the false teachers? Or is it introduced by the author of Colossians in order to align these powers clearly on the side of the cosmos and thus to strip them of their power? A comparison with Galatians 4:3, 8f. supports the latter alternative.

In any case 2:16–18 and 20–23 and, in the light of 2:22, also 2:8 show that the author regards the 'angels', the '*stoicheia* of the cosmos' and the 'principalities and powers' (1:16; 2:10, 15) as the source of the 'human doctrines' (2:22) which he opposes, just as Paul does in Galatians 4:8ff.

It is at the same time both specific and ambiguous when Colossians 2:18 speaks of the heretic as *ha heoraken embateuōn*. Since *embateuein* is attested as a technical term of the mysteries, apparently for entering the shrine, many exegetes argue that the heretical cult of the Colossians had the character of a mystery. The 'entry' (= initiation?) would then in certain cases have been preceded by a vision (*ha heoraken*), and Apul., *Met.* XI, 27 is cited in support: 'entering what he has seen'. Or the *ha* can be taken to refer to the 'self-abasement and worship of angels' mentioned above: 'which he had seen at his initiation'. Or one can incorporate the following words as well: 'conceited without cause by that which he has seen at his initiation (or: at his visionary entrance into the upper world)'.

But it is by no means necessary to interpret *embateuein* on the basis of the language of the mysteries. So others take the 'entry' of the post-mortal ascent of the soul: the (Gnostic) visionary enters what he has seen before in a vision or in ecstasy. It can also be translated 'investigating what he has seen' or 'taking possession of what he has seen'. In each case an ecstatic visionary 'seeing' is a mark of the false teachers, but this is not necessarily related to the religion of the mysteries.

All in all, the opponents in Colossians give us a unique example of a speculative Hellenistic Gnosis on the one hand and Jewish ethics and practices on the other merging into one another. Again the absence of any hint that the author was fighting on two fronts prevents our trying to postulate different groups of false teachers. But it is also understandable that scholars are reluctant to see here a false teaching peculiar to Colossae and with no religio-historical analogies.

However, the ambiguity of the often very indefinite references to the false teachings enables scholars to bring together these variegated data so as to give a definite form to this heresy. Yet this procedure also leads to very different descriptions of that heresy. In general it is true that, the more specific the description of the heresy, the more the statements of Colossians are distorted in one direction or another; the more these statements are taken at their face value, the less precise the resultant picture of the heresy.

This picture extends from Gnostics in the strict sense of the word via all the many suggested forms of Jewish-Christian syncretism to a legalistic Judaism. The solution of this intractable problem is, I think, to be solved by means of the 'interpolation hypothesis' proposed already in the last century.[19]

Colossians contains both a prescript (1:1–2) and a proem (1:3–8) in a thoroughly authentic Pauline fashion as well as a complete Pauline conclusion to the letter. In 4:18b we have the usual closing greeting; 4:10–18a contains an extensive list of greetings, which invites comparison especially with Romans 16:3–16 as a formal parallel; 4:7–9 contains the personal remarks which Paul usually includes at the end of a letter; 4:2–6 is a request for prayer for the apostle, a similarly stereotyped item in the epistolary form employed by Paul (cf. 1 Thessalonians 5:25; 3:11 = Thessalonians E; 2 Thessalonians 3:1f.; Romans 15:30–32). Of the other regular items of Paul's epistolary endings we apparently have in 3:12–14 the closing ethical exhortations and in 3:15a the 'climax', the (Jewish) prayer for peace (cf. Romans 16:20a: Philippians 4:9b; 1 Thessalonians 5:23; 2 Thessalonians 3:16; 2 Corinthians 13:11, etc.). If this analysis is correct, then the author of the canonical Colossians has later inserted 3:15c–4:1 into the conclusion of the letter, i.e. the domestic code of 3:18–4:1 and the exhortation to true worship of God in 3:16, together with the linking passages of 3:15b and 17, which already anticipate the theme of 'thanksgiving' in 4:2 (cf. 1:12).

There is no evidence in antiquity of a pseudonymous letter requiring from its author such an authentically composed seal of its genuineness as we find in the beginning and end of Colossians (contrast Ephesians!).

However, if we have here an authentic epistolary framework with interpolations, then there may be two 'layers' in the body of the letter. The body of the original Pauline letter to Colossae contained, I suggest, 1:24–29; 2:1a, 4f., 16f., 20–23; 3:1–11. This connects smoothly with the original introductory passage of 1:1–8 and with the original conclusion in 3:12–15a; 4:2–18.

In this letter Paul warned the Christians of Colossae, who were not known to him personally, against Judaizing legalism. The background to this was the practice of former 'God-fearing' Gentile Christians originating from the synagogue of which we know from Romans 14:1ff.; 1 Corinthians 8:1ff.; 10:23ff.: they continued to observe Jewish purity regulations and feast-days and, where the ritual purity of meat and wine, usually linked with pagan cults in the Hellenistic world, could not be guaranteed, they declined to consume them at all. This custom had nothing to do with dualistic asceticism. Paul reacted to the Colossians' behaviour more on grounds of principle than in Romans 14f. and 1 Corinthians 8 and 10, for he knew of no argument between 'strong' and 'weak' already taking place there, whereas he did in the case of Rome and Corinth. However he did not fear their falling away from Christ or from faith to serve the law, as was the case in Galatia.

The deutero-Pauline author of our Colossians has re-directed Paul's original polemic against the Gnostic heretics of his own time. He formulates his own anti-heretical statements in 2:1, 18 as in essence a doublet of the original references in 2:4, 16, 20–23 (cf. also 2:14 with 2:21). Only the 'taking his stand on visions' and the 'puffed up without reason' of 2:18 (cf. 1 Corinthians 4:6, 18f.; 5:2; 8:1; 13:4) were not found in that original.

If the author of the canonical Colossians wished to combine his anti-Gnostic ideas with the original Pauline letter, then he needed to insert certain interpretations and the linking passages which he composed at 1:13, 16b, 18c; 2:8, 10, 15, 18f.

Thus arose the tension between the monistic idea of Christ as the head and reconciler of *all* powers and the more dualistic one in 2:15 (cf. 1:13). The former the deutero-Pauline author formulated in 1:16–20 and 2:9–12, adopting and supplementing the hymn to Christ of 1:15–20. The latter led directly into the polemic against the heretics regarded as Gnostics in 2:16ff. Following on from Paul's letter (2:20), he accepted the Gnostic view that the cosmos was ruled or threatened by demonic powers. In 2:15, as 2:14 shows, he himself may have been thinking of the powers as created by God (1:15–17) but fallen, as in Jewish demonology (cf. 1 Corinthians 2:8; 2 Corinthians 4:4); sinners belong to them but their rights over sinners (the 'bond' of 2:14) have been taken away from them by Christ's death, so that they are now powerless (cf. 1:18b–20).

These observations have not settled the occasion of the composition of the canonical Colossians. The characterization of the heresy is generally fuzzy and the interpolator's descriptions in 2:8 and 18f. are rather inadequate taken in isolation. These factors and the non-polemical secondary parts of chapters 1, 3 and 4 militate against assuming that the author of our Colossians was actually involved in an argument with Gnostic heretics who were threatening the unity of the congregation. He expected the latter to stand firm in their faith (1:23) and to remain true to the teaching handed down to them (2:7f.); he describes the Gnostic heretics of his day as being outside the body of Christ (2:18f.). This polemic is more likely a setting out of theological principles than a polemic against a threat actually confronting the Colossian church. It does not follow that no concrete needs occasioned the letter as the following consideration of Ephesians will show.

An important part of the anti-Gnostic principles laid down here is the (already traditional) anti-dualistic statement that all was created through Christ, and that correspondingly all was redeemed by him (1:15–20, 23; 2:10; cf. 1:28). Its deutero-Pauline character is shown by its concentration on the 'forgiveness of sins' (1:13f., 20; 2:13f.). But it is this that reveals the letter's anti-Gnostic thrust: it is not the pneumatic that is redeemed, but the sinner. Corresponding to the 'Christological concentration' are the repeated references to Christ's sufficiency: in him 'all the treasures of wisdom and knowledge are hidden' (2:2f., 8f.; 1:9f., 19); terms like *sophia*, *gnōsis*, *epignōsis* and *sunesis pneumatikē* are clearly Gnostic in origin.

VI

The arguments against the Pauline authorship of Ephesians are so numerous and weighty that it is generally regarded today as a deutero-Pauline document.

All analyses have to start from the close relationship between Colossians and Philemon (as regards their setting) on the one hand, and between Colossians and Ephesians (as regards their content) on the other. Thus Ephesians and Philemon are linked indirectly. It seems that in these three letters we have an originally independent collection of letters (like 1–3 John and the Pastoral Epistles). The 'Catholic' address of Ephesians fits in with this.

There are many reasons both for seeing the same hand at work in the writing of Colossians and Ephesians and for attributing them to different authors. What I have said about Colossians offers a solution to this dilemma: the genuine letter of Paul to Colossae was supplemented by the author of Ephesians.

If this is correct, then the answers to the questions of the occasion for the writing of Ephesians and for the deutero-Pauline editing of Colossians must be sought together. Many scholars, we should note, have commented on Ephesians' lack of a setting. It is true that its purpose is far from clear. Yet it contains a characteristic theme, the unity of Jewish and gentile Christians in the one people of God (2:11–22). The letter addresses gentile Christians in particular (2:1–10): they should regard their conversion as sharing in the inheritance (3:6) of Christ's gifts, which are given to both

Jewish and gentile Christians (3:1–21). Already in the opening passage of the letter the unity of the church in this respect is solemnly asserted (1:22f.); the exhortations of 4:1–6 and 25–32 call for mutual acceptance and justify this call anew by appealing to the unity of Christ's body (4:7–16).

Many writers have puzzled over the specific occasion for this characteristic theme of Ephesians. A probable historical setting for Ephesians is provided by the predicament of the '*aposunagōgos*'. In the course of the Pharisaic restoration of the synagogue after the destruction of Jerusalem those Christian groups that up till then had lived within the synagogue community sought to join the (post-) Pauline churches, which from the start had been organized outside the synagogue's sphere of jurisdiction. The chief purpose of Ephesians was to secure the acceptance by the gentile Christians from the Pauline communities of their Christian brothers who came from the synagogue and at the same time to acquaint the latter with the Pauline tradition.

This suggested historical setting gives an immediate practical relevance to the warnings against falling back into pagan immorality (4:17–24; 5:1–21; cf. even 2:1ff.); they are warned in particular against unchastity and avarice (4:19ff.; 5:3ff.). Without conceding anything on matters of doctrine to Christians from the synagogues (cf. especially 2:15), the (Pauline) churches join in acknowledging with them the morality of the synagogue in accordance with their own traditions of teaching (4:20f.). The use of the (synagogue's) domestic code in 5:22–6:9 serves the same purpose.

We can assume the same setting and purpose for the corresponding deutero-Pauline passages of Colossians (1:9–23; 2:19; 3:15*b*–4:1); these call for harmony and (following Paul himself: 3:5–11) enjoin the same 'synagogue' morality of the domestic codes. Philemon was included in this collection since, in keeping with this purpose, it provided a clear example of this moral teaching.

If Colossians thus includes Ephesians' central theme as a subsidiary theme of its own, the anti-Gnostic polemic characteristic of the deutero-Pauline Colossians is, on the other hand, almost entirely lacking from Ephesians; but not quite entirely as 4:12–14 (cf. Colossians 2:8), 20f. and 5:6ff. in particular show. The repeated references to the apostolic foundation of the one church (2:20; 3:5, 7; 4:11f.) may also have an anti-enthusiastic thrust. Because of the striking distinction between 'Christ' and 'Jesus' in 4:20f., H. Schlier [20] sees here a reference 'to a Gnosis which separates Christ and Jesus, as with the Gnostics opposed in 1 John and by Ignatius of Antioch'.

Taken in conjuction with parallel statements in Colossians, other statements in Ephesians may also be interpreted as having a deliberate anti-Gnostic purpose. That is especially true of the anti-dualistic statement that *all* was created and redeemed (through Christ): 1:10; 3:9; cf. 3:15. It is likewise true of the emphasis on the dethroning and subjecting of all powers (1:20ff.; 3:10; cf. 2:2; 6:12) and of the description of redemption as the forgiveness of sins through Christ's blood (1:17; 2:5, 13f., 16; 5:2, 25). Here, consciously or unconsciously, Gnostic terminology is used (1:8f.,

17f.; 3:10; 4:13; 5:5, 17). In 3:10 too we seem to have a deliberate anti-Gnostic polemic in the statement that God's plan of salvation has now for the first time been made known to the (demonic) world-powers (cf. 1:20ff.; 2:2; 6:12) *by the church*.

The interweaving of the two themes, the unity of the church and the anti-Gnostic polemic, in both Ephesians and Colossians suggests that the latter theme was also made necessary by the predicament of the *'aposunagōgos'*.

In Colossians, it will be recalled, we saw how its anti-Gnostic polemic was not in response to any acute threat posed by the activity of Gnostic missionaries. The same is true of the less obtrusive polemical utterances of Ephesians.

In that case the anti-Gnostic polemic of the two letters was occasioned by the position of the *'aposunagōgos'* in one of two ways: either representatives of a Jewish-Christian Gnosis were barred from the synagogue and came to the attention of the deutero-Pauline author of the letters, or the unity of (post-) Pauline Christianity and of a Christianity based on the synagogue, a unity propounded by the author of Ephesians and Colossians, was opposed by more enthusiastic members of the Pauline churches.

In the former case the polemic would be directed against a markedly Jewish-Christian Gnosis. That is not the case here. Above all, the Gnostics seem to have protested at the acceptance of the moral teaching of the synagogue (4:19ff.; 5:6f.), even if there are no clear libertine traits of the false teachers to be detected.

Therefore the second suggestion is preferable. The situation created by the circumstances of the *'aposunagōgos'* necessitated a re-forming of the churches and led to reflection on the dogmatic basis of the unified church thus created (4:12–14). In this respect it led to a conflict with Gnosis or the Gnosticizing wing of the Pauline churches. The 'Catholic' church increasingly rejected all traces of Gnosis. It is the considerable proportion of Gnostic terms and ideas in the language of the deutero-Pauline author of Ephesians and Colossians which shows that the repudiation of Gnostic ideas was a later process. Earlier these various traditions must have been relatively close to one another.

NOTES

1. R. McL. Wilson, *Gnosis and the New Testament*, Oxford 1968, 55.
2. 'Die gnostischen Elemente im Neuen Testament als hermeneutisches Problem' in (ed.) K.-W. Tröger, *Gnosis und Neues Testament*, Berlin 1973, 359–381; 'Zur Herkunft der gnostischen Elemente in der Sprache des Paulus' in (ed.) B. Aland, *Gnosis: Festschrift für H. Jonas*, Göttingen 1978, 385–414; *Die theologische Anthropologie des Paulus*, Stuttgart 1980.
3. *A Paraphrase and Annotations upon ... the New Testament*, London 1653.

4. *Institutiones historiae ecclesiasticae Novi Testamenti*, Frankfurt/ Leipzig 1726.

5. *Entwurf einer vollständigen Historie der Ketzereien* ..., Leipzig 1762–1785.

6. *Einleitung in die göttlichen Schriften des Neuen Bundes*, Göttingen 1750, 1788[4].

7. *An Inquiry into the Heresies of the Apostolic Age*, Oxford 1829.

8. D. Schenkel, *De ecclesia Corinthia primaeva factionibus turbata*, Basel 1838; A. Schlatter, *Die korinthische Theologie*, BFChTh 18:2, Gütersloh 1914; F. Godet, *Commentaire sur la première épître aux Corinthiens*, Neuchâtel 1886–7.

9. These exceptions include H.-M. Schenke, K. M. Fischer, *Einleitung in die Schriften des Neuen Testaments* I, Gütersloh 1978, 43ff., 82ff., 95f., 128, 146; E. E. Ellis, 'Paul and His Opponents' in *Prophecy and Hermeneutics in Early Christianity*, Tübingen 1978, 80–115; G. Lüdemann, 'Zum Antipaulinismus im frühen Christentum', *EvTh* 40, 1980, 437–455.

10. *Freiheitspredigt und Schwarmgeister in Korinth*, BFChTh 12:3, Gütersloh 1908; *Die Volkommenen im Philipperbrief und die Enthusiasten in Thessalonich*, BFChTh 13:6, Gütersloh 1909; *Der Römerbrief als historisches Problem*, BFChTh 17:2, Gütersloh 1913; *Gesetz und Geist: Untersuchung zur Vorgeschichte des Galaterbriefes*, BFChTh 23:6, Gütersloh 1919.

11. *Gnosticism in Corinth*, Nashville 1971; ET of 1956; *Paul and the Gnostics*, Nashville 1972; ET of 1965.

12. P. Vielhauer, *Geschichte der urchristlichen Literatur*, Berlin/New York 1975, 119.

13. R. McL. Wilson, 'Gnostics – in Galatia?' *StEv* 4 = *TU* 102, Berlin 1968, 367.

14. H.-M. Schenke, K. M. Fischer, op. cit. (n. 9), 46f.

15. *The Singular Problem of Galatians*, HThS 14, Cambridge, Mass. 1929.

16. R. McL. Wilson, loc. cit. (n. 13), 358–367.

17. Ibid., 365.

18. Op. cit. (n. 1), 43; cf. 55, 58.

19. C. H. Weisse, *Philosophische Dogmatik* I, Leipzig 1855, 146, and *Beiträge zur Kritik der paulinischen Briefe* ..., Leipzig 1867, 59f.; F. Hitzig, *Zur Kritik paulinischer Briefe*, Leipzig 1870, 22f., 26; H. J. Holtzmann, *Kritik der Epheser- und Kolosserbriefe*, Leipzig 1872; O. Pfleiderer, *Der Paulinismus*, Leipzig 1873, 370f.; C. Masson, *L'épître de Saint Paul aux Colossiens*, CNT (N) 10, Neuchâtel 1950, 159; P. Benoit, 'L'hymne christologique de Colossiens 1, 15–20' in (ed.) J. Neusner, *Christianity, Judaism and Other Greco-Roman Cults: Studies for Morton Smith at Sixty*, SJLA 12, Leiden 1975, 226–263, esp. 254.

20. *Der Brief an die Epheser: Ein Kommentar*, Düsseldorf 1957, 217.

IX

GNOSIS AND THE APOCALYPSE OF JOHN

by

Professor C. K. Barrett, Durham

An invitation to contribute to this *Festschrift*, and thus to have the pleasure and privilege of a share in the honouring of an old and good friend, was not to be refused. A request however to write on Gnosticism in relation to the Johannine literature was another matter, for several reasons. In the first place, who knows so much about Gnosticism and the Fourth Gospel as Robin Wilson? To write on such a subject in a volume dedicated to him could only make the writer look a fool. In the second place, fool or not, I have already written on the subject, and would have little that is really fresh to say; moreover, my own immediate interests have moved on from John to Acts. It occurred to me that I might go on to consider the Johannine Epistles instead of the Gospel. There would be not a little to be said for this, but the epistles do not offer an untouched field, and where for example Dodd[1] and Bultmann[2] have reaped it is unlikely that much will be left for the gleaner. It might however have been interesting to see how, and if, ideas and relationships that have been detected in the first epistle are reflected in the practical circumstances disclosed by the second and third. It seems that, at this period, theological issues connected with Gnosticism (Jesus Christ coming in the flesh; 2 John 7) evoked strong ecclesiastical measures (2 John 9–11; 3 John 9f.). I decided however to take the bull by the horns and deal with a subject which, so far as I know, has been less frequently discussed: Gnosis and the Book of Revelation. At first sight the relation between the two may seem to be nil, but the matter may prove worthy of consideration.

A moment's reflection is, in fact, sufficient to show that the topic is a reasonable one. It is a cheering thought that in *Gnosis and the New Testament* (Oxford 1968) Dr Wilson's references to Revelation seem to be limited to a consideration of the question whether various Gnostic documents quote or allude to the book – an important question to which we shall return but one that is not sufficient to determine the relation between the thought of Revelation (and of Apocalyptic in general) and Gnosticism.

A second preliminary observation is that there seems to have existed a Johannine school, community, or circle,[3] of which John the Divine, the author of Revelation, was a member, and that if some members of the circle were deeply implicated in the beginnings of the Gnostic movement it is unlikely that John the Divine should have had no contact with it at all.

Again, there is a relation of some kind (on which study of Revelation may throw light) between Apocalyptic and Gnosticism. In an early study of Gnosticism[4] F. C. Burkitt took the view that the developing Christian Gnosticism of the second century was intended in part to replace the no longer credible eschatological mythology of Apocalyptic. '... "Chiliasm" had begun to fade into the background of the Christian consciousness. In the East the Apocalypse of John was already dropping out of favour, and documents such as the Apocalypse of Peter began to take its place, documents in which attention was concentrated on the state of good and bad souls immediately after death, rather than on a general resurrection at an anticipated return of Christ to earth with attendant rewards and punishments' (op. cit., 90f.). This view is open to criticism as perhaps an over-simplification of the facts. It has given place in some more recent studies to a more positive understanding of the relation between Apocalyptic and Gnosticism. This was powerfully put by R. M. Grant,[5] though he too begins from the view that disappointed Apocalypticism was one source of Gnosticism. What were Jewish believers to do when predictions not merely that Jews would become the rulers of the world but that their city and temple would remain inviolate were proved false? 'Faith was shaken in God, his covenant, his law, and his promises. Out of such shaking, we should claim, came the impetus toward Gnostic ways of thinking, doubtless not for the first time with the fall of Jerusalem but reinforced by this catastrophe' (op. cit., 34). 'When his predictions were not realized, the apocalypticist of the first century had several options. (1) He could postpone the time of fulfillment and rewrite his apocalypse; such revisions were actually made. (2) He could abandon his religion entirely. (3) He could look for escape rather than victory, and could then reinterpret his sacred writings in order to show that the revelation had been misunderstood. It would appear that most Gnostic teachers did reinterpret not only the Old Testament but also some of the apocalyptic writings or their ingredients' (op. cit., 35).

Later, Dr Grant brings out specific connections between Apocalyptic and Gnosticism. 'Origen suggests that a Gnostic doctrine known to Celsus came from the book of Enoch [Orig., Cels. v, 52, 54]; in Pistis Sophia we read that the Books of Ieu were written by Enoch in paradise [Pist. Soph. 99, 134]; and the later Manichees and Bogomils used both 1 Enoch and 2 Enoch [See also Söderberg, La religion des Cathares, 130, n. 1, 131]. The Ascension of Isaiah, part of which may have originated at Qumran [D. Flusser, 'The Apocryphal Book of Ascensio Isaiae and the Dead Sea Sect,' Israel Exploration Journal 3 (1953), 30–47], was used by the Archontics [Epiphanius, Haer. 40, 2:2]. More significant is the way in which the apocalypse form flourished in various Gnostic sects. Many of the books found at Nag-Hammadi are apocalypses – one of Adam to Seth, one of Dositheus, one of Sêêm or the Great Seth. The Gnostic Justin wrote a book called Baruch, presumably because he knew something of the tradition in which revelations were ascribed to the Old Testament personage (though for Justin Baruch has become an angel). [Note that Irenaeus, *Haer*. II, 24:2 (Harvey 336) regards Baruch as the name of God]' (op. cit., 41f.).[6] This clear and positive relation between Apocalyptic and Gnosticism has been recently supported by Christopher Rowland.[7] 'Knowing one's origins and destiny is just as much a concern of apocalyptic as [of] gnosticism, though in the former this knowledge has not yet become in itself a means of salvation' (op. cit., 21). It may be that Revelation has something to contribute here (see below, pp. 134f.).[8]

Finally among preliminary observations we should note that Revelation is the first Christian book to refer by name to a Gnostic sect or group. At 2:6,15 it refers to the Nicolaitans, who were evidently active at Ephesus and at Pergamum. It seems probable that the teaching of Balaam (2:14) and Jezebel the false prophetess (2:20) were connected with the same erroneous doctrine and that this included *ta bathea tou satana* (2:24); see further below. It is of course clear that the author of Revelation looked on this sect and its teaching with severe disfavour. This is not to say that he was necessarily uninfluenced by it. His colleague, the author of the Fourth Gospel, was both Gnostic and anti-Gnostic,[9] and there is no reason why John the Divine should not have shared this double attitude. In any case the Gnostic movement existed in his environment, and action and reaction must have been inevitable.

It is at this point that we may begin to make a more particular study of Revelation and its relation to Gnosticism. Who were the Nicolaitans?[10] The short, and correct, answer is: we do not know. Patristic statements rest upon the references in Revelation, helped out by the conjecture[11] that the sect of Nicolaitans was founded by the Nicolas of Acts 6. Thus Irenaeus, *Haer*. I, 26:3: The Nicolaitans are the followers of that Nicolas who was one of the seven first ordained to the diaconate by the apostles. They lead lives of unrestrained indulgence. The character of these men is very plainly pointed out in the Apocalypse of John, as teaching that it is a matter of indifference to practise adultery, and to eat things sacrificed to idols. Wherefore the Word has also spoken of them thus: 'But this thou hast that thou hatest the deeds of the Nicolaitans, which I also hate.' *Haer*. III, 11:1 adds nothing of substance to this, nor do other patristic writers, except that Clement of Alexandria does his best to save the reputation of Nicolas (*Strom*. III, 4:25; Eusebius, *Hist. Eccl*. III, 29:1–4).

Since the fathers seem to have had no information about the Nicolaitans that we do not ourselves have we turn to the passages in Revelation. The first, 2:6, tells us only that their works were, in the writer's opinion, odious. The second, 2:15, compares the teaching of the Nicolaitans with that of Balaam, who taught Balak to put a stumblingblock before the children of Israel; this consisted (taking the infinitive *phagein* to be epexegetical of *skandalon*) in leading them to eat food sacrificed to idols and to commit fornication. This suggests a further parallel in 2:20 in the woman Jezebel, who calls herself a prophetess and teaches my servants to commit fornication and to eat food sacrificed to idols. The combination of food sacrificed to idols and fornication recalls the so-called Apostolic Decree (Acts 15:20, 29; 21:25) and the Old Testament allusion in 1 Corinthians 10:6–10. The letter to Thyatira speaks also of those who claim to have knowledge of *ta bathea tou satana*, which was evidently a current phrase (*hōs legousin*, 2:24). This is important because it points in a Gnostic direction[12] and suggests that the action of the Nicolaitans, which John condemns, arose not out of mere licentiousness but out of false doctrine, indeed out of a kind of Satanology. The phrase is commonly interpreted in one of two ways.[13] It is sometimes claimed that the author deliberately perverted what the persons in question said. They professed to know the deep things of God (cf. 1 Corinthians 2:10); John the Divine countered: Deep things of Satan I call them. This is not impossible; compare for example the Old Testament substitution of *bōšet* for *ba'al*,[14] and, perhaps a better comparison, Colossians 2:8, where the writer appears to mean something like 'philosophy – empty deceit I call it'. Nevertheless this interpretation does not seem to do justice to *hōs legousin*. The usual alternative is to suppose that the Jezebelites (no doubt Nicolaitans) took the view that Christians should be aware by personal participation of the idolatrous worship and practice that went on around them. Given that heathen sacrifice and temple prostitution were the work of demons it was proper that Christians – who of course could not be harmed by the demons because they were protected by gnosis or sacraments or both – should know by experience what the demons were doing. They might safely eat idolatrous food and practise fornication, discover the deep things of Satan, and so beat him at his own game. This could have been represented as a logical step beyond Paulinism, though it involved a step that Paul refused to take. He went along with his Corinthians in accepting the argument that since both food and the organs that digest it are alike on the way to destruction Christians were bound by no food laws (1 Corinthians 6:12f.; 8:1, 4; 10:23, 25, 27), but he declined to draw a parallel conclusion regarding fornication, since sexual union is not (though it may appear so) the work of one organ but the action of the *sōma*, the whole human person, who is to be united to Christ. It could have been argued against Paul, how can we know the power of Christ to keep the body that has been united to him if it is never exposed to fornication? Or, how can sexual relations any more than eating affect the non-material spirit, which is all that matters?

These interpretations of *ta bathea tou satana*, especially the second, must be allowed to be possible, but I doubt whether either is satisfactory. Knowing the deep things of Satan is a boast, a claim of which certain people are proud; it seems to imply that Satan is one with whom it is well to be acquainted. In some of the later Gnostic systems the name Satan appears among the aeons and emanations.[15] There is however a good deal more to say than this.

The Nicolaitans are compared with Balaam (Revelation 2:14f.; the *houtōs* at the beginning of 2:15 connects Balaam's practice with the teaching of the Nicolaitans, thereby suggesting that teaching as the basis of immoral practice is what is common to the two). This calls to mind two other New Testament passages, which are undoubtedly related to each other: Jude 11 (They went in the way of Cain and for the sake of reward abandoned themselves to Balaam's error) and 2 Peter 2:15 (They left the straight path and went astray, following the way of Balaam the son of Bosor, who loved the reward of unrighteousness). The persons in question here appear to practise moral licence (possibly appealing to Paul's example, 2 Peter 3:15f.). Their free attitude to angels and other authorities (Jude 8; 2 Peter 2:10, 11) may be connected with the claim to know the deep things of Satan. Their questioning of the Parousia (2 Peter 3:4) has been connected[16] with a statement attributed to Hippolytus, in which it is alleged that Nicolas was the first to assert that the resurrection had already happened; he understood by 'resurrection' that 'we believe in Christ and receive the washing', but denied a resurrection of the flesh.

The name Satan occurs five times in the Seven Letters (2:9, 13(*bis*), 24; 3:9); subsequently in Revelation three times (12:9; 20:2, 7). In the first two of these Satan is explicitly identified with *ho drakōn, ho ophis ho archaios*. This means that we may reasonably expect to find a connection between those who profess to know the depths of Satan and the sect known as the Ophites (or Naassenes, the alternative name being derived from *naḥaš*, serpent; cf. also the Cainites, noting Jude 11).[17] The snake is not only a widespread religious symbol; it recalls the myth of Genesis 3, where the snake is the being who encourages man to take (what is thought to be) life-giving knowledge by eating the fruit of the forbidden tree. The snake thus becomes man's champion against the jealous God of the Old Testament who wishes to deny man knowledge; the patron saint, as it were, of Gnostics.[18]

There is no space in this paper, nor would it be relevant, to pursue the little that is known of the later history of Ophites, Nicolaitans, Cainites, and Carpocratians. It is enough to observe that there seems good reason to believe that early Gnostic groups existed in Asia Minor when Revelation was written. Their doctrine was antinomian; John the Divine was aware of it, and fought against it.

This leads to the questions that this paper must answer if its existence in this *Festschrift* is to be justified. Is Revelation simply a work opposed to the Gnostic movement? Does it have any positive relevance to the study of that movement?

There are several ways in which this question may be approached. We may ask, for example, what the Christian Gnostic heretics of the second century and later made of Revelation as a book. The answer to this question appears to be, Not very much. Dr Wilson, in *Gnosis and the New Testament* (above, p. 125), draws attention to the following passages.[19]

The Apocalypse of Adam 78:18–26:
> The third kingdom says of him that he came from a virgin
> womb. He was cast out of his city, he and his mother; he was

brought to a desert place. He was nourished there. He came and received glory and power. And thus he came to the water.

On this passage Dr Wilson (op. cit., 67f., 138) notes Böhlig's suggestion that there may be a reference to Revelation 12:5, or to its mythological background. His conclusion is cautious: 'In short, while we may perhaps suspect an allusion to Revelation 12:5 in the Apocalypse of Adam, we cannot be certain; we have to make allowance for the possibility of other influences' (op. cit., 68). No doubt it is wise to be cautious. When however the context is considered the repeated references to the child's mother as a virgin suggest, though they do not prove, that the author was a Christian,[20] and 78:9–14 (And a bird came, took the child who was born and brought him onto a high mountain. And he was nourished by the bird of heaven. An angel came forth there) adds to the possible parallels with Revelation 12 (v. 5, *hērpasthē*; 14, *hai duo pteruges tou aetou tou megalou*; 7, *ho Michaēl*)

The Apocryphon of John 2:16–20:
> Now [I have come to teach] you what is [and what was] and what will come to [pass], that [you may know the] things which are not revealed [and the things which are revealed, and to teach] you the [... about the] perfect [Man].

Cf. Revelation 1:19.

4:21, 22:
> This is the spring of the water of life which gives to [all] the aeons and in every form.

Cf. Revelation 22:1.

As far as these parallels are concerned (those alleged with other parts of the New Testament are not under consideration here) it is impossible not to share much of Dr Wilson's scepticism. 'Even such allusions [to the New Testament] as have been detected must be considered doubtful' (op. cit., 105).

The Sophia of Jesus Christ 111:16–20:
> And [the] gods of the gods by their wisdom revealed gods. By their wisdom they revealed lords. And the lords of the lords revealed lords by their thinking.

Dr Wilson (op. cit., 115), writing before the complete publication of the texts, refers to the titles 'God of gods' and 'King of kings', and notes that these 'may reflect knowledge of Revelation 17:14; 19:16'. One must now be even more cautious in drawing any conclusion about a literary relation here.

This is not a complete list of references to Revelation, and of course Dr Wilson does not suggest that it is. Nor will any such claim be made in the present brief discussion. A few passages, however, are interesting enough to add, especially a group from the Gospel of Truth. Of these the first is the most important.

The Gospel of Truth 19:34–20:14:
> There was revealed in their heart the living book of the living – the one written in the thought and the mind [of the] Father, and which from before the foundation of the all was within the incomprehensible (parts) of him – that (book) which no one was able to take since it is reserved for the one who will take it and will be slain. No one could have appeared among those who believed in salvation unless that book had intervened. For this reason the merciful one, the faithful one, Jesus, was patient in accepting sufferings until he took that book, since he knows that his death is life for many.

This passage recalls especially Revelation 5, in which the author laments that no one is found worthy to open the sealed book. He is cheered by the elder who tells him that the Lion of the tribe of Judah, the Root of David, has conquered so as to open the book and its seven seals. He looks, and sees not a lion but a lamb standing as though slain. The Lamb's victory leads to the ascriptions of praise that fill the rest of the chapter. Other chapters in Revelation refer to the book, described as the book of life, sometimes as the Lamb's book of life (3:5; 13:8; 17:8; 20:12, 15; 21:27). Sometimes the Lamb is said to have been slain from the foundation of the world (13:8; cf. 17:8). At Revelation 19:11 the rider on the white horse is said to be faithful and true. Cf. also Gos. Truth 21:23: He enrolled them in advance.

26:2–4:
> It is a drawn sword, with two edges, cutting on either side.

Cf. Revelation 2:12; also 2:16; 19:15.

32:27–30:
> ... from the day from above, which has no night, and from the light which does not sink because it is perfect.

This recalls, somewhat distantly, Revelation 22:5.

39:15–20:
> But the one who exists exists also with his name, and he knows himself [or; he is the only one who knows it]. And to give himself a name is (the prerogative of) the Father. The Son is his name.

The Name is treated from 38:6 to 41:3. Cf. especially Revelation 19:12 (a name which no one knows but he himself).

42:18–22:
> ... nor have they envy nor groaning nor death within them, but they rest in him who is at rest.

This recalls Revelation 21:4; cf. 7:17; 20:14.

It seems very probable that the author of the Gospel of Truth had read Revelation and occasionally recalled its language. We cannot say so much of any other Gnostic author though from time to time there are hints of possible acquaintance.[21] It would be rash to claim too much, but it is probably safe to say that Gnostic writers did not regard Revelation as an anti-Gnostic work.[22] Their attitude to Apocalyptic as a form of literature and theology is perhaps best indicated by the fact that in the Nag Hammadi Library five works are described as apocalypses (of Paul, first of James, second of James, of Adam, of Peter; possibly we should add Zostrianos). The fact is important, though Yvonne Janssens may exaggerate when she writes,[23] 'What is very clear is that the Gnostics had a fondness for the literary *genre* of Apocalyptic (at least a fifth of the Nag Hammadi library is "apocalypses"!), doubtless to aid the presentation of their teaching. The form of these apocalypses is in general, I think, near enough to Judaeo-Christian Apocalyptic. Yet there is a difference in the secret which is often entrusted to the seer and which cannot be revealed except to chosen Gnostics or fellow "spiritual" persons.'[24] This minimizes the difference between the Gnostic and other apocalypses, which is considerable. It remains, however, true that the Gnostics did not avoid apocalyptic on principle; a corresponding truth is that the great anti-Gnostic writers, notably Irenaeus and Hippolytus, use Apocalyptic (quoting Revelation freely) not to rebut the arguments of the Gnostics but to describe the unpleasant destiny in store for them.[25]

A second approach to the question before us is by way of analogy. Revelation is a Christian work with deep roots in Judaism. Does non-Christian Judaism provide us with information about the relation between Apocalyptic and Gnosticism?

It need not be said that Apocalyptic, though taken up and to a great extent preserved in Christian circles, is a Jewish phenomenon, with origins in the Old Testament. It has too often been treated as a singular line of development unrelated to other movements in Judaism and calling for separate treatment. That this is an error was long ago decisively demonstrated by W. D. Davies in relation to rabbinic Judaism. In his still important article of over thirty years ago[26] Dr Davies made three points. (1) 'In its piety and in its attitude to the Torah Apocalyptic was at one with Pharisaism' (op. cit., 22). (2) 'There is a community of eschatological doctrine between the Pharisees and the Apocalyptists' (op. cit., 23). Dr Davies mentions Akiba's championing of the cause of Bar Kokba, and comments, 'Nothing could more point to the reality of eschatological beliefs among the Rabbis and to the falsity of the customary distinction between fanatic Apocalypticism and sober orthodoxy' (ibidem). (3) 'The view is to be suspected that Apocalyptic stands for a popular interest, while Pharisaism is "scholastic". By its very nature Apocalyptic is a gnosis meant for the initiated: it dealt with visions given to the elect: it had an esoteric character however much its ideas might be diffused by preachers like the *'ober gᵉlila'ah'* (op. cit., 24).[27] It is no doubt true that in this passage Dr Davies is not using the word 'gnosis' in the narrow sense, that is, with reference to what is commonly understood by the Gnostic movement; it remains significant, and may in fact lead beyond the point that Dr Davies himself was concerned to make. For the main content of Pharisaism, of academic Judaism, is not a private gnosis but a legal system practised in the courts and taught openly by public instruction. It presupposes the existence of an intellectual élite, but the only limitations imposed upon its dissemination were the inward limitations of mental capacity. Pharisaism, Rabbinism, did however have a mystical element, frowned upon,[28] but in fact contributing significantly to the development of Judaism. 'Nun ist bekannt, dass die leitenden Kreise der alten Synagoge allezeit mit einem gewissen Argwohn über der Reinerhaltung des monotheistischen Gottesgedankens gewacht haben. Aber trotz aller Vorsicht drangen gnostische Irrlehren selbst in die Kreise der Schriftgelehrten ein.'[29] For the connection between such speculations, mystical experiences, and apocalyptic, it is perhaps sufficient to quote the fundamental Mishnah text.[30]

Chagigah 2:1:
> The forbidden degrees may not be expounded before three persons, nor the Story of Creation before two, nor [the chapter of] the Chariot before one alone, unless he is a Sage that understands of his own knowledge. Whosoever gives his mind to four things it were better for him if he had not come into the world – what is above? what is beneath? what was beforetime? and what will be hereafter?

There is no space here for a full discussion of the matter, but there is much to support the conclusion recently drawn by Dr Rowland: 'While fully accepting the problems presented by the rabbinic material and the dangers of building too much on an insecure foundation, it seems to me that there was probably an essential continuity between the religious outlook of the apocalypticists and that of the earliest exponents of *merkabah*-mysticism among the rabbis. Both seem to bear witness to the possibility that the study of Scripture could, in certain instances, lead to direct apprehension of the divine world' (op. cit., 444; see also 306–348).

This conclusion, that in Judaism there is a kinship and propinquity between Apocalyptic and the sort of mystical speculation that is one, and indeed a major, component among the phenomena of Gnosticism, will lead to one more observation.

This may begin from the fact that there is at least some contact between Revelation and the chapter of the Chariot (Ezekiel 1; cf. also 8; 10) which rabbinic Judaism handled with such caution. The following parallels, some clearer than others, are worth noting.

Revelation	Ezekiel
1:13	1:26
1:15	1:24
1:17	1:28
4:2	1:26
4:3	1:27f.
4:5	1:13
4:6	1:5,18,22; 10:12
4:7	1:10
4:8	1:18; 10:12
8:5	10:2

These parallels, though of varying weight, are sufficient to show that the Chariot vision was familiar to John and that he wrote with it in mind.[31] The Old Testament picture of the Garden of Eden is also used to supply some of the imagery of Revelation.[32] These observations could, of course, have no more than literary significance, but in the circumstances of the first century it is unlikely that the material had no deeper meaning. John stands within a tradition that combined mystical and apocalyptic-eschatological elements.

John's world-view, and not least his imaginative understanding of God, have not a little in common with developed Gnosticism. The universe is controlled by good and evil hierarchies of spiritual beings. There is indeed one God, of whom little can be said save that he is *ho ōn kai ho ēn kai ho erchomenos* (1:4) – an expression (intentionally) beyond both declining and construing. But this God shares his throne[33] with another, a slain lamb (5:6). In the vicinity of the throne are twenty-four elders, four living creatures, and seven spirits. Except that they are not provided with names they recall the aeons and emanations that stand between the ineffable Gnostic God and creation.[34] There are corresponding evil powers, which fortunately this paper need not attempt to sort out or arrange in order: the snake, the dragon, the devil, Satan, the beast, another beast, the great harlot, the false prophet, an assortment of demons.

Again, in both Gnosticism and Revelation salvation consists in the ultimate separation of two sets of beings. 'If anyone was not found written in the book of life he was cast into the lake of fire' (20:15; cf. 21:8; 22:3–5,14,15). It is true that there is a marked difference here. The elect whose destiny is to be in the city of God are what they are, not because of an innate pneumatic purity, but because they have washed their robes and made them white in the blood of the Lamb (7:14). Even among them, however, there appears to be an élite group who manifest a radical opposition to the flesh in that they are celibates: the 144,000 who follow the Lamb wherever he goes and who alone can learn the new song which they sing before the throne (14:1–5). And it is of course true that Revelation is about the unveiling of secrets. I quoted above (p. 127) words of Dr Rowland's; they may be said to call for an addition in the light of Revelation 5:5. After the letters to the seven churches the main substance of Revelation is introduced by the visions of chapters 4 and 5. Chapter 4 opens with the vision of the throne of God. God himself does not appear, but the various beings mentioned above surround the throne, and from it proceed thunders and lightnings. The Living Creatures sing the Trisagion (4:8), and the Elders, Worthy art thou (4:11). Next is introduced the sealed book (5:1–4), which is either the book of the living (that is, the saved), or the book of human destiny, which will include the names of the saved; and it is only the slain Lamb, who occupies the throne of God (5:6), who is able to open the book. It is the opening of its seals (6:1, 3, 5, 7, 9, 12; 8:1, leading to the seven angels, and so on) that sets the story of salvation in motion. The *style* of Revelation is to say: When the Lamb opened the first seal, I saw ... and I heard ... . The *style* of Gnosis would be to quote the contents of chapter 1 of the book, but the underlying sense is the same. Salvation consists in the fact that the Lion of the tribe of Judah, the Root of David, has overcome so as to open the book and thus disclose its contents.[35]

If any general conclusion is to be drawn from this paper, in which it has been impossible to study the contents of Revelation as a whole, it must be that the religious thought of the early Christian period constitutes a very complicated story. The sharp lines that are often drawn between law and mysticism, Hellenism and Judaism, Gnosticism and Apocalyptic, may possess a measure of didactic convenience, but they run the risk of fostering serious error. How did the mind of John the Divine work? That he abhorred idolatry (which for him, though not for Paul, was necessarily involved in eating *eidōlothuta*) and sexual and other kinds of immorality is clear. But he could fall into a trance (1:10) and see many visions; and he regarded his book as having infallible and incontestable authority (22:6,18,19); it would not be wrong to say that it contained the true gnosis. To know this secret revelation was the way to blessedness (1:3; 22:7). Not that reading it would benefit any but the elect; the time for conversion was past (22:11). He wrote Apocalyptic.[36] This meant however that there was revealed to him the truth about God and human destiny which is now visible in the heavenly world and is to become universally known, truth by which those who can receive it live; and what is this but Gnosticism? Certainly there is a great difference in emphasis. Apocalyptic, including the Johannine Apocalypse, is interested in the mysterious unfolding of history, which it sets against a clear time-scale. It builds upon the sacred books of the past, noting which of their prophecies had already been fulfilled and which retained predictive force. It is thus not a flight from history, as some have maintained[37] and as Gnosticism is: salvation happens for the people of God in, though at the end of, history. To become Christian, Gnosticism has to be historicized; this is not necessary for Apocalyptic since it already has a necessary historical element. To become Christian, Apolcalyptic has to give a share in God's throne to the slain Lamb, concerning itself with the middle of history as well as its end. This John has done; whether he has worked out all the implications of this move, and whether his myths need demythologizing, are further questions. Perhaps this was the point at which his colleague in the Johannine Circle thought it necessary to write a gospel.

NOTES

1. *The Johannine Epistles, MNTC*, London 1946.
2. *Die drei Johannesbriefe, KEK*, Göttingen 1967.
3. See, among a number of works, O. Cullmann, *Der johanneische Kreis*, Tübingen 1975; R. E. Brown, *The Community of the Beloved Disciple*, London 1979.
4. *Church and Gnosis*, Cambridge 1932.
5. *Gnosticism and Early Christianity*, New York 1959. Cf. O. Cullmann, *Le Problème littéraire et historique du roman pseudo-clémentin*, Paris 1930, 201: 'L'apocalyptique peut être considérée comme un côté particulier du gnosticisme'; also G. Kretschmar, in *RGG*³ II, 1657.
6. Material in square brackets is given by Grant in footnotes.
7. *The Open Heaven*, London 1982.
8. A notable supporter of a very different view was A. Schlatter. See *Die Theologie des Neuen Testaments*, 2. Teil, Calw and Stuttgart 1910, especially 138–142 ('Der Johanneische Dualismus'), 142–3 ('Die Johanneische Metaphysik'), and, with special reference to Jezebel and the Nicolaitans, *The Church in the New Testament Period*, London 1955, 293–5. H. Conzelmann, *Grundriss der Theologie des Neuen Testaments*, Munich 1967, 347–8, sets Apocalyptic and Gnosis over against each other as respectively right-wing and left-wing ways of expressing 'die Jenseitigkeit des Heils'.
9. C. K. Barrett, *Essays on John*, London 1982, 128–130.
10. A. Hilgenfeld, *Die Ketzergeschichte des Urchristentums*, repr. Hildesheim 1963, 408–11, is still a valuable collection of material. See also 250–77, 'Die ophitischen Häresien'.
11. N. Brox, *VigChr* 19, 1965, 23–30 (especially 30) thinks it more than conjecture.
12. See the opposite view in W. Bousset, *Die Offenbarung Johannis, KEK*, Göttingen 1906, 237 – not 'eine ausgebildete gnostische Schule'.
13. Clearly set out by R. H. Charles, *The Revelation of St John, ICC*, Edinburgh 1920, I, 73f. See also H. Schlier, *Bathos, ThWNT* I, 515f.
14. So Jeremiah 3:24; 11:13; Hosea 9:10; and in compounds.
15. For example in the scheme of Justin the Gnostic, Hipp., *Ref.* V, 26:4.
16. R. Seeberg, *Lehrbuch der Dogmengeschichte* I, Leipzig and Erlangen 1920, 282–4.
17. See Hilgenfeld (n. 10).
18. Bibliography in *RGG*³ IV, 1659.
19. I have adjusted the references to those in *The Nag Hammadi Library in English*, translated under the direction of J. M. Robinson, Leiden 1977, and have used that translation.
20. See however G. W. MacRae in *The Nag Hammadi Library*, 256.
21. E.g., Gos. Thom. 32:10; 42:8–12; 43:12–23; 44:34, 35.
22. There were those who believed that the Gnostic Cerinthus wrote Revelation; see Eusebius, *Hist. Eccl.* VII, 25:2 (III, 28:2 has been taken to mean that Gaius taught that Cerinthus wrote Revelation, but this does not seem to be the meaning of the text). According to Grant,

Gnosticism (n. 5), 98, Cerinthian Gnosticism was based on 'Christian apocalyptic, primarily the Apocalypse of John'.

23. In (ed.) J. Lambrecht, *L'Apocalypse johannique et l'Apocalyptique dans le Nouveau Testament, BEThL* 53, Gembloux 1980, 75.
24. See Wilson (p. 125), 130–139; also Grant, quoted on pp. 126, 127.
25. E.g. Irenaeus, *Haer.* II, 31:3.
26. *ET* 59, 1948, 233–7; repr. in W. D. Davies, *Christian Origins and Judaism*, London 1962, 19–30.
27. See also the article by T. W. Manson in *Aux Sources de la tradition chrétienne, Mélanges offerts à M. Maurice Goguel*, Neuchâtel and Paris 1950, 139–145.
28. See the well-known passage about the four who 'entered into Paradise' (T. Chag. 2:3; b.Chag. 14*b*; j.Chag. 77*b*; conveniently given in synoptic form in Rowland, *Heaven*, 310–12).
29. Str.-B. II, 307.
30. On this passage, taken with Aboth 3:1, see W. D. Davies in *Christian History and Interpretation: Studies presented to John Knox*, Cambridge 1967, 150f.
31. See a much fuller discussion in I. Gruenwald, *Apocalyptic and Merkavah Mysticism, AGJU* 14, Leiden/Köln 1980, 62–9.
32. Revelation 2:7; 12:9, 17; 22:1, 2.
33. Whether any other being may be said to share the throne of God was precisely the disputed issue in mystical Judaism and the controversies it evoked.
34. Note however the use of Amen as a name at Revelation 3:14, and cf. Hipp., *Ref.* V, 26:3.
35. On the Gnostic side, cf. Burkitt (as in n. 4), 90: 'The Gnostics were, in the last resort, Christians and had no "explanation" for Jesus. He remained more real to them as a "Saviour" than the fantastic demonic organization from which they understood that He was saving them.'
36. I believe that there is a difference between Apocalyptic and Prophecy, and that John wrote Apocalyptic, but cannot go into the question here.
37. Rowland, *Heaven*, 445, is rightly cautious on this matter, but it is doubtful whether John the Divine and his associates had much opportunity to escape from reality.

X

PROLEGOMENA TO THE STUDY OF THE NEW TESTAMENT AND GNOSIS

by

Professor Frederik Wisse, Montreal

As Robert McL. Wilson was quick to realize, the discovery of the Nag Hammadi codices started a new era in the study of Gnosticism. Wilson has been one of the pioneers of this new era and his wise and cautious evaluation of the new material has been a major steadying factor in the last three decades of Nag Hammadi studies.

These years were characterized not only by a bewildering array of opinions based on a limited and often erroneous understanding of the texts, but also by the dominance of issues and assumptions which stem from the pre-Nag Hammadi era of Gnostic studies. It is only recently that scholarship has begun to free itself from the burden of inherited misconceptions and false assumptions.

It is now widely recognized that Jean Doresse's characterization of the Nag Hammadi codices as a Gnostic or even a Sethian-Gnostic library was unwarranted.[1] The original owners and users were more likely heterodox ascetics who had joined one of the Pachomian monasteries which had been founded during the first half of the fourth century C.E. near the present town of Nag Hammadi.[2] This means that the individual tractates can no longer be assumed to be Gnostic, but must be shown to be Gnostic on internal grounds alone. It is not enough to be able to claim that a writing can be read in a Gnostic way or that it seems to presuppose Gnostic ideas, for that can be said of many ancient writings which are clearly not Gnostic in origin. Thus a significant number of Nag Hammadi texts can no longer serve as primary evidence of Gnosticism. Since these include such well-known tractates as the Gospel of Thomas and the Gospel of Truth, the consequences for the relationship between the New Testament and Gnosis are considerable.[3] It will require a good deal of difficult and painful rethinking. Of course, we cannot exclude the possibility that some in this group of heterodox writings will eventually prove to be Gnostic; the

138

situation is that our present knowledge of Gnosticism in its various forms does not give us a secure basis to call them Gnostic. For the time being, they cannot be adduced as evidence for the claim that parallel concepts or arguments employed or refuted in the New Testament are Gnostic in origin.

Another far-reaching assumption made by Doresse concerning the Nag Hammadi codices should also be questioned. He took it for granted that the Gnostic books contained sacred, sectarian teachings.[4] Scholarship has generally followed him in this tempting assumption, in spite of the difficulties this posed.[5] Doresse's guess that the codices were the holy books of one sect became untenable as soon as the varied content of the collection became better known. Instead it was conjectured that the codices presented us with the sacred writings of a number of Gnostic sects which somehow had been collected for heresiological purposes[6] or for use by a person or persons with a remarkable eclectic taste.[7] Whatever be the case, the individual writings were thought to reflect the beliefs of distinct groups. Much scholarly effort was spent on assigning the tractates to specific sects mentioned by the Church Fathers such as the Valentinians, Sethians, Basilideans, Barbelo-Gnostics, Simonians, Ophites or Hermetics. The inconclusive and often conflicting results of those attempts should have been sufficient reason to question the starting assumption.

In this approach to the Nag Hammadi texts, scholars took their cue from the ancient Christian heresiologists, not realizing that these contemporary opponents of Gnosticism most likely knew little more about the exact origin and purpose of Gnostic literature than we do today. As I have argued elsewhere,[8] the tradition of picturing Gnostics as sectarians with distinctive doctrines goes back to Justin Martyr. For Justin the word *hairesis* may still have carried the meaning 'school' in the sense of a teacher who attracted a number of disciples or followers. Justin himself headed such a school in Rome and there can be little doubt that this applied also to Valentinus, Basilides, Ptolemy and Marcion. When such teachers were 'excommunicated' the result would not automatically be the birth of a sect characterized by a distinctive teaching at variance with emerging orthodoxy. This would only be the case if the conflict was basically doctrinal and if the teacher in question imposed an authority structure on his followers similar to the one in orthodoxy. We have good reasons to believe that this was seldom the case.

The real reason for the expulsion of some of the heads of 'schools' was more likely a conflict with the church authorities over the right to teach than over heresy. This may lie behind Tertullian's report that Valentinus left the church when he failed in his bid to become the bishop of Rome.[9] With his rival in the bishop's seat his position in the church became untenable. At the time that this happened Valentinus already had been an acclaimed teacher for many years, both in Alexandria and Rome;[10] it is unlikely that his teaching was orthodox before his break with the church and became heretical only afterwards. Rather it would appear that in the middle of the second century the bishop of Rome began to limit the freedom of the various 'schools' which had operated unchecked in the city up to that point, and which may have caused unrest among the believers as well as tension with the hierarchy. As a consequence Valentinus and Marcion were forced to leave, and their teaching which had been tolerated before was now declared heretical. Heresy at this point was not yet teaching which conflicted with official doctrine, but rather the distinctive teaching of persons who were no longer in communion with the church.

By bringing the teaching function under hierarchical control the foundation of orthodoxy had been laid.[11] It guaranteed a semblance of unity and continuity in teaching. However, since this development appears to have been the reason why Christian teachers like Valentinus broke with the church or were forced to leave, they would not be inclined to imitate this development. Valentinianism did not become another 'orthodoxy' with a stable set of doctrines and practices jealously guarded by a hierarchy; rather it continued the uncontrolled heterodox and tolerant situation which had existed in the Roman Church in the first half of the second century.

Since the drawing power of Valentinus, Marcion and other heresiarchs did not end with their expulsion, the need arose to discredit their teaching in the eyes of the orthodox faithful. Justin Martyr set the pattern for heresiological tradition by linking the heresiarchs of his time with the legendary figure of Simon Magus, who had been condemned by the apostle Peter himself, and who was now declared to be the originator of the tradition of falsehood. Justin's treatment implied the existence of a chain of sect leaders, each with his own heretical teaching and followers but somehow linked to his predecessors. Later heresiologists simply added their opponents to the established list and attributed similar sectarian characteristics to them.[12]

This is the view of heresy which Irenaeus inherited and which determined his description of the Gnostic individuals and literature which he knew at first hand. Apart from the catalogue of heresies which he incorporated in his *Adversus haereses*,[13] Irenaeus used 'commentaries of the disciples of Valentinus' and he 'conversed with some of them'.[14] There is no reason to doubt the accuracy of the reports of what he read and heard, but we have every reason to question the framework in which he places the new information. He took it for granted that the people who called themselves disciples of Valentinus must be members of a sect and that the books which they used must contain the normative teachings of the Valentinian sect.

How unlikely these assumptions are is evident from Irenaeus' own description. He is very much aware that the Gnostic commentaries and oral reports do not agree with the teachings of Valentinus and Ptolemy as reported in the catalogue of heresies. He is greatly frustrated by the 'instability of their teaching'. He laments that 'there are not two or three who agree on the same subject; but as to details and names they argue the opposite'.[15] This is exactly the same impression as is left on the modern reader of the Nag Hammadi texts. Even among the tractates which appear somehow to be related, such as the 'Sethian' group, there is no stable myth or technical vocabulary which can bring some order or unity in the bewildering diversity.[16] At times within a single tractate one can find seemingly contradictory statements and *muthologoumena*.[17]

Irenaeus thought he had an explanation for this. The catalogue of heresies which he inherited from previous heresiologists claimed that the Gnostic sects multiplied because all Gnostics want to be teachers and each wants to develop his own set of teachings.[18] This fits his understanding of the contrast between truth, which is characterized by unity, constancy and coherence, and falsehood, which is typified by diversity, discontinuity and incoherence.[19]

Thus, to account for the diversity among the teachings of the Valentinians, Irenaeus has to picture them as fragmented into different branches each with its own teaching.[20] Since he defined a sect in terms of a distinctive configuration of teachings, each Gnostic writing which did not conform to previously reported sectarian teaching was taken to be evidence of a new branch or sect.[21]

Modern interpreters of the Nag Hammadi texts face the same predicament. Apart from the Hermetic tractates in Codex VI, none of the tractates fits comfortably into the sect descriptions of the heresiologists. For those which have affinities with the ancient reports of the teachings of the Valentinians one would have to assume that they represent a previously unknown branch of the sect. This would be a continuation of the basic mistake that Irenaeus and his successors made. In order to account for heresiological reports and the Gnostic writings we must free ourselves from the model which pictures the Gnostics as members of sects and their writings as sectarian teaching.

Irenaeus himself furnishes us with a vivid picture of a 'Valentinian', Marcus the magician. This religious charlatan appears to have been an itinerant preacher who claimed to be an improvement on Valentinus.[22] His allegiance to Valentinus appears to have been little more than that he borrowed some ideas and *muthologoumena* from Valentinian writings. Irenaeus leaves the impression that Marcus and the other Gnostic wandering preachers did not establish sects but moved on after preying on Christian women for the sake of money and sex. Those who had been physically and/or spiritually seduced by them generally returned to the orthodox fold, greatly regretting their error and folly. It is unlikely that Marcus called himself a Valentinian. No doubt he claimed to be a Christian teacher and as such was able to attract followers from among the orthodox believers. The little evidence we have indicated that Christian Gnostics normally remained part of the Christian community.[23] The sect names are inventions of the heresiologists and not Gnostic self-designations.[24] Even when Gnostics were forced to leave the church, they were not likely to imitate the orthodox church and authority structure but would form loose associations which left sufficient room for speculative and esoteric thought, most likely combined with individualistic, ascetic practice.[25]

It is this context which provides the natural '*Sitz im Leben*' of the Gnostic writings found among the Nag Hammadi texts. They do not reflect the normative beliefs of a structured community, nor were they designed to function as the holy books of a sect or sects. They are the true product of heterodoxy, i.e. a syncretistic situation conducive to speculative thought and without hierarchical control. As such we are dealing with a literary rather than a sectarian phenomenon. It is very similar to the origin and function of Orphic, Neo-Pythagorean and Middle Platonist literature for which it is also becoming increasingly clear that there is no organized sect in the background.[26] These writings reflect only the speculations and visions of individuals and the literary traditions which they used and imitated. One expects to find such individuals among itinerant preachers, magicians, sages, philosophers, ascetics, visionaries or holy men, roles which gradually began to merge in the second and third centuries C.E.

This would account for the frustrating diversity and incoherence of most of the Gnostic texts. It would appear that both the ancient heresiologist and the modern interpreter have tended to do too much justice to them! By treating them as sectarian teaching there is the tendency to create order where there is none. The so-called developed, Gnostic 'systems' of the second century C.E. may well be the invention of the ancient and modern interpreter rather than being intended by the Gnostic authors. The summary of the sectarian 'teaching' distilled from the Gnostic texts by the ancient heresiologist or modern scholar is far too structured and coherent. The *muthologoumena* have been pushed into the mould of orthodox teaching, which is alien to these heterodox speculations.

The consequences of this for the relationship between the New Testament and Gnosticism are far-reaching. We can no longer expect that the second and third century Gnostic 'systems' will give us a secure set of characteristics of Gnosticism. Neither can we appeal to a technical Gnostic vocabulary. Both have been used as major clues to find Gnostic influences or Gnostic opponents in the New Testament. The Nag Hammadi texts show how misdirected these efforts are.[27] Our working definition of Gnosticism will need to be more formal. It must do justice to the profound heterodoxy of the Gnostic writings. No doubt it will include the élitist, esoteric, syncretistic and anti-authoritarian attitudes of the Gnostics. The intense acosmic and ascetic spirit of the Gnostics must receive its rightful place. It is still unclear whether we will be able to become much more definite than this.

It is interesting to note that this 'definition' of Gnosticism fits well those New Testament phenomena for which a Gnostic explanation has always seemed likely. For example, the 'opponents' in the Pastoral Epistles, who have caused commentators so much difficulty, can now be accounted for. It was a mistake to try to combine the listed characteristics of the false teachers into the coherent beliefs of a Gnostic sect. Indeed, the early Catholic author is warning his readers against Gnostics, but only as a general threat and not as a specific group or sect. The impression left is that of a number of itinerant teachers who tried to impress women (2 Timothy 3:6) and who expected to be paid for their services (Titus 1:11). They were adept in speculative myths (1 Timothy 1:4; 4:7; 2 Timothy 4:4; Titus 3:9) and claimed a higher esoteric knowledge (1 Timothy 6:20). Their practice was ascetic and expressed their disdain for creation (1 Timothy 4:3f.).

It is significant that the only mention of a specific teaching in the Pastorals is with reference to two teachers whose names are given: Hymenaeus and Philetus.[28] They are most likely the real opponents of the author. He places them in the context of the despised Gnostics just as the heresiologists did with their contemporary opponents. The author also used the clever device, perfected by the heresiologists, of linking the contemporary Gnostics with the 'heretics' of the past. For the Paulinist author these are the circumcision party (Titus 1:10), the teachers of the law (1 Timothy 1:7), whom the great Apostle had already refuted.

The author uses a further argument against those who reject the 'sound doctrine' and authority structure of early Catholicism. The Gnostic false teachers are seen as a fulfilment of the apocalyptic prophecies about the false teachers of the last days (1 Timothy 4:1–3; 2 Timothy 3:1–9; 4:3–4).[29] As time went by this argument lost its effectiveness and plays no significant role in the heresiological tradition which began with Justin Martyr. This suggests a date for the Pastorals in the early part of the second century C.E.

Also the problematic relationship between Gnosticism and the Gospel of John will come to appear in a new light. The focus should shift away from the unanswerable question whether the author did borrow, or could have borrowed, a dualistic vocabulary, the redeemer myth, certain literary forms and a playing down of the sacraments, future eschatology and ethics from Gnosticism. Not only are these characteristics also to be found outside Gnosticism, but they are not really typical features of Christian Gnostic writings. The question should be whether the Gospel of John stands in the uncontrolled, speculative tradition of Gnostic literature and whether it shares in some way the Gnostic's pessimistic world view and élitist self-understanding. I think the answer is affirmative.

The author of the Fourth Gospel obviously did not feel bound by the early traditions about Jesus which were incorporated in the Synoptic Gospels, and his reinterpretation of Jesus is in many ways as daring as that found in Gnostic gospels. The framework of salvation has been refocussed in terms of a vulgar, Greek dualism between flesh and spirit or this evil world and the realm of light. One could even apply Harnack's definition of Gnosticism to the Gospel of John and see it as an acute Hellenization of Christianity.

The supposed anti-Gnosticism of the Gospel and Epistles of John is part of a modern attempt to rescue John from the hands of the Gnosticizers. As we see from their writings, Gnostics had little difficulty affirming the incarnation or the virgin birth,[30] though, as in the case of the author of the Gospel of John and many others in the early church, the real interest was in the divine presence. It is also meaningless to point out that the identity of the knowledge of God and knowledge of the self is lacking in the Fourth Gospel. One looks in vain for this modern abstraction in Gnostic writings.

Of course, the Gospel of John is not Gnostic, not because of inherent reasons, but because it received a secure place in emerging orthodoxy. All pre-orthodox, early Christian literature shares to some extent the idiosyncratic and heterodox character of Gnostic literature. There were not yet clear limits within which these authors had to stay in order to be accepted by a Christian audience. The success of the Gnostic teachers, in spite of the often grotesque nature of their claims, is proof of this. The assumption, which dominates New Testament studies today, that the Christian literature which precedes early Catholicism reflects the 'orthodoxy' and experiences of different 'schools' or communities is highly questionable in the light of this. It stretches the imagination how and why a text would be written in this early period which could reflect the history and beliefs of a distinct community.[31] The argument presented above on the way the Church Fathers misconstrued Gnostic and other heterodox writings may apply also to these recent approaches to some of the New Testament writings.

NOTES

1. *The Secret Books of the Egyptian Gnostics: An Introduction to the Gnostic Coptic Manuscripts Discovered at Chenoboskion*, New York 1960, 251.
2. F. Wisse, 'Gnosticism and Early Monasticism in Egypt', in *Gnosis: Festschrift für Hans Jonas*, Göttingen 1978, 431–440.
3. Others in this group are: The Apocryphon of James (I. *2*), The Treatise on the Resurrection (I. *4*), The Exegesis on the Soul (II. *6*), The Book of Thomas the Contender (II. *7*), The Dialogue of the Saviour (III. *5*), The Apocalypse of Paul (V. *2*), The Acts of Peter and the Twelve Apostles (VI. *1*), The Thunder, Perfect Mind (VI. *2*), Authoritative Teaching (VI. *3*), The Teachings of Silvanus (VII. *4*), The Interpretation of Knowledge (XI. *1*), and The Sentences of Sextus (XII. *1*).
4. Doresse, op. cit., 249.
5. E.g. H.-M. Schenke, 'The Phenomenon and Significance of Gnostic Sethianism', in (ed.) B. Layton, *The Rediscovery of Gnosticism*, II, *Sethian Gnosticism*, Leiden 1981, 589.
6. See T. Säve-Söderbergh, 'Holy Scriptures or Apologetic Documentations? The "Sitz im Leben" of the Nag Hammadi Library', in (ed.) J. E. Ménard, *Les textes de Nag Hammadi: colloque du centre d'histoire des religions*, *NHS* 7, Leiden 1975, 3–14, and my critique in 'Gnosticism and Early Monasticism in Egypt' (n. 2), 435f.
7. Martin Krause thinks that the codices were buried together with the owner ('Die Texte von Nag Hammadi', in *Gnosis* (n. 2), 243). However, there is no sign that the jar in which the books were found was buried in a cemetery and the several duplicates among the tractates speak against a single owner.
8. 'The Nag Hammadi Library and the Heresiologists', *VigChr* 25, 1971, 205–223.
9. *Val.*, 4.
10. See A. Hilgenfeld, *Die Ketzergeschichte des Urchristentums*, Leipzig 1884/Darmstadt 1966, 285f.
11. This did not happen everywhere at the same time. In Alexandria

control was finally established under Athanasius. The monastic movement provided in its early days a haven for heterodox thought.

12. A striking example of this found in Hipp., *Ref.* X, 11–12 where the bishop of Rome, Callistus, is placed in the catalogue of heresies.
13. *Haer.* I, 23–28 and most likely also 11–12.
14. *Haer.* I, Preface.
15. *Haer.* I, 11:1.
16. See F. Wisse, 'Stalking Those Elusive Sethians', in (ed.) Layton, *The Rediscovery of Gnosticism*, II (n. 5), 571–575.
17. See 'The Nag Hammadi Library and the Heresiologists' (n. 8), 219f.
18. *Haer.* I, 28:1.
19. *Haer.* I, 9:5–11:1.
20. *Haer.* I, Preface and 11.
21. See 'The Nag Hammadi Library and the Heresiologists' (n. 8), 218–19.
22. *Haer.* I, 13.
23. See K. Koschorke, *Die Polemik der Gnostiker gegen das kirchliche Christentum*, *NHS* 12, Leiden 1978, 177f.
24. Ibid.
25. See 'Gnosticism and Early Monasticism in Egypt' (n. 2), 439f.
26. See W. Burkert, 'Craft versus Sect: The Problem of Orphics and Pythagoreans', in (eds) B. F. Meyer, E. P. Sanders, *Jewish and Christian Self-Definition*, III, London 1982, 1–22, 183–189. This applies also to most of the apocryphal and apocalyptic literature.
27. See F. Wisse, 'The "Opponents" in the New Testament in Light of the Nag Hammadi Writings' in (ed.) B. Barc, *Colloque international sur les textes de Nag Hammadi*, *BCNH Ét* 1, Québec/Louvain 1981, 99–120.
28. On the view of the resurrection in Gnostic writings see my comments in 'The "Opponents" in the New Testament in Light of the Nag Hammadi Writings' (n. 27), 108–114.
29. The same argument is used in 1 John, 2 Peter and especially Jude; see F. Wisse, 'The Epistle of Jude in the History of Heresiology', in (ed.) M. Krause, *Essays on the Nag Hammadi Texts in Honour of Alexander Böhlig*, *NHS* 3, Leiden 1972, 133–143.
30. See 'The "Opponents" in the New Testament ...' (n. 27), 117–119.
31. The details given in recent literature on the community of 'Q' and the Johannine community represents the historical critical method applied *ad absurdum*.

XI

ADAM AND EVE, CHRIST AND THE CHURCH:

A Survey of Second Century Controversies Concerning Marriage

by

Professor Elaine H. Pagels, Princeton

All scholars now engaged in patristic and Nag Hammadi studies are indebted to the major contributions of Professor R. McL. Wilson. Since the present sketch of research in progress evinces my own indebtedness especially to his books, *Gnosis and the New Testament* and *The Gospel of Philip*, I am delighted to contribute it to the *Festschrift* honouring his achievements. For discussion and criticism of the work presented here, I am grateful, too, to several colleagues: Professors Gilles Quispel, Thomas Boslooper, and Peter Brown.

Some Christians, who 'proudly say that they are imitating the Lord, who did not marry', complains Clement of Alexandria, themselves reject marriage, and so 'boast that they understand the gospel better than anyone else' (*Strom.* III, 49). Clement recognizes that the bitter disputes that divided his Christian contemporaries involve not only complex doctrinal issues, but, often directly correlated with these, controversies over practice – especially sexual practice. From the second century, indeed, we can trace the development of different 'understandings of the gospel' as it is read in terms of *practice* – views that range from radically ascetic versions to the anti-ascetic (or, more accurately, modified ascetic) versions that Clement and his 'orthodox' colleagues endorse.

Harnack characterizes the four themes of early Christian preaching as follows: creation, salvation, resurrection, and sexual purity.[1] And, as he notes, Christian writers from Paul to the Apostolic Fathers and Apologists agree that what distinguishes Christians from unbelievers in practical terms is, above all, their purity. 'We who formerly delighted in *porneia*', Justin boasts, '... now embrace chastity alone' (I *Apol.* 14). Even outsiders could verify his boast: Galen, like Justin, admired not only the Christians' contempt of death, but especially their 'abstinence from the use of sexual organs' (*De Platonis Rei Publicae Summariis*, ed. Kraus-Walzer, fr. 1).

But what constitutes the 'purity' that the gospel requires? For generations (indeed, we might add, for nearly two millennia) following Jesus' death, this question has proved explosively controversial. Does the gospel require marital fidelity – or renunciation of sexual relations even within marriage? Did Christ confirm the ordinance of marriage, or did he come to liberate us from its bondage? Did Jesus and Paul condemn, as *porneia*, only violations of marriage, or marital intercourse itself?

Such controversies took, in the early church, diverse forms. Since antagonists on all sides claimed for opposing positions the authority of Jesus and Paul, they most often waged exegetical battles over passages that all held in common reverence, especially a cluster of synoptic sayings concerning marriage, i.e. Mark 10:2–10 par; 12:18–27 par; Luke 20:34, and Paul's Corinthian letters. Ascetically inclined Christians and their opponents each chose to emphasize, of course, those passages from the common sources that seemed to support their respective views. And those on both sides invoked, as well, other allegedly 'evangelic' and 'apostolic' sources: on one side, such sources as the Gospel of the Egyptians, and, on the other, such works as the Pastoral letters. Above all, the story of Adam and Eve, which both Jesus and Paul, following Jewish tradition, had introduced into discussions of marriage and sexual relationships, formed the storm centre of the controversy.

Let us briefly recall, then, those passages in which, all Christians agreed, Jesus established the pattern. According to synoptic tradition, Jesus refers to the Paradise story only once. Replying to the Pharisees' question concerning the grounds for divorce, he alludes to Genesis 1:27 and 2:24, placing marriage into the context of God's original purpose in creation. But citing the text traditionally understood as the divine ordinance of marriage, Jesus substitutes for the traditional text ('*they* shall become one flesh') a version (also used by the Damascene Jews) that implies that God had instituted monogamous marriage ('*the two* shall become one flesh', Mark 10:8 par). Then, ignoring his interlocutor's expectation that he would enter into contemporary debate concerning the legitimate grounds for divorce, Jesus astonished his audience by dismissing the whole subject: 'What God has joined together, let not man put asunder' (Mark 10:9). Mark's version, apparently the earliest, categorically declares the indissolubility of marriage.

Without entering into the complex question of the relationship of this statement to other Jewish tradition, let us note here only one simple point: Jesus' teaching challenges the dominant consensus concerning the structure and purpose of marriage. His Jewish contemporaries, whatever their differences, generally agree that its purpose lies in fulfilling the first divine command (Genesis 1:28: 'be fruitful and multiply'). That primary obligation directs the use of sexuality into patterns of marriage designed to serve the purpose of procreation. One rabbinic source interprets each phrase of Genesis 2:24 as defining the structure of marriage, prohibiting such practices as incest, adultery, and homosexuality that hinder the production of legitimate offspring.[2] Both polygamy (however infrequent in Jesus' time, and despite the minority opposition of Damascene Jews) and divorce served to facilitate fulfilment of that primary obligation. Religious law, for example, enjoined a man married ten years to a barren woman to divorce her and remarry, or to take another wife as well, in order to beget children. Such prescriptions, as well as the elaborate regulations concerning marital intercourse, demonstrate the same point: the religious obligation to procreate not only directed the structure of marriage, but took precedence over marital obligations themselves.

But Jesus, as synoptic tradition depicts him, radically challenges this consensus. He ignores, apparently, the command to procreate, assumed in Jewish tradition to be the purpose of marriage. Even *Matthew's* version, which softens Jesus' categorical prohibition with a loophole ('except for *porneia*', Matthew 19:9; cf. 5:31) allows for divorce only in cases of the wife's infidelity – not her infertility. This teaching, then, reverses traditional priorities: here, marital obligations take precedence over the obligation to procreate. Even more astonishing, in terms of Jewish tradition, is Jesus' endorsement – and his exemplification – of a new possibility: rejecting both forms of religious duty in favour of voluntary celibacy. Matthew adds to Jesus' statement on marriage his praise of those who 'make themselves eunuchs for the sake of the kingdom of heaven' (Matthew 19:12). Luke adds Jesus' praise of the barren woman (Luke 23:29) and places in the present tense his declaration concerning the state of marriage in relation to the resurrection:

> The sons of this age marry and are given in marriage; but those who are accounted worthy to attain to that age and to the resurrection from the dead neither marry nor are given in marriage, for they cannot die any more, because they are equal to angels, and are sons of God, being sons of the resurrection.   (Luke 20:34–36)

Such statements could not fail to horrify Jewish traditionalists. The barren woman, traditionally seen as cursed, Jesus blesses; a eunuch, whom rabbinic commentators despise for his sexual incapacity (and hence his incapacity to fulfil the primary divine command, Genesis 1:28), Jesus praises. Even more, Jesus encourages his disciples to follow his own example in rejecting family obligations altogether – whether to parents, relatives, wives, or children (Mark 10:28–31 par, note especially the variant in Luke 18:28–30).

His zealous disciple Paul goes even further. Paul, too, alludes to Genesis 2:24 only once. Shockingly, he wrenches this passage out of its traditional context, the discussion of marriage, to apply it instead to one of the worst forms of *porneia*. The most casual sexual encounter, Paul implies, makes a man 'one flesh' with his partner – even with a prostitute! 'Do you not know that whoever joins himself to a prostitute becomes one body with her? For, as it is written, "the two shall be one flesh" ' (1 Corinthians 6:16). Paul goes on to contrast such sexual union with the believer's spiritual union with

Christ: 'But whoever joins to the Lord becomes one spirit with him' (1 Corinthians 6:17).

Where Jesus' teaching indicates that marital obligations take precedence over those of procreation, Paul gives voluntary celibacy precedence over marriage itself. While Paul accepts 'the Lord's' dictum that marriage is indissoluble (1 Corinthians 7:10–11) and, like Jesus, ignores the obligation to procreate, he describes its purpose in solely negative terms. Although 'not sin', marriage serves intemperate believers only to prevent *porneia* (1 Corinthians 7:1–9). If Paul allows to men and woman a 'new mutuality' in marriage, this consists, at best, in mutual 'anxiety', 'trouble', and 'bondage' (1 Corinthians 7:32–35; cf. 7:3–5, 39–40; Romans 7:2). Since those who marry participate thereby in the temporal 'scheme of this world', even 'those who have wives' should live 'as if they had none' (1 Corinthians 7:29).

Some of Paul's followers read similarly the implications of his teaching in 1 Corinthians 15. Marriage, they argued, belongs to the lesser creation of the 'first Adam', whom Paul degrades from the glorious primal man celebrated in rabbinic tradition to a 'man of earth' in order to exalt the 'second Adam', the 'man of heaven', who (as Tertullian and Jerome noted) remained celibate.[3] Paul's followers debated, too, the implications of 2 Corinthians 11:2–3. Does Paul imply that the serpent violated Eve's bridal purity, either by seducing her himself, or by initiating her into sexual intercourse with Adam? Later interpreters saw in such passages the transformation of the traditional prophetic image of Israel as God's 'wife' into that of the 'new Israel' as Christ's perpetually virginal 'bride'.

This brief sketch, although far from giving a full account of Jesus' or Paul's views, may serve our present purpose by recalling certain passages that were to become, for generations of Christians, *loci classici* in the debates that raged over Christian sexual practice.

Although Paul surely intended his letters to the Corinthians to help resolve community disputes (prominently including those concerning sexuality and marriage) they aroused more. From the second century, as noted above, we can trace not only the development of contradictory interpretations of Paul's 'gospel' read in terms of doctrine (i.e. the 'Gnostic Paul' and the anti-Gnostic Paul),[4] but also, corresponding – and equally controversial – interpretations of Paul's 'gospel' read in terms of practice.

Some of his most ardent admirers, apparently distressed at those who claimed his (and Jesus') authority to 'forbid marriage' (1 Timothy 4:3), wrote, in Paul's name, letters designed to 'correct' such misappropriation of the apostle's teaching. The deutero-Pauline letters included in the New Testament, despite their theological divergences, all express basic agreement on such matters. All challenge radically ascetic interpretations of Paul, presenting instead an anti-ascetic version of his teaching that is far more consonant with Jewish tradition.

The 'Paul' of Ephesians, for example, invokes Genesis 2:24 in its traditional context, as he addresses exhortation to husbands and wives (Ephesians 5:21–33). Here 'Paul' goes on to interpret the union of Adam and Eve as prefiguring the 'great mystery' of Christ's union with his church

(5:32). Yet the passage shows that this 'great mystery' offers a paradigm for actual Christian marriage. Directly opposing ascetic extremism, this 'Paul' declares that 'no one ever hates his own flesh, but nourishes and cherishes it' (5:29). He follows, too, the patriarchal pattern established in Genesis 3, as he enjoins the husband to love his wife, and the wife, in turn, to submit in reverence to her husband. The 'Paul' of Hebrews, as well, perhaps recalling the Genesis tradition, commands that 'marriage be held in honour among all, and the marriage bed be unpolluted' (Hebrews 13:4). The 'Paul' of 1 Timothy, attacking as demonically inspired those 'liars' who 'forbid marriage and enjoin abstinence from goods which God created', insists that 'everything created by God is good, and nothing is to be rejected if it is received with thanksgiving, for then it is consecrated by the word of God and prayer' (4:1–5).

This author assumes not only that leaders of the Christian communities, like their Jewish contemporaries, are married men, but, assuming Jesus' requirement of monogamy, declares that their rule over their wives and children must exemplify their qualifications to manage 'God's church' (1 Timothy 3:1–5). Contrary to the Paul of 1 Corinthians, who urges widows to remain celibate, the 'Paul' of 1 Timothy 'would have younger widows remarry and bear children' (5:14f.). The presence of such unmarried women would, he warns, endanger the community's reputation.

The Pastoral 'Paul' abruptly censures, too, Paul's assumption (cf. 1 Corinthians 11:5f.) that some women (perhaps only virgins and celibates, cf. 1 Corinthians 14:33–35) will participate in public prayer and prophecy (1 Timothy 2:11f.). The story of Eve's sin demonstrates not only woman's natural susceptibility to deceit but also defines her present role in terms consonant with the consensus of Jewish tradition. Chastened by recalling Eve's sin and punishment, deprived of any authority, the woman must silently submit to her husband, although, the author allows, 'she will be saved through childbearing' if she accompanies this with modest behaviour (1 Timothy 2:13–15).

Purged of his radicalism, this 'Paul' not only ignores encouragement to voluntary celibacy (especially for women) but takes marriage for granted as the normal condition for all believers. Denouncing those who prohibit it, he reaffirms instead a reformed and stricter version of Jewish tradition. The institution of marriage, now understood as monogamous and indissoluble, expressed the creator's goodness, as its patriarchal structure demonstrates his judgement on Eve's sin. Although extant sources give few indications of what may have provoked such a picture of Paul, the letters attributed to Peter, which offer similar injunctions concerning marriage (1 Peter 3:1–7), suggest that 'ignorant and unstable' admirers of Paul 'twisted to their own destruction' (2 Peter 3:15f.) not only his theological teachings, but also his directions concerning sexual practice.

Writers revered as the 'Apostolic Fathers' of the church seized upon this tamed and domesticated version of the apostle as a primary weapon against ascetic extremists. Most assumed, with the deutero-Pauline author(s), that marital morality forms the normal basis of Christian life.

The author of the Epistle to Diognetus declares that 'Christians marry, as do all (others); they beget children; but they do not destroy foetuses' (5:6). Barnabas, in agreement with Jewish ethical tradition, declares that those who follow the 'way of light' abstain from all sexual practices that violate marriage or frustrate its fulfilment in legitimate procreation (10:1–12; 19:4f.). Like pious Jews, Christians are to repudiate fornication, adultery, homosexuality, abortion, and infanticide. Polycarp, Ignatius, and the author of 1 and 2 Clement, all endorse, as well, the deutero-Pauline pattern. Women are to submit to the 'rule of obedience' which faith requires (cf. 1 Cl. 1:3; 21:6–7). Both partners are to 'form their union with the approval of the bishop, so that their marriage may be according to God, and not according to their lust' (Ignatius, *Pol.* 5:2; cf. 1 Thessalonians 4:3–5). The longer recension of Ignatius' letter to the Philadelphians directs wives to be submissive, and husbands to 'love your wives ... as your own body, and the partners of your life, and your helpmates in the procreation of children' (*Phld.* 4).

Yet unlike Barnabas and the Epistle to Diognetus, Clement, Polycarp, and Ignatius cite, together with the deutero–Pauline author(s), his authentic letters, acknowledging those who remain 'pure in the flesh'. Each expresses, however, in regard to celibate Christians, a wary reserve, and warns that such spiritual athletes risk liabilities corresponding to their achievement. The author of 1 Clement, apparently including himself in their number, addresses celibates only to caution them against boasting as if their own zeal had acquired 'the gift of continence' which, he insists, only the Lord can bestow (1 Cl. 38:2). Polycarp distinguishes the virgins from the bishops (*Phil.* 5:3); his fellow bishop, Ignatius, is willing to allow them to 'remain in purity' so long as they maintain humble submission to episcopal authority. But if the celibate boasts, Ignatius declares, 'he is undone; if he becomes known apart from the bishop, he is destroyed' (*Pol.* 5:2). The longer recension of his letter to the Philadelphians censures any who 'consider marriage an abomination' (*Phld.* 4, long recension). And the writer of 1 Corinthians would have been astonished, to say the least, to find himself included in a list of those holy men, 'Peter and Paul, who were married men', and no less distressed to learn the positive interpretation of his alleged matrimony: '... for they entered into these marriages not for the sake of carnal desires, but out of regard for human procreation' (loc. cit.).

Would Paul have considered himself – or his Lord – any better served by those who revere both as champions of *enkrateia*? Enthusiastic converts, especially those not grounded in Jewish tradition, sometimes read 'the gospel' very differently. Tatian, writing his book *On Perfection According to the Saviour*, insisted that true disciples must 'imitate the Lord himself, who never married', and follow as well the example of his most celebrated apostle. Clement's polemic suggests that Tatian went on to point out that Peter, although married, left his wife and children when he began to follow Christ (*Strom.* III, 52); further, that Philip, the father of four daughters, dedicated them all to virginity. Tatian may have used 2 Corinthians 11:2f. to show that the church, being, in Paul's words, a 'pure bride betrothed to her one husband' required of its members the same purity as those betrothed to the virgin Christ himself (*Strom.* III, 74).

To prove that Jesus' and Paul's teaching corresponds with their example, Tatian relies primarily upon the selection of passages noted above – Jesus' sayings recorded in Matthew and Luke, and upon 1 Corinthians. Clement insinuates that his opponent attributes marriage to Satan (*Strom.* III, 80f.), but Tatian's ingenious reworking of Matthew 19:4–9 suggests that he attributed it instead to Adam. Tatian inserted into his reading of the text minor glosses that changed the whole meaning: 'When God had made male and female, He joined them together; (*and Adam said*), "Because of this (*bond*) a man shall leave his father and mother, and the two shall become one flesh" '. Tatian's redaction acknowledges that God created sexual differences, but indicates that Adam, not God, instituted marriage.[6] This transgression, in turn, allowed Satan to introduce the first couple to sexual intercourse (*porneia*, as Tatian reads it, cf. *Strom.* III, 82), earning Adam's expulsion from Paradise. Tatian points out that Jesus himself declared that 'marrying and giving in marriage' increased the pollution in the world that incurred the flood (*Strom.* III, 49, cf. Matthew 24:37–39). The Saviour's teaching, Tatian insists, demands that the believer break with 'the sins of the world': 'You cannot serve God and mammon' (*Strom.* III, 81; cf. Matthew 6:24). Tatian takes the Saviour's injunction to 'lay not up for yourselves treasures upon earth' (*Strom.* III, 86; cf. Matthew 6:19) to mean that the believer must renounce both wealth *and* offspring. As Tatian sees it, Christ himself reversed the positive value his Jewish contemporaries placed upon procreation, praising the man who 'makes himself a eunuch for the kingdom of heaven' (Matthew 19:12) and blessing the barren woman, the 'wombs that never bore, and the breasts that never gave suck' (Luke 23:29).

Paul confirms the radical discontinuity between law and gospel, Tatian continues, by contrasting the 'old man' with the 'new' (*Strom.* III, 82). Reference to 1 Corinthians 15 seems to underlie Tatian's theological scheme: Adam, born from earth, remained under the law that ordered procreation, marriage, divorce; Christ, the 'new man from heaven', liberates his own from all these constraints. Tatian apparently reads 1 Corinthians 6 as evidence of the antithesis between the sexual union exemplified in Adam and Eve and the believers' spiritual union with Christ. Tatian probably sees himself following Paul's lead when he characterizes marriage as a 'bond' (cf. 1 Corinthians 7:15, 27, 39). Paul's metaphor of Israel's bondage to the law as woman 'bound to her husband' (Romans 7:2) signifies, he says, the flesh bound in corruption (*Strom.* III, 80). For the same apostle, as Tatian notes, describes how Satan seduced Eve, originally intended to be a 'pure bride presented to her own husband', thus drawing the human race from purity, and plunging it instead into the corruption of sexual intercourse (*porneia, Strom.* III, 80). Because of this (*porneia*; cf. 1 Corinthians 7:2), Tatian says, Paul allows for the possibility of marriage, although only for those still too weak to endure celibacy. And even now, Tatian explains from 1 Corinthians 7:5, Satan tempts married

Christians from the celibacy required for prayer back into the *porneia* of their sexual relationship 'through lack of self-control' (*Strom.* III, 81). Interpreting I Corinthians 7:5f., Tatian writes,

> While agreement to be continent makes prayer possible, intercourse of corruption destroys it. By the disparaging way in which he allows it, (Paul) forbids it. For although he allowed them to come together again because of Satan and the temptation to incontinence, he indicated that the man who takes advantage of this permission will be serving two masters, God, if there is agreement, and, if there is no such agreement, incontinence, fornication (*porneia*), and the devil.
> (*Strom.* III, 81)

Clement, facing what he must have seen as the difficult task of discrediting Tatian's exegesis, finds himself impelled to resort to considerable exegetical ingenuity. First, he declares, Christ's example does not apply to his human followers. The reason why Jesus did not marry, Clement says, is that, 'in the first place, the Lord had his own bride, the church; and, in the second place, he was not an ordinary man' (*Strom.* III, 49). And while Clement admits that Paul described the church as a 'pure virgin', he dismisses her example, as he does that of Christ: 'the church cannot marry another, having obtained a bridegroom: but each of us individually has the right to marry the woman he wishes according to the law; I mean here first marriage' (*Strom.* III, 74).

What about the apostles? Against Tatian, Clement declares that 'Peter and Philip had children', and even adds that 'Philip gave his daughters in marriage' (*Strom.* III, 52)! What about Paul? Clement, like Ignatius' redactor, declares that 'even Paul did not hesitate in one letter to address his wife' (so he interprets Philippians 4:3), adding that 'the only reason he did not take her around with him is that it would have been an inconvenience for his ministry' (*Strom.* III, 53).

Turning to Tatian's interpretation of Jesus' sayings, Clement, instead of quoting the positive Lukan version that Tatian probably cited, quotes the negative version of Matthew 24:19. Admitting that the saying is problematic, he says that it 'is to be understood allegorically' (*Strom.* III, 49). He charges that Tatian takes Jesus' praise of eunuchs (Matthew 19:12) out of its context, the discussion of marriage. What Jesus meant, he insists, was that a married man, who has divorced his wife because of adultery, should not *remarry* (*Strom.* III, 50).

Luckily for Clement, when he goes on to attack Tatian's exegesis of 1 Corinthians, he finds in the deutero-Pauline letters the ammunition he needs. Clement replies 'to those who revile marriage' in the words of 'the blessed Paul' recorded in 1 Timothy 4:1–3 (*Strom.* III, 51, 85). Having enlisted Timothy's 'Paul' on his side, he then proceeds to the more difficult ground of 1 Corinthians 7. Repeatedly emphasizing the identity of 'the self-same man' as the author of the whole New Testament Pauline corpus

(*Strom.* III, 53; cf. 76), Clement skilfully interweaves passages from the Roman and Corinthian letters with those from Timothy, Titus, Colossians, and Ephesians, to prove that Paul affirms marriage and procreation. One example illustrates his technique:

> If 'the law is holy' (Romans 7:12), marriage is holy. This 'mystery' the apostle refers to 'Christ and the church' (Ephesians 5:32) ... Thus fornication (*porneia*) and marriage are different things, as far apart as God from the devil.   (*Strom.* III, 84)

Indeed, Clement adds, citing 1 Timothy 3:12, '(Paul) entirely approves the man who is husband of one wife, whether he be priest, deacon, or layman, if he conducts his marriage blamelessly, "for he (*sic!*) shall be saved through childbearing" ' (1 Timothy 2:15; *Strom.* III, 90). Such a Catholic view of the Pauline corpus enables Clement to conclude that the apostle affirms both marriage and celibacy:

> In general all the epistles of the apostle teach self-control (*enkrateia*) and continence and contain numerous instructions about marriage, begetting children, and domestic life. But they nowhere exclude self-controlled marriage.   (*Strom.* III, 86)

Julius Cassianus presents Clement with similar problems. Cassianus, like Tatian, bases his practical exposition of the gospel, *On Continence or Celibacy*, upon evidence drawn from the Genesis passages, reading these through sayings of Jesus and Paul. Like many others, Cassianus envisions the primordial human creation in purely spiritual terms. Citing 2 Corinthians 11:3–4, he contends that the primal transgression, the deception of Eve, signifies how Satan, represented, appropriately, in the form of a serpent, 'took the use of intercourse from the irrational animals, and persuaded Adam to have sexual union with Eve' (*Strom.* III, 102). Following this transgression, the man and woman were clothed with bodies, the 'coats of skins' (Genesis 3:21), and excluded from Paradise, bereft of their original spiritual nature (*Strom.* III, 95).

Neither the Saviour himself nor the true 'Father in heaven' (cf. *Strom.* III, 87, 94) intended (much less condoned) the present human condition:

> And let no one say that because we have these members, in that the female body is shaped this way and the male that way, the one to receive, the other to give seed, sexual intercourse is allowed by God. For if this arrangement had been made by God, whom we seek to attain, (Christ) would not have pronounced eunuchs blessed (cf. Matthew 19:12) nor would the prophet have said that we are 'not an unfruitful tree' (Isaiah 56:3), using the tree to illustrate the man who chooses to emasculate himself of any such notion.   (*Strom.* III, 91)

Supplementing sayings known from synoptic tradition with those from the Gospel of the Egyptians, Cassianus explains that Christ redeems those who 'trample on the robe of shame', our bodily 'garment', and restores us to that spiritual condition in which 'there is no male nor female' (*Strom.* III, 92).

Responding to Cassianus, Clement interprets the saying from the apocryphal Gospel allegorically, rejects the literal interpretation of Luke 14:26, and, most important, reinterprets Matthew 19:12: 'a "eunuch" does not mean a man who has been castrated, nor even an unmarried man', he declares, but one who is 'unproductive and unfruitful both in conduct and in word' (*Strom.* III, 99). Here again Clement interweaves references to 1 Corinthians with those from the Pastoral letters, claiming that the 'marital debt' Paul mentions (1 Corinthians 7:3) refers not merely to sexual intercourse, but 'to the obligation of marriage, procreation' (*Strom.* III, 107). In fulfilling this obligation, he adds, the wife may serve her husband as a 'help-meet' (cf. Genesis 2:18) not only in the home, 'but in Christian faith' (*Strom.* III, 108).

Clement rejects, above all, the claim that Adam and Eve sinned by engaging in sexual intercourse, 'as if the first couple did not have such union by nature' (*Strom.* III, 102). Rather, he declares, 'nature led them, like the irrational animals, to procreate' (*Strom.* III, 103). What, then, was their sin? Not *what* they did, Clement replies, but *how* they did it. Adam 'desired the fruit of marriage before the proper time, and fell into sin' (*Strom.* III, 94). Adam and Eve, then, like impatient adolescents, 'were impelled to do it more quickly than was proper because they were still young, and had been seduced by deceit' (*Strom.* III, 103). Alluding to the double meaning of the Hebrew term *yāḍaʻ*, Clement says that although the fruit of the tree of knowledge may signify 'carnal knowledge' ('the intercourse of man and woman in marriage'), those who partake of it need not incur sin. On the contrary, Genesis 4:1 ('Adam knew his wife') suggests to Clement a positive interpretation: practising intercourse with discernment involves knowledge. Thus, he concludes, 'marriage can be used rightly or wrongly; this is the tree of knowledge, if we do not transgress in marriage' (*Strom.* III, 104).

Yet Clement and his colleagues recognize that ascetic Christianity powerfully attracted (seduced, they would say) many enthusiastic converts. Marcion, although 'more continent than the apostle' as Tertullian ridicules him (*Marc.* V, 7), may have won, in some areas, a majority of believers. Tertullian attests (as Clement had, in relation to Tatian and Julius Cassianus) that the contest with Marcion involved nothing less than the 'true gospel': 'I say that *my* gospel is the true one', declares Tertullian; 'Marcion, that *his* is' (*Marc.* IV, 4). Marcion based his 'pure form of the gospel' not only, as his contemporaries had, on certain evangelic and apostolic sayings, but specifically on passages from Luke and those letters of Paul which he accepted as authentic (1 and 2 Corinthians, Romans, 1 and 2 Thessalonians, and Ephesians, rejecting 1 and 2 Timothy and Titus).

If the creator's law commands procreation (cf. Genesis 1:28) and orders both marriage (Genesis 2:23–24) and divorce, Christ's gospel, Marcion insists, proves its antithesis. The Saviour blesses the barren (Luke 23:29), rejects marriage for 'those counted worthy of the resurrection' (Luke 20:35), and categorically prohibits divorce. Like Tatian, Marcion claims Paul's authority for equating marriage with *porneia*, and censures marital intercourse (cf. 1 Thessalonians 4:3). Both the Lord himself, Marcion emphasizes (cf. Luke 12:35–40), and his apostle (2 Corinthians 11:3f.) envision Christ as a 'bridegroom' and his church as the 'pure bride'. Marcion, too, sees in the marriage of Adam and Eve the symbol of the sexual union which forms the antithesis of spiritual union with Christ (cf. 1 Corinthians 6:15; *Marc.* IV, 34). He goes on to read Ephesians 5:31f. in terms of the same antithesis: in contrast to the fleshly union of human marriage, Christ offers to the church, his 'bride', a pure union of spiritual love (*Marc.* V, 18).

Marcion's exegesis, as Tertullian recognizes, depends upon specific exegetical assumptions. Attacking Marcion, consequently, Tertullian articulates an essential principle of anti-ascetic exegesis. Referring to such passages as Ephesians 5:32 and 2 Corinthians 11:3–4, he insists that 'an image cannot be combined and compared with what is opposed to the real nature of the thing (*res*) with which it is compared' (*Marc.* V, 12). Rather, he insists, 'the image participates in honour with reality' (*Marc.* V, 18). Therefore, Tertullian continues, Paul, speaking of human marriage as signifying the 'great mystery, Christ and the church' (Ephesians 5:32), intends to interpret, not to annihilate, the 'mystery' included within human marriage. As Tertullian sees it, the sexual union reflected in Adam and Eve complements, rather than contrasts with, the spiritual union of Christ and his church.

Yet Clement and Tertullian bear unwilling witness to the immense success of ascetic versions of 'the gospel' they attack. The popularity of the apocryphal Acts demonstrates, too, that ascetic versions of the gospel could flourish – perhaps even more insidiously – apart from identifiable theological 'heresy'. What connects these with such teachers as Tatian and Cassianus is their practical conviction that sexual intercourse has no place in Christian life.[7] To support this conviction, their authors use typological and exegetical patterns similar to those that Clement and Tertullian condemn in the works of Tatian, Cassianus, and Marcion.

Writing 'out of love for Paul', the author of the well-known Acts of Paul takes the apostle – and his Lord – at what he believes to be their word. Strikingly, this author alludes to the Pastorals only to set the scene, censuring Demas, who, 'in love with this present world' (2 Timothy 4:10) deserted Paul, Alexander, the coppersmith, who did the apostle 'great harm' (2 Timothy 4:14), and Hermogenes, whom the Pastoral Paul includes among 'all those in Asia' who 'turned away from me' (2 Timothy 1:15) apparently offended by the 'bitter' severity of his preaching (cf. Act. Pl and Thekl. 1). Following the pattern we have observed, this author goes on to base his account primarily upon certain dominical sayings (most often cited in their Matthean form) and upon apostolic teachings largely derived from 1 Corinthians. His teaching 'concerning continence and the resurrection' exemplifies his technique, as he revises the beatitudes by combining them with images drawn from 1 Corinthians 6 and 7:

> Blessed are they who have kept the flesh pure, for they shall
> become a temple of God (cf. 1 Corinthians 6:13–20;
> 2 Corinthians 6:16–7:1) ... Blessed are they who have wives as if
> they had them not (1 Corinthians 7:29), for they shall inherit
> God (cf. Matthew 5:4) ... Blessed are they who through love of
> God have departed from the form of this world (cf.
> 1 Corinthians 7:31) for they shall judge angels (cf. 1 Corinthians
> 6:3) ... (Act. P1 and Thekl. 5–6)

Thekla's story celebrates the achievement of one who resists family pressure, social ostracism, threats of rape, torture, and sentences of death, and, finally, even the apostle's own hesitation, to follow 'the word of the virgin life as it is spoken by Paul' (Act. P1 and Thekl. 7; cf. 1 Corinthians 7:8, 25–35). Thekla sees herself simply as 'the handmaid of the living God' (Act. P1 and Thekl. 37). Other Acts go further, explicitly contrasting the celibate's bridal purity with the pollutions of sexuality incurred through the fall. The virgin disciple of the Acts of John, promising darkly to 'reveal more fully the mystery of marital union', declares that 'it is a device of the serpent, ... an ambush of Satan, a device of the jealous one, ... a shedding of blood ..., a falling from reason, a token of punishment ... a comedy of the devil, hatred of life ...' (Act. Jn fr. 3 in the Ps.-Titus Epistle, Henn.-Wilson II, 160, 209f.). The Acts of Thomas identifies the 'great serpent', who boasts that he incited a pure and beautiful young couple to engage in intercourse (and 'other shameful things' too dreadful to mention), with the one who deceived Eve, and bound the heavenly angels themselves 'in lusts for women' (Act. Thom. 31–33).

The author of the Acts of Thomas expands, too, Jesus' parable of the marriage feast (cf. Matthew 22:1–14 par) to contrast a marriage arranged by an earthly king ('the Lord of this world'?) with the spiritual marriage to Christ. Following the wedding, as the bridegroom lifts the veil of the bridal chamber to consummate his marriage, he discovers the Lord Jesus, appearing in Thomas' form, conversing with his bride. 'And the Lord sat down on the bed, and commanded them, too, to sit on the chairs (!)' as he urged them to 'abandon this filthy intercourse'. Those who repudiate their filial obligation to procreate receive 'the incorruptible and true marriage' (Act. Thom. 11–16). Ascetic exegesis of 1 Corinthians 6 seems to underlie the scene. The bride, converted to chastity, declares that, in rejecting temporal marriage, she is 'bound in another marriage' with Christ himself (Act. Thom. 14). The bridegroom, too, praises the Lord 'who redeemed me from the fall, and led me to the better' (Act. Thom. 15).

Juxtaposing the images of earthly and heavenly marriage, the author seems to assume (perhaps, like Tatian, from 2 Corinthians 11:3f.) that Eve herself originally was meant to remain a 'pure bride' in spiritual union with Adam. Her sin, as she engaged in sexual intercourse, includes, as *porneia*, marital intercourse; this too, is 'adultery', that violates that prior spiritual union.[8]

The author applies the same paradigm to each Christian convert. Mygdonia, converted to the faith, learns that the Saviour, in condemning adultery, refers not simply to violations of sexual fidelity, but to the whole 'sordid communion' with her husband that threatens to deprive her of 'true communion' with Christ (Act. Thom. 88). Mygdonia, lying veiled upon her bed, finally cries out that she no longer belongs to him, but to Christ (Act. Thom. 98). Hitting her husband on the face, she runs from him naked, ripping down the bedroom curtains to cover herself as she escapes to sleep with her nurse. Rejecting his anguished pleas, she accepts baptism. Thenceforth she eloquently repudiates her previous marriage, the 'fellowship of corruption', for the eternal marriage she enjoys with Jesus, her 'pure bridegroom' (cf. especially Act. Thom. 117–125).

The Acts of Andrew, like those of Thomas, celebrate the chastity that undoes the sin of Adam and Eve. Here Andrew reassures his convert Maximilla, as she is distressed by her husband's threats and pleas:

> I know, Maximilla my child, that you are moved to resist the whole allurement of sexual intercourse, because you wish to be separated from a polluted and foul way of life ... And I rightly see in you Eve repenting, and in myself Adam being converted: for what she suffered in ignorance you are now bringing to a happy conclusion because you are converted: or what the mind suffered which was brought down by her and was estranged from itself, I put right with you who know that you yourself are being drawn up. For you yourself, who did not experience the same things, have healed her affliction; and I, by taking refuge with God, have perfected (Adam's) imperfection ... As Adam died in Eve because of the harmony of their relationship, so even now I live in you, who keep the command of the Lord ...
> (Act. Andr. 5–7)

For all their differences, the majority of the apocryphal Acts agree that sexuality entered human experience through the fall, at Satan's instigation. From that 'work of corruption', which involved humanity in marriage and procreation, the Acts proclaim the gospel as a message of deliverance. The message of Christ restores dedicated celibates to paradisical innocence, as those who anticipate and share in the 'holy and incorruptible' marriage with their heavenly bridegroom.[9]

Such extreme versions of Jesus' and Paul's 'gospel' did not, of course, go unchallenged, even among those who, in Clement's words, admired monogamous marriage, while preferring celibacy.[10] The author of the Acts of Xanthippe alludes to Ephesians 5:23ff. (and perhaps to its parallels) to prove that 'Paul' taught not marital abstinence, but marital fidelity: 'I have taught wives to love their husbands, and fear them as masters, and husbands to observe fidelity to their wives' (Act. Xanthippe 20).

If certain ascetic authors tend to see Adam and Eve as representing mere sexual union, the human institution of marriage, others, equally ascetically inclined, adopt an opposite pattern of exegesis. The Apocryphon of John, for example, directly refers Genesis 2:24f. to spiritual, primordial union.

Here Adam recognizes in Eve, his spiritual partner, 'the luminous *epinoia*', exclaiming, in the words of Genesis 2:23, 'This is indeed bone from my bones, and flesh from my flesh' (Ap. John II, 23:4–11). Joining with her, he receives, as his 'helper' (cf. Genesis 2:18), the spiritual power of wisdom, 'who was called life' (Ap. John 20:18, 19). But forces hostile to spirituality intervene: the chief archon, fashioning a fleshly copy of Adam's spiritual counterpart, lulls Adam into the 'sleep' of oblivion (cf. Genesis 2:21ff.) and finally seduces her himself, thus implanting sexual desire within her. For this reason, the author concludes, sexual intercourse continues to the present day (Ap. John 24:26–31) opposing spirituality by drawing humanity instead into marriage, intercourse, procreation, and so into death. The practical implications are clear: only those who repudiate sexual desire and intercourse can achieve the spiritual purity humanity lost in the fall.

This paradigm of primordial spiritual union, violated through the introduction of its fleshly antithesis, appearing in many variants, seems to underlie many of the Nag Hammadi texts (i.e., Apoc. Adam, Orig. World, Hyp. Arch., Gos. Eg., Eugnostos, Gos. Thom., Gos. Phil.). For our present purpose of sketching out basic exegetical patterns, let us consider a second text that, like the Apocryphon of John, directly cites Genesis 2:23f. The Exegesis on the Soul contrasts the soul's pure marriage with carnal marriage 'encumbered with the annoyance of physical desire' (132:27–35). This author, too, reads Genesis 2:23f. not in reference to the latter, but to the former:

> The prophet said concerning the first man and the first woman,
> 'They will become one flesh' (Genesis 2:24). For they were
> originally joined together when they were with the Father, before
> the woman led astray the man, who is her brother.

Strikingly, this author, too, intends to read the Genesis passage allegorically through 'Paul's' eyes, citing passages from both 1 Corinthians and Ephesians to show, in the first place, that the soul's alienation expresses itself in sexual terms: 'the prostitution of the soul' leads to 'prostitution of the body as well' (Exeg. Soul 130:35–131:13). Secondly, the author intends to show that references to the man's lordship over his wife, like his other references to marriage, are to be taken symbolically. Having in mind, apparently, such passages as 1 Corinthians 6:16f., 2 Corinthians 11:3f. and Ephesians 5:23ff. (as well as the synoptic image of Christ as 'bridegroom'), the author explains that:

> The Father sent from heaven (the soul's) husband, who is her
> brother, the firstborn. Then the bridegroom came down to the
> bride. She gave up her former prostitution and cleansed herself
> of the pollutions of her adulterers, and was renewed, so as to be
> a bride.   (Exeg. Soul 132:7–12)

As her heavenly bridegroom impregnates the soul with the seed 'that is the lifegiving spirit' she becomes spiritually fruitful (133:31–134:6).

Reading Genesis 2:23f. allegorically, primarily through Ephesians 5:21–33, often in conjunction with passages drawn from 1 Corinthians, the author of the Exegesis on the Soul sums up through the image of marriage the whole of creation and redemption. This cosmological drama takes place in three acts. The first depicts the spiritual union, represented in Adam and Eve, in a state of primordial innocence; the second, their division and separation, which implicates them in sexuality (and death); the third, the coming of the 'pure bridegroom' to redeem his adulterous and prostituted bride. Restoring her to her original purity, he celebrates with her the 'mystery' of spiritual marriage (cf. Ephesians 5:32). This basic scheme, probably already implicit in such works as the Acts of Thomas and Acts of Andrew, undergoes many variants, and comes to play a major role in Christian exegesis of Genesis – and corresponding attitudes toward marriage and sexuality – throughout the next several centuries.

Yet if some Christians find in such sources as Genesis 2–3, Matthew 19, 1 Corinthians, and Ephesians 5 support for radically ascetic versions of 'the gospel', Valentinian Christians use the same sources – and even the same dramatic scheme – to draw from them opposite implications, both theological and practical.

How do Valentinian exegetes interpret the story of Adam and Eve – and its consummation in the 'mystery of Christ and the church'? Historians, confronted with a bewildering array of variant exegeses, often of the same passages, have tended either to agree with Irenaeus that Valentinian exegesis is hopelessly arbitrary (cf. *Haer.* II, 27:1–3)[11] or to agree with C. Barth that such different exegeses probably evince the work of different teachers, and show 'that the exegete does not consider himself bound to any single definitive interpretation'.[12] Both the heresiologists and the sources themselves indicate, certainly, that the exegesis of various teachers often differs. But once we recognize the basic *structure* and *method* underlying Valentinian exegesis, we can discern, even in the variety of extant sources, a certain thematic – and apparently traditional – consistency.

Like other theologians we noted above, the Valentinians narrate the drama of creation and redemption in three 'acts': first, primordial union; second, the separation and division of the two partners; third, their reconciliation and reunion in 'perfect marriage'. Valentinian exegetes tell this story in three different stages that correspond to each of these themes: first, in relation to the *plērōma*; second, to the *kenōma*; and third, to the *kosmos*. And while one theme dominates each stage of the drama (union, in the *plērōma*; separation, in the *kenōma*; reconciliation and reunion, in the *kosmos*), the threefold process itself unfolds, in turn, in each of the stages, leading to its further development in the next.[13]

This structure allows the Valentinian exegete to interpret the passages relating to Adam and Eve (or Christ and the church) in varying ways, depending upon which stage of the drama he intends to explicate. And the typology of Adam/Eve, Christ/church, I suggest, offers a key to understanding the fundamental pattern underlying the profusion of sources.

According to Irenaeus, Valentinus himself, describing the 'origin of all things', relates how the ineffable source of all being, dyadic in nature, brings forth the Father (or *nous*) and truth (*alētheia*). This primary tetrad brings forth, in turn, the syzygies *logos* and *zōē, anthrōpos* and *ekklēsia* (*Haer.* I, 11:1). Valentinian exegesis of the Johannine prologue suggests that the first of these syzygies symbolizes the primordial union later figured in Adam and Eve; the second, that of Christ and his church.[14] For as Eve ('life' = *Zōē*) was originally within Adam (cf. Genesis 2), so, Valentinian exegetes explain from John 1:4, 'in him (the *logos*) was *zōē*, the *suzugos*' (*Exc. Theod.* 6:4; *Haer.* I, 8:5). The feminine being, 'life' (*zōē* = Eve), in harmony with her masculine *suzugos, logos*, brings forth the second syzygy of the second tetrad: *anthrōpos* and *ekklēsia*, the primordial archetype of Christ and the church. So, Ptolemy explains, it is the divine life (*zōē* = Eve) who 'illuminates and reveals' those human beings who participate in the church (*ekklēsia; Haer.* I, 8:5). Interpreting the first 'act' of the drama, Marcus explains that Genesis 1:1 refers, in this context, to the origin of the primary tetrad, and Genesis 1:2 to that of the second (*Haer.* I, 18:1).

But of the divine aeons produced from this second syzygy (*anthrōpos/ekklēsia*) one, 'separating from the rest, and falling from its original order, produced the rest of the universe' (*Haer.* I, 11:1). Prefiguring Eve's alienation from Adam, Sophia's separation from her divine spouse (*thelētos*, 'what has been willed') transgresses the Father's will. So the author of A Valentinian Exposition (apparently interpreting spiritually the Genesis passage on marriage, 2:23f., and procreation, 1:28), explains that 'the will of the Father' is twofold: that 'no one should be in the *plērōma* without a *suzugos*', and 'always produce and bear fruit' (Val. Exp. 36:29–34).

The first act, like the others that follow, concludes in a scene of reconciliation and reunion as Sophia is 'restored to her own *suzugos*' (*Haer.* I, 2:4). Furthermore, to prevent further disjunctions in the *plērōma*, Christ teaches to all the aeons 'the nature of their syzygies' (*Haer.* I, 2:5), while his own *suzugos*, the Holy Spirit, equalizes and restores the whole pleromic being into joyful harmony.

Yet the conclusion of the first act, as we noted before, sets the stage for the second. Left unresolved, excluded from the *plērōma*, remains Sophia's 'desire' (*enthumēsis*). Produced apart from her *suzugos*, this element of Sophia remains, consequently, 'barren', 'a female and unformed fruit'.[15] Only reunion with her spiritual 'husband' can purify this element of Sophia, release her from suffering, and make her 'fruitful'. Moved by compassion, the pleromic aeons, themselves now capable of 'bearing fruit', since their own restoration in syzygy, send forth to her the Saviour as her divine husband. Receiving him with joy, she joins with him, becomes pregnant, and gives birth to their offspring, which is 'the church' (*ekklēsia, Haer.* I, 5:6).

Produced 'in the image of the *ekklēsia* above' (*Haer.* I, 5:6), the seed of the church that she bears, like its pleromic prototype, itself consists of a syzygy (*anthrōpos/ekklēsia*). So the author of *Exc. Theod.* 21, interpreting Genesis 1:27 in terms of the *kenōma*, explains that the verse ('in the image of God he created them; male and female he created them') refers to Sophia's 'finest production', as she bears *anthrōpos*, the masculine element of the seed, symbolizing the elect, and *ekklēsia*, the feminine element that symbolizes the 'calling'. The author draws further the parallel with Adam and Eve:

> ... so also, in the case of Adam, the male remained in him, but all the female seed was taken from him and became Eve, from whom the females are derived, as the males are from him. (*Exc. Theod.* 21:2–3)

Having given birth to the church in the nascent form of the seed, Sophia and her divine husband, Jesus, together plan to build for their offspring a 'house' to nurture and raise that 'seed' to maturity – the *kosmos* (cf. *Exc. Theod.* 47:1). Since events in the *kenōma* prefigure those in the *kosmos*, 'the church is rightly said to have been chosen before the foundation of the *kosmos*' (*Exc. Theod.* 41:2). So the second act, like the first, consummates in a scene of spiritual marriage and intercourse (cf. *Exc. Theod.* 13:1; 17:1) and sets the stage for act three.

When they go on to describe the actual process of human creation in the *kosmos*, how the spiritual 'seed' of the church becomes 'implanted' in human beings, Valentinian authors read the Adam and Eve story in yet other ways.[16] Here Adam may represent the *psuchē*, and Eve, hidden within him, the *pneuma*. According to the author of *Exc. Theod.* 50:1ff., Genesis 2:7a (*labōn choun apo tēs gēs*) indicates how the creator first fashioned for Adam an 'earthly and hylic' soul. 'Irrational and consubstantial with the beasts', this hylic soul is what Genesis 3:1 depicts as the 'serpent', the 'biter of the heel' (Genesis 3:15; *Exc. Theod.* 53:1–2). Yet, the author insists, this hylic soul is not to be confused with physical matter. For Adam was 'created in paradise, in the fourth heaven', where 'earthly flesh does not ascend' (*Exc. Theod.* 51:2). Rather, like the devil himself (with whom it is *homoousios*), this element consists of a debased form of spiritual *ousia*, one born from 'the weakness which is a product of the woman above' (*Exc. Theod.* 67:1).

Following this, the creator breathes into the hylic soul the 'breath of life' (Genesis 2:7b), the higher element of the soul, which remains hidden within the first like the soul within the flesh, or, indeed, like Eve within Adam. So Adam's recognition of Eve as 'bone of my bones and flesh of my flesh' (Genesis 2:23) refers, on one level, to this twofold nature of the soul itself (*Exc. Theod.* 51:1–3). Yet hidden even deeper, within the *divine* part of the soul, is the spirit itself. Thus the same passage, taken on another level, may refer to Eve, hidden and contained within Adam as the *pneuma* is concealed within the *psuchē*, as 'spiritual marrow' within the 'bone' of the 'rational and heavenly soul' (*Exc. Theod.* 53:5).

Eve's separation from Adam, then, bears multiple connotations. On one level, it signifies the severance of the original harmony of *psuchē* and *pneuma* within Adam. His 'sleep' (Genesis 2:21), therefore, shows the soul becoming oblivious to *pneuma*, as it separates from that divine element

(*Exc. Theod.* 2:2). Read on another level, the separation of Adam and Eve may symbolize how the pneumatic element of the church divided from its harmony with the psychic element.

In either case, each member of the syzygy, weakened by their separation, becomes vulnerable to seduction by the evil powers. For being constituted in syzygy, neither member of the divided pair can stand alone. Alienated from one another, each plunges into inferior relationships. Eve's sin, according to the author of the Gospel of Philip, was adultery. That Eve 'commits adultery' with the serpent signifies, for him, how pneumatic being, separated from its union with *psuchē*, joins instead with *hulē* (Gos. Phil. 42). Since 'every association which came into being between those unlike one another is adultery' (loc. cit.), *pneuma*'s union with *hulē* violates her original nature. Although 'when Eve was in Adam, there was no death', from their separation 'death came into being' (Gos. Phil. 71). So Eve, although born as the offspring of divine wisdom, becomes the 'little wisdom', the wisdom 'which knows death' (Gos. Phil. 39).

Adam undergoes an analogous experience. Rendered vulnerable to evil powers through disobedience (Gos. Phil. 61), he (or the *psuchē*, cf. Gos. Phil. 9) becomes enslaved to them. Separated from his spiritual *suzugos*, he does not partake of the tree of life (*zōē*), which would nurture his true humanity, but 'from the tree which produced beasts, and becoming a beast, he begat beasts' (Gos. Phil. 84). Like Eve, who also joins with the 'beast', the 'serpent' that symbolizes the hylic element, so Adam, too, becomes identified with *hulē*. Fed 'from the tree which produced beasts', the hylic nature increases its hold over him.

Once he is clothed with the physical body (the 'coats of skin' of Genesis 3:21; cf. *Exc. Theod.* 55:1) Adam finds that his hylic nature, alienated from the rational soul and from spirit, drives him 'into seed and procreation' as if he were now 'incapable of standing apart' from his identification with bodily impulses (*Exc. Theod.* 55:1–3). Thus Adam becomes the prototype of fallen humanity. The author of *Exc. Theod.* 56 concludes this exegesis by citing 1 Corinthians 15:47: 'therefore our father Adam is "the first man from earth, earthy" ' (*Exc. Theod.* 56:1–2). The author of the Gospel of Philip apparently alludes to the same passage to contrast Adam, the 'earthly man', with Christ, the 'man from heaven' (Gos. Phil. 28; cf. also log. 23, which cites 1 Corinthians 15:50).

Such theologians offer the closest analogy I have seen in second century sources to the doctrine later enunciated by Augustine: 'All who are begotten in the world are begotten of nature' (Gos. Phil. 30) in a process vitiated by sin that generates them inevitably toward spiritual and physical death. Yet the Valentinians insist (as will Augustine, adopting a very different line of argument) that such theology does not intend to indict sexuality *per se*, but only that debased form of sexuality resulting from the fall. One Valentinian, rejecting the usual interpretation of a passage from the Gospel of the Egyptians, declares that Christ does not impugn birth itself, 'since (birth) is necessary for the salvation of believers' (*Exc. Theod.* 67:1). The same teacher declares, indeed, that, had Adam 'sown from the *psychic* and *pneumatic* elements, *as well as* from the hylic', had he, that is, maintained the three elements of his being in their original harmony, his progeny would have been 'equal and righteous, and the teaching would have been in all' (*Exc. Theod.* 56:2). But the disjunction within the primordial couple (and, consequently, within Adam himself) effectively separated Adam's procreative energy from its harmony with *psuchē* and *pneuma*, and so brought suffering and death upon him and his descendants. The author of the Gospel of Philip, following Paul (cf. Romans 7) sees Adam, consequently, as bound under the law, capable of discerning good from evil, but wholly incapable of using his knowledge to make himself good, or to remove from himself the evil that has overtaken him (Gos. Phil. 94).

To repair this disruption – specifically, that of the psychic element, symbolized by Adam – 'the pneumatic element was sent forth, so that it might here be joined and united in syzygy with the psychic' (*Haer.* I, 6:1):

> Therefore the Saviour (embodying the pneumatic element) came, in order that he might remove the separation which was from the beginning, and again unite the two, and that he might give life (*zōē* = Eve/*pneuma*) to those who died in the separation, and unite them ... But the woman is united to her husband in the bridal chamber.   (Gos. Phil. 78–79)

Christ came, then, to reunite Adam and Eve, and to consummate their reunion by restoring to himself his own alienated (and internally divided) bride, the *church*. The author of the Gospel of Philip, speaking a 'mystery' (cf. Ephesians 5:32), describes how Jesus, embodying spiritual harmony, himself came forth from the union of the 'Father of the all' with the 'virgin who came down', that is, the Mother, the Holy Spirit (Gos. Phil. 82). Following Wilson's reading, we learn that 'he' (apparently the Saviour) revealed 'the great bridal chamber', that is, the *plērōma*. 'Because of this', the author continues, 'his body, which came into being on that day, came out of the bridal chamber'.

Problematic as the passage may be, I suggest that its author, having just alluded to Ephesians 5:32, has in mind the corporate image of Christ's 'body', the *church*. As the Saviour himself comes into being from a conjunction of spiritual powers, so does 'his body', the church, 'in the manner of him who came into being from the bridegroom and the bride'. This interpretation renders comprehensible the conclusion of this passage: 'so ... it is fitting for each one of the disciples to enter into his Rest', the rest that symbolizes the consummation of the divine marriage. If this is his meaning, the author of the Gospel of Philip follows a traditional pattern of Valentinian imagery which takes from Romans 12 and 1 Corinthians 12 (combined with allusions to Colossians and Ephesians) the collective image of the church as Christ's 'body'. The author of *Exc. Theod.* 42:3 agrees: Christ 'put on the body of Jesus, which is *homoousios* with the church'.

But what constitutes that 'body of Christ'? Our sources show that this question split Valentinian theologians among themselves.[17] The eastern branch of Valentinus' followers insisted that Christ's 'body' – the church – is purely 'spiritual', that is, that the church consists only of the pneumatic elect. So 'Theodotus says' that 'the visible part of Jesus was Sophia, the *ekklēsia* of the superior seed, and he put it on through the flesh' (*Exc. Theod.* 26:1). But the western Valentinians argued instead that Christ's 'body' consists of two elements, psychic and pneumatic. Hence the church includes both the masculine element (the elect) represented by Adam, and the feminine element (the called) represented by Eve. Describing Christ's cosmic manifestation, the author of *Exc. Theod.* 58:1 says that

> Jesus Christ received to himself the *ekklēsia*, that is, the elect and the called, the pneumatic from the Mother, and the psychic through the *oikonomia*; and he saved and raised (from both these elements) what was *homoousios* with him.

The author of the Interpretation of Knowledge (NHC XI. *1*) agrees. Citing the Pauline image of Christ's body, he insists that all Christians, both psychic and pneumatic, belong to the 'one body' which Christ heads. The author of A Valentinian Exposition (NHC XI. *2*), too, identifies Sophia (an image of the church) as herself 'a *suzugos* of *anthrōpos* and *ekklēsia*' (31:36–37).

When Christ unites with his church in marriage, all who praise 'the Father in the Son, and the Father in the Church' participate in that marriage (Val. Exp. 40:21f.). The author of the Tripartite Tractate declares that 'we in the flesh are his church' (125:4f.). Yet he sees that the elect share with Christ a unique *sungeneia*: 'the pneumatic race immediately became a body of its head' (118:28–35) since 'the election shares body and essence (*ousia*) with the Saviour, since it is like a bridal chamber because of its union with him' (122:12–17; cf. also 116:1–8). Yet the author shows his affiliation with the western school when he adds that the 'calling' has 'the place of those who rejoiced at the union of the bridegroom and the bride' (122:20–24). For he emphasizes that the 'calling', lacking full recognition of Christ, 'needed a place of instruction' which the cosmos provided for them. But at the eschatological transformation, he concludes, 'all the members of the body ... shall be restored in a single place, and receive the restoration simultaneously, when they have been manifested as the whole body – the restoration into the pleroma' (123:16–22).[18]

The consummation, then, shall restore the primordial union lost when Eve separated from Adam. According to the Interpretation of Knowledge, similarly, Jesus invites the church to 'Enter (into his "body", the church) through the rib whence you came, and hide yourself from the beasts' (10:34–37). The Tripartite Tractate, alluding to both Genesis and such passages as Galatians 3:28, declares that 'the end will receive a unitary existence just like the beginning, where there is no male nor female ... but Christ is all in all ... The restoration to that which previously was is a unity' (132:20–133:8). In that marriage 'Christ is one with her' (with the *ekklēsia*), in the bridal chamber, 'which is the love of God the Father' (138:10–11).[19]

Because part of the church remained in the condition symbolized by

Adam in his separation from Eve, or *psuchē* alienated from *pneuma*, western Valentinians explain that Christ came into the world 'to save the psychic element' (*Haer.* I, 6:1). But since first he 'put on' the 'psychic Christ' (*Exc. Theod.* 59:3), and 'even this psychic Christ, whom he put on, was invisible', he received 'a body spun for him out of the invisible psychic *ousia*' (*Exc. Theod.* 59:3–4), so that, becoming *homoousios* with Adam, he 'came into the perceptible world'. Such sources as the Interpretation of Knowledge, the Tripartite Tractate and the Gospel of Truth describe Christ's incarnation in terms that seem intended to refute any charge of docetism. For the Saviour 'not only took upon himself the death of those he intended to save', but wholly accepted the human 'smallness', allowing himself 'to be conceived and born as an infant in body and soul' (Tri. Trac. 115:3–11). Yet unlike the rest of humanity, the Saviour's conception occurred 'without sin, stain, or pollution'.

But if, since Adam, human sexuality had come to be dominated by hylic passions, how could anyone generated through sexual intercourse remain free from pollution? To answer this question, apparently, Valentinian theologians interpret the virgin birth as a symbol for the Holy Spirit's participation in his conception. While the rest of humanity, then, was generated from Adam in his alienation from Eve (and so from *pneuma*), Christ alone was born from a dynamic union of spiritual powers (cf. Gos. Phil. 82; *Exc. Theod.* 68; *Haer.* I, 15:3). Valentinian exegetes interpret Gabriel's announcement to Mary ('The Holy Spirit shall come upon you, and the power of the Most High shall overshadow you', Luke 1:35) as referring to the joint participation, in Jesus' conception, of the two primordial syzygies that form the second tetrad. These two, *logos* and *zōē*, *anthrōpos* and *ekklēsia*, prefigure, as noted above, Adam and Eve, Christ and the church (*Haer.* I, 15:3; *Exc. Theod.* 60). And if the author of the Gospel of Philip, for example, considers bodily existence 'despicable' in comparison with that of the soul that animates it (Gos. Phil. 22), he warns that far from simply despising the body, one must recognize its indispensability as an instrument of revelation: 'do not despise the lamb' (the actual body of Christ, cf. Heracleon, fr. 10).[20]

Valentinian references to Christ's 'body', then, often include ambiguity that plays upon its various connotations. The author of *Exc. Theod.* 61 concludes his account of how the Saviour 'destroyed death, and raised up the mortal body' by explaining that 'in this way, therefore, the psychic elements are raised and saved' (61:8). Heracleon, too, envisages in ecclesiological terms the 'resurrection of the body'. Commenting on John 2:19 ('destroy this temple and in three days I will raise it up ... he spoke of the temple of his body'), Heracleon explains that the resurrection 'on the third day' is the 'resurrection of the church (*ekklēsia*)' (fr. 15).

Heracleon sees, too, in the Samaritan woman of John 4 an image of the church, whose experience vividly recapitulates that of Eve. The Saviour finds 'the pneumatic *ekklēsia*', like her prototype, 'lost in the deep matter of error' (fr. 23). Her suffering, like Eve's, is expressed in sexual terms. Alienated from her 'true husband', she has involved herself in adultery, having joined herself with 'six men' whose number signifies immersion in 'all the hylic evil with which she was intermingled, and with which she consorted when she prostituted herself, contrary to reason' (fr. 18). But when the Saviour approaches her, he tells her to 'call her husband', indicating, Heracleon says, that her husband 'is her *plērōma*, so that, on coming with him to the Saviour, she may obtain from him power and union and the mingling with her *plērōma*' (fr. 18).

Having longed to be 'released from her immorality', the church recognizes immediately the truth of Christ's revelation, and so demonstrates 'the faith that was inseparable from her nature' (fr. 17). Acknowledging her previous 'ignorance of God and the things essential for her life', she joyfully receives her reconciliation with her spiritual *suzugos*. So, Heracleon adds, 'the church received Christ, and believed concerning him that he alone understood all things' (fr. 25). While remaining herself in communion with the Saviour, her joy impels her to return 'to the world', to 'preach the good news of Christ's coming to the calling' (fr. 27), that is, to the psychic members of the church. For, having reconciled her own spiritual nature in union with her *suzugos*, the pneumatic *ekklēsia* devotes herself to sharing with Christ the work of reconciling those who, 'in Adam', still remain alienated from the spirit (*Eve*). For 'through the spirit and by the spirit', Heracleon says, 'the soul is drawn to the Saviour' (fr. 27). Together with the Saviour she works to fulfil 'the will of the Father' that 'all men should know the Father and be saved' (fr. 31). The author of the Gospel of Philip, apparently in a similar way, suggests that the 'three Maries' of log. 32 (the Saviour's virgin mother, her sister, and Magdalene) serve as images of Christ's spiritual *suzugos* in her triple manifestations, respectively, as Holy Spirit, wisdom (Eve), and as his 'companion' and bride, the church (Gos. Phil. 55).

The Valentinian model of spiritual harmony, based on the interdependence of all beings requires, then, the reconciliation of each member with all of the others in order to reach fulfilment. Even the Saviour himself, coming into the cosmos, needs to be joined with his 'bride', the church, in order to re-enter the pleromic 'bridechamber'. Each of Christ's 'angels' – the company of spiritual syzygies of the members of the pneumatic *ekklēsia* – needs, in turn, reunion with his 'bride' to celebrate that marriage. The western branch of Valentinians extended this process further: the pneumatic *ekklēsia*, recapitulating the experience of Eve, separated 'in the beginning' from her 'true husband', needs, as well, to be reunited with Adam, who may represent the psychic element separated from its original union in that one 'body of Christ'.

Such a vision of the process of redemption the Valentinians, citing Ephesians 5:32, call the 'mystery of marriage' (Gos. Phil. 60) or the 'mystery of syzygies' (*Haer*. I, 6:4).

> They say, too, that Paul has referred to the syzygies within the *plērōma*, revealing them by means of one; for, when writing of marital union in this life, he expressed himself in this way: 'This is a great mystery, but I speak of Christ and the church'. (*Haer*. I, 8:4)[21]

The Gnostic Christian receives baptism, then, not only, as psychics do, as a 'going into death' (cf. Gos. Phil. 109, 59; Romans 6:3f.) and purification from sins, but also as a reunion with the *suzugos* Adam lost in separating from Eve. The participant receives 'the gift of the Holy Spirit' (Gos. Phil. 59, 109). Yet the process baptism initiates (rebirth through the Holy Spirit) receives completion only in *chrism*, which effects, as well, rebirth in the image of her *suzugos*, Christ. Those receiving chrism are reborn from a complete syzygy becoming children 'of the bridal chamber' (Gos. Phil. 66; cf. 103; compare *Exc. Theod.* 68; 79–80:1–3). The author of the Gospel of Philip explains that:

> Through the Holy Spirit we are indeed born but we are born again through Christ. In the two we are anointed through the Spirit, and when we have been born we are united … None shall be able to see himself either in water (*baptism*) or in a mirror (*eucharist/bridechamber*) without light. Not again wilt thou be able to see in light (*chrism*) without water or mirror. For this reason it is fitting to baptize in the two, in light and water. But the light is the *chrism*. (Gos. Phil. 74–75)

So, the author explains,

> … The *chrism* is superior to baptism, for it is from the word 'chrism' that we have been called 'Christians', certainly not because of the word 'baptism'. And it is because of the chrism that 'the Christ' has his name … Whoever has been anointed possesses everything. He possesses the resurrection, the light, the cross, the Holy Spirit.   (Gos. Phil. 95)

Those who experience, through these first two sacraments, spiritual reconciliation, then receive the eucharist as a celebration of 'spiritual love' (Gos. Phil. 77), participating with Christ in the eucharistic prayer that consecrates the 'mystery of marriage' (Gos. Phil. 60): 'You who have joined the perfect, the light, with the Holy Spirit, unite the angels with us also, the images' (Gos. Phil. 26).

Partaking of the eucharistic bread and wine, the Gnostic Christian perceives these, in turn, as symbols of the masculine and feminine elements of the pleromic *syzygy*. Interpreting John 6:53, 'Whoever does not eat my flesh and drink my blood has no *life* in him', the author of the Gospel of Philip suggests that 'his flesh is the *logos* (in which dwells life, as Eve in Adam; cf. John 1:4), and his blood, the *Holy Spirit*. Whoever has received these has food and drink and clothing' (Gos. Phil. 23; cf. 100). Participation in this whole sacramental 'mystery', then, undoes the effects of Adam and Eve's transgression. The participant receives, first of all, 'clothing', having 'put on Christ', in baptism, to cover the nakedness that shamed the fallen Adam and Eve (Gos. Phil. 23). Secondly, while Adam, eating from the tree of knowledge, lost access to the tree of life, bringing death upon his progeny, Christ's coming restores to him – in the oil of *chrism* – the fruit of the tree of life (Gos. Phil. 92).

Thirdly, since Adam's progeny, following his transgression, could find 'no bread in the world', that is, nothing to nourish their true humanity, 'man used to feed like the beasts' from the trees that symbolize 'the enjoyment of things that are evil' (Tri. Trac. 107:1–2), nourishing only their hylic nature. But when Christ came, the perfect man, he brought bread from heaven (John 6:35) so that man might be nourished with human food (Gos. Phil. 15). Whoever partakes of that food (*logos* and *pneuma*) in the eucharist, receives the 'resurrection in the flesh', life that cancels the penalty of death (Gos. Phil. 23). The sacraments, as the author of the Gospel of Philip emphasizes, consecrate the whole person:

> The holy man is holy altogether, down to his body. For if he has received the bread he will make it holy, or the cup, or anything else that he receives, purifying them. And how will he not purify the body also? (Gos. Phil. 108)

The sacraments that together effect the 'mystery of marriage', then, integrate the whole of human experience, reuniting *psuchē* with *pneuma*, and integrating these with the body in a state of consecrated holiness.

From this, Irenaeus says, the Valentinians derive direct implications concerning sexual activity. Those who have experienced that 'mystery of syzygies' are enjoined to enact marital intercourse in ways that express their spiritual, psychic, and bodily integration, celebrating the act as a symbol of the divine pleromic harmony. But those who remain uninitiated are to refrain from sexual intercourse. For these, remaining bound in the state symbolized by Adam's separation from Eve, still experience their sexual impulses as dominated by 'the power of lust' (*Haer.* I, 6:4).

Yet while Gnostic Christians practise the 'mystery of syzygies' through acts of sexual intercourse (only, we infer, with other Gnostic Christians), the Gospel of Philip shows that they also celebrate that 'mystery' in their union with all who belong to the pneumatic church, the 'bride of Christ'. The eucharistic 'kiss of peace' expresses their oneness with one another, and produces spiritual 'fruit':

> For the perfect conceive through a kiss and give birth. Because of this we also kiss one another. We receive conception from the grace which is among us. (Gos. Phil. 31)

The same author urges the members of that 'body' to repudiate adultery (referring, apparently, to 'intercourse' with the hylic element; cf. Gos. Phil. 42) and to live in a way that becomes the pure 'bride of Christ':

> You who are with the Son of God, love not the world but love the Lord, that those you bring forth may not be like unto the world, but may be like the Lord. (Gos. Phil. 112)

Contrary to those who claim that 'the gospel' entirely excludes it, then, the Valentinians see in marriage not only the symbol of the gospel's 'great mystery' but also a practical paradigm for the whole process of sanctification. The Valentinians, consequently, reject both forms of ascetic exegesis – that which, on the one hand, interprets Adam and Eve as depicting merely sexual union (the fleshly antitype of Christ and the church) and that illustrated in the Exegesis on the Soul, which interprets them exclusively in symbolic terms (the spiritual prototype of Christ and the church). Referring to cosmic creation, Valentinian exegetes see in Adam and Eve all three elements of human nature. Their typology receives its fulfilment in the reunion of Christ with his church, which even in the present age joins the Gnostic Christian with Christ, reuniting spirit, soul, and body in a state of consecrated holiness.

Confronted with such diverse forms of 'heresy', Clement and Irenaeus find themselves compelled to reinterpret, in terms they consider 'orthodox' not only the Adam and Eve story, but also its implications for sexual and marital behaviour. In his concern to refute ascetic versions of the gospel, Clement seems to accept the Valentinians as allies who, like himself, 'approve of marriage' (*Strom*. III, 1). But Irenaeus detests the élitism that leads them to condone sexual union for the 'initiated', while urging abstinence upon the rest. Although he admits that some may live exemplary lives, he insinuates that the sexual imagery that dominates their theology serves as a cover for all kinds of sexual licence (cf. *Haer*. I, 6:3; 13:1–6).

Against 'all the heretics' Irenaeus and Clement insist, above all, that Adam's misuse of free will – not his sexual inclination – initiated the fall. The primary theme that dominates the Adam and Eve story, as Irenaeus reads it, is

> the ancient law of human liberty. God made man a free agent from the beginning, possessing the power, as he does his own soul, to obey God's commands. (*Haer*. IV, 37:1)

Nor was human free will vitiated, as the Valentinians claim, by Adam's sin. Even now, Irenaeus declares, 'God has preserved the will of man free and under his own control' (*Haer*. IV, 37:5; cf. IV, 37:1–4). Clement agrees, rejecting any hint of 'original sin' that could communicate to posterity the effects of Adam's sin:

> Let them tell us how a newly born child would commit fornication, or how that which has done nothing has fallen under the curse of Adam. (*Strom*. III, 100)

And, he adds, if

> ... woman is regarded as the cause of death because she gives birth, so also, for the same reason, she may be called the origin of life. In fact, the woman that first began transgression is called *life*, because she became ... the mother of righteous and unrighteous alike, since each one of us makes himself either righteous or disobedient. (*Strom*. III, 64–65)

But if they indict Adam and Eve's misuse of free will as the cause of the fall, Clement and Irenaeus agree that the union of Adam and Eve, once purely spiritual, became identified with marital intercourse (and this, consequently, tainted by sin) through the fall. For the first disobedience, both heresiologists agree, took sexual form. Irenaeus takes Genesis 2:25 ('they were both naked, and not ashamed') to mean that Adam and Eve, although married, remained virgins in Paradise before sin. Like Clement, Irenaeus implies that they transgressed by engaging in intercourse before they had reached maturity:

> ... for they, having been created a short time before, had no understanding of the procreation of children; for it was necessary that they should first come to adult age, and then 'multiply' from that time onward.   (*Haer*. III, 22:4)

The loss of Eve's virginity initiated those 'bonds of union' that signalled the fall. Consequently, Irenaeus continues, only Mary's abstinence from sexual intercourse, reversing that process, could undo the disastrous effects of that primal transgression (loc. cit., cf. also III, 21:10). Adam's guilty response, too, indicates his complicity. For, Irenaeus says, Adam showed his repentance by his conduct, 'by means of the girdle' (cf. Genesis 3:7):

> covering himself with fig leaves, while there were many other leaves which would have irritated his body in a less degree. He, however, adopted a dress conformable to his disobedience, being awed by the fear of God; and resisting the erring, lustful propensity of his flesh (since he had lost his natural disposition and childlike mind, and had come to the knowledge of evil), he girded a bridle of continence upon himself and his wife ... fearing God ... . (*Haer*. III, 23:5)

As a consequence of sin, even Christian marriage involves its participants in the lesser Adamic creation. Between the claim that Christ abolished marriage, and the Valentinian counterclaim that he effected its full sanctification, the heresiologists attempt to steer a middle course. Marriage, divinely ordained 'in the beginning' received, they admit, Christ's qualified endorsement. Irenaeus' exegesis of the Adam and Eve story, following the pattern Jesus established, clearly subordinates the command to procreate (Genesis 1:28) to the institution of marriage (Genesis 2:23f.). So far, Clement and Tertullian would agree.

But both, unlike either Irenaeus or his Valentinian opponents (and, for that matter, unlike Jesus and Paul), cite Genesis 1:28 (together with the deutero-Pauline letters) to claim that Christian marriage fulfils its purpose only in procreation. To support this claim, these writers develop patterns of exegesis we noted earlier in the writings of the Apostolic Fathers. Marriage, declares Tertullian, is 'for increase' (*Marc*.). Clement, adopting a pattern of interpretation known from rabbinic exegesis, goes further, connecting Genesis 1:28 with 1:27:

> (God) said, 'multiply' (Genesis 1:27). This ought to be understood as follows: by the possession of reason man is 'made in the image of God', in so far as he cooperates with God in human creation. (*Paed.* II, 83)

As Clement sees it, Christ both confirms traditional marital patterns and transforms them, signalling the moral process that 'the gospel' requires. Retaining its patriarchal structure (which expresses, Clement believes, the order of 'nature' as well as the penalty for sin), Christian marriage must be 'purged from pollution'. This includes not only practices that pollute pagan marriages (incest, adultery, 'unnatural intercourse', homosexuality, abortion, and infanticide) but also the polygamy and divorce that marred its Jewish predecessor (*Paed.* II, 92).

Marriage, now monogamous and indissoluble, as God originally intended, may become, for believers, a 'sacred image'. But to experience it as such, Christians must correct within themselves the disordered relation of passion and reason resulting from Adam's sin. The married Christian, then, must not only subordinate sexual desire to reason, but annihilate desire entirely, thus recovering what Adam lost – the full use of rational free will:

> Our ideal is not to experience desire at all ... We should do nothing from desire. Our will is to be directed only toward what is necessary. For we are children not of desire but of will. A man who marries for the sake of begetting children must practise continence so that it is not desire he feels for his wife ... that he may beget children with a chaste and controlled will. (*Strom.* III, 57–58)

To accomplish this, as one might imagine, is not easy. 'The gospel', as Clement reads it, not only restricts sexuality to marriage, now restored to its original monogamous and indissoluble form, but, even within that, to specific acts intended for procreation. To engage in marital intercourse for any other reason is to 'do injury to nature' (*Paed.* II, 95). Clement excludes not only such counter-productive practices as oral and anal intercourse, but also intercourse with a menstruating, pregnant, barren, or menopausal wife, and, for that matter, with one's wife 'in the morning', 'in the daytime', or 'after dinner'. Clement warns, indeed, that

> ... not even at night, although in darkness, is it fitting to carry on immodestly or indecently, but with modesty, so that whatever happens, happens in the light of reason ... for even that union which is legitimate is still dangerous, except in so far as it is engaged in procreation of children. (*Paed.* II, 97f.)

Yet even at best, Christian marriage remains inferior to chastity. 'Chaste marriage', in which both partners devote themselves to celibacy, is better than a sexually active one. To the gnostic Christian,

> ... his wife, after conception, is as a sister, and is judged as if of the same father; who only recalls her husband when she looks at the children; as one destined to become a sister in reality after putting off the flesh, which separates and limits the knowledge of those who are spiritual by the specific characteristics of the sexes. (*Strom.* VI, 100)

Only celibate spouses, who thereby recover, so to speak, their virginity (*Strom.* VII, 12), transcend the whole structure of bodily existence, and recover the spiritual equality Adam and Eve lost through the fall:

> ... for souls, by themselves, are equal. Souls are 'neither male nor female', when 'they no longer marry nor are given in marriage' (cf. Luke 20:35). (*Strom.* VI, 100)

Such, Clement says, was the marriage of the blessed apostles, and

> ... such their perfect control over their feelings even in the closest human relationships. So, too, the apostle says, 'Let him who marries be as if he were not married' (cf. 1 Corinthians 7:29), requiring that marriage should not be enslaved to passion ... thus the soul acquires a mental disposition corresponding to the gospel in every relation of life. (*Strom.* VII, 64)

The practice advocated by ascetic Christians, then, who would abolish marital intercourse, and the opposite practice advocated by Valentinian Christians, who revere it as the primary symbol for sanctification, each attracted a select (and, one imagines, very different) group of enthusiastic adherents. Clement and his orthodox colleagues rejected both, and, following the precedent of the Apostolic Fathers, invoked the Hebrew Bible and the deutero-Pauline letters to assure the majority of believers of God's continuing (if qualified) blessing on marriage. Rejecting, too, the egalitarian tendencies inherent in both ascetic and Valentinian practices, orthodox leaders reaffirmed the husband's traditional dominance over his wife as consonant with 'nature' as well as God's judgement upon Eve's sin. Other issues proved more controversial. During the centuries following Clement, orthodox Christians engaged in heated argument concerning precisely *what* new strictures 'the gospel' imposes on marriage – whether, for example, remarriage of the widowed violates the principle of monogamy: whether, and under what circumstances, intercourse or divorce may be considered to be 'licit'. Most tended to agree with Clement and Tertullian, unlike both Irenaeus and his Valentinian opponents (and, for that matter, unlike Jesus or Paul), that Christian marriage finds its sole legitimate purpose in procreation.

While refusing to exclude married Christians from the church, Clement and his colleagues refused to renounce the ascetic ideal. They invited to the 'angelic life' (cf. Luke 20:35f.) the zealous few who despised any compromise with the lesser state symbolized by the union of Adam and Eve. Continence and virginity, they agreed, promised their devotees the fullest participation in the spiritual marriage that Christ enjoys with his virgin 'bride'.

Contemporary patristic (especially Protestant) scholars often repeat the cliché that second century orthodox Christians maintained, against all 'heretics' (and especially against Gnostics) the 'goodness of creation', and, specifically, the 'goodness of marriage'. To some extent, of course, they did. Yet our brief sketch suggests that Irenaeus, Clement, and Tertullian express as much sceptical reserve as affirmation. Their theological heritage still dominates, of course, Christian theology and attitudes. For Christians of many denominations issues concerning practical implications of 'the gospel' remain at the centre of contemporary theological – and practical – controversy.

NOTES

1. A. von Harnack, *The Mission and Expansion of Christianity*, tr. and ed. J. Moffat, New York 1961, 98–100.
2. Gn. r. 18:5.
3. Tertullian, *De exhortatione castitatis 5; De monogamia 5, 8 passim*; Jerome, *Adversus Jovinianum* I, 16.
4. See, for example, E. Pagels, *The Gnostic Paul: Gnostic Exegesis of the Pauline Letters*, Philadelphia 1975.
5. A. Vööbus, *History of Asceticism in the Syrian Orient* I, Louvain 1958, 42f.
6. Irenaeus, *Haer*. III, 23:8.
7. For recent discussion, see S. Davies, *The Revolt of the Widows*, Southern Illinois University Press 1980, 12ff.
8. Sometimes, in the apocryphal acts, *moicheia* seems to bear its usual connotation of marital infidelity (including infidelity to one's spouse in a 'chaste marriage', Act. Thom. 51). More often, however, it appears to be used synonymously with *porneia* to connote any sexual intercourse, including marital union. According to Act. Thom. 28, for example, the apostle preaches abstinence from three primary sins, the first of which is *porneia*. Act. Thom. 84 identifies *moicheia* as 'the beginning of all evils', attributing to Eve's engagement in sexual union (whether with the serpent or Adam, the author does not explain) the sin of *moicheia*. According to Act. Thom. 42–49, a celibate woman responds to sexual temptation as to *moicheia* (Act. Thom. 43), apparently identified with the fruit of the 'bitter tree' (Act. Thom. 44) from which Satan beguiled Adam and Eve. Act. Thom. 85 praises Christ as the one who brings holiness, abolishing *porneia* which includes Mygdonia's 'sordid union' with her husband (Act. Thom. 88;

see also 101). Such observations tend to confirm the statement of S. Davies that, for one whose religious commitments 'are predicated on the conviction that one is related to Christ as a bride to a bridegroom ... marital and extramarital intercourse become equally adulterous' (op. cit., 84).

9. Among other recent discussions, see G. Quispel, *Makarius, das Thomasevangelium, und das Lied von der Perle, NT.S* 15, Leiden 1967; A. F. J. Klijn, *The Acts of Thomas*, Leiden 1962, especially 34–53; R. Murray, *Symbols of the Church and Kingdom: A Study in Early Syriac Tradition*, Cambridge 1977.

10. Cf. Clement, *Strom.* III, 4; Tertullian, *Marc.* I, 29.

11. A view sustained by some recent commentators. See, for example, W. von Loewenich, *Das Johannes-Verständnis im zweiten Jahrhundert*, Giessen 1932, 76.

12. C. Barth, *Die Interpretation des Neuen Testaments in der valentinianischen Gnosis, TU* 37:3, 1911, 98.

13. For further discussion of their exegetical method, see E. Pagels, *The Johannine Gospel in Gnostic Exegesis*, Philadelphia 1973, 20–50.

14. For discussion, see Pagels, op. cit., 20–35.

15. Cf. Irenaeus, *Haer.* I, 3:4; *Exc. Theod.* 67:4–68; 80:1–3; Gos. Phil. 36. (The numeration follows the editions of H. M. Schenke, *ThLZ* 84, 1959 and R. McL. Wilson, *The Gospel of Philip*, London 1962. References included here are from Prof. Wilson's translation.)

16. Essential to note, in this regard, as Prof. G. Quispel reminds me, are the distinctions between eastern and western sources in the *Excerpta*.

17. Cf. discussion in E. Pagels, 'Gnostic and Orthodox Views of Christ's Passion: Paradigms for the Christian's Response to Persecution?' in (ed.) B. Layton, *The Rediscovery of Gnosticism* I, Leiden 1980, 277–283.

18. Loc. cit.: see also the excellent discussion (especially of Interp. Know.) by K. Koschorke, *Die Polemik der Gnostiker gegen das kirchliche Christentum, NHS* 12, Leiden 1978.

19. For more technical discussion, see edition of the Tripartite Tractate, translated and edited by H. Attridge, with introduction and textual notes by Attridge and Pagels, Leiden, forthcoming 1983.

20. For specific references see W. Völker, *Quellen zur Geschichte der christlichen Gnosis, SQS* n.s.5, Tübingen 1932, 63–86.

21. Cf. the major article by R. M. Grant, 'The Mystery of Marriage in the Gospel of Philip', *VigChr* 15, 1961, 129ff.

XII

EARLY CHRISTIANS AND GNOSTICS IN GRAECO–ROMAN SOCIETY

by

Professor Robert M. Grant, Chicago

In honouring Robert McL. Wilson we try to limit our range by dealing with one aspect of the Gnostic phenomenon with which he has been so vigorously concerned. Here we deal with the elusive question about the place of the Gnostics or of some Gnostics – as compared with Christians – in the social structure of the Graeco-Roman world. F. C. Burkitt saw their leaders as creating a 'new theology' (surely this was right) and removing 'a stumbling-block in the way of the conversion of the thoughtful classes'.[1] The oddity of Burkitt's language corresponds to the elusiveness of his thought. It would be extremely difficult to pinpoint members of 'the thoughtful classes' – almost as difficult as finding a practising Gnostic in some Graeco–Roman city. This is not to say that attempts made by more recent scholars have been much more successful.[2] In the belief that a text is worth several theories based on presumed parallels, and even giving up an emphasis on 'cognitive dissonance',[3] we venture to assemble some of the evidence and try to see where it leads.

First, we shall discuss the relatively scarce but definite evidence about both Christians and Gnostics from the higher levels of society. Second, we shall look at the evidence about the accusations of deviant practice laid against both groups – to begin with, Christians in general, later on, when clearly differentiated, the Gnostics. Finally, we shall note Christian polemics about the relative size and importance of Gnostic groups.

1—SOCIAL STATUS

The most important evidence we possess comes from Pliny the Younger when legate in Bithynia and Pontus, early in the second century. He himself was of senatorial rank and must have known what he was talking about when he wrote to the emperor Trajan that the many Christians in Pontus were 'of every age, every rank, and both sexes' (*omnis aetatis, omnis ordinis, utriusque sexus, Ep.* X, 96:9). Tertullian does not change the meaning when for *ordo* he substitutes both *condicio* and *dignitas* (*Apol.* 1:7) or simply *dignitas* (*Scapul.* 5:2).

This statement, to be sure, tells us nothing about the status of Gnostics. It is not often that we have any information, real even if biased, about the Gnostic leaders, especially as regards their social status. In four instances, however, some information does exist. To be sure, we know virtually nothing about the position of Basilides at Alexandria, but the fragments of his son Isidore's writings reflect a fairly broad and eclectic acquaintance with the religious philosophies of his time and with some early Greek literature. They suggest that Isidore had received a rather good education and, presumably, that his father had encouraged him to obtain it.[4] Second, the heresiarch Marcion came from Pontus on the south shore of the Black Sea and brought enough money with him to make a generous gift to the church at Rome. When he was expelled, some years later, he apparently received his money back. Since the gift was important enough for Tertullian to criticize it, it must show that Marcion's social status was relatively high as far as money was concerned.[5] His picture of the world suggests, on the other hand, that he did not feel at home in the world or human society and looked for a complete break with both. Third, we have a legend about Epiphanes, the precocious son of the Gnostic Carpocrates, who was said to have died at seventeen after producing his treatise *On Justice* in which he argued in favour of common ownership of property and women, ridiculing the Mosaic law along the way. Worship was supposed to be centred at his tomb. But what is the social status of a god? More seriously, we note that his father came from Alexandria, presumably bringing thence the education he imparted to his son, while his mother came from Same on Cephallenia in the Ionian Sea. Presumably she was responsible for the expenses of the cult. If so, we should recognize Carpocrates, Alexandria (for such was her name), and Epiphanes as members of a local elite.[6] Last and clearest is the case of Bardaisan of Edessa. With the non-Gnostic Christian polymath Julius Africanus he was a welcome guest at the court of Abgar IX of Edessa, to whom he demonstrated his skill in archery. There could be no doubt about his status, though there has been some about his Gnosticism.[7]

Certainly there were varieties of Gnostics. Henry Chadwick has noted that for Clement of Alexandria both Basilides and Valentinus 'are men of eminence whom he always regards with respect, even though he is aware of important differences'.[8] On the other hand, Irenaeus is especially severe toward the Valentinian magician Marcus, who he says has seduced many women as far as the Rhone valley (*Haer.* I, 13:7). Marcus approached 'the most elegant women, the ones with purple-bordered dress, and the richest'.[9] Their status was obviously high, though presumably it declined when they tried to repay the magician for their religious experiences (I, 13:3). The Gnostic women who more than a century later were reported to their Egyptian bishop (as civil administrator) by Epiphanius cannot have ranked high (*Haer.* 26, 17); he refers to Gnostic couples who serve quantities of meat and wine 'even if they are poor' (26, 4:3).

And from these considerations we may move back to Christian women of high rank. Hippolytus tells of misguided apocalyptic-minded Christians in Syria who awaited the Lord's coming in mountains and highways, but were not arrested or executed as robbers by the governor because his wife was a Christian (*Dan. comm.* IV, 18). And Tertullian describes a Cappadocian governor who treated Christians cruelly because his wife had become a convert. He died eaten by worms 'alone in his palace' (*Scapul.* 3:4). Had he treated her cruelly too? We never hear of Gnostic wives of governors, though Lucian tells us that the proconsul of Asia married the daughter of Alexander the false prophet: that was bad enough.

Before finally turning to two Gnostics known through Origen's biography, we should look at Origen himself as a standard. His father had enough money so that Eusebius could draw attention to its confiscations (*Hist. Eccl.* VI, 2:13). Origen himself lived with a very rich woman who liked budding theologians (VI, 2:13). He had to be protected by Roman soldiers from local pagans who held him responsible for the martyrdoms of his converts (VI, 3:4–5; 4:1), later discussing theology with the governor of Arabia at Bostra, haled thence by official letters sent to the prefect of Egypt and the bishop of Alexandria (VI, 19:15), next theologizing with the empress Julia Mamaea (VI, 21:3), perhaps on the resurrection, on which Hippolytus had addressed a treatise to her,[10] and finally known as author of letters to the later emperor Philip the Arabian and his wife Severa (VI, 34). Presumably Arabian contacts were beneficial; Philip was born not far from Bostra. All this reflects a social status never low and apparently rising.

We meet two Gnostic representatives in Origen's biography. First is the adopted son of his rich benefactress. She gave him special honours and encouraged his theological lectures at her house. Origen (perhaps jealous?) refused absolutely to pray with him, for he knew him to be a heretic. Eusebius gives the story no proper conclusion (VI, 2:13–14). We see both Christians and Gnostics as objects of benefactions. The second example is provided by the much richer Ambrose, whom Origen converted from Valentinianism; he then subsidized Origen's work (VI, 18:1; 23:1–2). Jerome adds the detail that 'some' were disappointed when Ambrose did not remember Origen in his will (*De viris illustribus*, 56). Both examples, related to a Christian of high status, possess high status themselves. Could it be that Gnostics too were *omnis ordinis*?

2—ACCUSATIONS AND STATUS

The letter of Pliny to Trajan already reflects interest in various charges against Christians.[11] Here what is interesting is how Christians dealt with them. Justin in his *Second Apology* (12:4) refers to male and female slaves who when tortured accused their owners of murder and/or incest. Some decades later we find divergent reports. At Lyons or Vienne pagans were enraged when slaves confessed their owners' guilt (Eusebius, *Hist. Eccl.* V, 1:14–15), yet the apologist Athenagoras could speak thus: 'Slaves belong to us, some more, some fewer, whose observation we cannot escape; but none of them has ever told such lies about us' (*Suppl.* 35:3). Obviously the Christians are claiming to have a reasonably high status, one certainly higher than that of their accusers.

A different line of approach to the accusations, especially those involving sex, seems to be taken as early as the Epistle of Jude. Here the 'blemishes on your agape' are ascribed to nominal Christians who need firm correction. More specifically, Justin refers to reports of infamous deeds practised among heretics (Simonians, Menandrians, Marcionites) and adds that he does not know whether they really practise them or not; he only knows that these heretics are not persecuted or executed (*Apol.* I, 26:7). Similarly Irenaeus, apparently following Justin, admits that he does not know whether or not the Carpocratians actually do what he has described, but says that such practices are recommended in their literature (*Haer.* I, 25:5). He insists that Carpocratians and others like them are responsible for the accusations against 'the divine name of the church'. People 'suppose that we are all like them and either turn their ears away from the proclamation of the truth or else, seeing their conduct, defame all of us'. A similar problem would obviously arise from the activities of the Cainites (I, 31:2). Clement of Alexandria describes the Carpocratians in much the same way. They 'gather together for feasts (I would not call their meeting an Agape), men and women together. After they have sated their appetites ("on repletion Cypris, the goddess of love, enters", as it is said), then they ... practise *koinōnia* in such an Agape' (*Strom.* III, 10:1).

Perhaps it could be said that, building on the vigorous anti-heretical effort of the later second-century, theologians were now ready to cast the blame for the accusations against Christians on the Gnostics, thus exonerating members of the 'great church'. It may well be significant that (1) Celsus is willing to enter into a discussion of Christianity at all and that (2) he does not make such accusations against the church as a whole, while (3) he seems to reserve the blame for sectarian groups (*Cels.* V, 63).

Origen has some new ideas. In his view the accusations of crimes were spread by Jews 'when the teaching of Christianity began to be proclaimed' (*Cels.* VI, 27). This is not exactly what Justin had said, and Origen provides no evidence. He goes on to state that the rumour 'some time ago' persuaded the ignorant that Christians were like that. '*Even now* it deceives some who by such stories are repelled from approaching Christians even if only for a simple conversation' (tr. H. Chadwick; italics mine). Later on he says that 'these allegations are now condemned even by *hoi polloi* ... as being a false slander'. Most people (*hoi pleistoi*) know that they are false because they have lived with a great many (*pleistoi*) Christians (VI, 40). It appears that while the charges still float around they have become much less credible. Indeed, Eusebius says (*Hist. Eccl.* IV, 7:15) that 'no one today may dare to utter vile calumny against our faith' (tr. J. E. L. Oulton).

The point of what we have been citing is this: the situation of Christianity in the second century is not discontinuous from that in the third. The charges linger on and the bitterness continues. At the same time, there *is* a gradual clearing of the air. Why so? In search of an explanation we turn to what Christian authors have to say about some of the heretical sects they oppose. We have seen that Justin raised suspicions about some Gnostics, as did Irenaeus. The latter author goes beyond suspicion to definite statements. His opponents eat meats offered to idols, attend pagan festivals and gladiatorial combats, and either seduce their disciples or steal other men's wives (*Haer.* I, 6:3). Similarly the Basilidians practise 'all possible forms of debauchery' (I, 24:5). And so on. We might be reading Lucian's account of the exploits of the false prophet Alexander (c. 42). 'He duped the simpletons in this way from first to last, ruining women right and left as well as living with boys. Indeed, it was a great thing prized by each if he simply cast his eyes on a man's wife. ...' (Harmon, slightly revised). Irenaeus cites the case of a deacon's wife from Asia who after a time with Marcus was recovered by Christians (*Haer.* I, 13:5). While Irenaeus knows a few ascetic Gnostics, he is polemically concerned more with the libertines. In his society the emphasis was much the same. Earlier the Christians, now the Gnostics, were being accused of actions harmful to marriage and the family. A glance at A. Berger's *Encyclopedic Dictionary of Roman Law* immediately shows how offenders would be subject not only to social condemnation but also to legal penalties: *Adulterium, Incestus, Stuprum*, not to mention *Homicidium*. Beyond that came the general social attitudes which supported marriage and the family, notably under the Antonine emperors.[12] Justin himself describes the way in which a Roman Christian woman sought divorce because of sexual abuse (*Apol.* II, 2:1–8). We conclude that the charges against the Gnostics are intended to show that they are outcasts from Graeco-Roman society, whatever their social rank may have been. Conversely, a Gnostic like Basilides could state (or be reported as stating), 'We are men and the others are all swine and dogs' (Epiphanius, *Haer.* 24, 5). The allusion to Matthew 7:6 does not take away the force of his delusion about the social scene.

3—CHRISTIANS VERSUS GNOSTICS

Another way of dealing with Gnostics is utilized by Origen. It consists of explaining what insignificant nonentities they are, especially when compared with the great numbers of Christians. What about Simonians? 'Now of all the Simonians in the world it is not possible, I believe, to find thirty, and perhaps I have exaggerated the number. There are very few in Palestine, while in the rest of the world he is nowhere mentioned' – except by readers of the book of Acts (*Cels.* I, 57). Origen restates his 'facts' later on. 'There are no Simonians anywhere in the world. ... The Dositheans also did not flourish even in their early days; at the present time ... their whole number is said not to amount to thirty' (VI, 11). Again, when he finds Celsus naming Marcellians, Harpocratians, and followers of Mariamme or Martha, he avers that he has carefully studied Christian doctrines and philosophy as well, but has 'never met with these' (V, 62).

This is his approach to the supposedly Ophite diagram used by Celsus for the Gnostic universe. It comes from 'the Ophites, a most undistinguished sect in my opinion'. Origen has travelled widely and asked everywhere from those who professed to be learned, but he has never found anyone who would stand by the diagram (VI, 24). The opinions reflected in it are not held by Christians but by sectarians who either no longer exist or are very few and easily counted (VI, 26). Obviously Origen's statements are tendentious. The tendency, however, seems factually reliable. His opponents at Alexandria could easily correct it if there actually were many Gnostics around, or if their social status was higher than he admits.

To sum up to this point: there are two stages here, first around the time of Irenaeus when Christians (after Justin's lead) accuse Gnostics of immorality and thus indirectly point to their anti-social stance, second in the time of Origen when Christians can look down on Gnostics whose numbers, status, and importance are well below that of the Christian church. What happened? Presumably the work of the anti-heretical fathers took effect and Gnostics, excluded from the Christian community, began to wither away. (Earlier the Valentinian Ptolemaeus suggests that the major Gnostic mission field was within the church, not outside.) It may also be that the status of Christians generally improved from one stage to the next, but in my opinion this is not very clear.

Finally we should note some contrasting evaluations made by Gnostics and Christians. Gnostics often regarded themselves as freed not only from the Old Testament law but from moral laws in general. The followers of a certain Prodicus claimed to be 'by nature sons of the first God' and because of their 'gentility and freedom' to be able to live as they pleased. They were 'lords of the sabbath' (cf. Mark 2:27) and royal children, not subject to laws. Just as Paul, perhaps in a similar conflict, tried to call Corinthians back to reality ('not many well-born', 1 Corinthians 1:26), so Clement points out that the Prodical libertines actually live in fear of being arrested (*Strom*. III, 30). Their situation does not really suggest a very high social status. Then when Gnostics ('knowers' = the intelligentsia?) viewed Christians as *idiotae* ('non-specialists') who knew nothing, the charge did not make much of an impression (Irenaeus, *Haer*. I, 6:4).

Another difference can be seen in the intra-group attitudes of Gnostics, or at least some Gnostics, and Christians. Epiphanius tells us that visiting Gnostics, recognized by secret signs, are welcomed with lavish feasts of meat and wine, provided even by those who are poor; after hospitality comes promiscuity (see above). Presumably they would call this festivity an agape. Ignatius of Antioch claims that his opponents have no concern for (real) agape, that is, love of neighbour, or for the widow, the orphan, the person oppressed, or in bonds or (just) freed, or for the hungry and thirsty (*Smyrn*. 6:2). Polycarp of Smyrna shares Ignatius' view (*Phil*. 6:1). Is Ignatius slandering them? Not according to the Gospel of Thomas. Jesus' disciples ask if they should give alms (log. 6), and he tells them that if they give alms they will do harm to their spirits (log. 14).

By this point it will be evident that because of the remarkable diversity among Gnostics, in principle greater than that among ordinary Christians, it is difficult if not impossible to speak of any general social status they may have possessed. If Christians themselves, in Pliny's words, were *omnis ordinis*, such must have been the case with the Gnostics too. Yet one might well ask about the function of social status and its possibility apart from social relations, relations which *a priori* the Gnostics rejected. The words of A. D. Nock about early Christians we should apply primarily to Gnostics. They were 'decidedly isolated', he wrote.[13]

> If of Jewish origin, they were mostly now cut off from their own people and regarded as apostates; if of Gentile origin, they were set apart from the ordinary pleasures and small change of society, and they were liable to be looked on as very strange individuals, even stranger than those who had become Jewish proselytes, since proselytes were at least a known if not a popular type.

In the most literal meaning of the expression, the Gnostics lacked common sense, whatever their origins may have been.

Some of them, like members of 'the libertine gnostic sect of the Phibionites',[14] obviously turned away from ordinary (bourgeois?) social life, but unfortunately a text cited by Werner Foerster does not show that their attitude was self-conscious. 'They deride those who are occupied with civil life and purity and virginity as if they undertook their labour to no purpose'.[15] The word *politeia* in Epiphanius' context means 'ascetic discipline'[16] and the setting thus turns out to be ecclesiastical rather than simply sociological.

NOTES

1. F. C. Burkitt, *Church and Gnosis*, Cambridge 1932, 91.
2. Cf. E. M. Mendelson, 'Some Notes on a Sociological Approach to Gnosticism', in (ed.) U. Bianchi, *Le Origini dello Gnosticismo, SHR* 12, Leiden 1967, 668–75; H. G. Kippenberg, 'Versuch einer soziologischen Verortung des antiken Gnostizismus', *Numen* 17, 1970, 211–31; P. Munz, 'The Problem of "Die soziologische Verortung des antiken Gnostizismus" ', *Numen* 19, 1972, 41–51; P. Pokorný, 'Der soziale Hintergrund der Gnosis' in (ed.) K.-W. Tröger, *Gnosis und Neues Testament*, Gütersloh 1973, 77–87; H. A. Green, 'Suggested Sociological Themes in the Study of Gnosticism', *VigChr* 31, 1977, 169–80.
3. Cf. *Gnosticism and Early Christianity*, ed. 2, New York 1966, 13–14; more reserved in *Gnosticismo e cristianesimo primitivo*, Bologna 1976, 47–51.
4. Clement, *Strom.* II, 113–14; III, 1–3; VI, 53. Note that Isidore looks down on someone who might be *neos* or *penēs* or *katōpherēs*; the last word could mean either 'lewd' or in this context 'downwardly mobile'.

5. Tertullian *Praescr. Haer.* 30:2 says he gave the Roman church only 200 sesterces, but this is idiomatic for a large sum.

6. Clement, *Strom.* III, 5.

7. H. J. W. Drijvers, *Bardaisan of Edessa*, Assen 1966, 217f.

8. H. Chadwick, *Alexandrian Christianity*, New York 1954, 31. Naturally we do not take seriously Clement's reference to 'the noble Carpocratians', *Strom.* III, 10:1, though we note his preference for Valentinian spirituality over Carpocratian carnality, III, 29:3.

9. Cf. M. Reinhold, *History of Purple as a Status Symbol in Antiquity*, CollLat 116, 1970, 53–57 (a peak in the second century).

10. *Hippolytus Werke GCS* I:2, ed. H. Achelis, Leipzig 1897, 251–53.

11. On the charges cf. my article in (eds) R. van den Broek, M. J. Vermaseren, *Studies in Gnosticism and Hellenistic Religions Presented to G. Quispel*, *EPRO* 91, Leiden 1981, 161–70.

12. Cf. e.g., J. Carcopino, *La vie quotidienne à Rome*, Paris 1939, 97–124; J. P. V. D. Balsdon, *Roman Women*, London 1962, esp. 173–223; C. Rambaux, *Tertullien face aux morales des trois premières siècles*, Paris 1979, 204–58.

13. A. D. Nock, 'Gnosticism', *HThR* 57, 1964, 255–79 (272); repr. in (ed.) Z. Stewart, *Essays on Religion and the Ancient World*, Oxford 1972, II, 940–59 (953).

14. See Benko's article in *VigChr* 21, 1967, 103–19.

15. W. Foerster, *Gnosis*, ET ed. R.McL. Wilson, Oxford 1972, I, 324.

16. G. W. H. Lampe, *Patristic Greek Lexicon*, 1113 (b, bottom of column): 'of ascetic and monastic discipline', with an almost exact parallel in Epiphanius, *Haer.* 70, 14:5.

Additional note: Mention should also be made of A. F. Segal, 'Ruler of this World: Attitudes about Mediator Figures and the Importance of Sociology for Self-Definition' in (ed.) E. P. Sanders, *Jewish and Christian Self-Definition*, II, Philadelphia 1981, 245–68; G. E. M. de Ste Croix, *The Class Struggle in the Ancient Greek World*, Cornell 1981.

THE NAG HAMMADI TEXTS AND THE
NEW TESTAMENT

XIII

THE CHRISTIANIZATION OF GNOSTIC TEXTS

by

Professor Martin Krause, Münster

Professor Wilson has greatly advanced the study of the New Testament and Gnosis and Gnosticism by his various important contributions to it. It is therefore most welcome that this volume devoted to this subject is being produced for him as a modest expression of our gratitude. I was glad to accept the invitation to contribute to it, although the topic proposed by the editors is not a simple one; what I say here can thus only serve as a proposal for the solution of this problem.

The Gnostic writings contained in the Nag Hammadi library[1] have demonstrated more clearly than had previously been realized the complexity of Gnosticism and its syncretism – or at any rate that of the owner of this library.[2] Besides Hermetic writings, Wisdom teachings and philosophical texts, the library contains, as is well-known, non-Christian Gnostic works containing Old Testament and Jewish material or philosophical Gnostic teachings. It does not follow, however, from the absence of Christian material that these must be of *pre*-Christian origin. Professor Wilson has rather, in several works, pointed out that it is also possible that originally Christian Gnostic works may have been de-Christianized.[3] The Authoritative Teaching in Codex VI could, I think, be cited as a good example of such a development. Above all the Christian Gnostic texts from Nag Hammadi, together with the Coptic texts known to us before, in the Codices Askewianus, Brucianus and Berolinensis 8502, show us the disagreements on both sides between Gnosticism and Christianity.[4] As far as our sources go they indicate that these relatively infrequently took the form of polemic; only a few Gnostic texts attack statements in the Old Testament and doctrines of the Christian churches. Far more often, however, Gnosticism and Christianity accommodated themselves to one another in Egypt, in keeping with the syncretistic mode of thinking of the Egyptians in all ages and not for the first time in late antiquity. This resulted in a Christian Gnosticism, which left its mark in

Christian Gnostic writings. Amongst them we can distinguish two main groups: (1) works composed as Christian Gnostic texts, and (2) originally non-Christian Gnostic texts, which have later been worked over by Christian hands and thus transformed into Christian Gnostic works. J. Doresse dealt with this group of Christianized Gnostic texts under the heading 'Gnostics disguised as Christians'.[5] In it he included the Sophia of Jesus Christ and the Apocryphon of John. Besides that he distinguished a group of 'Gospels of Christianized Gnosticism';[6] under this heading he discussed a large number of Christian Gnostic writings which we mostly regard as Christian Gnostic works.

In 1975 I, like Doresse, counted among the 'non-Christian Gnostic texts, which have been worked over by Christian hands' the Sophia of Jesus Christ and the Apocryphon of John, but also the Hypostasis of the Archons, the Book of Thomas the Contender and the Acts of Peter and the Twelve Apostles as well.[7] K.-W. Tröger also agreed with Doresse and myself in including among the 'Christianized texts' the Sophia of Jesus Christ and the Apocryphon of John, but also added the Gospel of the Egyptians and the Trimorphic Protennoia.[8] Apart from a group of 'writings which are essentially Christian Gnostic' he distinguished a group of 'Gnostic writings which are essentially non-Christian but contain Christian elements'; in this he included the Hypostasis of the Archons and the 'tractate without a title' in Codex II (On the Origin of the World). In brackets he added Eugnostos the Blessed. He set a question mark against the Exegesis on the Soul and the Authoritative Teaching, which presumably means that he was not sure how to classify these texts.[9]

All three authors therefore only agree in classifying two works as Christianized texts, the Sophia of Jesus Christ and the Apocryphon of John.

In a greater number of cases Tröger's classification and mine are at variance. That is partly the result of his division of the group of Christianized texts into two: besides the 'Christianized texts' he identifies a further group of 'Gnostic writings, which are essentially non-Christian, but contain Christian elements'; these seem to me a sub-division of the group of 'Christianized texts'.

In fact, as far as the *quantitative* scope of Christianization is concerned, there are two groups of Christianized texts: (1) texts which have been very extensively worked over by Christian hands, and (2) texts which have been Christianized only by *smaller Christian insertions*.

The division of Nag Hammadi texts into groups and in particular the distinction between texts which have been more or less extensively Christianized remains subjective[10] as long as no attempt is made to work out *objective criteria*; these must then receive the approval of all scholars involved in the study of these sources. This article tries to suggest some such criteria.

On the basis of my long involvement with the Nag Hammadi texts I have more than once called for literary-critical studies of the individual writings.[11] Tröger suggests the following method:[12] 'The question of how the Christianization of texts has taken place is very much a matter of discerning literary processes and the treatment of material and traditions. We have to consider, e.g., the addition of Christian quotations, the setting of Gnostic material of pagan provenance within a Christian framework, the introduction of Jesus Christ into a Gnostic concept of the Redeemer and the adoption of Christian terminology. Only then can we decide how superficial or how fundamental the Christianization of a text has been in each individual instance.' If I understand him aright, he too is arguing for literary-critical investigations; for in my opinion they alone will show whether Christian material is an integral part of any particular text or is only a later addition. I cannot concur with the method proposed by W. C. Robinson Jnr for investigating a Christian Gnostic text, the Exegesis on the Soul:[13] briefly stated, this is to remove all Christian Gnostic material from a Christian Gnostic text and thus to reveal the non-Christian Gnostic original which forms the basis for a Christianization of the work in question. What Robinson overlooks by this procedure of his is the close intertwining of Gnostic and Christian material which can be demonstrated in certain passages;[14] this is a decisive criterion for tractates which were composed as Christian Gnostic texts.

Thus I would take issue with Tröger's classification of the Exegesis on the Soul – even if it was marked as questionable – amongst his second group of 'Gnostic writings, which are essentially non-Christian, but contain Christian elements'.[15] Rather it seems to me to fit better into his fourth group, the texts which are essentially 'Christian Gnostic'.

Although at present we are not yet in a position to prove it, we must assume that the Christianization of Gnosis, that is the adoption of Christian material, took place over a fairly long period of time. Since, for instance, we do not know the original form of the Gnostic system, we do not know either what Christian elements may conceivably have contributed to its formation, or whether even the figure of the Saviour in the Gnostic systems was not perhaps a Christian legacy. We can only say that in the Christian Gnostic systems the Saviour is identified with Christ. In the course of further contacts between Gnosis and Christianity Christian ideas and figures may time and again have been taken over. Thus we are as yet unable to date the Christianized Gnostic texts more accurately.

Unfortunately the number of scholars involved in the investigation of the Gnostic sources who have a proper training in Egyptology and are familiar with the great influence of syncretism at all periods in Egypt,[16] is very limited. Thus the study of Gnosis has not yet given the effects of syncretism the central role they merit. Although only a part of the Nag Hammadi texts was composed in Egypt, it was certainly in *Egypt* that they were all translated into Coptic. Both in translation and in copying the texts their wording could be altered by additions, glosses or omissions. The works extant in more than one copy,[17] which make their publication in a synopsis very difficult or quite impossible, clearly show how much the text was worked over in Egypt. That becomes yet plainer when we compare these sharply divergent Gnostic texts with the Biblical texts copied at the same time, which display fewer textual variants. The Gnostics were not the first to embark upon this process of accommodating some of their texts to another religion, in this case Christianity. In this they followed other religions: Christianity, for instance, as is well known, Christianized a large number of Old Testament apocrypha and pseudepigrapha with Christian additions.[18] The church fathers tell us that the Gnostics wrote Christian Gnostic works,[19] and it is also to be expected that new Christian Gnostic works arose through additions to, and interpolations in, older works.[20]

These criteria which I have mentioned are hard to evaluate and therefore subjective, but there are also *objective* ones for assessing the Christianizing of Gnostic texts. Most can be gleaned from a comparison of Eugnostos the Blessed with the Sophia of Jesus Christ.[21] If we leave aside the still controversial question, whether Eugnostos contains only a little material or any at all which can be interpreted as Christian,[22] it is today beyond question that Eugnostos served as the basis for the Christian Gnostic Sophia of Jesus Christ. That is important for our enquiry since it means that we can follow through the Christianizing of a Gnostic text and at the same time extract *objective* criteria for possible Christianizing in the case of other Christian Gnostic writings. Here a letter is transformed through additions, material found only in the Sophia of Jesus Christ, into a dialogue between the Saviour and his disciples and Mary. In this the Saviour mainly answers the disciples' questions and fulfils their requests. Only the questions are additions; the answers are taken from the text of Eugnostos.[23] A Christian 'frame-story' transfers the action to a mountain in Galilee. At the end of the dialogue the disciples begin to preach the gospel. We can see that the editing has not been successful but has left traces of its activity behind. Above all these involve contradictions within the text: the questions and requests do not in general correspond very well with the answers.

The Christianizing also consisted of the addition of a 'frame-story' at the beginning and end of the text. At the beginning it is stated when the event took place (after Jesus' resurrection), who were involved (his twelve male and seven female disciples), and what the location was (a mountain in Galilee); the risen Jesus appears there to answer or fulfil twelve questions and requests.

The 'frame-story' at the end tells how the Saviour vanishes and the disciples, filled with joy, begin to preach the gospel.

Besides various additions to the text[24] we find frequently quoted 'He who has ears to hear, let him hear!' (Matthew 11:15 and elsewhere). In addition there are further echoes of the New Testament.[25]

From these we can derive the following objective criteria for the Christianizing of Gnostic texts:

1. contradictions and unevennesses in the proceedings,
2. a Christian 'frame-story' at the beginning, in which the risen Jesus appears on a mountain to his disciples,
3. the body of the material presented as a dialogue, in which the Saviour answers the disciples' questions,
4. scriptural quotations, above all Matthew 11:15, and

5.   a 'frame-story' at the end: after the Saviour has disappeared the
     disciples begin to preach the gospel.

It is striking that criteria (2) to (5) appear in a large number of Christian
Gnostic writings which K. Rudolph was the first to examine and described
as a literary *genre*, the Gnostic 'dialogue'.[26]
   This raises a number of questions: (1) did the Christianization of
Gnostic texts first lead to the rise of the literary *genre* of the Gnostic
'dialogue'? Or (2) did the editor of the Gnostic original carry out the
Christian revision along the lines of an already familiar *genre*, the Gnostic
'dialogue'? (3) Are *all* Gnostic 'dialogues' – like the Sophia of Jesus Christ
– the product of Christianizing?
   The first two questions cannot be given a straightforward answer. The
second possibility seems the likelier. Because we have no other instance
such as we have in the case of Eugnostos and the Sophia of Jesus Christ,
the third question can only be answered by a literary-critical investigation
of the writings of this *genre*. If we find examples of the first criterion
mentioned, contradictions and unevennesses in the text, then we must
consider this text Christianized.
   A literary-critical study of the Apocryphon of John, which belongs to
this literary *genre*, has shown that this work too is the product of
Christianizing.[27] Moreover several texts have been combined in this
production: a cosmogony describing events up to the fall of Sophia, a
paraphrase of Genesis 1–7, and a treatise on the destiny of the soul; these
were transformed into a dialogue. Of the ten questions and answers only
the fourth to the ninth fit one another, and the answers are briefly
formulated. The other answers are very long and only answer the questions
posed to a small extent. The explanations which follow immediately after
the real answers continue the train of thought of what preceded the
respective questions. If we omit the first three questions and answers that
in no way impairs our understanding of the context. The text begins and
ends with a Christian 'frame-story'. At the beginning the risen Jesus
appears to John and answers questions. At the end, after the
disappearance of the Saviour, John proclaims to his fellow-disciples what
has been communicated to him. Since the work contains a series of biblical
quotations and echoes, all our five criteria for a Christianizing are met in
the case of the Apocryphon of John.
   The Book of Thomas the Contender only satisfies criteria (1) to (4).[28]
There is no 'frame-story' at the end of the work. The opening 'frame-story'
refers to another point of time (during Jesus' earthly life), another place
(not specified, but not a mountain) and to only one partner in the dialogue
(Judas Thomas), so that Mathaias is named as witness to the discussion. It
is an artificial discussion. The speeches are of varying length, ranging from
2 to 116 lines. Besides we can detect contradictions between the 'frame-
story' and the dialogue. Only Jesus' first and ninth to eleventh speeches
and Thomas' first, ninth and tenth take place between the two of them. In
the others Jesus addresses a plurality of hearers, and Thomas is spokesman
for a group of persons not mentioned by name.

We can detect a series of contradictions in the Acts of Peter and the Twelve Apostles too.[29] This tractate has a Christian 'frame-story' at beginning and end, but differs from the Gnostic 'dialogues' in that it takes place in the time of the activity of the apostles. The disciples are already engaged in mission. Thus when the Lord who has appeared to them departs from them in the 'frame-story' at the end, there is no description of the disciples' preaching. Only a small part of the work consists of dialogues; narrative is commoner. Thus this tractate does not belong to the category of the Gnostic 'dialogues'; yet it too contains what seem to me Christianized narratives: the Gnostic pearl-seller Lithargoel, with whom Christ is identified.

Here we should also mention briefly some further texts which Tröger describes as Gnostic texts with Christian elements or Christianized texts;[30] yet only our fourth criterion applies to them. The Christianization of the Hypostasis of the Archons[31] is quantitatively and also qualitatively less than that of the texts mentioned above. The Christian colouring at the beginning consists only of the addition of a quotation from the New Testament (Ephesians 6:12). Christian elements are only found again at the end, as Wilson has indicated:[32] the spirit of truth sent from the Father (II, 96:35; cf. John 14:26) and the unction of eternal life (II, 97:2f.). Sabaoth's repentance and rehabilitation (II, 95:15ff.) may also be a Christian element.[33]

The tractate, On the Origin of the World, in Codex II contains Christian elements;[34] it meets our fourth criterion: quotations from the New Testament, echoes of the New Testament, even two mentions of Jesus (II, 105:26; 114:17), although he plays no central role. There is no Christian 'frame-story', nor are there contradictions or dialogues.

The same is true of the next two texts: the Gospel of the Egyptians mentions Jesus three times and Christ six times,[35] once in the colophon. He is, however, closely connected with Seth who has the central role, and his supernatural character is predominant. A. Böhlig even supposes that 'the passages in which Christ appears' are 'entirely secondary'.[36] So literary-critical studies are called for here. On the other hand we find a series of echoes of the New Testament[37] and the Gnostic system described in this work is so advanced that it probably belongs to a late phase.

The Trimorphic Protennoia in Codex XIII[38] also contains a series of Christian elements, as Wilson has shown.[39] A literary-critical investigation is urgently called for in this case too, particularly in light of the fact that the Berlin *Arbeitskreis*[40] is of the opinion that this document is older than the Prologue to John's Gospel.[41]

The Trimorphic Protennoia and the Gospel of the Egyptians, which Tröger places in his fourth group, I would like to assign to his second.

In their time the group of Christianized 'dialogues' were seemingly held in high esteem, since in them Gnostic doctrines were put in the mouth of the risen Christ. So they could claim to equal in importance the message of the New Testament, if not to surpass it; for a part of these texts was 'secret teachings' which could only be disclosed to the disciples or the elect. It is therefore not surprising that the church fathers struggled against them because of this claim. The mere absence of a Christian 'frame-story' could thus in itself indicate a late date of composition of the text in question, since it could only have arisen after the phase when Christian Gnosis was at loggerheads with the church.

One of the many tasks still awaiting scholars is thus the literary-critical investigation of these texts, but there is also that of attempting a relative and absolute dating of them. This may be easier in the case of texts with cosmogonies, since it is possible to set them in order both within the Coptic Gnostic corpus and also in relation to the Gnostic systems described by the church fathers.[42] In addition the texts need further investigation with reference to the quality of their Christianizing. And here too we can hope for Professor Wilson's collaboration, as we wish him many more years of study once freed from teaching duties, so that he may gather a rich harvest into his barns.

NOTES

1. J. Doresse was the first to attempt to catalogue the library in terms of its relation to Christianity, *Les livres secrets des gnostiques d'Egypte*, Paris 1958, 170ff.; *The Secret Books of the Egyptian Gnostics*, London 1960, 146ff. (the following citations are from the ET). After my criticism of this categorizing in 1966, in (ed.) U. Bianchi, *The Origins of Gnosticism* ..., *SHR* 12, Leiden 1967, 67ff., I attempted a new categorizing in *NHS* 6, 1975, 79ff., and in *Gnosis*, *FS* for H. Jonas, Göttingen 1978, 238ff. K.-W. Tröger proposed a similar analysis in *Altes Testament – Frühjudentum – Gnosis*, Berlin 1980, 21. We need not consider here the categories proposed, from a different perspective, by C. Colpe in *RAC* XI, 1981, 537ff.
2. Krause in *Gnosis*, *FS* Jonas, 241ff. (with bibliography).
3. R. McL. Wilson in *NTS* 3, 1957, 236f.; *Gnosis and the New Testament*, Oxford 1968, *passim*; (ed.) E.A. Livingstone, *StPatr* 14, 1976, 243ff.; *NHS* 8, 1977, 50ff.
4. Krause in *NHS* 17, 1981, 47ff. (with bibliography).
5. Doresse, op. cit. (n. 1), 197–218.
6. Doresse, op. cit. (n. 1), 218–241.
7. *NHS* 6, 1975, 82ff.; in *Gnosis*, *FS* Jonas, 238f., I mentioned only the Sophia of Jesus Christ, the Apocryphon of John and the Hypostasis of the Archons.
8. Tröger, op. cit. (n. 1), 21.
9. Tröger, ibid.
10. Tröger, op. cit. (n. 1), 22, writes; 'The assigning of the Nag Hammadi texts to such categories is in many instances at the mercy of subjective judgements and also displays questionable "cases".'
11. E.g. in (ed.) Bianchi, op. cit. (n. 1), 75f.; *Gnosis*, *FS* Jonas, 237.
12. Tröger, op. cit. (n. 1), 20f.
13. W. C. Robinson Jnr in *NT* 12, 1970, 102ff.
14. Cf. Krause in *NHS* 7, 1975, 48 and n. 14.

15. Tröger, op. cit. (n. 1), 21.
16. Krause in *NHS* 17, 1981, 48ff.
17. The Apocryphon of John, Eugnostos the Blessed, the Sophia of Jesus Christ, the Gospel of the Egyptians, On the Origin of the World in Codex II and XIII.
18. Even statements of Greek philosophers were transformed into Christian writings through additions; cf. W. C. Till in *Mémoires de l'Institut Française* 67, 1934, 165ff.
19. Cf. H. C. Puech in Hennecke–Schneemelcher–Wilson, *New Testament Apocrypha* I, London 1963, 231ff.
20. On eliciting Gnostic texts from the writings of church fathers by the use of literary criticism cf. the important works of J. Frickel, e.g. *Muséon* 85, 1972, 425ff.
21. On the following cf. Krause in *Mullus, FS* for Theodor Klauser, Bonn 1964, 215ff. (with bibliography).
22. Wilson, *Gnosis* (cf. n. 3), 115f.; A. H. B. Logan in *NHS* 17, 1981, 75.
23. Only the last answer (III, 118:1–126:16) comes from the material peculiar to the Sophia.
24. Krause, op. cit. (n. 21), 219f.
25. Krause, op. cit. (n. 21), 220.
26. K. Rudolph in (ed.) P. Nagel, *Probleme der koptischen Literatur*, Halle–Wittenberg 1968, 85ff.; cf. my additional notes in *NHS* 8, 1977, 16ff.
27. Cf. on the following Krause in Foerster–Wilson, *Gnosis* I, Oxford 1972, 100f.
28. Cf. on the following Krause in Foerster–Wilson, *Gnosis* II, Oxford 1974, 110f.
29. Cf. Krause in *NHS* 3, 1972, 36ff.
30. Tröger, op. cit. (n. 1), 21.
31. Krause in Foerster–Wilson, *Gnosis* II, 40–44.
32. Wilson, op. cit. (n. 3), 125.
33. Wilson, op. cit. (n. 3), 126.
34. A. Böhlig, P. Labib, *Die koptisch-gnostische Schrift ohne Titel aus Codex II von Nag Hammadi*, Berlin 1962, 33f.; Wilson, op. cit. (n. 3), 127.
35. A. Böhlig, *Das Ägypterevangelium von Nag Hammadi*, Wiesbaden 1974, 29ff.
36. Böhlig, op. cit. (n. 35), 30. Cf. also IV, 56:27 and 59:17, where he plainly stands in *second* place: *ete pai pe pinoč ñčhš*.
37. Wilson in *StPatr* 14, 1976, 245ff.
38. Cf. the literature mentioned in *Gnosis, FS* Jonas, 239, n. 179, and also subsequently J. M. Robinson in (ed.) B. Layton, *The Rediscovery of Gnosticism* II, Leiden 1981, 643ff. with further literature.
39. Wilson in *NHS* 8, 1977, 53f.
40. *ThLZ* 99, 1974, 731ff.; cf. also Robinson, loc. cit. (n. 38), 647f.
41. Cf. most recently Robinson, loc. cit. (n. 38), 643ff.
42. Cf. A. H. B. Logan in *NHS* 17, 1981, 66ff.

XIV

THREE THOMAS PARABLES

by

Professor Helmut Koester, Cambridge, Mass.

In his treatment of the parables of the Gospel of Thomas, Professor Wilson said that with respect to some materials used by its author, 'it is difficult to imagine him selecting a word here, a saying there, and keeping part of another saying for use at a later stage. Explanations which are to be valid must take account of what we can learn of the writer's methods, and free citation from memory would appear nearer the mark than an extensive use of scissors and paste'.[1] In spite of this insight, the interpretation of the parables of the Gospel of Thomas during the last two decades has sometimes proceeded as if it could be taken for granted that the author of this gospel knew all or several of our Synoptic Gospels, and as if he deliberately drew on these written parables, making well-considered alterations in order to express his Gnostic thought.[2]

Most amazing in such interpretations are two things: (1) the certainty about literary dependence of the author upon one or several written sources; (2) the assurance that there could be no possible doubt about the Gnostic meaning of such parables.

Parables are told, sometimes with suggestive alterations; or else parables are copied and allegorized. These, at least, seem to be the two different ways in which parables were used in the early Christian period. In the first instance, the conscious use of written sources and their redaction is highly unlikely; in the latter case, written materials are probably always utilized and deliberately edited.

I

The Sower

The occurrence of this parable in 1 Clement 24:5 is often disregarded:

The sower went forth and cast each of the seeds into the earth and falling into the earth, parched and bare, they dissolve. Then from their dissolution the greatness of the providence of the master raises them up (*anistēsin auta*), and from one (grain) many grow and bring forth fruit.

No doubt, the same parable is told as in Mark 4:3–9 (Matthew 13:3–9; Luke 8:5–8) and Gos. Thom. 9. Any literary dependence would be difficult to prove. However, only 1 Clement 24 and Gos. Thom. 9 have the term 'and cast' or 'and scattered'. Still, 1 Clement hardly knew any of the other written versions preserved to us. What is the meaning of the obviously shortened version of this parable in 1 Clement 24? One might think that it is a parable about the gracious providence of God who provides food for humankind. Only the phrase 'he raised them up' indicates that the author is using this parable as an illustration for the resurrection. The context confirms this, though without this context one could not be sure, because of the strong emphasis upon divine providence as the originator of the fruit.[3] In any case, it is a parable told with suggestive alterations as they occur in the process of oral transmission, not an allegorical interpretation of a written text.

In the version of 1 Clement 24 we observed major alterations of what may have been a more original form of the parable. However, in the version of the same parable quoted in Gos. Thom. 9, there is nothing that indicates a deliberate departure from a more original form of the parable of the sower:

> Behold, the sower went out, took a handful (of seeds) and scattered them. Some fell on the road; the birds came and gathered them up. Others fell on rock, did not take root in the soil and did not produce ears. And others fell on thorns; they choked the seed(s) and worms ate them. And others fell on the good soil and produced good fruit; it bore sixty per measure and a hundred and twenty per measure.[4]

Again, the parable is simply narrated. Nothing indicates the use of a written source or points to the narrator's attempt to comment upon a written text. That the text, as it is reproduced here, gives no evidence of any of the redactorial elements which appear in the synoptic version,[5] has been observed repeatedly.[6] There is, however, no indication of a deliberate avoidance of such redactorial elements or of the allegorical interpretation which Mark 4:13–20 (Matthew 13:18–23; Luke 8:11–15) presents. It is thus not justifiable to state that the author eliminated such features, because of his Gnosticizing understanding of the parable.[7] It may be correct that, in Gos. Thom. 9, the subject of the last clause ('it bore sixty per measure ...') is 'the earth' and not 'the seed',[8] but that could also be argued for the corresponding clause in Mark 4:8. If the supposedly Gnostic author expressed his interpretation in this way only, he did it in such a subtle fashion that it can be discovered only by a trained philological eye. What does that prove? Nothing but an ambiguity in narrative style. It is one thing to observe subtle changes made by a redactor who edits a literary document. It is quite another situation if one deals with a document that is primarily a collection of traditional materials. 'The birds came and gathered them up', 'the worms ate them' (only in the Gospel of Thomas), 'the sun rose and burned them' (only in Mark and Matthew) – such sentences belong to the narrator. Gos. Thom. 9 does not exhibit any redactional traits. The discussion of a possible written source is entirely gratuitous. Nor does the Gospel of Thomas tell us anything about the intended interpretation, neither in the narrative itself, nor in its context. Thus, the interpretation must accept the parable as a story told. There is no reason to believe that the results will differ from our understanding of the original synoptic parable.

II

The longest parable told in the Gospel of Thomas appears in log. 64:

Jesus said: 'A man had received visitors. And when he had prepared the dinner, he sent his servants to invite the guests. He went to the first one and said to him: "My master invites you". He said, "I have claims against some merchants. They are coming to me this evening. I must go and give them my orders. I ask to be excused from the dinner". He went to another and said to him, "My master invited you". He said to him, "I have just bought a house and I am required for the day. I shall not have any spare time". He went to another and said to him, "My master invites you". He said to him, "My friend is going to get married, and I am to prepare the banquet. I shall not be able to come. I ask to be excused from the dinner". He went to another and said to him, "My master invites you". He said to him, "I have just bought a farm, and I am on my way to collect the rent. I shall not be able to come. I ask to be excused". The servant returned and said to his master, "Those whom you invited to dinner have asked to be excused". The master said to his servant, "Go outside to the streets and bring back those whom you happen to meet, so that they may dine". Businessmen and merchants will not enter the places of my Father'.

The synoptic parallels to this parable are Matthew 22:1–14 and Luke 14:15–24. Both Matthew and Luke evidently relied on written sources which each of them edited in a different way. Matthew altogether destroyed the original narrative and substituted an allegory about the invitations to Israel, their rejection (the messengers are beaten and killed), and the subsequent punishment, i.e. the destruction of Jerusalem. Luke preserves the original dimension of the narrative: certain individuals are invited, but have various excuses. A puzzling feature in Luke is the twofold invitation at the conclusion of the parable: first the servant is sent out to bring in the poor, maimed, blind, and lame (Luke 14:21); but when it appears that there is still room (14:22), he is sent out once more to bring people from the 'streets and hedges' (14:23). Obviously, the second invitation, paralleled in Matthew 22:9 and Gos. Thom. 64, is the original conclusion of the parable, whereas the first must be considered a secondary Lukan expansion.[9]

The version of this parable in the Gospel of Thomas shows no trace of any of the Matthean or Lukan peculiarities and redactional changes. There is no reason whatsoever to assume a knowledge of the synoptic versions for the Thomas parable. On the contrary, it would be very difficult to explain how the author of the Gospel of Thomas was able to get rid of all allegorical and paraenetic features introduced by Matthew and Luke – features which only modern critical scholarship identified as secondary elements. To be sure, there are elements in Thomas' parable which one may not want to ascribe to the (hypothetical) original parable of Jesus, e.g., the foreshortened introduction and the expansion of the invitations from three to four.[10] But does that point to a Gnostic interpretation? First of all, it reveals the interests of a narrator who transferred the parable from a rural environment to an urban milieu. Secondly, as the excuses brought forth by those invited appear to be real excuses and not only pretexts,[11] the narrator produces a different effect: the host is not angry since he was slighted (Luke 14:21); rather, he is desperate as nobody can come. Why should that be 'Gnostic'? Finally, the invitations seem to come unexpectedly. Thus, those invited are confronted with a decision they have to make on the spot. Does that mean that those who are involved in business are 'therefore not prepared for, even fundamentally incapable of, accepting the invitation to Gnosis'?[12] If the request for an immediate decision is typically Gnostic, then sayings such as Luke 9:62[13] would be Gnostic sayings, and the story of Jesus' encounter with the rich man (Mark 10:17–22) a Gnostic narrative.

The conclusion of the parable, 'Businessmen and merchants will not enter the kingdom of my Father', may have been added by the author of the Gospel of Thomas. There is nothing Gnostic in this conclusion. Rather, like Thomas' version of the parable itself, this statement reflects a social decision of certain early Christian groups. The wealthy in the middle class of the cities, merchants, shipowners, traders, etc., are excluded from membership. In this respect, Thomas' parable reflects the same situation as the Epistle of James. However, James 4:13–17 accepts members of these professions under certain conditions, while Thomas rejects them.[14] Strictly speaking, only the first three invitations are extended to members of this class (collecting a payment from a merchant, buying a house, arranging a marriage),[15] whereas the fourth introduces a member of a different class, i.e. of the land-owning upper class: he has bought 'a farm', most likely an estate from which he collects his income. It is the same class which is addressed by the curses of James 5:1–6. Perhaps this fourth invitation is a later addition, since members of this class were scarcely found in Christian churches at an early time. However, the author of the Gospel of Thomas made no attempt to reconcile this fourth invitation, extended to someone who is not a businessman, with the conclusion which explicitly rejects merchants and businessmen. This confirms the view that the author of this Gospel is a collector rather than a (Gnostic) interpreter.

III

Professor Wilson already observed with respect to the Parable of the Wicked Husbandmen that 'the striking thing about the version in the Gospel of Thomas (Saying 65) only appears when we compare it with Dodd's reconstruction (on the basis of the synoptic versions) of the original story, in which we should have "a climactic series of three" – two slaves and then the son. This is, in fact, precisely what we find in Thomas'.[16]

> He said, 'There was a good man who owned a vineyard. He leased it to tenant farmers so that they might work it and he might collect the produce from them. He sent his servant so that the tenants might give him the produce of the vineyard. They seized his servant and beat him, all but killing him. The servant went back and told his master. The master said, "Perhaps [they] did not recognize him". He sent another servant. The tenants beat this one as well. Then the owner sent his son and said, "Perhaps they will show respect to my son". Because the tenants knew that it was he who was the heir to the vineyard, they seized him and killed him. Let him who has ears hear'.

The synoptic versions of this story (Mark 12:1–9; Matthew 21:33–41; Luke 20:9–16) are clearly allegories about Israel who first rejected the prophets, then killed 'the son' (Jesus) and thus is no longer fit to keep the vineyard of God. This is expressed right at the beginning through the quotation of Isaiah 5:2[17] and especially at the end through the statement '(The owner of the vineyard) will come and destroy the tenants, and give the vineyard to others' (Mark 12:9).

The conclusion seems obvious: the Gospel of Thomas indeed preserved a more original and non-allegorical version of this parable.[18] Nevertheless, several interpreters have insisted that the Thomas version is dependent upon at least two of the Synoptic Gospels and that 'the absence of the elements which have to be interpreted allegorically can altogether be understood as a deliberately designed secondary de-allegorizing by the Gnostic narrator'.[19] It is interesting to note the certainty of such interpreters with respect to the Gnostic meaning of this parable: the restored text, 'perhaps they did not recognize him', is rejected in favour of 'perhaps he did not recognize them', since the Gnostic narrator wants to state that the servant went to the wrong people – only the true revealer, the Son, can be recognized.[20] The servants are only mistreated, not killed, because the 'deadly hatred of the world' is restricted to the true revealer.[21] When the saying about the stone which the builders rejected (Mark 12:10–11) is quoted in the following saying of the Gospel of Thomas (66), it is because 'the Gnostic who can "hear" knows that the stone which the builders rejected, the son whom the husbandmen killed, is the cornerstone, i.e. the revealer'.[22] The Gnostic editor also deleted all features referring to 'history of salvation'[23] – did he indeed know what *Heilsgeschichte* meant? He certainly had no difficulty in referring to Israel elsewhere.[24] And can one really assume that this author was interested in the death of Jesus, 'the

Son'? Where, in the Gospel of Thomas, is the evidence that the writer of this gospel ever reflected upon the death of the revealer, because the world hated him?

All that appears in such interpretations is prejudice. Since the author must be Gnostic, he is neither permitted to be independent of the canonical gospels, nor is he given a chance to tell a story. But that is apparently exactly what he is doing here. He tells the story well and in a concise fashion. Those who knew the problems which could arise with absentee owners of agricultural estates – not only in Palestine[25] – would understand this story without difficulties. What is its theological meaning? That is a difficult question, because the author does not tell us anything about his interpretation. An owner of such an agricultural estate was mentioned in the preceding parable (see above). That provides at least a reason for the association of these two parables in the composition of the writing.[26] Does the following saying (Gos. Thom. 66) about the stone which the builders rejected interpret the preceding parable? We do not know that either, since the author introduces that saying separately ('Jesus said'). The Synoptic Gospels connect the saying explicitly with the Parable of the Wicked Husbandmen (Mark 12:10–11 and parallels), but Thomas does not. Apparently, they were transmitted together, though it was Mark who invented the interpretation of the one by the other. As Thomas is silent about the relationship, we cannot guess his thoughts on this matter. Is it possible that the author of the Gospel of Thomas primarily collected stories, parables, and sayings of Jesus?

IV

It is not my intention in this brief essay to present the 'right' interpretation of Thomas' parables. On the contrary, I want to point out that we do not know enough about story-telling and parables in the time of early Christianity.

To be sure, we *do* know how Gnostic authors interpreted parables. One example may suffice:

> Let not the kingdom of heaven wither away. For it is like a date-palm [shoot] whose fruits poured down around it. It put forth leaves and, when they budded, they caused the productivity (of the date-palm) to dry up. Thus it is also with the fruit which came from this single root: when it (i.e. the fruit) was [picked], fruits were collected by many (harvesters). It would indeed be good if it were possible to produce these new plants now; (for then) you (sing.) would find it (i.e. the kingdom). (Ap. Jas 7:22–35).[27]

What was the original parable in this case? What is the interpretation suggested by the author? Both questions make the mind boggle, though there is no lack of interpretative comment. Indeed, the author's complex allegorization has made the reconstruction of an original parable a real conundrum. But even in a case where the original is better preserved, it is hazardous to infer a Gnostic interpretation. Ap. Jas 12:22–27 apparently quotes such a parable unaltered:

> For the kingdom of heaven is like an ear of grain which sprouted in a field. And when it ripened, it scattered its fruit and, in turn, filled the field with ears of grain for another year.[28]

Does this parable speak of the Gnosis that is scattered over the world? Or of the spreading of Gnosis through those who received it? The interpretation added by the author tells otherwise (Ap. Jas 12:27–30):

> You also: be zealous to reap for yourselves an ear of life in order that you may be filled with the kingdom.[29]

It is characteristic that the parables of the Gospel of Thomas do not contain such interpretative comments. Thus, we simply cannot know what such parables suggested to a possibly Gnostic author – not to speak of the notorious imprecision of the term 'Gnostic'. We cannot know whether the mustard seed (Gos. Thom. 20) is understood as the Gnostic revelation.[30] Nor is it possible to state with any degree of certainty that the big fish in the Parable of the Fishnet (Gos. Thom. 8) is the symbol of the greatness of Gnosis.[31] Nor is there any reason to assume that the pearl (Gos. Thom. 76) is the Gnostic self of the human being.[32]

In all those instances, the parables of the Gospel of Thomas retain their narrative character. They are still stories, not artificially constructed revisions of written documents.[33] Their similarity to the more original parables of Jesus – repeatedly admitted even by scholars who argue for their dependence upon the Synoptic Gospels – is not accidental. For a better understanding of the history of the tradition of Jesus' parables, it is of the utmost importance to recognize the true narrative character of Thomas' parables. In contrast to the allegorizing tendencies especially of Mark and Matthew, and in contrast to the complex process of Gnostic symbolic interpretation, the Gospel of Thomas shares with Jesus the ability to tell stories – to be sure, stories which are puzzling, challenging, tantalizing, and perplexing; stories which speak of ordinary events and, at the same time, transcend everyday experiences; stories in which new perspectives do not derive from the theological system of a redactor, but from the inventiveness of the narrator who adapts the story to a new situation.

Thomas' parables must first be understood in the context of a continuing tradition of parables as oral and written narrative. When we have learned more about the theological and cultural *Sitz im Leben* of this tradition, it will also be possible to discuss the specific meaning of these parables in the Gospel of Thomas, i.e. in a writing of clearly recognizable Gnostic proclivities.

NOTES

1. R. McL. Wilson, *Studies in the Gospel of Thomas*, London 1960, 100.
2. Most typical of this approach is the recent article of A. Lindemann, 'Zur Gleichnisinterpretation im Thomas-Evangelium', *ZNW* 71, 1980, 214–43. Relevant literature is listed in notes 2, 4, and 5. Lindemann's article exhibits the fallacies of a 'Gnostic' interpretation in such a typical fashion that I can restrict my critical remarks primarily to his essay.
3. Quite possibly 1 Clement also recalls the Pauline simile of the 'bare kernel' that must die first before it comes to life (1 Corinthians 15:36–38).
4. Translation by T. O. Lambdin in (ed.) J. M. Robinson, *The Nag Hammadi Library in English*, New York 1977; reprinted in R. Cameron, *The Other Gospels*, Philadelphia 1982.
5. E.g. the explicit object of the sowing: *ton sporon*, in Luke 8:5. That Gos. Thom. 9 otherwise seems to resemble the Lukan version is only due to its brevity. Actually, its text is more closely related to Mark, cf. 'it did not take root' with Mark 4:6 (Luke 8:6 says: 'it lacked humidity').
6. Most recently by Lindemann, op. cit. (n. 2), 222f. That the word 'behold' introduces the parable here as well as in Mark 4:3 (and Matthew 13:3), but is nowhere else found as an introduction of a synoptic parable, does not prove Thomas' dependence upon Mark. This word is probably not a part of the Markan redaction, since Mark adds his own introductory formula 'Listen'.
7. Lindemann (op. cit. (n. 2), 224) wants to show that the author only intended to emphasize the contrast 'between those who bear fruit (the Gnostics) and those who do not bear fruit (the non-Gnostics)'.
8. Lindemann, op. cit., 223.
9. Cf. R. Bultmann, *The History of the Synoptic Tradition*, New York 1968[2], 175; J. Jeremias, *The Parables of Jesus*, New York 1972[2], 63–65.
10. Certainly the last sentence, 'Businessmen and merchants shall not enter the kingdom of my Father', is a secondary application.
11. The Lukan version suggests that the excuses are not more than subterfuges; cf. Jeremias, op. cit. (n. 9), 179.
12. Lindemann, op. cit. (n. 2), 231.
13. 'No one who puts his hand to the plough and looks back is fit for the Kingdom of God'. See also the story of Zacchaeus, Luke 19:1–10.
14. See also the wails of the merchants and shipowners in Revelation 18:11–19.
15. The third activity, to be sure, does not necessarily relate to a member of a specific class, though it is unlikely for someone who belongs to the poor portion of the middle class or is a slave.
16. Wilson, op. cit. (n. 1), 101.
17. Mark 12:1; Matthew 21:33; mostly deleted in Luke 20:9, though 'he planted a vineyard' still reveals the dependence upon Isaiah 5:2, while Gos. Thom. 65 says 'owned a vineyard', i.e. it reveals no knowledge of

the secondary reference to the Isaiah passage.

18. This conclusion was already suggested by H. Montefiore in idem and H. E. W. Turner, *Thomas and the Evangelists*, *SBT* 35, London 1962, 63.

19. Lindemann, op. cit. (n. 2), 236. The term 'de-allegorizing' (*Entallegorisierung*) was first used in relation to this parable by M. Hengel, 'Das Gleichnis von den Weingärtnern Mc 12,1–12 im Lichte der Zenonpapyri und der rabbinischen Gleichnisse', *ZNW* 59, 1968, 5–6. It is difficult to understand why Hengel thus argues against the possible authenticity of Thomas' version of this parable, since he demonstrates in the same essay that exactly this version reflects very well the actual economic situation in Palestine during the Hellenistic period and even later.

20. Lindemann, op. cit. (n. 2), 236f.

21. Ibid., 237.

22. Ibid., 237; cf. 238.

23. Ibid., 236f. For those who do not quite believe that, it is pointed out that, according to K. R. Snodgrass ('The Parable of the Wicked Husbandmen: Is the Gospel of Thomas Version the Original?', *NTS* 21, 1975–76, 142–44), Thomas depends upon the Syriac version of Mark in which the allegorical verse Mark 12:4 is missing. Syr[s] indeed leaves out this verse. But it is a fourth-century manuscript, probably dependent upon Tatian's Diatessaron. Of the Gospel of Thomas, however, we have Greek fragments written *ca*. A.D. 200. Anachronistic arguments seem to be quite all right, if one wants to prove Thomas' dependence upon the canonical gospels.

24. It is instructive to compare Gos. Thom. 52: 'His disciples said to him, "Twenty-four prophets spoke in Israel, and all of them spoke in you". He said to them, "You have omitted the one living in your presence and have spoken of the dead" '.

25. Hengel, loc. cit. (n. 19), has provided excellent documentation for this.

26. This may also explain the characterization of the landlord as 'a *good* man': the author indicates that, in contrast to the preceding parable, the rich landowner is not the villain in this story.

27. Translation by R. Cameron, op. cit. (n. 4), 60.

28. Translation ibid., 62.

29. Ibid.

30. Lindemann, op. cit (n. 2), 225.

31. Ibid., 218.

32. E. Haenchen, *Die Botschaft des Thomasevangeliums*, *TBT* 6, Berlin 1961, 48.

33. Lindemann (ibid., 243) claims that the forms of these parables were created by a 'downright systematically working unified Gnostic redaction'.

XV

THE GOSPEL OF PHILIP AND THE NEW TESTAMENT

by

Professor Eric Segelberg, Halifax

The Gospel of Philip and its relation to the New Testament cannot entirely be studied without taking into account its relation to the Old Testament. First we have to observe that Old Testament quotations specifically indicated as having been taken from the Holy Scriptures do not occur. It seems fairly difficult to find any quotations at all either from the (Hebrew) Old Testament or from the intertestamental literature.[1] Personal names in the Gospel of Philip are not abundant. Among them three are from the Old Testament: Adam (9),[2] Eve (2) and Abraham (1). All three appear in Genesis and the text of the Gospel of Philip shows that they are more than mere names. Adam came into being from two virgins, the Spirit and the virgin earth (83); his soul came into being through a breath (80); there are two trees in Paradise. Adam ate from the tree which bore animals (84); death comes into being through the separation of Eve from Adam (71); salvation means restoring what went wrong at the beginning. Christ came to repair what went wrong from the beginning (78). Eve separated from Adam because she was never separated from him in the bridal chamber (79). Abraham is referred to as introducing the circumcision 'teaching us that it is proper to destroy the flesh' (123, p. 82:26ff.).

These references clearly show that the author or authors of the Gospel of Philip had access to basic Old Testament teaching about the beginning of the world and of the elect people of God in Abraham. The interpretation is related to that of the Jewish tradition, but it has taken a special form, because the author of the Gospel of Philip is anxious to show how a higher authority, his Gnostic 'religion', is the answer to conditions which prevailed in the beginning. Terms such as Echamoth and Echmoth indicate the direction in which to search for the late Jewish exegetic tradition behind the Gospel of Philip (39). Thus Old Testament traditions are used, but with this special tendency. A similarity with the much later Islamic tradition should also be noted.

This use of Old Testament tradition is fairly common in Gnostic texts including the vast Mandean corpus.[3]

The importance of the study of the relationship between the New Testament and the Gospel of Philip was of course already observed by Wilson,[4] and he accepts the possibility of some influence from Matthew and John and on one occasion from Luke, but none from Mark. He further accepts the presence of allusions, if not quotations, from some Pauline letters (Ròmans, 1 and 2 Corinthians, Galatians, Philippians) and also from Hebrews. Wilson takes this New Testament influence as an indication of the Gospel of Philip's coming into being at an early period in the history of the canon. Since then Ménard and others have suggested a number of other possible allusions in the text of the Gospel of Philip. Gaffron has made a very thorough analysis of the New Testament quotations, comparing them with the Greek text as well as with the Coptic texts available, both those used by Horner and those preserved in other manuscripts. He does not, however, trace the way in which these quotations are interpreted. We have to rely heavily on his results.

Gaffron has found twelve quotations, one of which occurs twice. There is no need to enter here upon his meticulous analysis. We only note four results which he presents (ibid., p. 45).

1. In four cases one can point to a Greek *Vorlage* and there is no evidence against a Greek original in the other cases.

2. One cannot *prove* any influence from Sahidic or Bohairic translations. In one case influence from a Subachmimic text type is possible (John 8:34, § 110) but Gaffron emphasizes that in other Johannine quotations no such influence is possible.

3. Although the way of quoting is not always very accurate, the Gospel of Philip seems to share some peculiarities with the Diatessaron and the Curetonian Syriac translation; in other cases the text type is that of the Codex Bezae, the Vetus Latina and the Vetus Syra. Gaffron consequently suggests that the Gospel of Philip presupposes the Western text of the second century.

4. The Gospel of Philip presents what are indisputable quotations from Matthew, John, 1 Corinthians and 1 Peter. How the author knew these texts cannot be shown. There is only one certain quotation from Luke; in another possible case it could equally well be taken from Matthew, which seems more plausible. When one cannot distinguish between quotations from Matthew and Mark the same kind of plausibility speaks in favour of Matthew.

Allusions to New Testament texts have been identified by Wilson, de Catanzaro, Ménard and Gaffron. Here we venture into an even more difficult area. What to us may sound like an allusion may not be as obvious to a Gnostic of the second or third centuries. We have the whole corpus of the New Testament at our disposal. We also have a number of other early

Christian Gnostic texts. But we sometimes disregard the fact that a large amount of such early writings has been lost. Some of their titles we know, but the Nag Hammadi find has shown that there were many more texts circulating at that time of which we were entirely ignorant. What may sound like an allusion to us may not have made the same impression long ago. Gaffron wisely adopts a rather cautious attitude, taking up only a limited number of more obvious allusions.

He first refers to three expressions which belong to the terminology of the Gospel of Philip, namely 'the kingdom of heaven', 'my heavenly father' and 'die äusserste Finsternis', all used exclusively by Matthew. This further reinforces our previous observation that the Gospel of Matthew has an important role to play in the Gospel of Philip.

In another section he investigates some other allusions such as 'the sons of the bridal chamber/of the bridegroom' (§ 122); 'the dogs eat of the crumbs that fall from their masters' table' (Matthew 15:27/Mark 7:28); 'see, your house will be deserted' (Matthew 23:38/Luke 13:35, Gos. Phil. § 125); 'there will not be left stone upon stone' (Matthew 24:3 par, Gos. Phil. § 125). In these cases also Gaffron finds that Matthew is the most likely source, whereas there is no evidence of the use of Mark or Luke.

The Gospel of John is also alluded to in such expressions as: 'the friend of the bridegroom' (Gos. Phil. § 122, John 3:29; 'bread from heaven' (John 6:31ff., Gos. Phil. § 15). A clear allusion is found in Gos. Phil. 96: 'The Father was in the Son and the Son in the Father' which can refer either to John 14:10f. or John 17:21. These and other instances indicate that the author of the Gospel of Philip knew John or belonged to a tradition which knew that Gospel. This is in harmony with what we know about the Valentinian school of Anatolian or Italian background. Acts seems to be unknown to the tradition of the Gospel of Philip. There are some possible allusions to Pauline texts and Hebrews (Gaffron, 55–59). There are no allusions to the Pastorals, the Catholic Epistles or Revelation (ibid., 59).

Gaffron sums up by saying that the Greek version of the Gospel of Philip knew both Matthew and John as a whole, Matthew perhaps without the preliminary history (*Vorgeschichte*). Whether the Greek version of the Gospel of Philip knew the whole of the Pauline epistles from which it quotes or merely certain useful quotations from them is a matter of debate; Gaffron inclines to the latter view. The passage quoted from Luke (the Good Samaritan) is such an impressive text that once heard it could readily be reproduced. It does not therefore indicate that the Gospel of Philip knew the whole of the Gospel.

The introductory form used for the Gospel quotations is general, not referring to any particular author or text. Of the thirteen quotations seven are not introduced at all. When introduced by a formula Jesus or the Logos is mentioned as the speaker or it is obvious from the context what is meant. It seems significant that the eight agrapha are introduced by similar formulas. Once 'the Saviour' (*psōtēr*) is subject, in four 'the Lord', the same term being obviously understood in two other cases. In the final case the subject is not quite clearly expressed (Gaffron, 61). The frequent use of the term 'Lord' is in contrast to the general assertion, based on Irenaeus

Haer. I, 1:3, that in Valentinian Gnosticism the term was not in use. Here is possibly a point where New Testament influence is recognizable.

A New Testament or rather Gospel keyword is 'the Son of Man'. It appears three times in the Gospel of Philip (§§ 54 and 102, both marred by lacunae, and 120). In 120 we read: 'There is the Son of Man and there is the son of the Son of Man. The Lord is the Son of Man and the son of the Son of Man is he who is created through the Son of Man.' (Gos. Phil. 81:14ff.). Here we find an interpretation of the Son of Man identifying him with the Lord, something which is not often completely unambiguous in the New Testament. Wilson has shown that the term is not unknown in Gnostic literature,[5] and the full edition of the Nag Hammadi texts bears out what he suspected, that the term is very common. This indicates that the Son of Man, although of New Testament origin, is so common among the Gnostics that one cannot use it to prove a direct relationship with the New Testament.

Before ending this part of our study we should observe that the Gospel of Philip does not indicate any distinction between canonical and apocryphal dominical words.

Let us now sum up: the Gospel of Philip seems to know some of our New Testament writings, and probably two Gospels more or less in the shape we know them today. There is also some knowledge of Pauline texts and 1 Peter. We find a number of direct quotations chosen in a way which indicates a certain exegetical and theological tendency. Nobody would suggest that in its choice of quotations the Gospel of Philip shows a desire to present a full and balanced exposition of the New Testament. Furthermore, in a number of ways it shows the influence of New Testament texts without quoting them directly. These allusions point in the same direction as the direct quotations. They indicate familiarity with some Gospel texts and further, Pauline, texts. Other epistles too have been suggested.

What would appear to be decisive for our understanding of the relationship of the Gospel of Philip to the New Testament texts is the quotation of other dominical words unknown to the New Testament and generally unknown to the apocryphal Gospels and other texts available. If we believe that the Gospel of Philip came into being about the middle of the second century we can accept that dominical words not preserved in the Gospels were circulating. Papias, although a bishop, was not entirely happy with the written Gospels as he knew them but relied on some, and probably a large number of, other words circulating among Christians and regarded as having dominical authority. To what extent they were influenced by Gnostic ways of thinking is beyond our knowledge. However, it is probable that most agrapha in the Gospel of Philip belong to a more Gnostic kind of tradition than the one known to Papias. It seems likely that, as far as quotations and allusions are concerned, the Gospel of Philip's relation to the New Testament is governed by a clearly Gnostic tradition of a Valentinian type. Thus there is here an authority higher than that of the New Testament itself, and it is this authority that guides the author/authors of the Gospel of Philip in their reading of New Testament

texts. It would seem then that we have here a parallel to the relationship of
the Gospel of Philip to the Old Testament: part of it is used but a way of
interpretation is adopted which is not that of the New Testament but
rather of a late Jewish type which has experienced strong Gnostic
influence.

The relationship of the Gospel of Philip to the New Testament should
also be tested in another way. How does the former's doctrine square with
the latter's? In this short study it will not be possible to look into this
problem in its entirety. But it seems advisable to look at one single aspect:
the sacramental system of the Gospel of Philip and its relationship to the
New Testament. This sacramental system has been dealt with by several
scholars and the most noteworthy contribution has undoubtedly been that
of Gaffron, whose thesis has already been referred to on several occasions.
As is well known, the system seems to contain five sacramental acts which
are referred to in logion 68 (p. 67:27f.) where it is said: 'The Lord [did]
everything in a mystery, a baptism and a chrism and a eucharist and a
redemption and a bridal chamber'. Of these at least two, baptism and
eucharist, can easily be related to New Testament texts, perhaps also
chrism, but *apolutrōsis* (redemption) and the bridal chamber are more
difficult to relate in the same way. Now this relation to the New Testament
is certainly a slightly more complex affair than the straightforward
identification made by a modern New Testament exegete. It is not entirely
impossible to imagine a Christian or a Gnostic of the second century
reading his various New Testament texts and finding references which are
suitable for establishing a New Testament background for chrism. We can
point to 1 John 2:20, 27. If one wants to prove a biblical background for
the 'bridal chamber' one has to adopt a rather advanced kind of exegesis,
of the type used by Jewish scholars of the New Testament period or the
early centuries C.E. Now logion 68 says: 'The Lord made everything in a
mystery ...'. The Gospel of Philip thus wants its readers to believe that the
Lord – that is Jesus Christ – is in some way responsible for the
establishment of the five sacraments. Again, this shows that the Gospel of
Philip has a certain degree of relationship to the New Testament but also
that there must exist sources, not available to us, from which one can
deduce that Jesus, the Lord, instituted those five sacraments.

If we examine some aspects of these sacraments we will again find a
relationship to the New Testament, but also another and higher authority
which is decisive for its interpretation.

Baptism was instituted by Jesus and he was himself baptized by John the
Baptist. The Gospel of Philip knows of Jesus' baptism although neither the
Baptist nor the Spirit in the shape of a dove seems to be referred to. Two of
the passages (§§ 81, 89) are in rather poor condition and need a good deal of
reconstruction. The third text, logion 109, shows that an interpretation of
a different kind from that of the church is at work: 'By perfecting the water
of baptism, Jesus emptied it of death. Thus we do go down into the water,
but we do not go down into death in order that we may not be poured out
into the spirit of the world. When that spirit blows, it brings the winter.

When the Holy Spirit breathes, the summer comes.' In his translation Isenberg does not succeed in showing that the Coptic text uses the same word for his 'emptied of death' and 'to be poured out' into the spirit of the world. The Coptic verb is *pōht ebol*. Till is perhaps more successful in his rendering: 'so goss er den Tod weg' and 'damit wir nicht hinweggegossen werden' respectively. This expression may refer to the external action involved. Another external act is mentioned: 'we do go down into the water, but we do not go down into death'. This going down and later ascending is known from another passage (§ 59). It seems that the Gnostics of the Gospel of Philip had accepted a biblical or early church tradition in their performance of the baptismal act, but the interpretation was different, because their understanding of death was different. Gaffron (ibid., 120ff.) deals with this in his explanation of logion 97. In the light of logion 43, there also appears to be a reference to the complete immersion of the baptizand, again in accordance with the normal Christian procedure.

Chrism as the anointing of the baptizand is certainly known from Christian texts of around A.D. 200. Tertullian (*Bapt.* 7) refers to it. In his *Apostolic Tradition* Hippolytus describes it and the prayers connected with it. There is no indication in these texts of its being a recent introduction. We can therefore take it for granted that the use of chrismation was known at least by A.D. 150. However a biblical background for it is not regarded as plausible, the text from 1 John 2:20, 27 being generally understood in a symbolic way. One should, however, keep in mind how strongly unction was established in Old Testament tradition as well as in Near Eastern rites in general.[6] The Christian tradition also understands the imposition of hands with prayer upon the newly baptized, and sometimes upon the baptizand before the rite of baptism, as an act preceding the rite of unction (Acts 8:15–17; 10:44ff.). A complex relationship is involved which cannot be discussed now.

Gaffron has taken up the problem of the origin of the Gnostic chrismation and among others pointed to the Gnostic interpretation of the Tree of Life in Paradise as an important source (ibid., 143f.). What is striking in the Gospel of Philip's conception of the chrism is the idea of its superiority to the baptism in water. In logion 95 we learn: 'The chrism is superior to baptism, for it is from the word "chrism" that we have been called "Christians", certainly not because of the word "baptism".' This saying is best understood against its likely Syriac background: $m^e\check{s}\bar{\imath}h\bar{a}$ – $m^e\check{s}\bar{\imath}h\bar{\imath}n$.

Furthermore the logion continues: 'It is because of the chrism that "the Christ" has his name. For the Father anointed the Son and the Son anointed the apostles and the apostles anointed us.' Thus we see how the Gospel of Philip reckons with a kind of succession of chrismation. Probably the author read such a rite into the story of Jesus' baptism. Possibly the imposition of hands on the apostles was regarded as their unction and the 'us' refers to these Christian Gnostics who, perhaps, had a feeling of not being too distant from the time of the apostles. We may regard it as probable that the New Testament has influenced this in some way. The reading into the texts of unction is not so difficult for an author living in a tradition which has adopted unction. One takes it for granted that the practice is part of the original tradition, even if that is not the case.

It seems doubtful whether logion 111 has baptismal unction in mind. The reference to the Good Samaritan (Luke 10:34) seems rather to refer to something different. The use of the word *neh* (oil) instead of *chrisma*, points in the same direction. The result of the anointing was healing: 'for love covers a multitude of sins' (1 Peter 4:8). There are other passages worth looking at in this context, but this would appear to be enough to make it clear that there is a possible connection between the Gospel of Philip and the New Testament in the case of chrism, at least a reading into the text of the situation in the second century. But the emphasis on the higher dignity of chrism over baptism seems to be hard to defend from a New Testament standpoint, if the fact that chrism (usually) appears to follow baptism is not regarded as an indication of superiority.

The eucharist is dealt with in six logia. There is an obvious similarity with New Testament tradition in the acceptance of bread and wine in this act. Water is also included in accordance with early tradition (§§ 100, 108). But the tradition of the Gospel of Philip goes far beyond that of the New Testament. Logion 26 presents a quotation from the liturgy saying: 'You who have joined the perfect, the light, with the Holy Spirit, unite the angels with us also, the images'. It is hard to accept this prayer as in accordance with New Testament thinking. Here another tradition is at work. Gaffron (ibid., 184) writes:

> this prayer probably contains a request for the Holy Spirit which descended into the cup, that is in combination (syzygy) with the 'perfect man'. The language is ... genuinely Gnostic. Jesus thanks (the Father) for the syzygy Christ-Holy Spirit or Soter-Achamoth.

Logion 23 reproduces John 6:53f. in a eucharistic fashion: 'Because of this he said, "He who shall not eat my flesh and drink my blood has not life in him". What is it? His flesh is the word, and his blood is the Holy Spirit. He who has received these has food and he has drink and clothing.' In his interpretation of this logion Gaffron lays stress on the fact that this understanding of John 6:53f. would have been accepted by any Catholic Christian at the time. But the author of the Gospel of Philip read it in a Gnostic way (ibid., 180).

Logion 108 has a more surprising twist: 'The holy man (Isenberg's translation, 'priest', seems slightly dubious because we have hardly any evidence of priests in this text; the term should properly be used to render *hiereus*, which is not a common term in the second century to denote a presbyter; moreover the Coptic expression seems to be referring to the perfect man[7]) is completely holy, down to his very body. For if he has taken the bread, will he consecrate it? Or the cup or anything else that he gets, does he consecrate them? Then how will he not consecrate the body also?' Gaffron expresses his interpretation thus: 'The "holy man" has so much *pneuma* that all that he touches gains a share in *pneuma* through this touch and thus is purged from mixture with matter.' (ibid., 178). The reality of 'consecration' is due not to the recitation of the dominical words or a prayer for the coming of the Holy Spirit but due to the holiness, fulness of Spirit of the agent. Here again we find a deviation from what we believe is the New Testament tradition.

The *apolutrōsis* (*sōte*) causes some trouble. It is included in logion 76 along with baptism and *numphōn* and is prefigured by one of the main parts of the temple in Jerusalem. It has possibly something to do with a rite of anointing (*neh*). If that is the case there might be a New Testament background to it in James 5:14 which refers to an act bringing both forgiveness of sins and healing. But we remain to a large extent in the dark about this important rite and feel inclined to ascribe its use in the Gospel of Philip mainly to a tradition with little connection with the New Testament.

The fifth sacrament, 'mysterium', largely remains a mystery. It is the supreme act, but there is no agreement among scholars either about its external nature or about its theology (Gaffron, 191–222). By looking upon it as the last sacrament (*Sterbesakrament*), however, Gaffron contributes something new to the discussion; this sacrament would then correspond to the Mandean *masiqta*. But further discussion is necessary before we can come to a more certain conclusion on this matter. As things stand there is little hope of finding a New Testament background or rite corresponding to this mysterium. Whatever may have been its nature, it indicates that another authority than the New Testament has been at work here.

Let us now summarize our results. There is direct or indirect Old Testament influence on the Gospel of Philip in some respects, but there is also another and supreme authority at work which seems to give the Old Testament texts another meaning than the 'catholic church' of the second century would attribute to them. There is also direct influence from some New Testament texts on the Gospel of Philip. Probably the author(s) of the Gospel of Philip knew the Gospels of Matthew and John, but whether in the shape we know them today or not cannot be determined. In addition some Pauline and Petrine verses are quoted. Some allusions to Gospel texts, mostly Matthaean, and a few other texts are certain and some more are possible. The quotations used are chosen in a tendentious way. They can hardly be described as mirroring even the vague orthodoxy of the second century. For the author(s) there is an authority higher than the New Testament. The agrapha quoted are mainly from unknown sources. In them must have been codified the Christian Gnostic tradition which shaped the Gospel of Philip. The mid second century or the early part of its second half is the period when one would expect to find this kind of incomplete collection of New Testament writings. We do not know, however, to what extent this Christian Gnostic group was later than the 'Catholics' in becoming aware of the formation of the New Testament. Thus the Gospel of Philip may be somewhat younger than is generally thought.

In its sacramental system the Gospel of Philip again shows an obvious relationship with the New Testament but in addition there is a higher authority which reinterprets both the rites known from the New Testament and adds other sacraments which have no clear existence in the New Testament. Thus in the matter of sacraments and probably also in other areas of doctrine we come across the same phenomenon as in the Gospel of Philip's relationship to the Old Testament and New Testament: a clear relationship but also the existence of another and more authoritative sacred source.

NOTES

1. Various attempts have been made to establish influence, e.g. S. Giversen, *Filipsevangeliet*, Copenhagen 1966, 101. H. G. Gaffron, *Studien zum koptischen Philipsevangelium unter besonderer Berücksichtigung der Sakramente*, Bonn 1969, observes that there are no OT quotations or references in Gos. Phil. He thinks, however, that the author may have known certain parts of the OT, esp. the Paradise story. This knowledge, he thinks, was based not on reading of the OT but on Gnostic school tradition.
2. The numbers refer to the logia or 'paragraphs' into which H. M. Schenke divided the work in his German translation in *ThLZ* 84, 1959, 1–26 = Leipoldt-Schenke, *Koptisch-gnostische Schriften aus den Papyrus-Codices von Nag-Hammadi*, Hamburg-Bergstedt 1960, 33–65f. and 81f. In this study the text of Walter Till, *Das Evangelium nach Philippos* (*PTS* 2, Berlin 1963), has been used. Occasionally Till's text has been compared with the facsimile edition. The logia are referred to according to the order in Till's edition. Wesley Isenberg's translation in (ed.) James M. Robinson, *The Nag Hammadi Library in English*, 131–151, has occasionally been referred to. In this study the Gospel of Philip is regarded as a unity without notice being taken of the fact that it has probably come into being during a certain period of time and that it may contain doctrines or traditions which are not always compatible.
3. Cf. E. Segelberg, 'Old and New Testament Figures in Mandaean Version' in (ed.) S. Hartman, *Syncretism*, *SIDA*, Stockholm 1969, 228–239.
4. *NTS* 9, 1963, 291–294.
5. *The Gospel of Philip*, London 1962, 179ff.
6. Cf. E. Segelberg, *Maṣbūtā*, Uppsala 1958, 155–160.
7. Isenberg, op. cit., 146 (77:2). Cf. E. Segelberg, 'Ministry in Some Gnostic Circles and in the Church', in (ed.) M. Parvio, *Ecclesia, Leiturgia, Ministerium*, T. Harjunpää *Festschrift*, Helsingfors 1977, 155–166.

XVI

THE BOOK OF THOMAS (NHC II. 7):
A REVISION OF A PSEUDEPIGRAPHICAL
EPISTLE OF JACOB THE CONTENDER

by

Professor Hans-Martin Schenke, Berlin

Strictly speaking the title of this paper is inadequate since it only partly covers what I am going to discuss. Also, cautious or suspicious readers should be encouraged to add a question mark after the subheading. It is the primary purpose of this paper to point out the overall relevance of the Book of Thomas (hereafter, declining the usual abbreviation, Bk Thom.) for New Testament scholarship. But, since the aspect referred to in the subtitle (involving literary criticism) is, in my opinion, the most exciting one, I wanted to emphasize it from the very outset. In the course of setting forth the various points of relevance, this aspect will only be the destination of our journey. The longer scholars are occupied with the Book of Thomas the more it becomes apparent that this writing is of extraordinary importance – not only in a very general sense, but also for New Testament scholarship in particular. In a sense this very document turns out to be a magnifying glass or mirror for New Testament problems, methods, and theories. The most important items can be summarized in six points.

1. In the beginning of the Book of Thomas, the dialogue setting presents not only important new material for the Syrian Judas Thomas tradition but also, more particularly, a new argument for the discussion on the Johannine figure of the Beloved Disciple (cf. Kirchner 1977: 802[9]; Schenke/Fischer 1979: 178). This argument should be of relevance even to those scholars who cannot share my view – and recognize it as a (further) corroboration of my thesis – that the legendary figure of Judas Thomas was in fact the model after which the Johannine redaction shaped its concept of the Beloved Disciple. The new argument lies in the declaration made by Jesus (Bk Thom. 138:7f. *ñtok ... pašbr ñmēe*); in this connection

213

we can disregard its curious introduction. Here, the Coptic *pašbr̄ m̄mēe* (line 8) is (or, at least, was) understood by all translators as meaning 'my true friend' (or something similar). Accordingly, the sentence *n̄tok … pasbr̄ m̄mēe* 'you are … my (only) true friend' would, in principle, pass for an equivalent of the Greek *su ei … ho philos mou ho alēthinos*, which is very close to the designation of the Johannine Beloved Disciple. In order to assess this 'closeness' it is necessary to reduce both to a common denominator. In the Gospel of John the Beloved Disciple is called:

$$ho\ mathētēs\ hon\ {ēgapa \atop ephilei}\ ho\ Iēsous\quad {(13{:}23;\ 19{:}26;\ 21{:}7,\ 20) \atop (20{:}2).}$$

Transformed into direct address, the literary mode of the Book of Thomas, it would read *su ei hon philō*. What is apparently missing here, if plain identity is demanded, is only an adverb *alēthōs*. But this comparative meaning ('love him more than the other ones') is, nevertheless, already present in the Johannine formula though only by implication. A nominal expression might be more in need of such an explication than a verbal one. At any rate, the uniqueness of the relationship between Jesus and the Beloved Disciple, which, according to the outcome of New Testament exegesis, the Gospel of John asserts, is equally present in the formulation of the Book of Thomas (especially through the combination of 'my' and 'true').

But now this entire interpretation seems to have been deprived of its foundation by Peter Nagel (1980). According to Nagel's argument, the translation 'my true friend' would only be possible if the text were *pašbēr m̄mēe* (instead of *pašbr̄ m̄mēe*), whereas the actual construct form *šbr̄-* must be a rendering of the element *sun-* (or *phil-*) of a Greek composite noun. Nagel for his part conjectures a twice mistaken *sunathlētēs* 'fellow contender' behind the expression in question (first misread into *sunalēthēs*, and this then only mechanically transferred into Coptic). Now, there are many things that could be said in both appreciation and criticism of Nagel's position. For instance, one would object that his solution presupposes more, and more serious, misunderstandings than the usual interpretation, even in his opinion, would imply. Scholars might feel motivated to follow Nagel's track but also to seek a solution free of new complications. But after my own attempts in this direction I should like to say that this road leads nowhere. In this connection, however, I want to confine my reply to Nagel to the essential. We have to begin with Nagel's premises, according to which there is a categorical difference between *šbr̄ m̄mēe* and *šbēr m̄mēe*. And it is precisely the existence of this difference that must be denied emphatically. In fact, there are on the whole four possible ways to express this same syntagmatic relation, namely *šbēr m̄mēe, šbr̄ m̄mēe, šbēr mēe*, and *šbr̄ mēe*; and each of these could be a rendering of a Greek *sun*-compound (as is very often the case when other words follow *šbr̄* or *šbēr*); but this need not be so. In all of the four cases the hierarchy of the two nouns, their mode of rection, is in principle the same – notwithstanding the variation of actual forms. In all four cases the basic meaning is the same, that is, 'friend in respect of truth'. What nuance this basic meaning adopts is only determined by the context. In our passage where the actual wording is only 'you are ... my friend in respect of truth', the predicate could mean either 'my (companion as) friend of truth' or 'my friend (who is so) in truth'. On account of the whole, i.e. double, predication of Thomas the second possibility must be regarded, already at the level of the Coptic translation, as that one which is far more likely. Besides, its decisive advantage lies in the fact that in this case (in contrast to the first possibility; but this cannot be explained here) the conception of the Greek model is entirely free from problems (*ho philos mou ho alēthinos*).

What has been explained so far can also be verified by examples or analogies for either part of *šbr mmēe*. That, even in its construct form, the word *šbēr* is capable of rendering the Greek noun *philos* is already indicated in the Sahidic New Testament by the passage Matthew 11:19 par Luke 7:34, where *šbr telōnēs* does not mean 'fellow tax collector' but renders the genitive construction *philos telōnōn*. For an example where the Coptic *rectum* represents a Greek adjective, we can refer to Proverbs 14:20 (P. Bodmer VI): *šare hñšbēr mste noušbr hēke* is a translation of *philoi misēsousin philous ptōchous*. Further, there is a passage which not only verifies the formal state of affairs with which we are primarily concerned here but which is – especially by its doubling of the object – almost a material parallel to the double predication of Thomas in the Book of Thomas. This passage is Acts 10:24, which reads according to the best witness to the Sahidic translation of the Bible: *eafmoute enefsungenēs mñ nefšbēr anankaios* (Chester Beatty Codex B) as a translation of *sunkalesamenos tous sungeneis autou kai tous anankaious philous*. The Sahidic text variants for the last part are *šbēr nanangaios* (BM Or. 7594), and *šbeer ñanankaion* (Bodleian Hunt. 394). The grammatical status of the word *šbēr* in the Chester Beatty manuscript is, however, despite its homography with the *absolutus*, the *constructus* (therefore *šbēr-*). Thus confronted here with a *status constructus šbēr-*, which, homographic with the *status absolutus*, is quite current in Sahidic, we may well ask whether it is possible, conversely, to understand the element *šbr* in our expressions *šbr mmēe* as a *status absolutus* which is only homographic with the *status constructus*. In this perspective a passage of Shenoute becomes important: *kata | the ñta oušbr | epōn pe ñ/hēgemonikos | r̄mñtre nai* (ed. Chass. 107:33–37) 'comme un ami commun, du gouvernement, me l'a certifié' (tr. Cherix 1979:29). Then again, the phenomenon could also be seen in connection with the special dialect of the Book of Thomas (influence of Achmimic), which does not seem to be identical with the dialect of the other documents of Codex II.

Trying to carry out the same search for analogies with regard also to the second part of *šbr mmēe* (our *mmēe* corresponds to *mme* in classical Sahidic), we should ask: are there other expressions in Sahidic texts with the element *mme* being preceded by a (real or apparent) *status constructus* and rendering a Greek adjective 'true'? And immediately our attention will be drawn towards the usage *ene m̄me*, especially towards those cases where it does not translate the single Greek noun *margarītēs* but the two-word expression *lithos timios* (1 Corinthians 3:12; Revelation 17:4; 18:12, 16; 21:19).

For the argument we are concerned with here, i.e. the high probability that the source for *pašbr̄ m̄mēe* in the Book of Thomas is a Greek *ho philos mou ho alēthinos*, still another fact may be of some importance: taken in this sense, *šbr̄ m̄mēe* would express, if one may say so, a natural concept. (Cf. from this point of view the indisputable 'true friend' (*šbēr m̄me*) in Teach. Silv. 95:14, 19f., *pistos hetairos* in Theognis 416 and *gnēsioi philoi* in Cl.Al., *Prot.* IX, 82:7.) Finally, this naturalness is reflected by the existence of the opposite concept, as an example of which we can take the Lycopolitan *šbēr ñkraf* 'false friend' (Man. *Psalm-Book* 64:4; 94:4).

2. On another level, i.e. not in the narrative framework but in the text itself, the Book of Thomas again displays striking parallels to the Gospel of John, and, what is more, to passages in John which are obscure and raise enormous exegetical difficulties, all of which are found in chapter 3. There are, altogether, three points of contact of that kind. The first two are contained in the passage 138:21–36, which reads:

> But Thomas said to the Lord: 'Therefore I beg you to tell me what I ask before your ascension. [An]d only if I hear from you (the truth) about the hidden things can I speak about them. And it is obvious to me that it is difficult to perform the truth before men.' The Saviour answered and said: 'If (in fact) the things that are visible to you are obscure to you, how can you hear about the things that are not visible? If it is difficult for you to perform the deeds of truth that are visible in the world, how indeed, then, will you perform those (deeds) that pertain to the exalted height and to the accomplishment which are not visible? And how will you be called "performer (of the truth)"? Therefore (it is valid): You are apprentices! And: You have not yet received the height of perfection.'

For the moment, we should not worry about the strange relationship between question and answer, which is nevertheless typical throughout the Book of Thomas. Rather, it is the mention of the performance of truth and the intensive manner in which this very topic is treated here to which we want to draw attention since these two aspects manifest an evident link with the well-known motif of *poiein tēn alētheian* in John 3:21 (and 1 John 1:6). Further, the two 'if'-sentences within the answer of the Saviour are important: they represent a still more interesting parallel to the Gospel of John, and in particular to John 3:12. Here the contact does not consist in the wording of a certain phrase but in the fact that whole sentences in both cases are formed after the same model and presuppose the same logic.

The third parallel is found in the passage 140:5–18. It reads:

Thomas answered and said: 'Lord, this indeed is why I am asking you like < — >, (namely) since I have understood that it is (only) you that is good for us, as you say.'
Again the Saviour answered and said: 'Therefore it is necessary for us to speak to you. For this is the doctrine for the perfect. If, now, you desire to be perfect, you must observe these (words). If (you will) not (observe them), your name is "Ignorant", since it is impossible that a wise man dwells with a fool. For the wise man is full of all wisdom. To the fool, however, the good and the bad things are the same. For, the wise man will feed on truth and "will be like a tree growing by the torrent".'

Here it is the surprising 'us' in the beginning of the Saviour's answer to which we want to draw attention, for it strongly recalls John 3:11 where the sudden shift from (first person) singular to plural is equally astonishing since it is made without discernible reason.

In my opinion, the exhibition of these three parallels has a value in itself. It is not intended to raise the question – nor to anticipate an answer in a definite direction – about which might be dependent on which. For it is possible that the phenomena of the Book of Thomas pointed out here are not located on one and the same level. And there is reason to suspect that their relation to the aforementioned phenomena in the Gospel of John can only be defined on a broader basis.

3. While points 1 and 2 have dealt with noteworthy details, we now turn to a matter which pertains to the Book of Thomas as a whole or, strictly speaking, to its material as a whole. The Book of Thomas is a new source for the form-critical investigation of the literature of early Christianity. It is especially relevant for the tradition of the sayings of Jesus. In several recent articles Helmut Koester has tried to demonstrate the importance of non-canonical early Christian writings for the sayings tradition (1979; 1980a; 1980b). From the Nag Hammadi documents it is the Gospel of Thomas, the Dialogue of the Saviour, and recently also the Apocryphon of James which in his view take the leading role. But the Book of Thomas he only just mentions, Now, in my opinion, the Book of Thomas should be fully included in his survey and ought to be given a central position there. The matter I have in mind is extensive, and to draw from this source will prove to be productive. Here I only want to exemplify this by one detail, that is, the relationship of two passages of the Book of Thomas with that famous saying which appears in the Gospel of Thomas as logion 2; the more so since this connection has already been mentioned by Koester (1980a: 242). These two passages read:

[Bless]ed is the wise man who s[ough]t [after the truth]. [For w]hen he had found it, he came to rest upon it forever and was not afraid of those who wanted to disturb him' (140:41–141:2).

And if you pray, you will find rest, < ... > that you have left
behind trouble and disgrace. For when you come forth from the
troubles and passions of the body, you will receive a place of
rest from the Good One. And you will rule with the Ruler, you
joined with him and he joined with you, from now on, for ever
a[nd] ever' (145:10–16).

It is quite obvious that these two sayings are related to each other and
that both belong to wisdom tradition. More strictly speaking, each of them
is a variant of the very productive and widely applicable sayings type
centring around the topics of 'seeking' and 'finding' (cf. Koester 1980a:
238–244). These two sayings may be used to interpret each other by those
traits in which they resemble one another and even by those in which they
differ. And both sayings are related to a third one, the one already
mentioned, which apparently held a special place in the tradition and is
best known to us from the Gospel of Thomas (log. 2). (For the variants and
relations of this logion cf., e.g., Koester 1980a: 242f.) Now, if these two
sayings in the Book of Thomas seem to depend on that third one – they
look like solutions, interpretations, applications of that compactly
structured one – this need not imply that it is the Gospel of Thomas itself
on which the Book of Thomas or an overall source of it (given its existence)
are dependent here. It might be that our sayings depend on that logion in a
state in which it was not yet, as a saying of Jesus, incorporated into the
Gospel of Thomas, i.e. when it existed as an autonomous saying of
Wisdom. In any case, as a basis for its application here we must postulate a
complete form for the saying, such as is nowhere preserved, which
included both the motif of *disturbance* preceding the astonishment
(preserved only in the Coptic version) and the motif of *coming to rest* after
becoming ruler (only preserved in Greek). Thus it would be necessary to
presuppose the whole saying in the following form or something like it:

> (Wisdom says:)
> He who seeks must not stop seeking
>   until he finds;
> and when he has found,
>   he will become disturbed;
> and when he has become disturbed,
>   he will be astonished;
> and when he has become astonished,
>   he will become ruler;
> and when he has become ruler,
>   he will find rest upon it.

The first saying quoted above from the Book of Thomas, that is the
beatitude, could be understood as an implicit answer to three (or four)
questions which were directed at the underlying logion: 1. What properly
is it that the seeking person seeks and finds? 2. Upon what does he come to
rest or to what does the *epi* in *epanapauesthai* refer? 3. How does he

become disturbed, that is to say, by what or by whom? (4. And how do the three motifs cohere in substance?) By the way, the description of salvation in this saying seems to aim at a situation within historical time whereas the parallel saying at the end of the Book of Thomas obviously has an eschatological orientation. Furthermore, there are some details and associations which are worth noticing. Since salvation is here promised to the man who is explicitly said only to be *seeking* the truth (that *finding* is nevertheless implied is shown by the introduction of the following sentence), it would be possible to say that this man, then, belongs to the second category of Philo, *Fug.* 119–176 (category 1: who neither seeks nor finds; category 2: who finds whenever he seeks; category 3: who seeks without finding; category 4: who finds without seeking). The statement of the text: *apsabe m̄ton m̄mof ehrai ejñ tmēe* deserves attention with regard to its language as well as its use of metaphor. There is a perfect parallel to this expression, in terms of actual Coptic wording, which John D. Turner has already pointed out (1975: 152). This parallel is Treat. Res. 44:1–3 which reads: (We received rest) *ñtarensouōn tmēe auō anm̄tan m̄man ahrēi ajōs* 'when we recognized the *truth*. And we came to rest upon *it*.' At the same time the metaphorical aspect of the passage is important: apparently truth can be conceived of as *something upon which* one can come to rest. Since behind the Coptic expression *m̄ton m̄mo* = *ehrai ejñ* a Greek *anapauesthai epi* may be supposed, we must direct our attention in addition to two Philo passages where the same construction occurs although there the place to rest on is not truth itself but the divine Logos or Virtue, respectively; cf. *Som.* I, 128: *hōs anapausomenos epi logō(i) theiō(i)* etc.; *Som.* I, 174: ... *tēn gēn, legō de tēn pamphorōtatēn kai eukarpotatēn aretēn, eph' hēs katheudei ho askētēs anapauomenos* etc. By the way, both times the reference is to Jacob (and in interpretation of Genesis 28:11,13); and this is very important for the material of the Book of Thomas since such Jacob topics occur again. Concerning the special use of metaphor in our expression 'coming to rest upon truth', first of all an essential aspect follows from the description of the consequences in the same sentence. From this it can be learned that the resting-place upon truth means unceasing safety and being taken out of disturbance. From the next sentence, which appears as an answer given by Thomas, it follows that the resting-place is imagined in such a way that one can come to rest *upon it* as well as *within it*. It further follows from it that the resting-place 'truth' must be identical with one's property (as the underlying Greek expression we can suppose *ta idia*) or with one's home. Would it be going too far to conclude that the resting-place is located *above* or *in the height*? At any rate it seems to follow from all this that the 'truth' mentioned here is imagined as an elevated, safe, homelike castle (cf. from this point of view also Philo, *Agric.* 65; and *Migr. Abr.* 28).

The motif expressed by *netouōše aštr̄tōrf* (141:2) is strongly reminiscent of a passage from Gos. Thom. log. 2, viz.:

auō hotan efšančine fnaštr̄tr̄
auō   efšanštortr̄ fnar̄špēre (32:16–18).

Rather than taking this for mere chance we are led – as already indicated or supposed – to assume dependence of this expression on the wisdom saying 'He who seeks must not stop seeking', etc. Once we take this for granted, a second synoptical view is worth while. Admittedly the exact meaning of *štortˀ* within this wisdom saying is enigmatical. But in the context of the wisdom saying itself everybody will understand the formulation quoted above as indicating a process simply connected to the 'one who seeks' (: 'becoming disturbed'). According to the Book of Thomas, however, the subject of this process has been understood as being the *patiens* of an action, hence the different wording (some others 'want to disturb him'). The original *fna/efšanšt(o)rtˀ* seemed to imply to the author of the Book of Thomas that the finding of the 'one who seeks' would immediately rouse hostile forces against him, which try to disturb him. Naturally it would be good to know whether this is a forced reinterpretation or, essentially, a legitimate explication of what is really meant by the enigmatic expression. But there is no answer for questions of this kind.

The second of the two passages of the Book of Thomas quoted above is the final promise of the document. It has obviously been formulated according to the pattern of the wisdom saying 'He who seeks must not stop seeking', etc. That this topos of wisdom occurs once again within our text and in such an outstanding position (though in a somewhat different application) should be considered as a further sign of its enormous significance. And Koester (1980a: 242f.) has made it probable that elsewhere this topos provided the clue for the whole arrangement of material; i.e. in the supposed main source of the tractate The Dialogue of the Saviour. In the beginning of the final promise here the catchword 'seeking' has been replaced by the catchword 'praying', which within the tradition of this topos is one of its equivalents (cf. Matthew 7:7f. par; and Koester 1980a: 238–244). Presumably this equivalent has been used here to provide a smooth link with the preceding exhortation. A consideration, now, that seems to me very important and is also necessary in order to understand the pointed brackets in the translation given above refers to *je* in line 11. The clause (1. 11f.) introduced by *je* causes more difficulties regarding its function in the sentence structure than is visible at first sight. To put it concisely, the state of affairs is thus: as a strictly causal clause (as it had been considered so far) it is illogical, as a sort of object clause it is lacking a natural verbal basis. Its illogicality follows from the tense used in this clause (the perfect only makes sense if one looks back from the moment of 'rest') as well as from the rivalry with the protatic 'if you pray'. Only the following readings would be logical: on the one hand, 'if you pray you will find rest *after* you have left behind trouble and disgrace'; on the other hand, either 'If you pray you will find rest', or 'You will find rest since you have left behind trouble and disgrace' (cf. the following sentence). In view of this dilemma into which the causal interpretation of *je* leads, it would seem more natural, so to speak, and more promising to resort to the alternative, viz. the possibility of an object-clause interpretation of *je*. In this case, to be sure, we have to suppose a gap in the flow of the sentence, an inadvertent omission, immediately before *je*. Such a hypothesis seems plausible, however, the more so since out of the stock of motifs of the underlying wisdom saying just that very verb seems to be missing, namely *thaumazein*/*r̄špēre*, which could have provided the basis of such a natural *je*-clause. (For the construction *r̄špēre je* within the Sahidic New Testament cf. Mark 15:44; Luke 11:38; John 3:7; 4:27; Galatians 1:6; 1 John 3:13.) Then it would be easiest to assume that the supposed omission consisted in a verbal expression like < *ñtetñr̄špēre* > : 'And if you pray you will find rest < and you will be astonished > that you have left behind the trouble and the disgrace.' By the way, this solution may also elucidate the motif of 'being astonished', which is enigmatic in itself; cf. *ho thaumasas* (Cl. Al., *Strom.* II, 45:5) and *fnar̄špēre* (Gos. Thom., log. 2; NHC II, 32:17f.). The respective passages in the Book and the Gospel of Thomas, application and source, throw light upon each other. And perhaps here again the Book of Thomas explicates what in the Gospel of Thomas is meant but not said.

However, the most difficult problem of this final promise consists in the application and development of the motifs of 'resting' and 'ruling'. This multidimensional and far-reaching problem centres on the 'neutral' (formulated not in the 1st but in the 3rd pers. sing.) designations 'the Good One' and 'the Ruler' (or 'the King'). But to pursue this problem would carry us beyond the perspective chosen at this stage. And so the mere indication may suffice here. Nevertheless, the vast complex of phenomena to which this one belongs will come under discussion in the following sections.

4. Even the dialogue framework of the Book of Thomas as a whole proves attractive for New Testament scholarship, especially once more for the exegesis of the Gospel of John. Obviously, the Book of Thomas and the Gospel of John are linked by the phenomenon of misunderstanding on the part of the Saviour's dialogue partner(s). But in the Book of Thomas it is relatively easy to find out that these 'misunderstandings' are just the accidental consequence of a process by which an originally continuous text was transformed into a dialogue. One may wonder whether it is more appropriate to attribute the 'results' to the incompetence of the 'dramatist' or to the objective difficulty of the task which he had set himself. At any rate, in the light of the Book of Thomas the question arises for the Gospel of John as well whether at least part of the so-called Johannine misunderstandings should not be explained in a similar fashion, i.e. in terms of literary criticism, and whether a working hypothesis of this kind (cf. Schenke/Fischer 1979: 187) can be verified. The Book of Thomas, then, would be important as a test model for the examination and reconsideration of exegetical methods which have been, or should be, applied to the Gospel of John. This not only pertains to the special case of the misunderstandings but to the whole of literary criticism of the Johannine discourses. These, it is true, are to a large extent one-sided dialogues. As to the individual stances in literary criticism, I have especially in mind the overall version of Rudolf Bultmann, characterized by the idea that a collection of *Gnostic* 'Offenbarungsreden' underlies the

dialogues (a source hypothesis which, in my opinion, has too hastily been put aside by scholarship; cf. Schenke/Fischer 1979: 182), as well as the 'partial' version, now propagated by Koester, according to which at least certain dialogues in John are based on sayings of Jesus, i.e. on material of the sayings tradition from a special sphere and a special stage of development. In the Book of Thomas the state of affairs is again much more manifest. Regarding the 'misunderstandings' here, Jesus and Thomas are in fact at cross-purposes. Other incriminating features add to this, especially in terms of content. And it is only all this taken together that makes the aforesaid source theory a natural conclusion.

That a procedure by way of literary criticism is indispensable if the Book of Thomas is properly to be understood, should be regarded as unquestionable. In fact, the question can merely be: *which kind* of literary criticism? A first attempt to build up a suitable theory has been made by Turner. According to his view, the Book of Thomas was compiled by a redactor from two sources. 'One work, section A' (= 138:4–142:21[26]) 'was a dialogue between Thomas and the Savior, perhaps entitled "The Book of Thomas the Contender writing to the Perfect". The other work, section B' (= 142:26–145:16) 'was a collection of the Savior's sayings gathered into a homiletical discourse (...) perhaps entitled "The Hidden Words which the Savior spoke, which I wrote down, even I, Matthaias". A redactor has prefixed section A to section B, and prefaced the whole with an *incipit* title composed on analogy with the original title to section B, and designating Matthaias as the scribe of the whole. The subscript title, designating Thomas as the scribe of the whole, was borrowed from the original title to section A, and suffixed to the newly-formed whole' (1975: 215). And in terms of content Turner places the two source documents and the new whole in the history of the *genre* of sayings of Jesus within a syncretistic (encratitic and slightly Gnosticizing) Christianity where the process would finally lead by way of the immanent interpretation of the sayings within collections of sayings to a reformulation of sayings in revelation dialogues (cf. 1975: 224f.).

All the problems and difficulties caused by the text which provide the background for the remarks made above have been raised by Turner. It is only on the strength of a different setting of priorities among the problems raised that I believe that, with the same method being applied, scholarship must come to a completely different result, viz. the one indicated above. Obviously the text has to be divided not in the middle, but throughout its length. It is the whole framework of the Book of Thomas or, what is almost the same, the dialogue between Jesus and Thomas, that is alone responsible for all the present curiosities and can be proved as having been forced subsequently upon the material. It is possible to fade out this framework without greater difficulties and it appears immediately that the text is quite comprehensible, beautiful, and important – which cannot be asserted of it in its present shape. I would say the framework has to be 'faded out' – it must not simply be subtracted or cut off. After the observations made so far on dialogicized sayings material (cf., e.g., Koester 1980a: 252) one must take into account the possibility that parts of the underlying material were used to construct the question of the dialogue partner. By the way, all this is not meant as a vague possibility but is the result of a detailed analysis of the whole document within a full-scale commentary on the Book of Thomas. I have carried out such a reconstruction of – if I may say so –the 'Eugnostos' of the Book of Thomas (or what is related to it in the same way as Eugnostos is to the Sophia of Jesus Christ).

5. The next point again is of some relevance to the sayings tradition or, in other words, to the christological concept of Jesus as the teacher of wisdom, especially with regard to its roots. This aspect results from the specific kind of text that emerges as the unique source from the procedure of literary criticism described. And for the moment the question whether the conception of such a source is taken seriously as a scholarly hypothesis or only regarded as a kind of exegetical experiment may be left open. Neither is it necessary for the reader to face my reconstruction in full. It will suffice if one simply abstracts the framework mentally and allows the material to make its impression on oneself. But it is especially important, of course, that one withdraws oneself from the view implicit in the 'frame-story' that Jesus is the speaker and 'I' of this material. Who is actually speaking here should rather be inferred from what is said.

Provided that it is legitimate to disregard the passage 141:10–13 (from *etbe tagapē ñtpistis* to *tšorp ñagapē*), which is unambiguously Christian but, in my opinion, can be proven to be a redactional gloss on the same level as the dialogue framework, the resulting state of affairs can be described as follows: there are, certainly, a few phrases and sentences which come so near to passages of the New Testament that, at first sight, one is inclined to regard them as reflections of those New Testament passages or, in other words, as depending on the respective writings or traditions of the New Testament. In addition to the parallels to John 3 discussed above, this especially applies to: the formula of introduction 'Truly I tell you' (142:27, 29f.); the second of the (three) beatitudes: 'Blessed are you who are reviled and not esteemed! On account of the love your Lord has for you' (145:3–5); the third beatitude: 'Blessed are you who weep and are oppressed by those witho[ut] hope! For you will be released from every bondage' (145:5–8); finally the exhortation that introduces the final promise: 'Watch and pray that you do not remain in the flesh but rather come forth from the bitter bondage of this life!' (145:5–10). But the New Testament phrases and sentences coming under consideration as sources belong just to those parts of the New Testament which themselves represent – or at least could represent – material taken over and inherited from Judaism (and/or Hellenism). That is, they are in themselves not specifically Christian. Thus it would be quite conceivable (analogous to our view of the relationship between the two passages of the Book of Thomas and Gos. Thom. log. 2) that these 'parallels' owe their familiar appearance not to Christianity but rather directly to those predecessors of Christianity. But even if we took such sentences of the Book of Thomas as of Christian character, this would have no real relevance to our question as to the essential nature of the material as a whole. For the bulk of the material obviously represents quite different and essentially non-Christian traditions and concepts. Also, we must not approach our question concerning the nature of the material from a 'static' point of view, expecting to find something fixed once and for all. Rather this material, being of paraenetical nature, is to be considered as being always in movement. Along these lines, one must suppose that its eventual make-up with a Christian framework was preceded by practical use made of it in the Christian groups concerned.

My point shall again be exemplified by an exegetical treatment of a single relevant passage. It is the sentence: '[Yo]u will send the[m d]own befo[re —— and] kill them daily in order that they might rise from death' (144:41–145:1). This talk about being killed and rising from death can certainly be regarded as the most obvious Christian motif of our text. By the way, the reconstruction of the Coptic wording is practically certain. The only remaining matter of uncertainty is the large lacuna at the beginning of line 42. But the preserved parts of the sentence are long enough, so that by and large there can be no doubt about its substance. The point is that the persecution of the disciples of wisdom by the unbelieving fools is a persecution to death, but that even this ultimate attempt to keep off wisdom fails because the persecuted are saved from death. By this we have already paraphrased the function of the final conjunction *jekaas* here; it is to be taken as equivalent to the respective *auō* in the centre of either of the preceding sentences. Obviously it can hardly express the intention of the killers. Rather, the Greek *hina* clause, which is to be supposed behind the *jekaas* clause here, belongs to the type used to denote a true consequence according to the intention of God. (Cf. Bauer 1958: 747:20–30.) The closest parallel is the *hina* clause in Luke 11:50. The clue to the particular way killing and rising from death is talked about here is to be found in the adverb *m̄mēne*, which probably corresponds to a Greek *kath' hēmeran*: the terms are used here in the well-known figurative manner (cf. Luke 9:23; 1 Corinthians 15:31; 2 Corinthians 4:11*a*) and denote the daily peril of one's life and being guarded daily against death. (For this kind of reference to reality with both expressions cf. also 2 Corinthians 6:9. For the figurative, especially moral, use of the concept of resurrection see, e.g., Teach. Silv. 106:17–21.) In this perspective it also appears that – in spite of the New Testament parallels referred to – nothing specifically and necessarily Christian is discernible about the way the Book of Thomas uses the expressions mentioned. The positive counterpart of this negative finding will immediately become evident if we take up the mystery of the lacuna. It may well be regarded as certain that what has been lost in the lacuna completed the preceding clause, which denotes an action that leads – or is intended to lead – to the killing mentioned immediately afterwards. An important further step is suggested by Bentley Layton; for he has found the only natural reconstruction for *n̄na̧/* [– – – at the end of line 41 (only preserved on a Doresse photo), namely as *n̄na̧/* [*hrn̄* (see the critical apparatus of his edition of Codex II). This invalidates the result of our former efforts to fill the lacuna (cf. Kirchner 1977: 802, 804[66]).

On the other hand, this preposition with its meaning 'before', 'in front of' (in the context of the preceding words) is very distinctive and restricts considerably the frame of expectation for what may still follow here. To think of an action which takes place *before men*, which means to think of trials with death sentences, seems to be excluded by the preceding 'send them *down*'. The element '*down*' suggests the image of a pit. And if the 'sending ... before' is no 'sending ... before' *men*, is it perhaps a 'sending ... before' *ferocious beasts* which are expected to kill the persons in question? (For the *preposition* from this point of view cf. Matthew 7:6 [Middle Egyptian]: *m̄pr'hioué n̄netnmargaritēs n̄nahrn nešeu*; and for the verb 'send' 2 Corinthians 4:9 [Sahidic]: *eutauo m̄mon epesēt* [for the Greek *kataballomenoi*].) As it is possible, in connection with the 'fire-extinguishing dew' occurring earlier in this text (144:15–17), to ascertain the influence of a topos of the Daniel legends (salvation from the burning furnace), it would not be surprising if in this passage of the Book of Thomas the actual twin concept of this topos was to be found, i.e. the 'sending down' ('casting down') into (and salvation from) the den of lions (cf. Daniel LXX, 6:6, 8, 13, 18; Bel and the Dragon LXX, 31–32). One would have to conceive of something like *henmouei* or *nimouei* 'lions' for the remaining space of the lacuna. That 'Daniel in the den of lions' had become a current motif in paraenesis becomes clear, e.g., in the Acts of Paul (Hennecke/Schneemelcher 1964: 269); 1 Clem. 45:6; and especially Cl. Al. *Strom.* II, 103, 104. In the passage of Clement of Alexandria we can also see how the topos can be used with a figurative sense. Such a generalized usage is presumably favoured by the specific role that the metaphor 'lion' (as the prototype of a ferocious man-killing beast) has always played in paraenesis and devotional language (cf., e.g., 2 Timothy 4:17; Hebrews 11:33; 1 Peter 5:8; Treat. Seth 55:9f.; Teach. Silv. 105:30f.; 108:10–14).

After all, let me modify the opening question about the nature of the (not essentially Christian) source of the Book of Thomas so as to ask now whether there is not agreement that it gives the impression of a piece of paraenetical wisdom literature of Hellenistic Judaism. By the way, this wisdom can be proved to be Platonizing and has essential parallels in Philo.

6. The last point results immediately from the preceding one and regards the possible relevance of the Book of Thomas for the difficult problems posed by the canonical Epistle of James. We are concerned here with nothing less than the question whether Arnold Meyer might have been right after all. Meyer (1930) believed, as is commonly known to New Testament scholarship, that the enigma of James was to be solved by recognizing that in fact it was an apocryphal Hellenistic Jewish epistle of the patriarch Jacob, with only some quite insignificant and superficial Christian interpolations. And this exciting hypothesis has been under discussion up to the present day. Though almost nobody has accepted it as a whole, there are not a few scholars who sympathize with it and try to assimilate essential aspects of it to their own interpretation. (Cf., e.g.,

Kümmel 1973: 358; Vielhauer 1975: 570f.; Schenke/Fischer 1979: 243f.)

The lines of connection which possibly exist between the Book of Thomas and James become most clearly visible from the set of problems implied in the subscript title. In order to point that out briefly (I have done it in full elsewhere) it is necessary to start right away from what is indeed a bare matter of fact which is self-evident to specialists in Coptic grammar though it does not yet dominate the general consciousness of Nag Hammadi scholars: the bipartite nature of the subscript title. In fact it reads: 'The Book of Thomas. The Contender writes to the Perfect' – and nothing else. It consists of two units of assertion, each entirely independent, from the syntactical point of view. By the way, the second unit represents one of the usual opening formulas of an epistle. It is from this base of bare facts that the crucial question, which is admittedly disputable, arises, namely whether this formal curiosity of the subscript title may not be directly connected with the overall literary character of the document as a Christian dialogization of a Jewish source. This, in fact, would provide a plausible explanation. For the first title, 'The Book of Thomas', covers the document as it is now or, in other words, is especially in accordance with its present dialogical framework. While there is no internally necessary connection between the two titles, the second title contains – with its mention of 'the contender' and 'the perfect ones' – just such concepts as are central to the material subjected to the framing. This means that the second title seems suitable to cover the supposed source of the Book of Thomas. And in the light of this material (with the dialogue frame faded out) even the enigmatic figure of 'the contender' emerges from anonymity. For in the milieu from which the supposed source is likely to come, that is to say, within the sphere of Platonizing Jewish wisdom tradition, the main witness to which is Philo of Alexandria, there is only *one* contender: he who contended with God, that is Jacob. Whenever in this sphere mention is made of '*the* athlete', as a synonym of which the designation '*the* ascetic' occurs as well, everybody knows that Jacob is meant. Here Jacob is conceived of as the ideal and prototype of the man who, though not yet possessing wisdom and virtue, in permanent struggle against the passions does not stop contending for them. That this understanding of Jacob is to be found in Philo is a well-known matter of fact. (Significantly enough, almost all the material we need here for our explanation of the Book of Thomas has already been collected by Meyer within the context of his aforementioned interpretation of James; cf. 1930: 197–202; 270–279.) In a sense, this view still depends on a further question, namely whether this Jacob conception of Philo, notwithstanding its involvement in the specific Philonic interpretation of the Scriptures, belongs to those ideas which Philo did not create himself but rather shared with his immediate spiritual environment. As far as I know, however, this question can be answered in the affirmative. Additional evidence is provided by the material of the Book of Thomas itself, which displays paraenetical Jacob motifs at essential points and to a considerable extent. Therefore it may be conjectured that the second part of the subscript title of the Book of Thomas was in fact the original title of its source and, consequently, this source had the form of a pseudepigraphical epistle of the God-contender Jacob, addressed to the perfect ones. And the 'dramatist' who created the present shape of our writing would also have to be held responsible for the editing of the subscript title to its present form. He would have reshaped not only the corpus of his source but also its subscript title, by formally putting it together *with* and, in effect, subsuming it *under* the new title conceived for the new shape of the document: 'The Book of Thomas'. It is only in this way that Thomas became the Contender. For the dramatist, of course, the contender was Thomas.

This source hypothesis for the Book of Thomas – provided that after all (when the complete evidence has been presented) it turns out to be well-founded and convincing – may, of course, be an important and exciting matter in itself. In the context of this paper, however, the main aspect to be emphasized is its fertilizing power for the exegetical work on James. What does it mean that on both sides, in the case of the Book of Thomas and of James, it is precisely an epistle of Jacob that seems to show up as the underlying source? In addition, the close relation of the two source documents will hardly be limited to their fictive labelling as epistles of Jacob, but will also apply to the material they contain. But here a lot of work remains to be done. Above all, it will be indispensable to re-examine Meyer's hypothesis on James thoroughly in the light of the Book of Thomas hypothesis pointed out here – and, of course, *vice versa*. In doing so, even the major obstacles to full scholarly acceptance of Meyer's theory may eventually fall, namely the purely Jewish-based interpretation of James 2:14–26 and his assertion, required as a premise, that the allegory of the names of Jacob, Rebecca, Isaac, and the twelve sons of Jacob had been the guiding principle for the arrangement of the material.

BIBLIOGRAPHY OF WORKS CITED

Bauer, W. 1958. *Griechisch-deutsches Wörterbuch zu den Schriften des Neuen Testaments und der übrigen urchristlichen Literatur⁵*, Berlin.

Cherix, P. 1979. *Étude de lexicographie copte. Chenouté: Le discours en présence de Flavien (Les noms et les verbes)*, *CRB* 18, Paris.

Hennecke, E.-Schneemelcher, W. 1964. *Neutestamentliche Apokryphen in deutscher Übersetzung³* II, Apostolisches, Apokalypsen und Verwandtes, Tübingen.

Kirchner, D. 1977. ' "Das Buch des Thomas". Die siebte Schrift aus Nag-Hammadi-Codex II eingeleitet und übersetzt vom Berliner Arbeitskreis für koptisch-gnostische Schriften', *ThLZ* 102, 793–804.

Koester, H. 1979. 'Dialog und Spruchüberlieferung in den gnostischen Texten von Nag Hammadi', *EvTh* 39, 532–556.

Koester, H. 1980a. 'Gnostic Writings as Witnesses for the Development of the Sayings Tradition' in (ed.) B. Layton, *The Rediscovery of Gnosticism. Proceedings of the International Conference on Gnosticism at Yale, New Haven, Connecticut, March 28–31, 1978* I, *The School of Valentinus, SHR* 41:1, Leiden, 238–256 (256–261).

Koester, H. 1980b. 'Apocryphal and Canonical Gospels', *HThR* 73, 105–130.

Kümmel, W. G. 1973. *Einleitung in das Neue Testament* (17th ed. of *Einleitung in das Neue Testament* by P. Feine and J. Behm), Heidelberg.

Layton, B. (ed.) 1982. 'Nag Hammadi Codex II, 2–7. Together with XIII, 2*, brit. lib. or. 4926(1) and p. oxy. 1, 654, 655. With contributions by many scholars' in: *The Coptic Gnostic Library edited with English translation, introduction and notes published under the auspices of The Institute for Antiquity and Christianity* (General editor J. M. Robinson), *NHS*, Leiden-in press.

Meyer, A. 1930. *Das Rätsel des Jacobusbriefes, BZNW* 10, Giessen.

Nagel, P. 1980. 'Thomas der Mitstreiter (zu NHC II, 7: p. 138,8)', *Mélanges offerts à M. Werner Vycichl, Société d'Égyptologie Genève, Bulletin* 4, 65–71.

Schenke, H.-M./Fischer, K. M. 1979. *Einleitung in die Schriften des Neuen Testaments* II, *Die Evangelien und die anderen neutestamentlichen Schriften,* Berlin.

Turner, J.D. 1975. *The Book of Thomas the Contender from Codex II of the Cairo Gnostic Library from Nag Hammadi (CG II, 7): The Coptic Text with Translation, Introduction and Commentary, SBLDS* 23, Missoula, Montana.

Vielhauer, P. 1975. *Geschichte der urchristlichen Literatur. Einleitung in das Neue Testament, die Apokryphen und die Apostolischen Väter,* Berlin.

XVII

THE TRIMORPHIC PROTENNOIA AND THE FOURTH GOSPEL

by

Doctor Yvonne Janssens, Montignies-sur-Sambre

I was delighted to accept the invitation to collaborate in this volume honouring Professor Wilson whom I have known for many years and whose knowledge and sound judgement I have always appreciated. But now that it comes to putting pen to paper I fear that I may have been rather rash: neither Trimorphic Protennoia nor the Fourth Gospel are easy texts to interpret! However the subject is a fascinating one, so in the end 'je ne regrette rien'.

Trimorphic Protennoia is a short text: it comprises only sixteen pages in the Coptic library from Nag Hammadi, and was found 'inside the front cover of Codex VI'.[1] On the last extant page is to be found the beginning of another Nag Hammadi text generally entitled On the Origin of the World (NHC II. 5 – untitled in the manuscript). For reasons not worth developing here, this detail has allowed an approximate determination of the pagination (missing from the manuscript) of Trimorphic Protennoia. My references always give two numbers, as is now customary, the first indicating the page, the second the line of the codex. I published an *editio princeps* with the first translation in French and a commentary – all too imperfect – in *Le Muséon* in 1974.[2] Almost simultaneously there appeared in the *Theologische Literaturzeitung* a German translation (under the overall supervision of Gesine Schenke).[3] This helped me to publish in the *Bibliothèque copte de Nag Hammadi* (Quebec) a new edition with a French translation, in an improved form and with an index, in 1978.[4] Unfortunately this still needs further correction! And finally there appeared an English translation by J. D. Turner in the collective volume edited by J. M. Robinson, publishing for the first time a complete English translation of all the Nag Hammadi texts (of which I had had no knowledge before my own publication).[5]

Trimorphic Protennoia is introduced straight away by a self-revelation: '[I am] the Pro[tennoia]' – and the formula 'I am' recurs more than twenty

229

times in its few pages. What is more, the work is expressed almost entirely in the first person singular, apart from a small number of passages in the second or first person plural generally referring to interlocutors of Protennoia, although this is not clearly indicated.

At first sight one can distinguish three definite divisions. Each of them begins with a self-revelation, respectively: 'I am Protennoia, the Thought ...' (35:1); 'I am the Voice that appeared ...' (42:4); 'I am the Word (the Logos) ...' (46:5). At the end of each part a sub-title specifies the subject to some extent. The title of the first part contains a small lacuna which can easily be filled: *p[log]os ñtprōtennoia*: 'The Word of the First Thought' (42:3). Unfortunately of the title of the second part (46:6) only four letters remain (a Greek feminine ending). The most acceptable conjecture is [*thimar*]*menē*, 'Heimarmene' or Destiny, which furthermore does have an important place in this second part. It is sometimes objected that it is abnormal to find in an ancient text a title comprising one single word.[6] However the papyrus is intact and blank before this word, which is placed in the middle of the line. One could suppose nevertheless that the title began on the preceding line (the papyrus is in a poor condition at the beginning of this page, as in all the concluding pages). Clearly all this remains extremely hypothetical. As for the third part, its title appears at the end of the work: 'The Word of the Epiphany' (50:21). It is immediately followed by the title of the whole: 'Trimorphic Protennoia. A Holy Scripture written by the Father, with perfect knowledge'.

These three parts correspond – by and large – to the three 'manifestations' of Protennoia, which justify the epithet 'trimorphic'. But the three parts themselves are not as distinctly divided: the first already deals with the three modes of presence – and adds even more to the list.

Let us dwell for a moment on the second theme: 'I am the Voice'. Some have translated this: 'I am the Call' – Gesine Schenke, for example (art. cit., n. 3: 'der Ruf'), and Colpe.[7] The latter stresses moreover that the call is a central theme ('Leitprädikat des Rufes') of Gnosis, which is indeed the case. For the Gnostic believes that he is imprisoned in matter until the moment the Saviour makes the call resound.[8] However, I would not go so far as to affirm that Protennoia *is* the call here: in the succession 'Thought – Voice – Word', Voice has the more logical place. Thought must be transformed into Voice to *emit* the Word. Voice here has the place occupied by the 'Mother' in another expression of this 'Gnostic triad', such as is found in this same text: 'The Father,[9] the Mother, the Son' (Trim. Prot. 37:22). And on the following page (38:15) we also learn that Protennoia is 'the Womb', *tote*.[10] It is therefore the Voice which 'gives birth', as it were. Regarding this triad, we should remember that in Hebrew the term 'Spirit' (*rûaḥ*) is feminine. The Mother is therefore, for the Gnostics, a fairly natural interpretation of the Spirit. The Greek word, *Pneuma*, is neuter, but Coptic, lacking a neuter, replaces it sometimes by a masculine, sometimes (and more often) by a feminine.

We should further make clear that two different Coptic terms (*smē* and *hroou*) are used for Voice in this text, both signifying 'call' as well as 'voice',[11] like their Greek equivalent, *phōnē*. I had consistently translated them by 'Voice'. In a commentary (which does not dwell specially on this point), Helderman,[12] in passing, translates various of the passages and renders *hroou* sometimes by 'voice' (Trim. Prot. 42:4: 'I am the Voice'), sometimes by 'call' (in 36:13ff. and 42:15). I believe that this is the right solution. The author of Trimorphic Protennoia – or its Coptic translator, if the original was in Greek – does not appear to make a real distinction between *smē* and *hroou*. But I am of the opinion (as no doubt Helderman is) that the same word should not always be taken in the same way: could the Greek *phōnē* perhaps be at the root of all this?[13]

And since my study is here concerned with a comparison between Trimorphic Protennoia and the Fourth Gospel, I should point out that John[14] also uses the term 'voice' (*phōnē*) in his Gospel. You even find there 'I am the Voice' (1:23)! But in the Fourth Gospel it is John the Baptist who utters this little phrase! The Valentinian Gnostic Heracleon, author of the very first known commentary on this Gospel, says on this subject: 'the word (the Logos) is the Saviour, the voice in the wilderness is represented by John, and the echo is the whole succession of prophets. The voice, because of its greater affinity with the Logos, becomes Logos ...'.[15] This seems to us very interesting for the interpretation of Trimorphic Protennoia: the double aspect of Protennoia thereby becomes clearer: 'I am the Voice ... I am the Word'. But in Heracleon, as in the Fourth Gospel, the 'Voice' (John the Baptist) is inferior to the Word – which is not the case with Trimorphic Protennoia, where Protennoia identifies herself equally with both the Voice and the Word.

There is another noteworthy passage in John using the term 'voice' (*phōnē* occurs sixteen times in the Fourth Gospel. Trimorphic Protennoia uses *hroou* twenty or so times and *smē* a good ten times): in the well-known parable of the 'Shepherd' in chapter 10: 'the sheep hear his voice (v. 3: *phōnē*) ... the sheep which belong to him, these he calls (v. 3: *phōnein*) ... they know his voice (v. 4: *phōnē*) ... they do not know the voice (v. 5: *phōnē*) of strangers ... I have other sheep ... they will hear my voice (v. 16: *phōnē*)'. And again in verse 17: 'My sheep hear my voice (*phōnē*) and I know them'. In each case one could probably substitute 'call' for 'voice': the sheep hear the call of the shepherd. In any case, in verse 3 the shepherd *calls* his sheep. Similarly in 5:37, 'You have never heard his voice' (that of the Father in this case), the sense could just as well be: 'you have not heard his call'.

In Trimorphic Protennoia we read for example: 'This voice (*hroou*) which we have heard is strange to us and we do not know it' (44:6f.). 'The Archigenetor ... did not recognize this voice' (or 'this call': *smē*) (44:29) ... 'hear ... the call (*smē*) of the Mother' (44:30f.). And in 46:9, it is again a matter of this 'voice (or call: *smē*) of the Mother'. If the examples are not all convincing, the two first passages quoted appear to me to offer serious parallels to the Fourth Gospel. Furthermore K. Fischer poses the question 'how far has John adopted Gnostic categories of thought?'[16] However I will postpone my reply for the moment. I have left unfinished the résumé of Trimorphic Protennoia: now it is time to return to it.

By means of a succession of self-revelations in 'I am' form (I have counted about ten of them in the first part, six or seven in the second and a similar number in the third), Protennoia makes known her profound nature. The first part reveals in particular her place in the heavenly world: she is Life, knowledge (*gnōsis* emanates from her: 36:10), the Thought of the Father (36:17), the Image of the Invisible Spirit (38:11), and already in this first part, the Womb (38:15). She is the invisible in the All, numberless, immeasurable, ineffable. The second part reveals more particularly her role here below: apart from being the Voice, she is the (male) Consort (42:5: although she is called 'the (female) Consort' in 42:8!), the Mother (42:9), the Womb (45:6: cf. 38:15. And so she has the same role in both worlds!). She produces the light (45:7) and is also the Aeon (45:8), the perfection of the All, i.e. Meirothea, the glory of the Mother (45:9f.). Finally, the third part reveals more particularly her role as Saviour and is therefore predominantly eschatological. She is the Logos (46:5 and 14), the Light (stated three times: 47:28, 29 and 30). She is 'their' beloved (that of the archons, according to the context, but probably it applies more to those whom she will call 'her own': 49:11), the Father of everyone (49:19f.), but is ungraspable (50:17). All this is very far from simple! However the Johannine specialists will have already noted the comparisons that could be made here.

Protennoia comes down three times – no doubt from 'heaven', as 45:31f. suggests, where after the failure of her second descent she proclaims: '(I poured out the Holy Spirit upon them) and I ascended to heaven. I entered into my light ... without my branch'. The first part deals at length with her first descent 'to the midst of Hades' (36:4). There she revealed herself 'in all those who knew me' (36:22f.), to 'those who are in Silence ... in darkness ... in the abyss' (37:12, 14, 15). But from the next page on, interpretation becomes more difficult. The text bears visible trace of recasting, of additions. We read, for example, on page 38: 'He gave Aeon to the Father of all the Aeons, that is to say to me, the Thought of the Father, the Protennoia, that is, Barbelo, the perfect glory, and the Invisible One, secret, immeasurable. I am the Image of the Invisible Spirit, and it is from me that the All received image ... (I who am) the Virgin who is called Meirothea, the unapproachable Womb, the ungraspable and immeasurable Voice. Then the perfect Son revealed himself to his Aeons, who emanated from him ... he glorified them ... He stood in the glory with which he glorified himself. They blessed the perfect Son, the Christ, the God who came into being by himself, and they gave glory saying: "He is, he is, the Son of God, the Son of God." ' The names Barbelo and the Virgin (*parthenos*) Meirothea only appear here.[17] The first recalls Barbelo-Gnosticism, the second Sethian Gnosis (in so far as these represent two distinct sects!), whereas Christ, Son of God, and even the theme of glory have a fine biblical ring! On the following page (39:13ff.) there also appears the great Light Elēlēth – who claims to be king (of the Aeons? – his domain is not specified here). Then it is the turn of 'the great Demon who rules in the depths of Hell and Chaos, lacking form and being imperfect, but possessing the form of the glory of those who were begotten in the darkness. Now he is called Sakla, that is Samaēl Ialtabaōth, he who received power which he stole from that guileless one whom he overcame at first, that is the Epinoia of the Light, (she) who came down, (and) from whom he came forth from the first'. To understand this last passage one has to refer to another Gnostic text (itself also pervaded by Christian themes), of which we possess no less than four versions: two short and two long. This is the Apocryphon of John, whose short version was already known to us through the Codex Berolinensis 8502 and which we have now recovered in three Nag Hammadi manuscripts: codices II and IV (long version) and codex III (short version). The codex II version is the best preserved of the long versions. By comparing the Apocryphon of John and Trimorphic Protennoia we can draw the conclusion that the 'great Demon' is the abortion born of the fall of Sophia (here called Epinoia). In 40:12ff. we in fact read: 'I (Protennoia) am going to come down into the world of mortals which is in that place since the day when this guileless Wisdom (*Sophia*) was conquered, she who went down'. This great Demon is called here Samaël (i.e. the blind god or the god of the blind), Ialtabaôth (or Ialdabaôth). In what follows he is regularly called the Archigenetôr. I cannot go into all the details and take the liberty of referring my reader to the commentary in my Quebec edition (ad loc.).

Trimorphic Protennoia then recounts the creation 'through Christ' (39:5–7) of four Aeons each with three names – of Sethian origin! 'And they all together blessed the perfect Son, the god who was begotten' (39:11–13). It is at this moment that 'the great Light Eleleth' – one of the four Aeons – says 'I am king' (39:15f.). 'And at that moment there also appeared the great Demon' (39:20f.) who 'began to produce Aeons in the likeness of the real Aeons' (40:5f.). 'But now' (says Protennoia), 'I have come down, and I have reached chaos and I was [near to] those who are mine' (40:29–31) – we will discover a little further on (41:1 and 16) that 'her own' are 'the Sons of the Light'. She has delivered them from all the bonds and has broken the chains of the demons of the underworld. She continues: 'I am the first to have come down because of my portion (*meros*) which remained, i.e. the Spirit which is in the soul ... I have spoken to the archons and to powers ... I have spoken my secrets (*musterion*) to those who are mine ... I have come down towards [those who have been] mine since the beginning' (41, *passim*).

In the second part – the second descent – Protennoia reveals herself as Voice, as female consort and Mother, and 'in the likeness of a woman'. 'And I have spoken to them; and I shall instruct them about the coming end of the Aeon, and I shall teach them about the beginning of the coming Aeon'. She made the call resound 'in the ears of those who have known me, that is the Sons of the Light' (42, *passim*). On the same page, it is specified that, on her first descent, she revealed herself 'through the Thought, in the likeness of my masculinity'. When the great Powers 'knew that the time of fulfilment had appeared, the elements trembled all together. And the foundations of the underworld and the vaults of chaos shook' (43). There was great anxiety also on the part of Destiny (*Heimarmene*) and its 'followers' (usually seen as the planets), that 'our whole dwelling has been shaken, and the whole circuit of our upward way has been destroyed, and the route ... which leads us to the Archigenetôr of our creation has ceased to be reliable for us'. Now the Powers are perplexed and 'ascend' to the Archigenētōr (the Creator) to question him and reproach him for his boasting (claiming to be the one true God! – a parody of the Old Testament frequent in Gnostic texts). 'This voice which we have heard is strange to us and we do not know it' (44). And a few lines further on: '... neither did even the Archigenētōr of our creation himself, about whom we boast, know this voice'. But Protennoia reassures them and 'calls them into the supreme and perfect light' where they will be glorified, receive the throne, the robe, the baptism. 'For it is I who have given form to the All ... it is I who sent breath into those who are mine. And I poured the Holy Spirit over them and ascended to heaven, I entered into my light ... without my branch (*klados*), I sat down ... among the Sons of the pure Light' (45). The subtitle Heimarmenē which appears here (46:4) is probably due to the fact that it is precisely in the domain of Destiny that Protennoia appeared in this second descent.

Finally the third part concerns the third descent of Protennoia, as Logos, 'sent to illuminate those who are in darkness' (46:31–33). She alone is 'the Logos, ineffable, spotless, immeasurable, inconceivable, a hidden light ... an immeasurable light, the source of the All, the root of the entire Aeon ... the breath of the Powers, the eye of the three dwelling-places (*monē*)' (46, *passim*). The last appellation requires some explanation. It was already stated in 37:21–2 that the Thought is in three dwelling-places (*monē*): the Father, the Mother, the Son. Being the 'light', she can consistently call herself here 'the eye of the three dwelling-places', the eye being 'the light of the body' (Matthew 6:22).

On page 47, Protennoia summarizes her three descents. The 'first time' has probably disappeared in a lacuna at the top of the page. 'The second time, I came in the [sound] of my voice, I gave form (*eikōn*) to those who received form till their fulfilment (*sunteleia*). The third time, I revealed myself to them in their tents (*skēnē*), I who am Logos. And I revealed myself in the likeness of their form, and I wore the garment of each of them, and I have hidden myself in them. And they have not known the one who empowers me ... And I have hidden myself in them, until I reveal myself to my brethren. And none of them has known me, even although it was I who was at work in them ... I am the Light which illuminates the All. I am the Light which rejoices in my brethren. For I have come down into the world of mortals because of the Spirit which has remained in [it]'. Page 48 lists the various intermediaries of salvation: those who present the robe, those who baptize, those who enthrone, those who glorify, those who take possession (five times three names) and finally, 'the five seals (*sphragis*) from the light of the Mother, the Protennoia' (48:31f.) which ensure participation in the mystery of knowledge. On page 49 'their Christ' reappears (but the top of the page has deteriorated). Then: 'I am their well-beloved ... for in that place I clothed myself like the son of the Archigenētōr. And I was like him until the end ... of the ignorance of chaos'. Then once more there is a reference to the three descents or appearances: 'And among the angels, I have appeared in their form, and among the Powers, as one of them, and among the sons of man as a son of man, I who

am father of everyone' (49:11–20), and another reference is made to the
effects of salvation: 'He who possesses the five seals ... stripped off (the)
robe of ignorance and put on a brilliant light ... Among such darkness will
be scattered and ignorance perish' (49:28–36 *passim*).

I give the ending in full (50:9–24): 'I have proclaimed to them the five
ineffable seals that I may dwell in them, and that they too may dwell in me.
I myself have put on Jesus, I have raised him from the accursed tree and I
have established him in the dwelling-places of his Father. And those who
kept watch over their dwelling-places did not know me. For, as for me, I
am ungraspable, I and my seed which is mine, I will establish it in the holy
Light, in an inaccessible Silence. Amen.

> The Word of the Epiphany   3
> Trimorphic Protennoia   3
> A Holy Scripture written-by-the-Father
> With perfect knowledge.'

(the four last lines are entirely in Greek).

According to certain interpreters, this last page may be an addition, a
later Christianization (the name of Jesus, for example, only occurs here).
According to some, too, the 'Father' writing 'in perfect knowledge' would
be Seth, 'father' of Sethian Gnosis. But Seth is never mentioned in this
work! Would the subject here not rather be Protennoia, who has asserted
that she herself is 'the Father'? In my opinion neither of the two solutions is
fully satisfactory: that the 'Revealer' should himself have *written* would
hardly be consistent with what happens in other revelation texts.

It is not without some trepidation that I approach the – burning –
question of the parallels between Trimorphic Protennoia and John. For
one group, the former is *one*, if not *the* source of John, and of the Prologue
in particular (in the third part: 'I am the Logos'). For others – and I was
one – it would be rather a case of Trimorphic Protennoia having
'plundered' the New Testament and especially the Fourth Gospel.
Trimorphic Protennoia would be in this instance then a de-
Christianization (which is one of Professor Wilson's hypotheses). A third
hypothesis has been advanced: that both the Fourth Gospel *and*
Trimorphic Protennoia have been inspired by an identical common
source: Jewish Wisdom literature (another opinion put forward by our
dedicatee).[18] There are still further possibilities to which I shall return.

In an earlier work,[19] I picked out certain parallel passages in the
Prologue of John and Trimorphic Protennoia. Here I will consider both
texts in their entirety, following the page order of Trimorphic Protennoia.
I will confine myself in general to citing possible parallels, leaving the task
of drawing conclusions to Johannine specialists.

Trim. Prot. 35:1ff.: '[I am] the Protennoia ... through whom the All
stands ... [she who] is prior to the All'. One could compare John 1:1–3: 'In
the beginning was the Word ... Everything came into being through him'.

Now let us stop for a moment at the opening formula: 'I am' (Greek *egō eimi*; here we have on each occasion the Coptic equivalent *anok pe*). Its frequent usage in the Fourth Gospel also has long intrigued exegetes. More than one has envisaged a Gnostic source. It is not surprising therefore if the discovery of Trimorphic Protennoia (we saw at the beginning of this article that the self-revelation in 'I am' form occurred twenty or so times in it) should have led to the supposition that in it we had *one*, if not *the*, Gnostic source of this formula. G. W. MacRae has made a very detailed study of the question.[20] He investigates 'both ... the origin of the Gnostic usage and its relationship to the New Testament', distinguishing the absolute use of the formula ('I am') and the employment of 'a predicative form of *ego eimi* as a claim to divine or transcendent identity'. His conclusion is that 'the use of "I am" with a variety of predicates in the manner of the Fourth Gospel' occurs in 'the Coptic Gnostic sources from the Nag Hammadi library'. But in the Apocryphon of John and others, the boast of the Demiurge: 'I, I am a jealous God and there is no other God but me' in all likelihood goes back to the Old Testament, more particularly Second Isaiah, which 'exercised a special influence on the development of Jewish apocalyptic thought. Its insistence on universalism and its open conflict with the claims of polytheistic paganism made it especially welcome to both apocalyptic and Hellenistic Judaism'. On the other hand, the use of 'I am' with a variety of predicates occurs in several texts from Nag Hammadi, particularly in The Thunder, Perfect Mind and the end of the long version of the Apocryphon of John in Codex II (30:11–31:28).[21] The formula is also current in the Isis aretalogies. According to MacRae, 'it seems highly likely that The Thunder owes its use of the first-person style to the aretalogy form, which, of course, had spread far beyond Egypt'. In short, even though MacRae suggests 'possible lines for comparison with the Fourth Gospel', I do not think that the use, although frequent, in both Trimorphic Protennoia and the Fourth Gospel, of the self-proclamation formula is sufficient proof of the influence of one of the two texts on the other, all the more so since John relates very *concrete* self-revelations like 'I am the Good Shepherd' (10:11 and 14) or 'I am the Vine' (15:1 and 5), something we do not find in Trimorphic Protennoia. MacRae does note, however, 'a (possible) parallel between some of the Gnostic sources in which the *egō*-proclamation appears and the Fourth Gospel – a parallel not so much in words or explicit allusions, as in religious outlook and religious discourse' (134).

We read next in Trimorphic Protennoia (35:6f.): 'I have three names, being alone perfect'. Thus there appears the notion of the 'triad', which will recur later in the form 'Father, Mother, Son' (see above), and which is in fact the Gnostic expression of the Christian Trinity. If we understand correctly, it is as it were an element of perfection. John is aware of the notion of Trinity (Father, Son, Holy Spirit), but nowhere does it appear so clearly, in a single expression.

Then there appears, even on the first page, the succession of negative attributes which will subsequently recur frequently: 'I am invisible (35:7 and 24) ... inaccessible (35:11), numberless (35:27), immeasurable, ineffable (35:28)'. None of these, to my knowledge, occurs in the Fourth

Gospel. The author shows on the contrary that the Father can be seen and known through a very tangible presence of the Son (e.g. 14:7ff.).

In line 12 we note: 'I am the life of my Epinoia'. Thanks to the Apocryphon of John (BG 53:4ff.) we know that the Epinoia of the Light is the good Spirit sent as helper to Adam, and that his helper is called *Zōē* (Life!). She is at work in the whole creation. This no doubt explains as well Protennoia's declaration here (35:19f. – still speaking of herself): 'moving in each and working in them all'. All this recalls – albeit very remotely – Jesus' self-revelation in John 14:6: 'I am the Way, the Truth and the *Life*' (*zōē*) and probably also the action of the Holy Spirit in us (particularly John 14:16 and 26).

We have passed over (35:16f.) the presence of Protennoia 'in the archons and angels and demons', entities which recur several times in Trimorphic Protennoia, always in the plural, with the exception of 40:5, in which reference is made to the 'great Demon' (which implies the existence of other demons too). The three terms are found in the Fourth Gospel, but *archōn* is certainly not used in the same sense, except perhaps in 14:30 and 16:11 where the reference is to the 'prince (*archōn*) of this world'. And 'demon' never appears in it in the Greek form *daimōn* (employed by Trimorphic Protennoia three times out of four), but always in the form *daimonion*.

We could note in passing 'every *hylic* (1.18, *hulikos*) soul', 'hylic' being a term frequent in Gnosis, but one not found anywhere in the entire New Testament.

Finally, in lines 21ff.: 'Those who are asleep I awaken; and I am sight for those who are in slumber'. I have already emphasized above the importance of the theme of the call in Gnosis: this call of the Saviour 'awakens those who are asleep' (that is the divine spark enclosed and sleeping in matter). Sometimes this theme is associated with John 11:11 in which Jesus says: 'Our friend Lazarus is sleeping, but I am going to waken him'. The terms, furthermore, are misinterpreted by the disciples (v. 12), but the evangelist immediately makes it clear that Jesus was referring to the death of Lazarus.

36:4f.: 'I [have descended to the] midst of Hades, I have shone on the darkness' strikes me as very similar to John 1:5: 'the light shines in the darkness' (cf. also 8:12).

And immediately after that (36:5f.): 'it is I who have caused the water to *well up*' perhaps recalls the water becoming a spring *welling up* in eternal life, in the episode of the Samaritan woman (John 4:14). The Valentinian Gnostic Heracleon comments, however: 'those who share in the blessings granted from above themselves cause to well up abundantly for the eternal life of the others what has been granted to them'. And again, with regard to John 4:13: 'the water which the Saviour gives comes from the Spirit and his power'.[22]

36:7f.: 'It is I who produced everything' once more recalls John 1:3: 'Everything came into being through him'.

36:22f.: 'I have revealed myself in all those who have known me'. The theme of knowledge is present in the Fourth Gospel. Even in the first chapter reference is made to witnesses who have *not* known Jesus (1:26). Even John the Baptist did not know him (vv. 31 and 33). But from the moment he saw him (vv. 32 and 34), he 'attests that *he* is the Son of God'. We shall have to return to this.

37:1–3: 'He who is hidden in us pays the products (*phoros*) of his fruits (*karpos*) to the water of life'. In my commentary (Quebec ed., 61f.) I explained that 'the products of his fruits' meant quite simply, 'fertility'. But what more particularly interests us here is 'the water of life'. This expression recurs twice more: in 41:23 and 48:20. The latter passage refers explicitly to the water of baptism: 'I handed him over to the baptizers; and they baptized him ... and they immersed him in the spring (*pēgē*) of the water of life' (48:12–21). In 37, 'he who is hidden within us' causes some difficulty. In 36:5ff., Protennoia said: 'it is I who have caused the water to well up, I who am hidden within waters'. In 45:21f.: 'I have hidden myself in everyone, I have revealed myself in them'. In 46:14ff.: 'I am the Logos ... hidden light, bearing a fruit of life, causing a living water to well up'. In 47:18 and 22: 'I have hidden myself in them'; and in line 23, the Logos continues: 'until I reveal myself to my brethren'. In 49:20f., again: 'I have hidden myself in all those (that is the 'sons of men'), until I reveal myself in my members'. All this leads us to suppose that, in this passage, 'he who is hidden in *us*' (the Gnostics) can only be the Logos. But in 41:22 reference is made to 'the *Spirit* who is in the soul'. In 45:28ff.: 'it is I who have sent the *breath* into those who are mine. And the eternal *Holy Spirit* I have shed upon them'. Be that as it may, the water of life, fertilized by a divine being, can only be the sacral water. And I think I can then compare with it 'the living water', the subject of the episode of the Samaritan woman (John 4:10f. and perhaps also v. 14: 'the water which I will give him will become in him a spring (*pēgē*) welling up in eternal *life*'), but this should be especially compared with Trim. Prot. 48:20f., which we have just quoted.

The text of page 37 continues (3 to 9): 'Then the Son who is perfect in every respect, that is the Logos who was begotten by the Voice ... being Light, revealed the infinite ones, and all the unknowables became known' – cf. John 1:5 and particularly 9.

And 'he appeared to those who are in darkness' (37:13f.): cf. 36:5. And 'he instructed those who are in the abyss' and they 'became Sons of the Light' (15 and 19f.): these 'Sons of the Light' will recur four more times in Trimorphic Protennoia: 41:1 and 16; 42:16 and 49:25. We read in the Fourth Gospel (12:36): 'While you have the light, believe in the light, so as to become sons of light'. But we never find this theme of *faith* in Trimorphic Protennoia. Furthermore, John also spoke of 'children of God', a phrase not found (at least in the plural) in Trimorphic Protennoia.

'And the sound begotten of my Thought being three dwelling-places (*monē*): the Father, the Mother, the Son ...' (20–22). In the commentary of my Quebec edition I compared John 14:2: 'In my Father's house are several dwelling-places (*monē*)'. While Professor Wilson certainly thought this reference 'more promising', J. M. Robinson objects that 'such a mythological background of the use of *monē* does not come to expression in John'.[23] If such had been my idea, he would have been entirely correct.

But it never entered my head! I am simply stating that *monē* is a rare word, that John is the only author in the entire New Testament to use it, and that the whole context is dominated by this idea of the 'presence' of God. John uses *monē* a second time in the same chapter, in v. 23: 'If anyone loves me, he will heed my word, and my Father will love him; we will come to him and we will establish our *dwelling-place* (*monē*) with him' (these are the only two occurrences). Protennoia employs it a second time too (in 46:29), but always in the sense of the three 'dwelling-places' of the divine triad, and thus in a clearly mythological sense of 'place', as Robinson rightly explains it, drawing his support from Gesine Schenke's thesis which I am unable to consult. All I wanted to emphasize was the sameness of *vocabulary* (but not of meaning). I would add to Robinson's exposition that *monē* figures on various occasions in the Gnostic texts: Hyp. Arch. 93:29; Acts Pet. 12 Apost. 5:25; Thund. 19:11; Tri. Trac. 70:17 and 100:30. A special investigation of these different usages would be required: the question thus remains open.[24]

Let us take up again on this page the presence of the theme of glory, so frequent in the Fourth Gospel: 37:24f.: 'a Logos ... which possesses all glory'; 37:31: 'it is I (Christ) who anointed him with glory'.

In our summary we have already drawn attention to the various Christian traits on page 38. Let us take up the notion of 'image' (*eikōn*) (present in the Bible, but not in John): 'I am the Image of the Invisible Spirit, and it is from me that the All has received image' (38:11f. – it recurs in 40:34, 45:24, 47:12 and 16). Note also 'the perfect Son, the Christ' (38:22), and in particular lines 23 to 25: 'they gave glory saying: "He is, he is, the Son of God, the Son of God"' which seem to me to be very similar to John 1:34: 'And I, I have seen and bear witness that this is the Son of God'.

Page 39 has nothing of interest for our comparison. On page 40 I merely draw attention to: 'I am going to come down into the world of mortals because of my portion (*meros*) which has been in that place since the day that the guileless Wisdom was conquered ...' (12–15). I purposely quote thus far to demonstrate that the mythology of the author has nothing in common with the theology of the Fourth Gospel. For Trimorphic Protennoia, the 'portion' is the divine spark (the *pneuma*, as we will see later) remaining in man after the fall of Sophia (this myth was already alluded to on the previous page). John only uses *meros* to express an idea of sharing. I refer more particularly to 13:8: 'If I do not wash you, you can have no part (*meros*) with me', which is clearly quite different![25]

In 40:29–31: '... I have come down and I have reached chaos and I was near to those who are mine' is at any rate a *little* more like the Johannine concept of 'his own' (only in the use of *terms*!).

Page 41 specifies in the first line that those who belong to Protennoia are 'the Sons of the Light'.[26] One might compare 'my own, that is the Sons of Light' (41:16) and again in lines 27–8: 'I have related my secrets to those who are mine'. This notion of 'one's own' recurs several more times in what follows. The term also appears in the Fourth Gospel (I cite at random 1:11 and 13:1), but does it refer to the same idea? In Trimorphic Protennoia 'one's own' are the Gnostics and the spirits of light.[27] They are such *by nature.* In John, Jesus speaks of 'those whom you have *given* me' (17:24), and of 'the love with which you loved me' (17:26),[28] two themes totally unknown in Trimorphic Protennoia. In 41:20ff.: 'I am the first to have descended because of my portion (*meros*) which has remained, that is the Spirit which is in the soul, which is born of the water of life and of the bath of the mysteries'. To a certain extent one is reminded of the discussion with Nicodemus in John 3, particularly verse 5: 'no one, unless he be born of water and the Spirit ...'.

On page 42:14ff., I would again emphasize: 'It is I who make the call sound in the ears of those who have *known* me, that is, the Sons of the Light'. The theme of knowledge is central in this text. On page 36, Protennoia had already said: 'it is from me that knowledge (*gnōsis*) derives' and two lines lower down: 'I am ... knowledge'. Once again, knowledge is present in the Fourth Gospel, but Jesus never says in it that he himself is this knowledge (an abstract term!). On this theme of knowledge, one might think for example of chapter 10 of John (the parable of the shepherd): 'the sheep which belong to him ... follow him because they know his voice' (v. 4). And in verses 14f.: 'I know my sheep and my sheep know me, just as my Father knows me and I know my Father ...'. But in the Bible, this knowledge implies love, and a love which extends even to death on the cross. In Trimorphic Protennoia it is a matter of 'knowledge of the infinite ones' (42:12), that is, Gnosis.

In Trim. Prot. 43:29, 'we did not know whose it is' perhaps prepares the way for what is to be read on page 44:5ff.: 'we did not know to whom we belong, because that voice we have heard is strange to us, and we do not know it'. In John 10:5 we find: 'They (the sheep) will never follow a stranger; but rather they will flee from him because they do not know the voice of strangers'.

44:27ff.: 'neither did even the Archigenētōr of our creation, about whom we boast, know this voice'. This is the widespread Gnostic theme of the ignorance of the Demiurge (here called Archigenētōr). One can see how much all this differs from the Fourth Gospel.

In 44:10f., 'let us weep and mourn' is very close to John 16:20: 'You will weep and mourn'.

We could also quote a few lines from page 45 which might suggest parallels in John: 'I am the perfection of the All ... casting a call of the voice to the ears of those who know me. And I call you into the supreme light ... if you enter it you will be glorified' (45:9–14). The conclusion of this page has already been quoted in the summary. I merely pause for a moment over the term *klados* (branch) which makes me think of John 15:6 (even although the same word is not used!): 'I am the vine, you are the branches (*klēmata*)'. The rest is once more up to Johannine specialists.

However it is mainly the third part, beginning 'I am the Logos', which offers numerous parallels with John, and with the Prologue in particular. To start with there is the term *Logos* itself, which, as is well known, John only employs in the Prologue. But he does say that 'the Logos became flesh' (1:14), an unthinkable assertion for a Gnostic. Protennoia, too, after having twice asserted 'I am the Logos' (46:5 and 14) does say on the last page 'I *put on* Jesus' (*aeiti ñiēs hiōōt*, 50:12f.). The body of Jesus was only a 'garment' with which she did not identify herself.

Having in any case already dealt with the question of parallels with the Prologue[29] – and to save space – I will merely quote (following the page order of Trimorphic Protennoia) the passages picked out in my earlier work. I will add the various terms or lines without a parallel in the Prologue of John.

46:5 and 14: 'I am the Logos'.
46:17f.: 'causing a living water to well up from the invisible spring' (cf. above on 36:6f. and 37:3).
46:24: 'the source of the All' – John 1:3.
46:27: 'the glory' – John *passim*.
46:29: '*monē*': see above on 37:22.
46:30: 'Logos': Prologue of John.
46:32f.: 'illuminate those who are in the darkness' – John 1:5.
47:14f.: 'I revealed myself to them in their tents' (*skēnē*) – John 1:14 (*eskēnōsen*).

On *skēnē* I draw attention to the important article of Helderman,[30] which I cannot analyse in detail here. From a close study of the use of this word in the New Testament and in its Coptic versions, he concludes among other things that *skēnē* is in fact a word adopted by Coptic but with the emphasis on durability. Personally I would add that, according to Cerfaux and Cambier (commenting on Revelation 15:5), 'There is, furthermore, alliteration between the Greek word *skēnē*, meaning "tent", and the Hebrew word *šᵉkînâ* which denotes the permanent presence of God, his dwelling'.[31] For Helderman, the 'tents' in Trimorphic Protennoia would signify the permanent dwelling of men, into which the Logos launched his call as in a theatrical 'scene' (also *skēnē*) (art. cit., 206).

47:18f.: 'They did not know him who empowers me' – John 1:10. Likewise 47:24: 'None of them knew me'.
47:29f.: 'I am the Light which illuminates the All. I am the Light ...' – John 1:9.
47:31: 'I have come down into the world' – John 1:9*b* (but Trimorphic Protennoia continues in line 32 – 'because of the Spirit which has remained in it').

Page 48 furnishes only very distant parallels with John: the antithesis light-darkness, lines 10ff.: 'the darkness ... I put on and stripped him of it. I put on him a shining light ...'. In line 20 there is 'the spring of the water of life' and in lines 24f., the expression 'to glorify'.

On page 49 the Docetism of the author is plain and hardly leaves any scope for parallelism. However one could note the expression 'son of man': 'among the sons of man, (I have appeared as a son of man)' (18f.) – John 1:51, etc. There is also 'Sons of the Light' (25) which we have already encountered (see above on 37:15) – John 12:36. The terms 'glory', 'light' and 'darkness' recur, in lines 27, 32 and 35 respectively. There is also a distant parallel in lines 21f.: 'I reveal myself among my members which are mine' which recalls, for example, John 1:11 ('his own').

As for page 50, I have quoted it in its entirety apart from the first – very faulty – lines in which is taken up at most the idea of 'gathering' one's own that is also to be found in John 14:3. In the following lines quoted above one finds: 'that I may dwell in them and that they too may dwell in me' – John 15:4ff.

And, once more (50:15): 'they did not know me' – John 1:10.

The idea that during this third 'epiphany' Protennoia will establish her 'seed' in the holy Light also to some extent recalls John 14:3.

What are we to conclude from all this? What I have particularly tried to emphasize is that while identical terms occur in Trimorphic Protennoia and the Fourth Gospel, they do not have the same meaning. Did John borrow them from Trimorphic Protennoia or *vice versa*? The first question to be answered would clearly be which of the two is the older – which is far from being established! It is very possible, as a number of exegetes maintain, that Trimorphic Protennoia underwent a later Christianization. But it is precisely in the 'Christian' passages that the 'kinship' with the Johannine Prologue is most marked! How could we then explain these Christian 'additions'?

Following upon the work of Bultmann, Conzelmann, Käsemann, and more recently Luise Schottroff, Elaine Pagels and others, critical scholarship has tended to maintain that the Fourth Gospel has one or several Gnostic sources, or at least bears the stamp of Gnostic influence,[32] while one would not go so far as to say, with Schottroff,[33] that John is a Gnostic, whose entire thought is structured by a rigid and undifferentiated dualism. I refer more particularly to Langbrandtner's – very well argued – thesis.[34] His method is a model one: he examines the text in extreme detail, almost verse by verse. He comes to the conclusion that there were two redactions of John (which I believe is possible, given the contradictions which have been noted). The first gave evidence of a theology at least akin to Gnostic thinking; what is more, the theology of this redaction *is* Gnostic (we should emphasize that Langbrandtner did not yet know of Trimorphic Protennoia!) and the final redactor sought particularly to correct these tendencies and re-establish orthodoxy. Here I believe he is wrong. Not everything is Gnostic which bears the mark of dualism: the dualism 'of decision' ('Entscheidungsdualismus') in John is a very different thing from the dualism 'of nature' in Gnosticism. The author's error, in my opinion, is in having relied too much upon the – albeit undeniable – points of contact between the Fourth Gospel and the Odes of Solomon. That the latter is Gnostic is not universally accepted.[35]

Other hypotheses are perhaps more subtly differentiated. Thus, according to Barbara Aland,[36] the Fourth Gospel, itself not yet Gnostic, marks a significant step towards Christian Gnosis. I would more readily agree with H. M. Schenke,[37] that at the time of the redaction of John, the boundaries between orthodoxy and Gnosticism had not yet been firmly defined. It is necessary, as J. M. Robinson rightly points out,[38] 'to ask whether the words and phrases, though current in Christian usage, are distinctive of Christianity in comparison with other Hellenistic religions'. I also willingly align myself with Professor Wilson's position: 'How can we distinguish a de-Christianised text from one that is purely gnostic in origin?'[39] At the Messina colloquium in 1966 he was already saying: 'the New Testament period was not a period of pure and unsullied doctrine, free from all taint of heresy, but a period in which there was a considerable degree of theological experiment, some of which ultimately came to be branded as heretical'.[40] In the discussion following Robinson's paper,[41] he states on this very subject: 'there are parallels in thought which may indicate only a common background'. With this I whole-heartedly agree. But at present I leave the last word to specialists in the Fourth Gospel.

NOTES

1. See J. M. Robinson, 'Inside the Front Cover of Codex VI', in *Essays on the Nag Hammadi Texts in Honour of A. Böhlig*, NHS 3, Leiden 1972, 74–87.
2. 'Le Codex XIII de Nag Hammadi', in *Muséon* 87, 1974, 341–413.
3. ' "Die dreigestaltige Protennoia", eingeleitet und übersetzt vom Berliner Arbeitskreis für koptisch-gnostische Schriften', *ThLZ* 99, 1974, 731–46.
4. *La Prôtennoia Trimorphe*, BCNH Université Laval, Section 'Textes', fasc. 4, Québec 1978.
5. 'Trimorphic Protennoia (XIII, *1*)'. Introduced and translated by J. D. Turner in (ed.) J. M. Robinson, *The Nag Hammadi Library in English*, Leiden 1977, 461–70.
6. C. Colpe, 'Heidnische, jüdische und christliche Überlieferung in den Schriften aus Nag Hammadi III' in *JAC* 17, 1974, 121, n. 36.
7. Ibid., 119–121.
8. See e.g., W. Langbrandtner, *Weltferner Gott oder Gott der Liebe*, Frankfurt 1977, 296–302.
9. Coptic expresses 'the Thought' by a masculine, *pmeeue*.
10. I wrongly took this as the Greek adverb (frequently borrowed by Coptic), whereas it was really a Coptic dialectal form of *tate*!
11. Cf. W.E. Crum, *A Coptic Dictionary*, Oxford 1939, 334b (*smē*); 704b (*hroou*).
12. J. Helderman, ' "In ihren Zelten ...", Bemerkungen zu Codex XIII Nag Hammadi p. 47: 14–18 im Hinblick auf Joh. I, 14', in (eds) T. Baarda, A. F. J. Klijn, W. C. van Unnik, *Miscellanea Neotestamentica* I, *NT.S* 47, Leiden 1978, 181–211.
13. E.g., in Trim. Prot. 42:14f. 'it is I who make the *call* resound' is clearly a much more acceptable translation than mine.
14. To aid my exposition I call the author of the Fourth Gospel 'John', even though it is now almost certain that it was not Christ's disciple who wrote it.

15. Cf. *Muséon* 72, 1959, 106 (Greek text), 128 (French translation).
16. K. M. Fischer, 'Der johanneische Christus und der gnostische Erlöser', in (ed.) K. W. Tröger, *Gnosis und Neues Testament*, Berlin 1973, 245–266 (the phrase cited is on 250).
17. 'Me[iroth]ea' however recurs on its own at 45:9.
18. Cf. the discussion following J. M. Robinson's paper at the Yale Congress in (ed.) B. Layton, *The Rediscovery of Gnosticism* II, *SHR* 41:2, Leiden 1981, 664.
19. 'Une source gnostique du Prologue?' in *L'Evangile de Jean: Sources, rédaction, théologie, BEThL* 44, Gembloux 1977, 355–358.
20. 'The *Ego*-Proclamation in Gnostic Sources' in (ed.) E. Bammel, *The Trial of Jesus, SBT* 2nd series, 13, London 1970, 122–134.
21. Cf. my edition of Trim. Prot., 11f.
22. W. Völker, *Quellen zur Geschichte der christlichen Gnosis, SQS* NS 5, Tübingen 1932, fr. 17, and my edition of Heracleon with translation and commentary in *Muséon* 72, 1959, 110–111 and 133.
23. Art. cit. (n. 18), 656f.
24. Cf. also the very interesting discussion following Robinson's Yale paper, loc. cit. (n. 18), 662ff.
25. Cf. perhaps Langbrandtner, op. cit. (n. 8), 93.
26. Cf. above on 36:5.
27. Cf. Colpe, art. cit. (n. 6), 122.
28. See e.g. B. Rigaux, 'Les destinataires du IVe Ev. à la lumière de Jn 17' in *RTL* 1, 1970, 289–319 (esp. 295f. and 316ff.). According to K. Rudolph, *Die Gnosis, Wesen und Geschichte einer spätantiken Religion*, Göttingen 1980^2, 300, the theme of 'one's own' could come from Jewish Wisdom literature.
29. See n. 19.
30. See n. 12.
31. L. Cerfaux, J. Cambier, 'L'Apocalypse de saint Jean lue aux chrétiens', *LeDiv* 17, Paris 1955, 137.
32. See e.g. Rudolph, op. cit. (n. 28: 164 *inter alia*).
33. *Der Glaubende und die feindliche Welt, WMANT* 37, Neukirchen 1970.
34. Op. cit. (n. 8).
35. Cf. e.g. M. Lattke, 'Die Oden Salomos in ihrer Bedeutung für Neues Testament und Gnosis', *OBO* 25, 1–2, Göttingen 1979.
36. 'Gnosis und Christentum' in (ed.) Layton, op. cit. (n. 18) I, 319ff. See esp. 340–342.
37. 'Die neutestamentliche Christologie und der gnostische Erlöser', in (ed.) Tröger, *Gnosis und Neues Testament*, 228.
38. 'Sethians and Johannine Thought: The *Trimorphic Protennoia* and the Prologue of the Gospel of John' in (ed.) Layton, op. cit. (n. 18) II, 643–670 (the phrase cited is on p. 655).
39. 'The *Trimorphic Protennoia*' in *Gnosis and Gnosticism, NHS* 8, Leiden 1977, 52.
40. 'Gnosis, Gnosticism and the New Testament', in (ed.) U. Bianchi, *Le Origini dello Gnosticismo, SHR* 12, Leiden 1967, 525.
41. See n. 18.

R. McL. WILSON

BIBLIOGRAPHY OF PUBLISHED WORKS
1952–1981

Compiled by

R. A. Piper, St Andrews

1952
'Nomos: The Biblical Significance of the Law' in *SJTh* 5, 36–48.

1953
'Philo and the Fourth Gospel' in *ET* 65, 47–49.
'Soteria' in *SJTh* 6, 406–416.

1955
'Gnostic Origins' in *VigChr* 9, 193–211.
Reviews:
> (Ed.) F. L. Cross, *The Jung Codex: A Newly Recovered Gnostic Papyrus. Three Studies by H.-C. Puech, G. Quispel and W. C. van Unnik* in *ET* 66, 296; and in *NTS* 1, 309–313.
> J. Héring, *L'Épître aux Hébreux* (*CNT(N)* 12) in *SJTh* 8, 440–441.

1956
'Coptisms in the Epistle to the Hebrews?' in *NT* 1, 322–324.
'Erinys in Gnosticism?' in *JThS* n.s. 7, 248–251.
'The Fourth Gospel and Hellenistic Thought' in *NT* 1, 225–227.
Reviews:
> W. F. Howard, *The Fourth Gospel in Recent Criticism and Interpretation* (rev. by C. K. Barrett) in *SJTh* 9, 206.
> (Ed.) D. E. Nineham, *Studies in the Gospels: Essays in Memory of R. H. Lightfoot* in *SJTh* 9, 77–79.
> H. J. Schoeps, *Urgemeinde, Judenchristentum, Gnosis* in *SJTh* 9, 315–316.

1957

'The Early History of the Exegesis of Gen. 1.26' in (eds) K. Aland and F. L. Cross, *StPatr* 1: *Papers Presented to the Second International Conference on Patristic Studies Held at Christ Church, Oxford, 1955*, Part 1 (= *TU* 63, Berlin), 420–437.

'Did Jesus Speak Greek?' in *ET* 68, 121–122.

'Gnostic Origins Again' in *VigChr* 11, 93–110.

'The New Testament in the Gnostic Gospel of Mary' in *NTS* 3, 236–243.

'Simon, Dositheus and the Dead Sea Scrolls' in *ZRGG* 9, 21–30.

'Some Recent British Publications of New Testament and Patristic Studies' in *ZRGG* 9, 364–368.

Reviews:

> C. K. Barrett, *The New Testament Background: Selected Documents* in *SJTh* 10, 309–312.
>
> E. E. Ellis, *Paul's Use of the Old Testament* in *SJTh* 10, 428–432.
>
> C. T. Fritsch, *The Qumran Community: Its History and Scrolls* in *SJTh* 10, 107–109.
>
> I. Moir, '*Codex Climaci Rescriptus Graecus*' (*TaS* n.s. 2) in *SJTh* 10, 106.

1958

The Gnostic Problem: A Study of the Relations between Hellenistic Judaism and the Gnostic Heresy (London), reprinted 1964.

'Further "Unknown Sayings of Jesus" ' in *ET* 69, 182.

Reviews:

> M. Albertz, *Botschaft des Neuen Testamentes* II: *Die Entfaltung der Botschaft*, Halbband 2: *Der Inhalt der Botschaft* in *SJTh* 11, 207–209.
>
> S. G. F. Brandon, *The Fall of Jerusalem and the Christian Church*[2] in *SJTh* 11, 318–319.
>
> H. Braun, *Spätjüdisch-häretischer und frühchristlicher Radikalismus* (*BHTh* 24) in *SJTh* 11, 108–110.
>
> (Ed.) F. L. Cross, *The Oxford Dictionary of the Christian Church* in *ZRGG* 10, 258–260.
>
> J. Jeremias, *Jésus et les païens* in *SJTh* 11, 205–206.
>
> H. Köster, *Synoptische Überlieferung bei den apostolischen Vätern* (*TU* 65) in *NTS* 5, 144–146.
>
> C. Masson, *Les deux Épîtres de Saint Paul aux Thessaloniciens* (*CNT(N)* 11a) in *SJTh* 11, 319–320.
>
> O. Prunet, *La morale chrétienne d'après les écrits johanniques* in *SJTh* 11, 216–217.
>
> H. H. Rowley, *The Dead Sea Scrolls and the New Testament* in *SJTh* 11, 436–437.
>
> Tyndale Lectures: P. E. Hughes, *Scripture and Myth, an Examination of Rudolf Bultmann's Plea for Demythologization*; F. F. Bruce, *The Teacher of Righteousness in the Qumran Texts*; A. M. Stibbs, *God Became Man* in *SJTh* 11, 96–97.

1959

'Some Recent Studies in the Lucan Infancy Narratives' and 'Farrer and Streeter on the Minor Agreements of Matthew and Luke against Mark' in (eds) K. Aland, F. L. Cross, J. Daniélou, H. Riesenfeld and W. C. van Unnik, *StEv* 1: *Papers Presented to the International Congress on 'The Four Gospels in 1957' Held at Christ Church, Oxford, 1957* (= *TU* 73, Berlin), 235–253 and 254–257.

'The Coptic "Gospel of Thomas" ' in *NTS* 5, 273–276.

'Genesis 1.26 and the New Testament' in *Bijdr.* 20, 117–125.

'The Gnostic Library of Nag Hammadi' in *SJTh* 12, 161–170.

'The Gospel of Thomas' in *ET* 70, 324–325.

'The Gospel of Thomas' in *Pulpit Digest* 40 (December), 13–16.

'Light on the Sayings of Jesus: Interpreting the "Gospel of Thomas" ' in *The Daily Telegraph and Morning Post* No. 32,337 (Monday, 6th April; London), 10.

'Some Recent British Publications' in *ZRGG* 11, 77–79.

'Recent British Publications III' in *ZRGG* 11, 380–383.

'Some Recent Studies in Gnosticism' in *NTS* 6, 32–44.

Reviews:

> J. Doresse, *Les livres secrets des gnostiques d'Égypte* in *ET* 70, 104.
>
> L. Goppelt, *Christentum und Judentum im ersten und zweiten Jahrhundert* (*BFChTh.M* 55) in *SJTh* 12, 101–104.
>
> D. W. Gundry, *Religions. A Preliminary Historical and Theological Study* in *ZRGG* 11, 179.
>
> A. R. C. Leaney, *The Gospel according to St. Luke* (*BNTC*) in *SJTh* 12, 433–434.
>
> F. J. Leenhardt, *L'Épître de Saint Paul aux Romains* (*CNT(N)* 6) in *SJTh* 12, 435–436.
>
> H. E. del Medico, *The Riddle of the Scrolls* in *SJTh* 12, 447–448.
>
> G. Strecker, *Das Judenchristentum in den Pseudoklementinen* (*TU* 70) in *JThS* n.s. 10, 156–158.
>
> R. V. G. Tasker, *The Second Epistle of Paul to the Corinthians* in *SJTh* 12, 207–208.
>
> V. Taylor, *The Person of Christ in New Testament Teaching* in *ZRGG* 11, 185–187.

1960

Studies in the Gospel of Thomas (London).

'Light on Sayings of Jesus: Interpreting the "Gospel of Thomas" ' in *BiTr* 11, 132–135.

'Some Recent British Publications IV' in *ZRGG* 12, 257–262.

' "Thomas" and the Growth of the Gospels' in *HThR* 53, 231–250.

'Thomas and the Synoptic Gospels' in *ET* 72, 36–39.

Reviews:

> F. F. Bruce, *Biblical Exegesis in the Qumran Texts* in *SJTh* 13, 96.
>
> J. Daniélou, *Théologie du judéo-christianisme* in *SJTh* 13, 323–326.
>
> J. Doresse, *The Secret Books of the Egyptian Gnostics* (Tr. P. Mairet) in *ET* 72, 19; and in *Theol.* 63, 390–391.

R. M. Grant, *Gnosticism and Early Christianity* in *ET* 72, 74; and in *ThTo* 17, 116–118.

R. M. Grant and D. N. Freedman, *The Secret Sayings of Jesus, with an English Translation of the Gospel of Thomas* in *ET* 71, 234.

(Ed.) A. J. B. Higgins, *New Testament Essays. Studies in Memory of T. W. Manson* in *ZRGG* 12, 90–91.

G. A. F. Knight, *A Christian Theology of the Old Testament* in *ZRGG* 12, 89.

1961

Contributor of ET to (eds) M. Malinine, H.-C. Puech, G. Quispel and W. Till, *Evangelium Veritatis Supplementum: Codex Jung F. XVII^r–F. XVIII^v (p. 33–36)* (*SJI* 6, Zürich and Stuttgart).

'Recent British Publications V' in *ZRGG* 13, 70–74.

Reviews:

J. Barr, *The Semantics of Biblical Language* in *ET* 72, 330.

J. Doresse, *The Secret Books of the Egyptian Gnostics* (Tr. P. Mairet) in *JSSt* 6, 109–112.

E. S. Drower, *The Secret Adam: A Study of Nasorean Gnosis*; M. A. Larson, *The Religion of the Occident*; and E. O. James, *The Ancient Gods* in *Theol.* 64, 27–29.

E. Evans, *Tertullian's Treatise on the Resurrection. The Text Edited with an Introduction, Translation and Commentary* in *ZRGG* 13, 286–287.

B. Gärtner, *The Theology of the Gospel of Thomas* (Tr. E. J. Sharpe) in *ZRGG* 13, 285–286.

F. C. Grant, *The Gospels, Their Origin and Their Growth* in *SJTh* 14, 304–307.

(Ed.) R. M. Grant, *Gnosticism: An Anthology* in *ET* 73, 16.

R. M. Grant and D. N. Freedman, *The Secret Sayings of Jesus, with an English Translation of the Gospel of Thomas* in *JSSt* 6, 112–114.

K. Grobel, *The Gospel of Truth: A Valentinian Meditation on the Gospel* in *SJTh* 14, 96–99.

A. J. B. Higgins, *The Historicity of the Fourth Gospel* in *SJTh* 14, 309–310.

S. H. Hooke, *Alpha and Omega* in *SJTh* 14, 428–430.

H. Lietzmann, *Kleine Schriften: I. Studien zur spätantiken Religionsgeschichte* (*TU* 67) in *NTS* 7, 173–174.

W. C. van Unnik, *Evangelien aus dem Nilsand* in *ET* 72, 127.

D. S. Wallace-Hadrill, *Eusebius of Caesarea* in *ZRGG* 13, 197–198.

1962

The Gospel of Philip: Translated from the Coptic text, with an Introduction and Commentary (London/New York).

'Gnosis' in (eds) B. Reicke and L. Rost, *BHH* 1: A-G (Göttingen), 580–581.

'Mark' (commentary) and 'Pagan Religion at the Coming of Christianity' in (eds) M. Black and H. H. Rowley, *PCB* (Edinburgh), 712–718 and 799–819.

Reviews:

A. Adam, *Die Psalmen des Thomas und das Perlenlied als Zeugnisse vorchristlicher Gnosis* (*BZNW* 24) in *Gn.* 34, 522–523.

J. Barr, *The Semantics of Biblical Language* in *NTS* 8, 282–283.

F. W. Beare, *The Earliest Records of Jesus: A Companion to Huck's Synopsis of the First Three Gospels* in *British Weekly* (1 November), 2.

(Eds) M. Black and H. H. Rowley, *PCB* in *The Times Literary Supplement* No. 3159 (14 September), 693.

C. Colpe, *Die religionsgeschichtliche Schule. Darstellung und Kritik ihres Bildes vom gnostischen Erlösermythus* (*FRLANT* 78) in *Gn.* 34, 571–574.

B. Gärtner, *The Theology of the Gospel of Thomas* (Tr. E. J. Sharpe) in *NTS* 8, 283–285; and in *ThTo* 19, 127–128.

(Ed.) R. M. Grant, *Gnosticism: An Anthology* in *SJTh* 15, 214–215; and in *Theol.* 65, 72–74.

E. Haenchen, *Die Botschaft des Thomas-Evangeliums* (*TBT* 6) in *SJTh* 15, 327–330.

R. P. C. Hanson, *Tradition in the Early Church* (*LHD*) in *British Weekly* (6 December), 15.

H. Hegermann, *Die Vorstellung vom Schöpfungsmittler im hellenistischen Judentum und Urchristentum* (*TU* 82) in *Gn.* 34, 836–837.

J. Héring, *The First Epistle of Saint Paul to the Corinthians* (Tr. A. W. Heathcote/P. J. Allcock) in *British Weekly* (5 July), 2.

C. F. D. Moule, *The Birth of the New Testament* (*BNTC* Companion Volume 1); and W. Klassen and G. F. Snyder, *Current Issues in New Testament Interpretation. Essays in Honor of Otto A. Piper* in *British Weekly* (18 October), 5.

J. C. O'Neill, *The Theology of Acts in Its Historical Setting* in *SJTh* 15, 434–436.

W. Schmithals, *Die Gnosis in Korinth. Eine Untersuchung zu den Korintherbriefen* (*FRLANT* 66) in *SJTh* 15, 324–327.

W. Wilkens, *Die Entstehungsgeschichte des vierten Evangeliums* in *SJTh* 15, 431–433.

H. A. Wolfson, *Religious Philosophy. A Group of Essays* in *Gn.* 34, 727–728.

1963

Ed. of ET of E. Hennecke, *New Testament Apocrypha* I: *Gospels and Related Writings*, ed. by W. Schneemelcher (London), including a fresh tr. of the Gospel of Thomas (Appendix 1) and a précis of tr. of the Gospel of Truth (Appendix 2) by R. McL. Wilson.

Collaborator with (eds) M. Malinine, H.-C. Puech, G. Quispel, W. Till and J. Zandee in *De Resurrectione (Epistula ad Rheginum): Codex Jung F. XXII^r–F. XXV^v (p. 43–50)* (Zürich and Stuttgart).

'The New Testament in the Nag Hammadi Gospel of Philip' in *NTS* 9, 291–294.

'A Note on the Gospel of Truth (33.8–9)' in *NTS* 9, 295–298.

Reviews:

H. Baltensweiler, *Die Verklärung Jesu* (*AThANT* 33) in *SJTh* 16, 215–216.

(Eds) A. Böhlig and P. Labib, *Die Koptisch-gnostische Schrift ohne Titel aus Codex II von Nag Hammadi im Koptischen Museum zu Alt-Kairo* (*Deutsche Akad. d. Wiss. zu Berlin. Inst. f. Orientforsch.* 58) in *Gn.* 35, 591–595.

G. Bornkamm, G. Barth and H.-J. Held, *Tradition and Interpretation in Matthew* in *British Weekly* (28 March), 2.

B. Gärtner, *John 6 and the Jewish Passover* (*CNT* 17) in *SJTh* 16, 92–93.

R. M. Grant, *A Historical Introduction to the New Testament* in *British Weekly* (20 June), 2.

A. M. Hunter, *Paul and his Predecessors*[2] in *Gn.* 35, 215–216.

M. Krause and P. Labib, *Die drei Versionen des Apokryphon des Johannes im Koptischen Museum zu Alt-Kairo* (*ADAIK* 1) in *Gn.* 35, 833–835.

W. G. Kümmel, *Man in the New Testament* (Tr. J. J. Vincent) in *British Weekly* (14 February), 2.

E. Lövestam, *Son and Saviour: A Study of Acts 13, 32–37* (*CNT* 18) in *SJTh* 16, 94–95.

G. Lundström, *The Kingdom of God in the Teaching of Jesus*; N. Perrin, *The Kingdom of God in the Teaching of Jesus*; and J. E. Yates, *The Spirit and the Kingdom* in *British Weekly* (14 November), 12.

J.-É. Ménard, *L'Évangile de Vérité. Rétroversion grecque et commentaire* in *ThZ* 19, 145–146.

B. M. Metzger, *List of Words Occurring Frequently in the Coptic New Testament* in *SJTh* 16, 217–218.

C. Mondésert, *Philon d'Alexandrie: Legum Allegoriae I-III. Introduction, Traduction et Notes* in *JThS* n.s. 14, 121–122.

P. Prigent, *Apocalypse 12. Histoire de l'exégèse* (*BGBE* 2) in *SJTh* 16, 93–94.

G. Scholem, *Ursprung und Anfänge der Kabbala* (*SJ* 3) in *ZRGG* 15, 295–298.

E. F. Sutcliffe, *The Monks of Qumran* in *SJTh* 16, 323–324.

H. E. W. Turner and H. Montefiore, *Thomas and the Evangelists* (*SBT* 35) in *JEH* 14, 119; and in *JThS* n.s. 14, 265.

J. Zandee, *The Terminology of Plotinus and of Some Gnostic Writings, Mainly the Fourth Treatise of the Jung Codex* (*UNHAII* 11) in *NTS* 9, 401.

1964

'The Gospel of Philip' in (eds) C. W. Dugmore and C. Duggan, *SCH(L)* 1, London, 98–103.

'The Gospel of Thomas' in (ed.) F. L. Cross, *StEv* 3: *Papers Presented to the Second International Congress on New Testament Studies Held at Christ Church, Oxford, 1961, Part 2: The New Testament Message* (= *TU* 88, Berlin), 447–459.

Reviews:

> H. Anderson, *Jesus and Christian Origins*; A. Ehrhardt, *The Framework of the New Testament Stories*; and A. Farrer, *The Revelation of St John the Divine* in *British Weekly* (27 August), 2 and 12.
>
> W. H. Brownlee, *The Meaning of the Qumran Scrolls for the Bible (with Special Attention to the Book of Isaiah)* in *SJTh* 17, 493–494.
>
> R. Bultmann, *The History of the Synoptic Tradition* (Tr. J. Marsh) in *British Weekly* (9 January), 2.
>
> *Calvin's Commentaries: The Second Epistle of Paul the Apostle to the Corinthians and the Epistles to Timothy, Titus and Philemon* (Tr. T. A. Smail) in *British Weekly* (21 May), 6.
>
> T. Henshaw, *New Testament Literature*; A. W. Heathcote, *An Introduction to the Letters of St. Paul*; and F. Foulkes, *The Epistle of Paul to the Ephesians* in *SJTh* 17, 490–493.
>
> G. Jeremias, *Der Lehrer der Gerechtigkeit* (*StUNT* 2) in *ZRGG* 16, 386–388.
>
> B. M. Metzger, *Chapters in the History of New Testament Textual Criticism* (*NTTS* 4) in *SJTh* 17, 363–365.
>
> B. M. Metzger, *The Text of the New Testament*; and J. Dupont, *The Sources of Acts: The Present Position* in *British Weekly* (23 April), 2.
>
> C. F. Potter, *The Lost Years of Jesus* in *SJTh* 17, 102–103.

1965

Ed. of ET of E. Hennecke, *New Testament Apocrypha* II: *Writings Relating to the Apostles, Apocalypses, and Related Subjects, Index to Volumes I and II*, ed. by W. Schneemelcher (London).

'Response to G. Quispel's "Gnosticism and the New Testament" ' in (ed.) J. P. Hyatt, *The Bible in Modern Scholarship: Papers Read at the 100th Meeting of the Society of Biblical Literature, December 28–30, 1964* (Nashville/New York), 272–278.

'John Allegro and the Dead Sea Scrolls: Scrolls and the Scriptures' in *British Weekly* (30 December), 7.

Reviews:

> J. Dupont, *The Sources of Acts: The Present Position* in *SJTh* 18, 234–235.
>
> E. Evans, *Tertullian's Homily on Baptism. The Text Edited with an Introduction, Translation and Commentary* in *ZRGG* 17, 373.
>
> L. A. Garrard, *Athens or Jerusalem? A Study in Christian Comprehension* in *ET* 77, 80–81.
>
> J. C. Hurd Jr, *The Origin of 1 Corinthians* in *British Weekly* (17 June), 4.

F. Legge, *Fore-runners and Rivals of Christianity, Being Studies in Religious History from 330 B.C. to 330 A.D.* in *SJTh* 18, 496–499.

W. Schmithals, *Paul and James* (*SBT* 46); and H.-E. Tödt, *The Son of Man in the Synoptic Tradition* in *British Weekly* (12 August), 4.

G. Strecker, *Der Weg der Gerechtigkeit: Untersuchung zur Theologie des Matthäus* (*FRLANT* 82) in *ZRGG* 17, 370–372.

1966

'Second Thoughts: XI. The Gnostic Gospels from Nag Hammadi' in *ET* 78, 36–41.

Reviews:

Calvin's Commentaries: The Acts of the Apostles 14–28 (Tr. J. W. Fraser) in *British Weekly* (5 May), 4.

A. J. B. Higgins, *Jesus and the Son of Man* in *RelLife* 35, 325–326.

M. Hornschuh, *Studien zur Epistula Apostolorum* (*PTS* 5) in *JEH* 17, 105.

J. Jeremias, *The Eucharistic Words of Jesus* (Tr. N. Perrin) in *British Weekly* (7 July), 4.

G. E. Ladd, *Jesus and the Kingdom. The Eschatology of Biblical Realism* in *British Weekly* (10 February), 6.

A. R. C. Leaney, *The Rule of Qumran and Its Meaning* in *British Weekly* (21 April), Suppl. ii; and in *SJTh* 19, 504–506.

B. M. Metzger, *The Text of the New Testament*, and S. Neill, *The Interpretation of the New Testament 1861–1961* in *SJTh* 19, 491–493.

H. J. Schonfield, *The Passover Plot* in *British Weekly* (17 February), 4.

W. Schrage, *Das Verhältnis des Thomas-Evangeliums zur synoptischen Tradition und zu den koptischen Evangelienübersetzungen. Zugleich ein Beitrag zur gnostischen Synoptikerdeutung* (*BZNW* 29) in *VigChr* 19, 118–123.

N. Turner, *Grammatical Insights into the New Testament* in *British Weekly* (9 June), 4.

B. F. Westcott, *The Epistles of St John* in *British Weekly* (8 December), 4.

1967

'Gnosis, Gnosticism and the New Testament' in (ed.) U. Bianchi, *Le Origini dello Gnosticismo: Colloquio di Messina, 13–18 Aprile 1966; Testi e Discussioni* (*SHR* 12, Leiden), 511–526 (discussion, 526–527); 'Addenda et Postscripta', 691–702.

Articles in (ed.) P. Edwards, *EncPh* (New York/London): 'Mani and Manichaeism', V, 149–150; 'Marcion', V, 155–156; 'Numenius of Apamea', V, 530–531; 'Simon Magus', VII, 444–445; 'Valentinus and Valentinianism', VIII, 226–227.

Reviews:

O. Cullmann, *Salvation in History* in *British Weekly* (22 June), 8.

E. E. Ellis, *The Gospel of Luke (NCeB)* in *British Weekly* (20 April), 12.

R. M. Grant, *The Formation of the New Testament*; and C. H. Talbert, *Luke and the Gnostics* in *RelLife* 36, 147–149.

R. M. Grant, *Gnosticism and Early Christianity*[2] in *CQR* 168, 378–379.

M. D. Hooker, *The Son of Man in Mark* in *British Weekly* (1 June), 12.

R. Kasser, *L'Évangile selon Saint Jean et les Versions Coptes de la Bible (BT[N])* in *SJTh* 20, 489–490.

J. Knox, *The Humanity and Divinity of Christ: A Study of Pattern in Christology* in *British Weekly* (24 August), 8.

C. F. D. Moule, *The Phenomenon of the New Testament (SBT* 2nd ser. 1) in *British Weekly* (9 March), 4.

N. Perrin, *Rediscovering the Teaching of Jesus* in *British Weekly* (23 February), 4.

J. A. Phillips, *The Form of Christ in the World: A Study of Bonhoeffer's Christology* in *British Weekly* (17 August), 8.

G. Quispel, *Ptolémée: Lettre à Flora. Analyse, texte critique, traduction, commentaire et index grec*[2] *(SC* 24) in *Gn.* 39, 721–722.

P. Ricca, *Die Eschatologie des Vierten Evangeliums* in *SJTh* 20, 245–246.

1968

Gnosis and the New Testament (Philadelphia/Oxford).

Collaborator with (eds) M. Malinine, H.-C. Puech, G. Quispel, W. Till, R. Kasser and J. Zandee in *Epistula Iacobi apocrypha, Codex Jung F. I^r–F. VIII^v (p. 1–16)* (Zürich and Stuttgart).

'Gnostics – in Galatia?' in (ed.) F. L. Cross, *StEv* 4: *Papers Presented to the Third International Congress on New Testament Studies Held at Christ Church, Oxford, 1965,* Part 1: *The New Testament Scriptures (= TU* 102, Berlin), 358–367.

Reviews:

C. K. Barrett, *The First Epistle to the Corinthians (BNTC)* in *British Weekly* (18 April), 4.

(Ed.) U. Bianchi, *Le Origini dello Gnosticismo. Colloquio di Messina, 13–18 Aprile 1966 (SHR* 12); and R. Haardt, *Die Gnosis. Wesen und Zeugnisse* in *Gn.* 40, 451–455.

R. E. Brown, *Jesus, God and Man* in *British Weekly* (21 March), 4.

F. G. Downing, *The Church and Jesus. A Study in History, Philosophy and Theology (SBT* 2nd ser. 10) in *British Weekly* (19 December), 4.

R. Haardt, *Die Gnosis. Wesen und Zeugnisse* in *Bib.* 49, 273–275.

D. Hill, *Greek Words and Hebrew Meanings* in *British Weekly* (25 January), 4.

J. H. E. Hull, *The Holy Spirit in the Acts of the Apostles* in *British Weekly* (11 April), 4.

A. M. Hunter, *According to John* in *British Weekly* (26 December), 4.

H. Langerbeck, *Aufsätze zur Gnosis*, ed. H. Dörries (*AAWG.PH* 69) in *JThS* n.s. 19, 293–294; and in *ThZ* 24, 143–144.

X. Léon-Dufour, *The Gospels and the Jesus of History* (Tr./Ed. J. McHugh) in *British Weekly* (23 May), 4.

W. Marxsen, *Introduction to the New Testament* (Tr. G. Buswell) in *SJTh* 21, 497–499.

D. E. Nineham, *The Gospel of St Mark* (*PGC*); and W. J. Harrington, *The Gospel According to St Luke* in *British Weekly* (18 July), 4.

R. Summers, *The Secret Sayings of the Living Jesus: Studies in the Coptic Gospel According to Thomas* in *RelLife* 37, 643–644.

1969

La Gnose et le Nouveau Testament, Preface J.-É. Ménard, Tr. J. Fleury (Paris/Tournai/Rome).

'The New *Passion of Jesus* in the Light of the New Testament and the Apocrypha' in (eds) E. E. Ellis and M. Wilcox, *Neotestamentica et Semitica. Studies in Honour of Matthew Black* (Edinburgh), 264–271.

Reviews:

M. Arnaldez *et al.*, *Philon d'Alexandrie. Colloques nationaux du Centre national de la recherche scientifique. Lyon, 11–15 Septembre 1966* in *Gn.* 41, 411–413.

(Ed.) W. Barclay, *The Bible and History* in *SJTh* 22, 226–228.

C. J. Barker, *The Acts of the Apostles* in *British Weekly* (18 December), 4.

(Ed.) M. Black, *The Scrolls and Christianity* in *British Weekly* (24 April), 4.

H. Conzelmann, *An Outline of the Theology of the New Testament* in *British Weekly* (19 June), 4.

E. Käsemann, *New Testament Questions of Today* in *British Weekly* (17 July), 4.

J.-É. Ménard, *L'Évangile selon Philippe. Introduction, texte, traduction, commentaire* in *VigChr* 23, 311–317.

J. Rohde, *Rediscovering the Teaching of the Evangelists* in *British Weekly* (27 February), 4.

J. N. Sanders and B. A. Mastin, *The Gospel According to St John* (*BNTC*) in *British Weekly* (13 February), 4.

J. Smith, *A Priest for Ever* in *British Weekly* (8 May), 4.

W. Wink, *John the Baptist in the Gospel Tradition* (*MSSNTS* 7) in *SJTh* 22, 113–114.

1970

Gnosis und Neues Testament, Tr. L. Kaufmann (*Urban-Taschenbücher* 118, Stuttgart).

Reviews:

J. M. Allegro, *The Sacred Mushroom and the Cross* in *British Weekly* (28 May), 7.

(Ed.) E. Bammel, *The Trial of Jesus. Cambridge Studies in Honour of C. F. D. Moule* (*SBT* 2nd ser., 13) in *British Weekly* (23 July), 4.

(Ed.) R. Batey, *New Testament Issues*; and C. Cross, *Who Was Jesus?* in *British Weekly* (24 September), 4.

C. F. Evans, *Resurrection and the New Testament* (*SBT* 2nd ser., 12) in *British Weekly* (19 March), 4.

L. Goppelt, *Apostolic and Post-Apostolic Times* (Tr. R.A. Guelich) in *British Weekly* (23 April), 4.

M. L. Peel, *The Epistle to Rheginos* in *JThS* n.s. 21, 179–181.

M. J. Suggs, *Wisdom, Christology, and Law in Matthew's Gospel* in *RelLife* 39, 619–620.

1971

Ed. of ET of E. Haenchen, *The Acts of the Apostles: A Commentary* (Oxford).

'The Literary Forms of the New Testament' in (ed.) C. M. Laymon, *The Interpreter's One-Volume Commentary on the Bible* (Nashville/New York; London/Glasgow, 1972), 1124–1128.

'Gnosticism in the Light of Recent Research' in *Kairos* 13, 282–288.

Reviews:

F. H. Borsch, *The Christian and Gnostic Son of Man* in *SJTh* 24, 237–238.

C. H. Dodd, *The Founder of Christianity* in *British Weekly* (19 February), 9.

J. C. King, *A Christian View of the Mushroom Myth* in *SJTh* 24, 104–105.

J. C. O'Neill, *The Theology of Acts*[2] in *British Weekly* (1 January), 12.

C. H. Talbert, *Luke and the Gnostics* in *ET* 82, 157.

1972

Ed. of ET of W. Foerster, *Gnosis. A Selection of Gnostic Texts, I. Patristic Evidence* (Oxford).

'How Gnostic were the Corinthians?' in *NTS* 19, 65–74.

'Jewish Christianity and Gnosticism' in *RSR* 60, 261–272.

'Philo of Alexandria and Gnosticism' in *Kairos* 14, 213–219.

Reviews:

R. Haardt, *Gnosis: Character and Testimony* (Tr. J. F. Hendry) in *ET* 83, 219.

M. Krause and K. Rudolph, *Die Gnosis II. Koptische und Mandäische Quellen* in *BiOr* 29, 86–87.

J. M. Robinson and H. Koester, *Trajectories through Early Christianity* in *JThS* n.s. 23, 475–477.

R. Williamson, *Philo and the Epistle to the Hebrews* (*ALGHJ* 4) in *BiOr* 29, 228–229.

E. M. Yamauchi, *Gnostic Ethics and Mandaean Origins* (*HThS* 24) in *JThS* n.s. 23, 234–235.

1973

Collaborator with (eds) R. Kasser, M. Malinine, H.-C. Puech, G. Quispel, J. Zandee and W. Vycichl in *Tractatus Tripartitus, Pars 1: De Supernis, Codex Jung F. XXVI^r–F. LII^v (p. 51–104)* (Bern).

'The Spirit in Gnostic Literature' in (eds) B. Lindars and S. S. Smalley, *Christ and Spirit in the New Testament. Studies in Honour of Charles Francis Digby Moule* (Cambridge), 345–355.

Reviews:

    S. R. C. Lilla, *Clement of Alexandria: A Study in Christian Platonism and Gnosticism (OTM)* in *JEH* 24, 286–288.

    E. M. Yamauchi, *Pre-Christian Gnosticism: A Survey of the Proposed Evidence* in *ET* 84, 379.

1974

Ed. of ET of W. Foerster, *Gnosis. A Selection of Gnostic Texts, II. Coptic and Mandean Sources* (Oxford).

'From Gnosis to Gnosticism' in *Mélanges d'Histoire des Religions, offerts à Henri-Charles Puech* (Paris), 423–429.

' "Jewish Gnosis" and Gnostic Origins: A Survey' in *HUCA* 45, 177–189.

'Nag Hammadi: A Progress Report' in *ET* 85, 196–201.

Reviews:

    L. Morris, *Apocalyptic* in *SJTh* 27, 371–372.

    (Ed.) K.-W. Tröger, *Gnosis und Neues Testament. Studien aus Religionswissenschaft und Theologie* in *ThLZ* 99, 829–833.

1975

Collaborator with (eds) R. Kasser, M. Malinine, H.-C. Puech, G. Quispel, J. Zandee and W. Vycichl in *Tractatus Tripartitus, Pars II: De Creatione Hominis, et Pars III: De Generibus Tribus, Codex Jung F. LII^v–F. LXX^r (p. 104–140); Oratio Pauli Apostoli; Evangelium Veritatis, Supplementum Photographicum* (Bern).

'Old Testament Exegesis in the Gnostic Exegesis on the Soul' in (ed.) M. Krause, *Essays on the Nag Hammadi Texts, in Honour of Pahor Labib (NHS 6, Leiden)*, 217–224.

'The Trials of a Translator: Some Translation Problems in the Nag Hammadi Texts' in (ed.) J.-É. Ménard, *Les Textes de Nag Hammadi. Colloque du Centre d'Histoire des Religions, Strasbourg, 23–25 octobre 1974 (NHS 7, Leiden)*, 32–40.

Articles in (ed.) M. C. Tenney *et al., The Zondervan Pictorial Encyclopedia of the Bible* (Grand Rapids): 'Basilides, Gospel of', I, 486–487; 'Dositheus, Apocalypse of', II, 157; 'Egyptians, Gospel of', II, 258–259; 'Eugnostos, Letter of', II, 415; 'James, Apocalypse of', III, 395–396; 'Mary, Birth (or Descent) of', IV, 106; 'Paul, Apocalypse of', IV, 623–624; 'Peter and the Twelve Apostles, Acts of', IV, 722; 'Philip, Gospel of', IV, 759; 'Thomas, Gospel of', V, 735–736.

Reviews:

    T. H. C. van Eijk, *La résurrection des morts chez les pères apostoliques (ThH 25)* in *JThS* n.s. 26, 462–463.

1976

'The Gospel of the Egyptians' in (ed.) E. A. Livingstone, *StPatr* 14: *Papers Presented to the Sixth International Conference on Patristic Studies Held in Oxford 1971*, Part 3: *Tertullian, Origenism, Gnostica, Cappadocian Fathers, Augustiniana* (= *TU* 117, Berlin), 243–250.

Articles in (ed.) K. Crim, *IDB: Supplementary Volume* (Nashville): 'Apocrypha, NT', 34–36; 'Philip, Gospel of', 664–665.

Reviews:

> F. F. Bruce, *The 'Secret' Gospel of Mark* (*WoodL* 1974) in *SJTh* 29, 197.
>
> C. Elsas, *Neuplatonische und gnostische Weltablehnung in der Schule Plotins* (*RVV* 34) in *BiOr* 33, 405–406.
>
> (Ed.) H. Quecke, *Die Briefe Pachoms: Griechischer Text der Handschrift W. 145 der Chester Beatty Library* (*TPL* 11) in *JEH* 27, 308–309.
>
> M. Tardieu, *Trois Mythes Gnostiques* (*EAug*) in *JThS* n.s. 27, 215–217.

1977

'The Gnostics and the Old Testament' in (ed.) G. Widengren, with D. Hellholm, *Proceedings of the International Colloquium on Gnosticism, Stockholm, August 20–25, 1973* (*VHAAH.FF* 17, Stockholm/Leiden), 164–168.

'The *Trimorphic Protennoia*' in (ed.) M. Krause, *Gnosis and Gnosticism. Papers Read at the Seventh International Conference on Patristic Studies (Oxford, September 8th–13th, 1975)* (*NHS* 8, Leiden), 50–54.

Reviews:

> (Eds) H. W. Attridge and R. A. Oden, *De Dea Syria* (*SBLTT* Graeco-Roman Religion 1); (ed.) M. W. Meyer, *The 'Mithras Liturgy'* (*SBLTT* Graeco-Roman Religion 2) in *ET* 88, 280.
>
> O. Cullmann, *Der johanneische Kreis. Zum Ursprung des Johannesevangeliums* in *BiOr* 34, 407–408.
>
> M. McNamara, *The Apocrypha in the Irish Church* in *ET* 88, 184.

1978

Ed. of *The Future of Coptic Studies* (*Coptic Studies* 1, Leiden).

Ed. of *Nag Hammadi and Gnosis. Papers Read at the First International Congress of Coptology, Cairo, December 1976* (*NHS* 14, Leiden).

'II. Apokryphen des Neuen Testaments' in *TRE* III (Berlin/New York), 316–362.

'Jewish Literary Propaganda' in (eds) A. Benoit, M. Philonenko and C. Vogel, *Paganisme, Judaïsme, Christianisme; Influences et affrontements dans le Monde Antique. Mélanges offerts à Marcel Simon* (Paris), 61–71.

'One Text, Four Translations: Some Reflections on the Nag Hammadi Gospel of the Egyptians' in (ed.) B. Aland, with U. Bianchi, M. Krause, J. M. Robinson and G. Widengren, *Gnosis. Festschrift für Hans Jonas* (Göttingen), 441–448.

'Slippery Words II. Gnosis, Gnostic, Gnosticism' in *ET* 89, 296–301.
Reviews:
  (Ed.) J. M. Robinson, *The Nag Hammadi Library in English*; and K.
  Rudolph, *Die Gnosis: Wesen und Geschichte einer spätantiken
  Religion* in *ET* 90, 26–27.
  D. Trakatellis, *Ho Huperbatikos Theos tou Eugnostou* in *JThS* n.s.
  29, 632–633.

1979

Ed. (with E. Best) of *Text and Interpretation. Studies in the New Testament
Presented to Matthew Black* (Cambridge).
'Philippians in Fayyumic' in (eds) E. Best and R. McL. Wilson, *Text and
Interpretation. Studies in the New Testament Presented to Matthew
Black* (Cambridge), 245–250.
Ed. (with D. M. Parrott) of ET, Introduction and Notes on 'The Acts of
Peter and the Twelve Apostles: NHC VI, I:1, 1–12, 22' in (ed.) D. M.
Parrott, *Nag Hammadi Codices V, 2–5 and VI with Papyrus Berolinensis
8502, 1 and 4* (*NHS* 11, Leiden), 197–229.
Ed. (with G.W. MacRae) of ET, Introduction and Notes on 'The Gospel
According to Mary: BG I:7, 1–19, 5' in (ed.) D. M. Parrott, *Nag
Hammadi Codices V, 2–5 and VI with Papyrus Berolinensis 8502, 1 and 4*
(*NHS* 11, Leiden), 453–471.
'Simon and Gnostic Origins' in (ed.) J. Kremer, *Les Actes des Apôtres:
Traditions, rédaction, théologie* (*BEThL* 48, Leuven), 485–491.

1980

'Valentinianism and the *Gospel of Truth*' in (ed.) B. Layton, *The
Rediscovery of Gnosticism: Proceedings of the International Conference
on Gnosticism at Yale, New Haven, Connecticut, March 28–31, 1978* I:
The School of Valentinus (*SHR* 41:1, Leiden), 133–145.
Reviews:
  F. T. Fallon, *The Enthronement of Sabaoth: Jewish Elements in
  Gnostic Creation Myths* (*NHS* 10) in *JThS* n.s. 31, 191–193.
  E. Pagels, *The Gnostic Gospels* in *ET* 91, 343–344.

1981

'Gnosis and the Mysteries' in (eds) R. van den Broek and M. J.
Vermaseren, *Studies in Gnosticism and Hellenistic Religions, Presented
to Gilles Quispel on the Occasion of his 65th Birthday* (*EPRO* 91,
Leiden), 451–457.
'Twenty Years After' in (ed.) B. Barc, *Colloque international sur les textes
de Nag Hammadi, Québec, 22–25 août 1978* (*BCNH Ét* 1;
Québec/Louvain), 59–67.